UNIVERSITY OF CINCINNATI

CLASSICAL STUDIES,

I

UNIVERSITY OF CINCINNATI
CLASSICAL STUDIES

VOLUME I

EDITED BY

D. W. Bradeen, C. G. Boulter, A. Cameron,
J. L. Caskey, P. Topping, C. R. Trahman, J. M. Vail

LECTURES

IN MEMORY OF

LOUISE TAFT

SEMPLE

FIRST SERIES · 1961-1965

Carl W. Blegen	Bernard Ashmole
Giorgio de Santillana	W. K. C. Guthrie
Benjamin D. Meritt	Henry T. Rowell
Romilly Jenkins	Gerald F. Else

PRINCETON UNIVERSITY PRESS

FOR THE UNIVERSITY OF CINCINNATI

1967

Acknowledgment is made to Random House
for the quotation on p. 77 from
The Collected Poetry of W. H. Auden, 1945, pp. 109-10.

Printed in the United States of America
by Princeton University Press

PREFACE

THE LECTURES published in this volume were delivered at the University of Cincinnati from time to time over a period beginning in October 1961 and ending in January 1965. Each pair has appeared before now in a preliminary printing which was distributed to a limited number of colleagues.

The series was instituted as a memorial to Louise Taft Semple and as an acknowledgment of the privilege and the responsibility which she left to us. Upon her death in March 1961, it was learned that she had established a trust fund to support classical studies at the University, providing in this way an enduring continuation of benefactions which she had given during many years of her life. Her intentions were made clear in the Trust Agreement, where it was stated that the income from the fund should be used, under the direction of the Trustees, "solely for the purpose of promoting the study of the classics, such term to be interpreted in its broadest sense as the endeavor to make vital and constructive in the civilization of our country the spiritual, intellectual and esthetic inheritance we have received from the Greek and Roman civilizations." It was further stipulated that recommendations for the use of the income should be made by the Department of Classics, subject to the approval of the Board of Directors of the University.

As was characteristic of Mrs. Semple, her earlier gifts in this sphere (and in many others) were made anonymously; similarly the Classics Fund, as it is called, was presented not in her own name but as an adjunct to a more general endowment for humanistic studies, which had been established some thirty years earlier in memory of her father, Charles Phelps Taft, by her mother, Annie Sinton Taft. Mrs. Semple sought no special recognition for herself, but it would have been contrary to her nature to impose secrecy upon her successors. Therefore we feel it proper to record this brief outline of the origin of the fund.

Financial backing was by no means her only contribution to the welfare of this Department and its undertakings. Professor William T. Semple, her husband, was its Head for thirty years, and his observation, insight, and imagination were determining factors in its development. He discussed his reflections and plans with her; her sound intuition and critical response were often decisive. This combination of resources led to the gathering of an exceptionally able group of professors, the provision of fellowships for undergraduates and graduate students, large expansion of the John Miller Burnam classical library, to which was added an important collection of modern Greek books, support of research and a series of fruitful excavations in Aegean lands, means for suitable publication of the results, and opportunities to bring visiting lecturers to Cincinnati.

In 1961 the members of the departmental faculty, contemplating the paths that Mrs. Semple's gift had opened for the future, came to feel that one form of acknowledgment—indeed one clear obligation—was to make known the fields in which some of their special interests lay. Rather than attempting to offer accounts of their own work, however, they invited others to speak on topics in these fields. A number of the guests followed the suggestion that in one part of the lectures they might deal with progress of studies up to now, and in another with certain major problems still unsolved; but no specific limits were set.

The results, embodied in the lectures here presented, reveal a wide range, including pre-classical archaeology and Greek art, Greek and Latin literature, Greek philosophy, ancient and Byzantine history. There is a preponderance of the Hellenic over the Roman, reflecting undoubtedly a tendency of the moment in classical studies. This ought not to be taken as a judgment of their relative importance or as an index of the attention that they command in this department of our University.

We would close with a word of thanks to those who participated in the series of lectures for the time and thought which they devoted to the presentation of their ideas and for the pleasure and stimulation which they afforded to their audiences. The lectures are printed substantially as they were given, in this first of a series of volumes which we propose to issue occasionally in the future as other papers call for publication in this form.

THE EDITORS

CONTENTS

The Mycenaean Age

The Trojan War, The Dorian Invasion, and Other Problems

By CARL W. BLEGEN

Delivered October 31 and November 1, 1961

FOREWORD

I T IS A GREAT HONOR and a deep pleasure to have the
privilege of initiating this series of lectures that have been
planned in memory of Louise Taft Semple, donor of the
magnificent endowment for the promotion of classical studies in
the University of Cincinnati. She and her husband, William
T. Semple, were also the generous benefactors who organized
and sponsored the archaeological expedition of the University
of Cincinnati and, with their financial support, made possible the
expedition's work over a long period of years at one world-
famous site, Troy, and at another not previously well known,
but now receiving general recognition, the Palace of Nestor at
Pylos. The excavations at Troy, conducted on a large scale,
often with more than one hundred workmen, were continued
through seven annual campaigns from 1932 to 1938; and the
uncovering of Nestor's palace which has been carried on during
the past ten seasons, beginning in 1952, is not yet quite finished.

Much of the work done by the Cincinnati Expeditions both
at Troy and at Pylos has been concerned with the pre-classical
period, and particularly with Mycenaean civilization which is
now beginning to be recognized as the first blossoming of what
may be called Greek culture. Louise Semple felt a keen interest
in this early phase of Hellenic life and expression, taking part in
the excavation of chamber tombs at Prosymna in Argolis, and
in the uncovering of the contemporary remains left by Troy VI
and VIIa. It is therefore not inappropriate, in this series dedicated to her memory, to devote the first lectures to the Mycenaean Age and some of its problems.

CARL W. BLEGEN

1

THE MYCENAEAN AGE
THE TROJAN WAR,
THE DORIAN INVASION
AND OTHER PROBLEMS

EIGHTY-FIVE YEARS have passed since those autumn
weeks in 1876 when Heinrich Schliemann and his wife
Sophia discovered the unplundered royal Shaft Graves
at Mycenae and introduced to a startled world the matchless
collection of gold, silver, bronze, and other objects that were
recovered in those graves. A genuine tribute is due to these two
people, who, lacking trained assistants, lacking the equipment
and facilities of modern expeditions, uncovered, collected, and
preserved hundreds and even thousands of small delicate items
without damage to anything and without seriously mixing grave
groups. Schliemann believed that these treasures represented
the culture of the epic era so vividly reflected in the Homeric
poems, and he was convinced that they had belonged to actual
historical personages who took part in an actual Trojan war.
Indeed he was sure that he had found the tomb and the bones
of King Agamemnon himself. The general public which had
been impressed by Schliemann's earlier success in finding the
site of Troy, which also had yielded up its many gold, silver
and bronze hoards, accepted Schliemann's broad conclusions and
much of his evaluation of the Mycenaean remains. Almost all
the classical scholars in England gave a friendly, not to say
enthusiastic, reception to the news from Mycenae, and many
of the German archaeologists, too, reacted favorably. But part
of the world still took a skeptical attitude, and it is entertaining
—these many decades after the event—to note the astonishing
alternative explanations of the royal graves and their contents

that were seriously offered by some of the well-known scholars of that day. One held that these wonderful jewels, weapons, and implements were remains left by the Celts; another identified them as of Gothic origin from the time of the Heruli in the third century after Christ, or of Alaric at the end of the fourth century; yet another regarded them, in part, as Byzantine; they were also judged to be Carian, or Indian, or at least oriental; and one critic maintained that they were products of Scythian art, wholly different from anything Greek.[1]

Time was on Schliemann's side, for he was of course essentially right; and he is fully entitled to the credit for first lifting the veil that covered the Mycenaean world. He was greatly and ably assisted in his later excavations by Wilhelm Dörpfeld, who both at Troy and at Tiryns brought careful architectural method and measurement into the field operations, and who drew the excellent plans of the walls and buildings that were uncovered, an example that set a model of clarity for later archaeological draftsmen. But Schliemann's discoveries were only the very beginning, and vastly more still remained to be found and interpreted.

The first great broadening of knowledge regarding Mycenaean civilization we owe to the patient industry of Christos Tsountas who as a young man in the eighties and nineties, carried out wide explorations at Mycenae itself and elsewhere. It was he who found and opened most of the nine tholos tombs that are now familiar landmarks in the neighborhood of the Mycenaean citadel, and he also discovered and cleared more than a hundred chamber tombs in the same general area. The tholos tombs, all of which had been plundered, were obviously royal sepulchres, later in date than the shaft graves, and they might represent a subsequent dynasty of rulers. The chamber tombs, which in their long period of use overlapped both the

[1] P. Gardner in *J.H.S.*, I, 1880, pp. 94-106, defends Schliemann's views in answer to attacks made by L. Stephani in *Compte Rendu de la Commission Impériale Archéologique pour l'année 1877*, St. Petersburg, 1880. The appearance of the butterfly as a decorative motive on the gold jewelry convinced Stephani that some of the jewelry must be attributed to the third century after Christ or later. U. Köhler suggested a Carian origin in his article "Ueber die Zeit und den Ursprung der Grabanlagen in Mykene und Spata," *Ath. Mitt.*, III, 1878, pp. 1-13.

Shaft Graves and the tholoi, were the burial places not of kings but of private citizens. They shed much hitherto wanting light not only on private burial customs but on Mycenaean life and culture as a whole. Tsountas, who later became a distinguished professor in the University of Athens, likewise excavated part of the palace at the summit of the acropolis and some smaller houses on the lower slopes of the hill. He was also fortunate enough to recover from a grave pit that escaped the attention of plunderers in a tholos tomb at Vaphio in Laconia, many further treasures as well as the two famous gold cups with scenes of capturing and taming wild bulls. In 1893 he was able to publish a systematic survey of Mycenaean culture in most of its aspects, an admirable analysis, which appeared in an expanded English version in 1896, and which has not yet been altogether superseded, even in 1961, by a better interpretation.

A new era in Mycenaean studies dawned with the work of Sir Arthur Evans in the opening decade of our century. His great excavations at Knossos from 1900 to 1905 and later revealed an old, long-established metropolitan culture that had worked out its own independent development through a millennium and a half or more; at intervals it blossomed forth in special splendor, as illustrated by three successive stages of construction. These were ascribed by Evans to three chronological eras, the Early, Middle, and Late periods of the Bronze Age. This division, with each period subdivided into three phases, I, II, and III, formed the substantial framework for the useful, not to say indispensable, chronological system he created. Though there have been major and minor criticisms, it was adopted by most archaeologists, extended, and applied wherever possible throughout the Aegean and indeed in the whole eastern Mediterranean. Evans also gave a name to this Cretan culture, calling it Minoan from the Cretan King Minos, well known in Greek tradition; and the three stages could be conveniently indicated by prefixing Early, Middle and Late before Minoan.

One of the most important achievements of Minoan culture was the invention of writing and the keeping of written records. Evans recognized at least three different kinds of scripts: the earliest called a hieroglyphic system, and somewhat later two linear systems, which he named Linear A and Linear B scripts. Most of the documents were inscribed on clay tablets, the survival of which depended mainly, or perhaps exclusively, on chance baking in the fires that, as a rule, eventually destroyed the palaces. Records in the Linear A script have been found in the Messara and in many other places in Crete, inscribed on stone, metal and clay; but those in the Linear B form have not yet come to light at Cretan sites outside Knossos.

In the Late Minoan Period, represented by the third and last of the great palaces, Evans believed he could recognize the roots and origins of almost all the characteristic elements (in architecture, gold work, metal work, jewelry, fresco painting, pottery, and so on) that had already become known in Mycenaean culture; he concluded therefore that the latter was directly derived from the Minoan. He argued that so effective an imposition of a whole culture could only have been carried out by conquest and domination. He thus postulated an invasion of the Greek mainland on a large scale and a long period of actual Minoan rule during which the Mycenaean area became a "mainland branch of Minoan culture."

This view of Minoan-Mycenaean relations prevailed for some time among many archaeologists. It is obvious that there was considerable traffic between Crete and the Greek mainland, and Minoan trading stations were almost surely established at strategic coastal points. This may be deduced from the fact that an island just off the port of Megara and a harbor in eastern Laconia in later times were still called Minoa; and at least four trading ports on various islands in the Aegean bore the same name. Athenian tradition, too, remembered that king Minos for a time exacted an annual tribute of seven youths and seven maidens from Athens until the hero Theseus volunteered to end the intolerable oppression or die in the attempt. He slew the Minotaur and freed the city from Minos' power. This story suggests that the Cretans may once have had a foothold of some sort in Attica, if not elsewhere.

As the work of exploration and excavation of Mycenaean sites in continental Greece continued, those who conducted the digging and became intimately familiar with the monuments and the various kinds of objects recovered found the domination theory less and less convincing. Certainly the Mycenaean people owed a vast debt to Minoan influence, but underneath the surface appeared a solid core of distinctive non-Minoan character, obviously a heritage cherished and maintained from a long preceding era of free untrammeled development. To the mainland school of archaeologists it thus began to seem clear that the relations with Minoan Crete had more probably begun in a peaceful manner, possibly first by friendly trade and barter; and perhaps the goods exchanged were at the outset carried largely in Minoan ships; Minoan sea power certainly won its way into and established itself in later Greek tradition.

From a culture much more sophisticated than their own the mainlanders perhaps borrowed, copied, adapted and modified all that pleased them. In the end, having become warlike and powerful, they built ships of their own, raided Crete, captured Knossos, and carried off whatever booty they liked, human as well as inanimate goods; and then, inspired by the elegance they had seen in the island, when they returned to their homes they set about building comparable large palaces for themselves, though they laid them out according to their own distinctive plans. The principal structure had a monumental façade facing a court; one passed through it and a vestibule into a spacious hall of state with the royal throne set against the wall at the right and in the center an enormous circular ceremonial hearth. The whole building was finished and decorated throughout in the Cretan manner—perhaps by actual Cretan artists and artisans. Virtually all the Mycenaean palaces that have been found on the mainland of Greece belong, at any rate, to the third phase of the Late Bronze Age, long after construction of that kind in Crete had ceased.

Evans' chronological scheme of Early, Middle and Late Minoan, each divided into three sub-periods I, II, III, had soon established itself firmly; but in time it became customary to reserve for objects recovered in Crete the name Minoan, and to use for things found in the Cyclades and on the mainland corresponding phrases Early, Middle and Late Cycladic and Early, Middle and Late Helladic as distinguishing geographical terms.

The years between World Wars I and II were fruitful in the field of Mycenaean studies. Renewed investigations in and about the great centers of Tiryns and Mycenae clarified many problems. K. Müller's searching examination and publication of the fortification walls and the palace at Tiryns, revealed the sequence of construction of the many elements that make up the whole complex. G. Karo's superb publication of the objects found by Schliemann and Stamatakis in the Shaft Graves at Mycenae provided the first complete scholarly description and interpretation of this invaluable material.

The new excavation at Mycenae undertaken by the British School in Athens under the direction of A. J. B. Wace, cast much fresh illumination on the chronology of the great walls and the tholos tombs as well as on the history of the Grave Circle just inside the Lion Gate. Many smaller settlements too yielded to the spade their treasures of various kinds, especially their evidence for pottery sequence, burial customs and the life of the ordinary people. Swedish Expeditions worked at Ásine, Dendra, Berbati, all in Argolis, and in northern Messenia; the French School at Argos and in Phocis; the American School at several Corinthian sites (Korakou, Gonia, Zygouries), Prosymna (Argive Heraeum), and on the north slope of the Athenian Acropolis, and, in cooperation with the Fogg Museum, under the direction of Hetty Goldman, at Eutresis in Boeotia. Archaeological researches in Rhodes and Cyprus as well as in Syria and beyond likewise brought to light much fresh Mycenaean pottery and other material, clear evidence of the widespread extent of Mycenaean trade, if not colonization, around the eastern end of the Mediterranean.

In southwestern Messenia, not far to the north of the Bay of Navarino, a Mycenaean palace of considerable size was discovered shortly before the outbreak of the second World War, in April 1939, by a joint Hellenic-American expedition which was conducted by K. Kourouniotis, representing the Greek Archaeological Service, and C. W. Blegen representing the University of Cincinnati. One of the trial trenches exposed an

Archives Room that contained more than six hundred clay tablets and fragments of tablets inscribed in the Linear B script. They were the first of their kind to come to light on the Greek mainland, although twenty-eight large pottery jars for wine or oil, bearing painted characters of the Linear B script, had many years earlier been found by A. Keramopoullos in the ruins of the Mycenaean Palace at Thebes, the House of Kadmos. Other inscribed jars and fragments have been recovered at Orchomenos in Boeotia, Eleusis, Mycenae and Tiryns.

During the war, in 1940, Furumark's great work on Mycenaean Pottery was published, a comprehensive analysis and classification of all the pertinent material, so far as available in publications. This was the first detailed systematic treatise on the subject, and it is a notable landmark in the realm of Mycenaean ceramics. The chronological order of the successive classes and styles of Mycenaean pottery, as fixed by Furumark, has now become a system of sequence dating, which has been widely accepted. It may be used independently of absolute calendar years, though it has some fairly well established points of attachment to that system. Taking as a basis Evans' general framework for Late Minoan, Furumark postulates the following classes for the Mycenaean area in the Late Bronze Age: Mycenaean I, Mycenaean II A and II B, Mycenaean III A 1, III A 2 early, III A 2 late, Mycenaean III B, Mycenaean III C 1 early, III C 1 late, III C 2. He thus makes ten successive categories of styles extending through a period of some 450 years.

Regular archaeological field work in Greek lands was inevitably precluded during the war and its aftermath, and almost a decade passed before progress could be resumed. The museums had been for the most part emptied and their contents buried in bomb-proof shelters under ground for safety. Many of the buildings themselves had suffered damage and had to be reconstructed or replaced. It was only in 1957 that the unrivalled Mycenaean Room in the National Museum at Athens was again opened to public view, with its wonderful treasures displayed in the modern manner.

The past decade has been remarkably rich both in its yield

of fresh archaeological material and in the progress that has been made in Mycenaean studies. Most noteworthy at Mycenae itself was the discovery of a second royal grave circle lying outside the citadel so close to the Tomb of Clytemnestra that it had suffered damage when the latter was built. Its excavation by J. Papadimitriou and G. Mylonas in 1952, 1953, and 1954 revealed 24 graves of various shapes and sizes, for the most part contemporary with, but apparently beginning somewhat earlier than, those first found in 1876 by Schliemann inside the fortification wall. Like all new discoveries, this one, too, raised a host of fresh and interesting problems. For convenience the old circle excavated by Schliemann inside the fortification walls is now called Grave Circle A, and the newly found one outside the fortress has been named Grave Circle B. Although many theories have been evolved, no one has yet been able to explain satisfactorily why there are two such circles of the same period.

Three large substantial houses were uncovered by A. J. B. Wace on a terrace to the west of the acropolis, and some neighboring buildings of the same kind were later excavated by the Ephor N. Verdelis. In these houses inscribed tablets in Linear B were brought to light for the first time at Mycenae in 1952. Inside the citadel itself houses and walls have been searchingly examined and re-examined by Professor Wace and by Professor G. Mylonas, and also by Dr. Papadimitriou and Lord William Taylour, who were the first to find inscribed tablets within the fortification walls.

Reconstruction of the Cyclopean Walls at Tiryns led to the recovery of much pottery and numerous fragments of frescoes. Further tombs at Dendra, excavated by Swedish archaeologists and the Ephor Verdelis, have given up bronzes of unique interest as well as other remains. The pre-classical site at Lerna, with stratified deposits extending from Neolithic times through the Late Mycenaean Age, was excavated by the American School of Classical Studies at Athens under the direction of J. L. Caskey. In western Messenia the extensive remains of the Palace of Nestor were almost wholly exposed to view, along with some houses of the lower surrounding town, by the University of Cincinnati Expedition, which likewise cleared two nearby tholos tombs and several chamber tombs. In a much wider area many tholos tombs, chamber tombs and settlements were found and excavated by Professor S. Marinatos, who recovered jewelry of gold and silver, inlaid daggers, many fine gems, amber and quantities of pottery. From these and other explorations by Valmin, Kourouniotis, Yalouris and McDonald, it has become clear that Messenia in Mycenaean times was more densely populated than almost any other part of Greece; and the settlements seem to have roots going back into the Middle Helladic Period.

In other parts of the country, too, many additional discoveries of Mycenaean remains have been reported. Attica has produced its quota, especially in the Agora of Athens and in the cemetery of chamber tombs at Perati which is being investigated by S. Iakovides. Much new material has also been brought to light at Gla in Boeotia by the Ephor J. Threpsiades, both in and about the walls and the gateways, as well as in the palace on the summit of the hill. The Ephor D. Theochares in Thessaly has uncovered some parts of a large Mycenaean palace at the key site of Iolkos in Volo, the port from which the Argonautic Expedition set forth; and he has found an important tholos tomb in the vicinity of Pharsala.

The foregoing list, which is far from exhaustive, will serve to give some idea of the steady copious inflow of fresh Mycenaean accessions into the museums of Greece from day to day, week to week, and year to year. In the meantime during the same decade study and co-ordination of what was already available has likewise marched forward. In the spring of 1951, copies of all the texts inscribed on the tablets found at ancient Pylos in 1939 were published by Emmett Bennett, Jr., of Cincinnati, and these documents were thus made accessible to linguistic scholars and those interested in the problem of decipherment. In February 1952 volume II of Evans' *Scripta Minoa* appeared, containing a large part of the Linear B material found by Evans half a century earlier in the Palace of Minos at Knossos. These new publications, providing hitherto inaccessible material for further testing, stimulated a fresh attack on the linguistic puzzle offered by the Linear B script.

The culminating and most sensational achievement of all came at the beginning of June 1952 when Michael Ventris first issued his cautiously tentative suggestion that the Linear B script represents an early form of the Greek language. For this solution he speedily found abundant confirmation in a further wider application of the syllabic grid he had worked out. It took a good deal of courage to launch this theory, for it ran directly counter to one of Evans' most positive postulates, namely that the language of the Linear B script was Minoan and not Greek, a view that had long been generally accepted by most archaeologists and historians. Ventris' decipherment, which was circulated in *Work Note 20* and in a following Experimental Vocabulary, received an enthusiastic welcome from only a few scholars, but was met with reserve by many. His long technical account, written in collaboration with John Chadwick, and published in the *Journal of Hellenic Studies* in 1953,[2] elicited some further favorable notice; but a new tablet, ultimately called Ta 641, found at Pylos in broken pieces June 4 and June 10, 1952, settled the question for most people. It was cleaned and put together in Athens in the autumn, first studied and photographed in the following spring, and was not known to Ventris until the middle of May 1953. This tablet, with ideograms to illustrate the types, dealt with tripods and other vessels of larger and smaller sizes, some with three handles, some with four, and others without handles; and many of these descriptive terms, which were spelled out in full in the text, emerged clearly in Greek words when the test of Ventris' syllabary was applied.[3] It convinced most of the leading linguistic scholars, who were concerned with the problem, that the solution was fundamentally sound, although there were—and still are—many unresolved difficulties of transcription and interpretation. A few scholars have rejected the decipherment altogether and continue to do so; but none can deny that the

[2] M. G. F. Ventris and J. Chadwick, "Evidence for Greek Dialect in the Mycenaean Archives," *J.H.S.*, LXXIII, 1953, pp. 84-103. This was followed by their *Documents in Mycenaean Greek*, Cambridge, 1956, and by Chadwick's *The Decipherment of Linear B*, Cambridge, 1958.

[3] C. W. Blegen, "An Inscribed Tablet from Pylos," *Arch. Eph.*, 1953-1954 (1955), pp. 59-62.

texts, as read in accordance with Ventris' syllabary, yield multitudes of real Greek words as well as whole phrases, along with
many personal names and place names that are unquestionably
Hellenic.

The presence of Greek speech on the mainland in the late
phases of the Bronze Age need not have unduly startled the
students of linguistics, for one of the most distinguished among
them, C. D. Buck, had long ago cogently pointed out that the
distribution of the later Greek dialects demonstrates that the
introduction of the Greek language into Greece occurred at
least as early as the fourteenth century B.C.[4] Moreover in his
memorable Sather Lectures of 1930-1931 Martin P. Nilsson
had convincingly shown that Greek mythology and the Greek
epics spring from roots that go far back into the Mycenaean
period.[5] Excavators in the field, too, had called attention to the
lack of any archaeological evidence to indicate a break in culture
and the arrival of a new people in Greece in the Late Bronze
Age. Indeed some held and still hold that the first Greeks must
have been the bearers of Middle Helladic culture who came
and established themselves in the peninsula some time between
2000 and 1800 B.C.

In any event the discovery of written Greek in the Linear
B script on Mycenaean tablets of the Late Bronze Age establishes the certainty of some of these deductions. Emmett Bennett, Jr., in his acute comparison of the weights and measures
used in the Linear A and Linear B systems, had noted that the
difference between those two forms of writing was not merely
or primarily a chronological one: it was obvious rather that they
represent two quite different languages and cultures, and he
inferred that the Linear A must be Minoan and Linear B Mycenaean.[6] This distinction has now won a wide acceptance.

The definite recognition of the Mycenaeans as Greeks calls
for something more than mere passing mention. Let it be an

[4] C. D. Buck, "The Language Situation in and about Greece in the Second
Millennium B.C.," *Classical Philology*, XXI, 1926, 1-26.
[5] M. P. Nilsson, *The Mycenaean Origin of Greek Mythology* (Sather Classical
Lectures, VIII), Berkeley, 1932.
[6] E. L. Bennett, Jr., "Fractional Quantities in Minoan Bookkeeping," *A.J.A.*,
LIV, 1950, pp. 204-222.

early stage in the history of that race, perhaps before Hellenic speech had yet been fully evolved. Nonetheless it demonstrates the inherent strength of the Greek people and their astonishing power of survival: they still exist and flourish today, retaining their distinctive character, their language, their exclusiveness along with their cohesiveness, despite intense individualism. Apart possibly from the Chinese, there are few, if any, other comparable peoples in their tenacity to endure. In their long history they have at least three times blossomed out into world leadership in culture: in the Late Mycenaean Age, in the classical period, and in the heyday of the Byzantine Empire. They have withstood the impact of innumerable invasions that brought hordes of foreign intruders into their land from the north, from the east, from the south, and from the west; they have endured subjection and occupation for centuries under alien rule, and yet they have always in the end absorbed the marauders and imposed their own Greek spirit, their way of thinking and their culture on the fusion of Hellenized survivors that remained. The poet Horace nearly two thousand years ago observed this remarkable power possessed by the Greeks.

The Mycenaean era corresponds with the Epic Age, the Heroic Age of Greece. To the Hellenes of classical times it was a real period, peopled with genuine persons of flesh and blood, who played their parts in events that truly occurred in actual places. Herodotus and Thucydides, the lyric and dramatic poets and all the other ancient writers were untouched by doubts about the historical reality of the Trojan War; nor did they hesitate to accept Agamemnon, Achilles, Diomedes, Nestor, Odysseus and the other heroes as the veritable leaders of the expeditionary force that invaded northwestern Asia Minor and laid siege to Troy.

Professional Homeric scholarship in the nineteenth century was to a great extent marked by a deep skepticism; the poems were ripped to shreds, the subject matter was regarded as fiction or fancy inspired by minor episodes and raids, transferred by the poet or poets from various other places to Troy, and the possibility that there was any substratum of historical truth was

THE MYCENAEAN AGE 17

brushed aside. In the light of the greatly broadened knowledge of the Mycenaean world and its Greek character that is available today most students of Homer have turned away from that negative attitude of the past century and are willing to recognize that the epic cycle and Greek tradition, though often embroidered by phantasy, are not wholly creations of the imagination, but rest on some basis of reality. The evidence from the epics, from tradition, from archaeology, from linguistics and from the Linear B tablets has recently been assembled and strikingly presented by D. Page in a brilliant book, *History and* the *Homeric Iliad* (Berkeley, 1959).

Schliemann was of course the discoverer of Troy in the 1870's, but the high mound of Hissarlik was composed of at least nine distinct and separate layers of debris, one lying above the other, representing a series of successive settlements; and he had difficulty in determining which one to identify as the Troy of Priam. At the outset he believed it must be the deepest and earliest of all the layers; but when he found in that deposit only the most primitive remains, with weapons and implements of stone and bone and handmade pottery, he shifted to the third layer; and later he changed again from the third to the second, counting from the bottom. But in his final campaign of 1890, having Dörpfeld as his collaborator, and digging far outside the walls of Troy II, he exposed high up in the sixth layer, in association with a large building of the megaron type, a quantity of Mycenaean pottery of the kinds with which he had become familiar at Mycenae. He realized at once that a further change was necessary. His death in December of that year prevented him from conducting the new excavation he had immediately planned. Dörpfeld, however, carried out the project with sensational success in 1893 and 1894, uncovering the magnificent fortification walls and the great palatial houses of Troy VI. He concluded that this citadel, shown by much associated imported pottery to be contemporary with Mycenae, must be recognized as the Homeric Troy.

The Cincinnati Expedition, which re-examined the entire sequence of layers in the years from 1932 to 1938, was able to differentiate 46 separate strata in the deposits that had accumulated on the site and felt obliged to make another relatively minor change in the identification; for the ruins of Troy VI appeared clearly to have been caused by a tremendous earthquake and not by human hands and fire. After the disaster, with no sign of any change of culture, the fortification walls were at once repaired; some houses were rehabilitated, many new ones, crowded close together, were erected over their ruined predecessors and wherever empty space could be found. This is the phase Troy VIIa, which forms the direct continuation of Troy VI. Almost every house was sooner or later equipped with large storage jars, evidently for wine and oil and food supplies. They ranged in number, depending on the size of the house, from two or three to nearly twenty. They were sunk deep down beneath the floors and were covered by flat stone lids at the floor level. This was surely a precautionary measure laying up supplies to withstand a siege. This town had lasted probably no more than one generation when it was destroyed in a devastating fire. Scattered about in the wreckage of houses and streets were recovered a few fragments of human bones, indicating that the destruction was accompanied by violence. The Cincinnati Expedition therefore concluded that Troy VIIa must be recognized as the ill-fated city that was besieged, captured, sacked and burned by the Achaean invaders. This view, although rejected by some scholars, has been generally accepted, and Dörpfeld himself suggested in 1935 that Troy VIIa should rather be called Troy VIi to indicate the direct continuity it represents.

Many fragments of imported Mycenaean pottery were found in the successive strata of deposits laid down in the time of Troy VI, giving an orderly chronological sequence from Late Helladic I to Late Helladic III. From the debris of the final phase, Troy VIh, which came to its end in the earthquake, a considerable quantity of Mycenaean potsherds was recovered. These pieces, clearly assignable to Late Helladic III, represented predominantly an early stage of that period, but they were accompanied by not a few fragments of a following later stage. These two divisions are now, since the publication of Furumark's book, known as Mycenaean III A and III B. In the deposit of the reconstruction period, after the earthquake, which we call Troy VIIa, Mycenaean sherds were much less numerous than in Phase VIh, although we collected more than 165 pieces, some from imported, some from locally manufactured pots. The bulk of this material represents the style of the later stage III B, but a good many examples must be ascribed to III A. Of great significance are a half dozen or more fragments which bear designs of the III A style painted on a local Tan Ware that is distinctive of Phase VIIa. This fact demonstrates that Troy VIIa existed at a time when pottery of the III A class was still being made and used, although it had already to some extent been displaced by the style of III B. Troy VIIa did not long survive, for its destruction was carried out while the III B ceramic style still retained its initial vigor and showed no signs of decline. No pieces of Furumark's III C style were recognized in this layer. The evidence thus reviewed gives us invaluable sequence datings, though their precise translation into absolute chronology in years B.C. may yet encounter some difficulties, as we shall see.

However that may be, it is now reasonably well established that Troy VIIa must be the Homeric Troy, if there ever was one, and also that it was sacked and burned before the middle stage of the ceramic style III B.

Excavations during the past ten years in southwestern Messenia have also contributed toward the clarification and solution of some problems connected with the Trojan War. The Mycenaean palace which has been almost completely uncovered on a commanding hilltop called Epano Englianos, only a few miles north of the bay of Navarino, is now known to a fairly wide public, but it may perhaps be useful for the argument to offer a brief survey of its character and contents.

It is a large complex, comprising four major and several minor buildings that occupy the southwestern half of the elevation. From a study of all the evidence available, we believe that the different elements of the palace were constructed one after the other, some relatively early in the ceramic phase Mycenaean III B. The hill had been previously occupied, perhaps by a smaller preceding palace and other buildings of Mycenaean

III A; those structures were demolished and for the most part removed and the top of the elevation seems to have been cut down and levelled in preparation for the erection of the new palace. Henceforth the acropolis was clearly reserved for the use of the ruler with his family and officials. A lower town using pottery of the III A style had existed on the sloping terraces below the citadel. Those houses were destroyed by fire, and they were succeeded by later habitations contemporary with the new palace and equipped with pottery of the III B class. They were in turn put to the torch at the same time as the palace on the hill. This sequence of two periods is clear, both on the hilltop and in the surrounding town.

In the central building of the palace the apartments of state were designed in the regular Mycenaean architectural manner —a gateway, a court, a porch, vestibule and throne room, all following one after the other along the same general axis. Along each side of the megaron was a corridor from which doorways opened into waiting rooms, store rooms of many kinds, magazines for olive oil and other supplies, and pantries, and a stairway that led to the upper story, where the sleeping rooms and the women's quarters were no doubt located. In the eastern angle of the building, a suite of one large room with a hearth and several smaller chambers may have been the apartments of the Queen. Nearby was also a bathroom with a terracotta tub still preserved in place in a clay setting, while a stand holding two large jars for water occupied a corner of the room. The floors throughout the building were coated with stucco, which in many rooms bore painted decoration; and frescoes adorned the walls in all the principal apartments. A pair of two connected rooms just beside the entrance gateway deserves particular mention, for this was probably the office of the Director of Internal Revenue and it was here that most of the inscribed tablets recovered in the palace were filed away in orderly arrangement.

The southwestern building was likewise a residential unit, probably the first element to be erected in the chronological order of construction. Fronting on a broad court, it had a large entrance hall with two columns in its façade and a single interior column in its axis. Passing through this hall and turning at right angles towards the left, one reached a much larger hall, no doubt the throne room, which had at least four, more probably six, interior columns; unfortunately erosion has carried away nearly all of the floor and details of the original arrangements are wholly lost. The unorthodox right-angled turn into the hall of state suggests that this is an early element from an initial stage before the later characteristic Mycenaean axial plan had been developed, probably at the very beginning of Phase III B. Behind these public rooms were the domestic quarters with store rooms and pantries, a bathroom and a stairway to the upper story.

The northeastern building of the palace, comprising seven rooms, several of large size, seems to have been the workshop of the establishment for the repair of equipment in metal, leather and other materials, perhaps also serving as an armory. Many inscribed tablets and fragments were found in the largest room. In the southeastern corner of the building is a small room which had an almost monumental façade with massive antabases, fronting on a little court. In the latter stands a squared block, plastered on all sides and bearing painted decoration, probably an altar; and what we have may perhaps be interpreted as a palace shrine.

Behind the workshop to the northwest, close beside the steep edge of the hill, is the wine magazine in which were uncovered remains of some thirty-five large wine jars. Many clay sealings also came to light; they had evidently served to certify the various kinds of vintages or flavors of the wines that were brought to this store room, and several of the sealings were inscribed with the Linear B ideogram that had earlier been identified as meaning wine.

In size, plan and general style the palace takes its place alongside those at Mycenae and Tiryns, with which it is certainly contemporary. There is no trace of a fortification wall around the acropolis, but the steep edge on all sides, ranging from ten to twenty feet and more in height, provided a good defensive line. Down below the citadel to the northwest, southwest, and southeast remains of houses forming the lower town extend downward on descending slopes and terraces. To the northeast and to the south of the hill, not far distant, are three tholos tombs, and some five hundred yards towards the west is a cemetery of chamber tombs. I have ventured to put in this brief description to make it clear that we are dealing with the capital and the administrative center of the whole surrounding district of western Messenia.

The palace was destroyed in a tremendous fire that wrecked all the units of the entire complex and at the same time laid the lower town in ruins. All the furniture, fittings and other objects of perishable nature that were in the various buildings on the fatal day were burned to ashes. The fire was so hot that even some pieces of gold melted into drops. With the exception of a few items in metal and stone that somehow were protected from the action of the heat, only the clay tablets and the pottery and the clay sealings came through with little if any damage. The tablets and the sealings indeed benefited from the disaster, for they had not previously been baked; they were fired by the conflagration hard and durable enough to survive. The vases, too, though often cracked and broken, for the most part suffered little irreparable injury except in a few areas, where perhaps under especially intense heat they became warped and twisted and even vitrified.

The pantries in the palace, which have already been mentioned, number eight all told, six in the central unit and two in the southwest wing. All seem to have been provided with wooden shelves along the walls. On these shelves the household "china" or crockery was kept, the pots apparently arranged in neat systematic order, shape by shape, some stacked one inside another when possible, some suspended on strings. When the wooden shelving burned down the vases fell to the floor and were for the most part shattered by the wreckage that accompanied and covered them. The chronological importance of these pots lies in the fact that they surely represent the ceramic shapes and styles that were in normal current use on the very day the palace was set afire and destroyed. The total number of pots found in the pantries exceeds 7500, representing twenty-five or more different shapes, nearly all of them plain, without painted decoration.

If a digression may be permitted for a moment or two it might be of interest in passing to mention a theory that has been offered to explain the keeping of so large a stock of vessels on hand. The suggestion was essentially that the king, as a kind of merchant prince, gained his livelihood by holding a monopoly of commerce in all fields, including ceramics. It is something of a strain on the imagination to think of the monarch who resided in this great palace with its stately Throne Room, frescoed walls, decorated floors and all the appurtenances of power and wealth, as a seller of plain simple domestic pots and pans. I should prefer to see here the ordinary dishes and utensils, perhaps for the use of the large staff required to maintain the establishment. The king undoubtedly had his own dinner service, whether made of gold to match his magnificent drinking goblet, described in the *Iliad*, or of less precious metal. The enormous number of kylikes or wine cups—2853 stems were counted by Marion Rawson, all from one pantry, which seems to have been used exclusively for goblets of this type—perhaps requires a special explanation. It is clear from the epic poems that in the Heroic Age no occasion was ever missed for pouring a libation and having a drink; the vast number of broken fragments of these cups found almost everywhere in the debris in and about the palace led us to believe that after the wine was drunk the kylix was thrown to the floor or against the wall and shattered. This would account for the need of a great many goblets. The custom of breaking wine cups in this way is known from many other regions and periods.

The whole collection of pottery displays a remarkable uniformity of style which assigns it to the latest stage of Mycenaean III B. No example of a krater-bowl—or "deep bowl" as it is often called—was found in any of the pantries, but seven or eight pots of this shape were recovered, in whole or in part, in other rooms of the palace. Among them several bear painted decoration in the late manner of Mycenaean III B. Two others, one plain, one with a pattern in a reserved zone, look like products of the Granary Class of Mycenaean III C. An urn-like jar, standing on three short legs and carrying a somewhat elaborate linear design, might be a forerunner in a late Phase of III B, of the Close Style that comes still later. It is curious that these deep bowls, which are so numerous at Mycenae and at other sites in Argolis both in Mycenaean III B and III C, occur so extremely rarely in Messenia. But on the other hand certain shapes that are popular in southwest Peloponnesus seem to be highly uncommon in Argolis. The overwhelming testimony of the pottery in any event fixes the sequence dating for the destruction of the palace of Nestor at the very end of Mycenaean III B.

The identification of this palace, it seems to me, does not require much discussion. As we have seen, save for its lack of a fortification wall, it is in almost all respects comparable to the contemporary palaces of the great lords at Tiryns and Mycenae, and it must have demanded for its construction and maintenance a royal family of little if at all less wealth and power than possessed by the ruling dynasties in Argolis. In all Greek tradition the only family in the late Mycenaean period which is famous as having those needed qualifications of property and political strength in southwestern Peloponnesus is that of the Neleids, the most distinguished representative of which was Nestor. By the Greeks of the classical age and later Nestor was always regarded as a Messenian. It was only in Strabo's time that Homeric scholars—in the absence of any and all recognizable remains to indicate the actual site of Nestor's Pylos—speculated whether it might not have been in Triphylia close to the Alpheios River. They were led to this conjecture by Nestor's mythical tales, recorded in the *Iliad*, of the dashing cattle raids he had carried out in his youth into Elis across the Alpheios, and the students of Homer were especially impressed by the speed of his going and returning with his booty. Some modern scholars who cherish the same deep faith in the absolute accuracy of the Homeric poets in details of geography and topography and the exact timing of travel in the heroic age, by ship and by chariot, still cling to the theory of a long-lost Pylos near the Alpheios River. The only actual mention of Nestor's palace in the Homeric poems is found in the *Odyssey* in the story of Telemachus' visit to Pylos in search of news of his father Odysseus. Although far from specific, the topographical indications in that account fit much better with the palace at Englianos than with any rival far to the north in Triphylia.[7] But there is yet no real rival. (By a curious and amusing coincidence the hill of Englianos today actually lies in the modern eparchy called Triphylia.)

We have noted that in the time of Nestor the establishment at Englianos, with a considerable lower town clustered about it, was the administrative seat of a centralized bureaucratic government; and the tablets show that its authority extended over many other towns in the surrounding region. One series of tablets refers to nine different places, always listed in the same order: this recalls the passage in the Catalogue of Ships, where Nestor is called the ruler over nine cities. But it must be admitted that the place names mentioned on the tablets, with one exception, are quite different from those in the Catalogue. In any case most scholars now accept the identification of the palace at Englianos as the home of Nestor.

The history of the palace, as worked out from the evidence provided by the archaeological remains, fits well against the background of Greek tradition and of the Homeric poems. We conclude that the earliest element of the palace was built at the very beginning of the Mycenaean III B phase. This would be the work of Neleus, the father of Nestor, who came from Iolkos in Thessaly to carve out a domain for himself. Somehow, either by peaceful means or by force, he acquired the site of Pylos; according to one version he obtained it as a gift from king Aphareus, but the burning and the razing of the structures of the III A period that previously stood on the citadel strongly suggest the use of violence. Neleus founded his capital, consolidated his position, surely built the first unit of the palace and ruled for a time. All his sons, with the exception of Nestor, were slain by Herakles; and when Neleus died Nestor succeeded to the throne. He reigned a long time—through three generations of men, in the graphic phrase of the epics. It was

[7] The best account of Nestor and the Neleids known to me is that given by R. Hampe, "Die Homerische Welt im Lichte der neuen Ausgrabungen. Nestor," in *Vermächtniss der antiken Kunst* (Heidelberg, 1950), pp. 11-70.

probably Nestor who built the central unit of the palace containing the megaron and its great hearth; it is possible that he also erected the Workshop and the Wine Magazine. He was already an old man when he joined the expedition against Troy for which he provided 90 ships with crews and equipment. He served with distinction as the trusty friend and principal counselor of Agamemnon who was the acknowledged supreme sovereign and commander in chief. Prudent in his conduct and in his relations with the gods, Nestor had the good fortune after the capture of Troy to return to his home without incidents or difficulties. He continued still to reign for a time: in the tenth year after his return, as recounted in the *Odyssey*, he was visited by the young Telemachus. How much longer Nestor survived is unknown. He died presumably about the middle of the long ceramic Phase III B and tradition records that he was succeeded by a son and a grandson, and possibly by a great grandson, whose names are not specifically given. The length of their reigns is nowhere mentioned; they must have been short in any event, since the palace itself was demolished at the end of Mycenaean III B. Tradition has it that in the end Pylos was captured, looted, and burned by the invading Dorians. The inhabitants fled, some of the Neleids taking refuge in Athens, where they founded at least two eupatrid Athenian families, one being that of Peisistratos, and others continuing on to Asia Minor to settle in Ionia. Pylos itself, abandoned, and never again reoccupied, was ultimately overgrown by vegetation and disappeared from human ken.

In recapitulation for a moment, we find that the palace of Nestor in southwestern Messenia was constructed at the beginning of the ceramic period of Mycenaean III B and was destroyed by violence at the end of that same period. On the eastern shore of the Aegean we have seen that Troy VIIa must be identified as the city of Priam and Homer, and that it was taken by force, burned and razed at a time a little before the middle of the pottery phase Mycenaean III B.

On the Helladic side of the Aegean Professor Oscar Broneer in publishing an account of his excavation of Mycenaean remains on the northern edge of the Athenian Acropolis and on the slopes below, called attention to the widespread ruins and devastation that afflicted the leading Mycenaean centers at the end of Mycenaean III B. He suggested that the war against Troy, carried out on an ambitious scale by a great coalition of Achaeans, must have been waged long before the end of Phase III B and certainly at a time when the Mycenaean world was still prosperous and strong. He also advanced his belief that the destruction of the Mycenaean strongholds must have been the work of the Dorian invaders.[8] The results of the Cincinnati excavations both at Troy and at Pylos have led us to the same conclusions and we agree fully with Professor Broneer's views. Since these recent developments, of no little interest and importance, have not yet been fully discussed it seems to me worthwhile to go into the evidence in somewhat more detail.

In the past few years it has come to be recognized that the end of the ceramic period of Mycenaean III B was marked almost everywhere on the Greek mainland by a trail of calamity and disaster. At Mycenae itself the palace and the buildings in the citadel were destroyed by fire, following which there was only a feeble reoccupation during the period of the ceramic style III C. Tiryns suffered a like fate at the same time: the palace was burned and wrecked and was later reconstructed only on a modest scale, if at all. The Palace of Nestor at ancient Pylos perished at the same time in a tremendous conflagration that laid waste the whole complex of structures, no doubt after they had been thoroughly looted. It was never again rebuilt and re-occupied. The House of Kadmos at Thebes came to its end in a similar disaster, almost surely to be dated to the same fateful juncture. The Mycenaean Palace at Gla in the Copaic basin was abandoned at the close of the pottery phase III B and was never re-inhabited, as the Ephor J. Threpsiades has kindly informed me.

But it was not only the royal residences and strongholds that suffered; many of the smaller Mycenaean settlements ceased to exist after the end of the III B period. The site at Berbati was deserted at that time, and there was no habitation in My-

---

[8] O. Broneer, "Athens in the Late Bronze Age," *Antiquity*, XXX, 1956, pp. 9-18.

cenaean III C, a fact made known to me by Professor Å. Åker-ström. The neighboring town of Prosymna, too, evidently failed to survive that dangerous turning: more than 1200 vases were recovered from some fifty chamber tombs, the bulk of them belonging to the style of Mycenaean III B; but not one vessel nor even a potsherd assignable to Mycenaean III C came to light. The country town of Zygouries, which with its Potter's Shop seems to have flourished in the days of Mycenaean III B, yielded no recognizable wares of Phase III C to show that it lasted into that era. Numerous settlements of modest size in western Messenia, which had apparently existed since the Middle Helladic period, were likewise forsaken by their occupants before they crossed the threshold into Mycenaean III C.

This list could undoubtedly be considerably amplified, if necessary, but it is long enough to establish the general thesis that the Mycenaean world on the Greek mainland had suffered a crushing blow and had for the most part been reduced to poverty and impotence at the end of Mycenaean III B. In one province alone, namely Attica, Mycenaean sites continue, both in Athens itself and in the Mesogeia, to be prosperous, and pottery of the III C style is found in abundance. This fact is in accord with Attic tradition which boasted that the Dorian invaders were unable to conquer Attica. In the Peloponnesus and in Boeotia, at any rate, the surviving settlements appear to have been small and feeble. Parenthetically it might be noted that in the Ionian islands toward the west, and in the east, especially in Rhodes and Cyprus and beyond in Asia Minor and along the Syrian and Palestinian coast, pottery of the Mycenaean III C style, or related to it, appears in some quantity, suggesting that the latest Mycenaean culture, or contacts with it, were still maintained in these regions.

The downfall of Mycenaean power sketched above indicates, as Professor Broneer recognized, that there could have been no Trojan expedition worth writing about in the time of Mycenaean III C. At that time the principal Mycenaean centers, which, as recorded in tradition and the Homeric poems, provided the major contingents of ships and men, had been destroyed and most of them were lying in ruins. This was not the moment when the great Achaean coalition could be organized to carry on a war overseas. Most of the settlements that still remained on the Greek mainland were undoubtedly devoting all their efforts to face the problem of their own survival. If a large expeditionary force ever was mobilized to cross the Aegean and attempt to capture the formidable fortress-stronghold of Troy it must have been at a time when the Mycenaean world was flourishing and undamaged and the many minor kingdoms and principalities were ready and willing to rally around their overlord in a united effort to win booty and glory. That could only be in the period when the great palaces still stood in their pomp and splendor and the smaller settlements were enjoying their greatest strength, while pottery of Mycenaean III B was at the height of its widespread popularity. It could not well have been earlier, that is to say in the time of the Mycenaean III A style, as some scholars would have it; for the big royal palaces with their spacious megara had not then been built, and it is unlikely that a supreme king had yet established himself as the recognized overlord of all.

The Dorian Invasion has for a long time been treated as an orphan or a stepchild, or perhaps it might better be compared with a displaced person. The Greeks of the classical era had no doubt about its authenticity; it was firmly embedded in tradition and folk memory and it shed light on many events and developments that lay far beyond the beginnings of written history. Some modern scholars have challenged or rejected it altogether as a figment of the imagination. But to many historians and students of linguistics it has seemed to be an antecedent event necessary to account for the subsequent distribution of dialects and the political division and condition of Greece. The chief difficulty has been that there appeared to be no clearly and unmistakably marked slot or groove in the background into which the invasion could be fitted.

Thucydides states that the Peloponnesus was conquered by the Dorians and the Heraclids eighty years after the fall of Troy. His authority is of course unquestioned, but he does not tell us just how he got the eighty years or exactly when Troy fell. The latter crucial information was supplied long afterwards through the calculations of Eratosthenes, a distinguished geographer and astronomer of the third century B.C., who reached his chronological results by computations of the aggregate length of the genealogies of the Spartan kings and others. But in this field much depended on just how many years were reckoned to a generation. Some chronographers, among them Eratosthenes, allowed forty years, some thirty-five, and still others only thirty; and naturally they arrived at very different results, ranging through a period of nearly two hundred years, from the later part of the fourteenth century B.C. to the end of the twelfth. Douris of Samos, who lived in the fourth century placed the fall of Troy in 1334 B.C. Ephorus, a historian also of the fourth century, assigned it to 1135 B.C. As worked out by Eratosthenes, the date for the taking of Troy—the peg from which the chronology of many other events was suspended—when transposed into absolute years was fixed at 1184-1183 B.C.; and the completion of the Dorian Invasion thus fell in 1104-1103. But the background of the Greek countryside at the latter date displays little or no real evidence of an extensive destruction and ravaging on a large scale by military operations. The whole area seems already for a long time to have been sparsely populated or almost deserted. It is nearly a century earlier that the telltale track of the Dorians must be recognized in the fire-scarred ruins of all the great palaces and the more important towns which, as we have seen, were blotted out at the end of Mycenaean III B. When the two systems are converted into absolute years there is a discrepancy of approximately one century between the genealogical chronology of Eratosthenes and the sequence dating given by Mycenaean pottery as worked out by Furumark. Something must be wrong with one or the other system. Before we go further we must consider Furumark's neat chronological table, which is as follows:

Myc.	I	1550-1500 B.C.
	II A	1500-1450
	II B	1450-1425
	III A:1	1425-1400

III A:2 early	1400-1375
III A:2 late	1375-1300
III B	1300-1230
III C:1 early	1230-1200
III C:1 late	1200-1125
III C:2	1125-1100

The beginning of the table, Mycenaean I and II, from 1550 to 1450 is based on Evans' dating of Minoan civilization at Knossos, which in turn goes back to synchronisations with Egypt. For the early part of Mycenaean III A Egyptian contacts give some relatively scanty support, but for the later phases of III A and III B, Mycenaean pots found in datable Egyptian contexts are more numerous. The transition from Mycenaean III B to III C still lacks specific confirmatory evidence, and the dating of the later III C phases depends mainly on indirect combinations. When the evidence is analysed in this way, the sure dependable support for the table appears to be rather skimpy— and it must be admitted that some additional irrefutable confirmation would be welcome—but by and large Furumark's system, founded on at least some specific relation to genuine Egyptian calendar dates, is far more trustworthy than anything based on the estimated durations of imperfect genealogies.

For working purposes Furumark's conclusions have been generally accepted by archaeologists, who take them, as they were meant, as approximate, with some leeway here and there. A few minor modifications have been proposed: Professor Wace suggested pushing back the beginning of III B to 1330 or 1340 B.C., but he presented no new evidence. Others have felt that the initial phase of Mycenaean III A might perhaps be adjusted downward close to 1400 B.C. Many excavators are content more broadly to assign III A to the fourteenth century, III B to the thirteenth and III C to the twelfth. One must, however, remember that it is the pottery sequence that forms the basis for dating, and new discoveries in one area or another may still impose a slight upward or downward shift alongside the scale of absolute years. At the moment my own view is that Troy VIIa came to its end by enemy action in the decade around

1270 or 1260, while Nestor's Pylos and the other great palaces on the mainland were pillaged and burned some two generations later near the close of that century.

J. Bérard in 1951 had arrived at approximately the same dates for the capture of Troy and the Dorian conquest; but, proceeding by a different way, he believed that the destruction of Mycenae occurred in the middle period of the pottery style of III C, if not later; and he placed the change from Mycenaean III B to III C about 1250 B.C. It seems to me, however, now to be well established that the change came not long before 1200 and that the real destruction of Mycenae coincided with it.[9]

One of the greatest problems in this field of research raises the fundamental questions: who were the Greeks and whence did they come? Many scholars have struggled with these queries and the answers have been both numerous and diverse. Before going further into these matters it might be well to note that there is no pure race of any consequence now in existence. There may have been some in the remote origins of the human species, but long before recorded or even archaeological history began all had become mixed and fused from many elements. It is a truism that every people is the product of its past. The inhabitants of the Helladic peninsula in the Stone Age and the Bronze Age were several times overrun by invaders who came from one direction or another. The newcomers presumably slew most of the men, but the women and children were no doubt spared and ultimately absorbed the strangers or were

[9] Other views and interpretations, differing more or less from those presented here: J. Bérard, "Recherches sur la chronologie de l'époque mycénienne," Acad. des Inscr., Mémoires, XV, 1960, pp. 1-64; H. Biesantz, "Die Minoischen Bildnis-gemmen," *Marburger Winckelmann-programm*, 1958, pp. 9-25; idem, "Die kretisch-mykenische Kunst," *Illustrierte Welt-kunstgeschichte*, I, pp. 369-410 (Zurich, 1959); K. Bittel, *Grundzüge der Vor- und Frühgeschichte Kleinasiens* (2 ed., Tübingen, 1950); idem, *Kleinasiatische Studien* (Istanbul, 1942); H. J. Kantor, *The Aegean and the Orient in the Second Millennium B.C.* (Arch. Inst. of America, *Monograph* I, Bloomington, 1947; also in *A.J.A.*, LI, 1947, pp. 1-103); F. Matz, *Kreta, Mykene, Troja: die minoische und die homerische Welt*, Stuttgart, 1956; F. Schachermeyr, *Poseidon und die Entstehung der griechischen Götterglaubens*, Bern, 1950; idem, "Prähistorische Kulturen Griechenlands," Pauly-Wissowa, *R.E.*, XXII (Halb-bd.XLIV), 1954, 1350-1548.

themselves absorbed into the ensuing fusion. In this way many
diverse elements of culture were inherited and adopted. It was
surely by a process of this kind that the Greeks came into being,
and through many centuries they gradually evolved into the
distinctive people they became. The ancestors that introduced
the Hellenic language which set the Greek way of thinking
made the most important contribution.

Most historians think that the first Hellenes or their ancestors
must have made their way into the Helladic peninsula from the
north. And if they had no ships, this conclusion seems logical.
In the past persistent efforts have been expended in attempts to
identify some particular artifacts as belonging distinctively to
the Dorians, almost surely the latest of the Greeks to arrive:
among the items suggested are certain bronze "spectacle" fibulae, or safety pins, for example, or broad short swords for slash-
ing strokes, or even the later well-known pottery of the Geometric style. Some students indeed have sought to discover a
trail of such objects running down from the north along the
eastern and western coasts of Greece, as if it were something in
the nature of a modern paper chase. But it soon became apparent that not a few examples of these artifacts could be found
in the interior of the country far away from the littoral; and,
moreover, the particular objects selected for the test could not
with certainty be shown to be products or possessions characteristic of the Dorians.

And now that the arrival of the Greeks, or their forebears,
seems to be receding into a far more remote period in the early
part of the second millennium, the difficulties of determining
how and from what place they came have been greatly increased.
Some experts in linguistics, moreover, are reluctant to believe
that the Greek language could possibly go back to so early a
time, since they are convinced that its development, once begun,
moved rapidly.

Professor John Myres of Oxford in his Sather Lectures, delivered in 1927,[10] discussed exhaustively and ingeniously all

[10] J. L. Myres, *Who were the Greeks?* (Sather Classical Lectures, VI), Berkeley,
1930.

the evidence he was able to gather regarding the origin of the Greeks. His analysis of this remarkable people probed deeply into their common heritage in descent, in speech, in religion, in culture and tradition. The reader who has faithfully perused the bulky volume—and in doing so has inevitably acquired a vast amount of information from the fresh and novel facets of the problem as it is here presented—when he reaches the end still wonders, as Professor Myres himself probably did, who were the Greeks.

The evidence from archaeology, as we have already seen, reveals no recognizable break in culture between the coming of the Middle Helladic people, about 1800 B.C., plus or minus a century, and the close of the Mycenaean period. Most of the excavators who have worked at sites of this era on the Greek mainland therefore believe that the Middle Helladic folk formed the initial wave of the Hellenic stock that entered Greece. Once established in control of the mainland, they settled down to a life of steady gradual progress and evolution. In the sixteenth century, if not perhaps even earlier, they came into contact with Minoan civilization. Whatever their form and character—whether carried out by peaceful methods or aggression—these relations became progressively closer, and Minoan influence increasingly permeated mainland culture. One archaeologist has well remarked that in the earlier stages of this relationship we seem to be dealing with a Minoanized Mycenaean civilization, and in its later stages with a Mycenaeanized Minoan way of life. As in all later periods, the Greeks of this early age evidently evinced a passionate interest in everything new which they could adopt and modify as they chose.

If we are right in taking the Middle Helladic people to be Greeks—perhaps in an embryonic state of linguistic development—one fact recently ascertained must not be left out of consideration in any attempt to determine how they reached Greek lands. That is the discovery made at Troy that the Sixth Settlement was built by newcomers who appeared on the scene at the same time that the Middle Helladic wave rolled over the western side of the Aegean. These two movements were not only contemporary, but they clearly represent the same general culture.[11] For in each region Gray Minyan Ware now appears as the predominating kind of pottery, made in the same characteristic angular shapes, in a fabric that could be produced only under reducing conditions in the kiln. It was the knowledge of how to build a kiln of this type that the invaders brought into Greece and into Asia Minor; the pots themselves were then duly turned and fired locally. Both to the east and to the west of the Aegean Sea Mattpainted Ware soon makes its appearance, more abundantly in Greece, perhaps because that region lay so much nearer the Cyclades, where pottery of that kind most probably was invented. The settlements on the Greek mainland were also favorably situated to fall deeper and more quickly under Minoan influence.

The coming of the Greeks then must have been effected by some means and route which facilitated access to both shores of the Aegean. A suggestion was long ago made (by me, in fact) that the movement could have been carried out by ships coming down from the Pontus through the Sea of Marmora and the Dardanelles, where one contingent might have landed and taken possession of the Troad while the main body continued on across the Aegean to Greece. That suggestion seems not to have aroused much enthusiasm from any quarter. If it is rejected, one can easily enough imagine an invasion on a broad front spreading across the eastern and central Balkans and moving into Thrace and Macedonia and beyond. But so far as concerns picking up fragments of Gray Minyan pottery that may have been dropped along this wide trail in a paper chase of our own, we are no better off than those who tried to follow the scent of the Dorians.

Professor Myres in his Sather Lectures, studying the pedigrees of the Homeric heroes, called attention to the fact that many of them had human ancestors going back only two or at most three generations before they came to their origin in a god.[12] According to his interpretation, the beginning of the genealogy in a divine ancestor marks the date at which the family of the hero first took its place on the Greek stage, or in

[11] For an opposing view see K. Bittel in *Gnomon*, XXVIII, 1956, pp. 243 ff.
[12] Myres, *op.cit.* (note 10), pp. 308 ff.

other words first arrived in Greece. Professor Gomme in his commentary on Thucydides thinks Myres' conclusion sound. If we accept this view we must agree that at some time, two or three generations before the Trojan War, there was an influx of heroic characters who founded the families that soon thereafter became the rulers of the chief sites of Mycenaean power. These might be the adventurers, or Vikings, as Professor Nilsson has called them, whose descendants—he thinks—later became the kings and chieftains of the epics.[13] Whether they themselves were Greeks who imposed their language on a non-Greek common people, or were non-Greeks who took over the speech of the Greek people they conquered, remains to be determined. However that may be, if we find this theory worthy of belief, we must envisage the arrival toward the end of the fourteenth century of a good many ambitious soldiers of fortune who seized the strategic key points of the Mycenaean world; once established there, they began to build their distinctive palaces, each possessing a great throne hall with a huge central hearth. Later, perhaps, they added—for security when they deemed it necessary—a massive fortification wall around the citadel as at Athens, Mycenae, and Tiryns.

The entrance of vikings on the scene is of course romantic, but the ingenious theory that the point at which a hero's ancestry goes up to a god marks the arrival of the family in Greece is not the only possible explanation. It might equally well signal the first rise to public power and leadership; or it could mean that a household had lifted itself to a stage of keeping written genealogical family records and using imagination to supply a divine forefather for the earlier period beyond the reach of memory.

In this survey we have hitherto dealt mainly with some of the larger problems concerning the Mycenaean world. There are of course many other matters, perhaps of lesser magnitude, some of which have stirred up much argument, not to say controversy. One of these disputed questions must certainly be mentioned here. It has to do with the relative dating of the Linear B tablets found by Sir Arthur Evans at Knossos and those recovered more recently at Pylos and Mycenae on the

---

[13] Nilsson, *op.cit.* (note 5), p. 85.

Greek mainland. In his annual excavation reports from 1900 and the following years, Evans records the discovery of many hundreds and even thousands of tablets and fragments both in the palace itself and outside it along the paved roadway leading to the Little Palace, as well as inside the latter. Most of these pieces were found, he says, in strata assigned to the end of the palace of Late Minoan II, some time between 1450 and 1400 B.C. in accordance with his system of dating. But not a few tablets, Evans reports, came from deposits containing pottery of later date, Late Minoan III. His final conclusion was that the clay tablets had been baked and thus preserved by the great fire that laid the Late Minoan II palace in ruins. Various explanations of this disaster have been suggested, such as a violent earthquake, or an internal dissension and revolution, or capture, sacking, and burning by invading Mycenaean forces from the mainland of Greece. This latter view had in time won fairly wide acceptance and few, if any, ventured to challenge Evans' dating of the event.

In 1939 came the discovery in the Pylian region of southwestern Peloponnesus of Nestor's palace, in which were ultimately recovered more than 1000 tablets and fragments inscribed in Linear B. These, too, had been baked hard in a tremendous fire which made possible their survival while the palace itself was almost totally consumed. The abundant pottery found on the floors and in the pantries dates the destruction to the end of Mycenaean III B, that is to say, about two hundred years or more after the palace at Knossos was destroyed. The Linear B tablets found in 1952 and later at Mycenae likewise come from a stratum assigned by the excavators on ceramic evidence close to or at the very end of the thirteenth century.

When compared, the tablets from Knossos and those from the mainland are almost indistinguishable, in shapes, in general arrangement of the guide lines and the writing, in the normal forms of the syllabic signs, in documentary character and bureaucratic type, and in purpose. It is true that there are some greater or minor variations in the shapes of certain characters, but little if at all more than might be expected in writing done by different hands. This striking physical similarity led some students to wonder if the two groups were really two whole centuries or more apart in their origin, or if some mistake in dating had possibly been made on the one side or the other. The evidence on the mainland side, from Pylos and Mycenae, seemed to be unshakable; that from Knossos was not altogether clear of doubt, since Evans himself reported finding some of the tablets in Late Minoan III contexts, though the great majority were attributed to Late Minoan II. An investigation of the journals and daybooks of the excavations—the records kept by Sir Arthur Evans himself and his chief associate Duncan Mackenzie, which are deposited in the Ashmolean Museum—was undertaken jointly by two scholars. One speedily became convinced that all the tablets from Knossos were found in strata of the reoccupation period, that is to say, a late, if not the latest, stage of Late Minoan III. The other investigator no less quickly reached the conclusion that the Linear B documents from Knossos definitely came from deposits that had been laid down in the time of the palace of Late Minoan II.[14] Two separate reports have now been promised.

One somewhat confusing complication is that in his great work, *The Palace of Minos*, Evans makes it clear that a good deal of pottery in the fully developed style of Late Minoan III A was actually found on the floors of the palace he calls Late Minoan II. This means of course that the disastrous fire that wrecked the palace must have occurred at a time when Late Minoan III pottery had already come into general use.

The whole problem has become much more complex following Ventris's decipherment of the Linear B script and his demonstration that the language is an early form of Greek. Evans had naturally believed it to be Minoan—anything else was unthinkable to him—and on that assumption, the baking and preservation of the tablets by the fire that destroyed the palace of Late Minoan II could be plausibly and logically de-

[14] The controversy has been carried on chiefly in the press, for the most part in the London *Observer* (beginning July 3 and 10, 1960) and the *Listener* (Oct. 27, 1960). Professor L. R. Palmer's work, *Mycenaeans and Minoans* (London, 1961; New York, 1962), presents vigorous arguments for dating the Knossian tablets in the thirteenth century. Current bibliography is given promptly in *Nestor*, published by E. L. Bennett, Jr., Institute for Research in the Humanities, University of Wisconsin.

duced. Those who still reject Ventris's solution hold firmly to that view. But those who accept the language of the tablets as Hellenic now face a somewhat difficult choice of alternatives.

On the one hand they must explain how it was possible that documents in Greek came to be written in great numbers in a palace of Late Minoan II. The most likely explanation that has been proposed suggests that Mycenaean marauders from the mainland had already before this time seized and occupied the palace and established domination over Crete from this center. Certain Mycenaean pots of Late Helladic II types which have been found at Knossos have induced some archaeologists to argue that a conquest of this kind may well have been carried out. It still remains, however, to determine just how and when an invasion from the mainland could have been effected without leaving visible traces of violence and damage to the palace itself. Moreover, if we accept the view that the invaders succeeded in taking over the entire establishment, consolidating their power, and introducing their highly bureaucratic form of administration, as shown by the tablets, we are left completely in the dark so far as explaining the devastating fire that subsequently brought the palace down. Not that there is any lack of hypotheses and conjectures about it!

On the other hand is the bold alternative of rejecting altogether the conclusions of the excavators that the tablets come from the palace of Late Minoan II, and maintaining instead that they belong to a late phase of Late Minoan III. Apart from calling into question the judgment of Sir Arthur Evans and Mackenzie, this view involves the further presupposition that the palace was to a great extent, if not entirely, rehabilitated after the fire and was reoccupied and used as an administrative center of government for two hundred years and more. It requires still another assumption, namely that the building once again, toward the end of the Late Minoan III period, was burned to the ground in a fire by which the tablets were baked hard enough to be preserved. The excavators had characterized the reoccupation as an insignificant settlement of squatters among the ruins. Little or no archaeological evidence is now available, since it has all been dug away.

It is obvious, in view of these many uncertainties and guesses, that the whole problem demands further intensive study and clarification. We must in any event wait to see if the investigation of the records of the excavations can shed new and decisive light on the matter. Pending that, no one is in a position to express an authoritative opinion. There is evidently much to be said on both sides, and the arguments will have to be heard and considered.

The striking similarity of the tablets from the two regions, Crete and the mainland, obviously reflecting in both areas the same meticulous bureaucratic system of administration, seems to me to indicate an approximate contemporaneity of the documents and not a separation of two centuries or more. There are, moreover, some objects recorded and pictured on the Knossian tablets that look as if they represent types (swords, arrowheads, and pottery) that have not yet been certainly found to appear in contexts earlier than Late Minoan III. I am wondering if it is not perhaps possible that the continued occupation of the L.M. II palace in Period L.M. III, which Evans himself observed and reported, might not have lasted a good deal longer than has been thought. A possibility of this kind might conceivably reduce by several decades, at least, the temporal gap between the two opposing views, though it would probably satisfy few if any of the champions of either side.

Although it has evoked lively debate, with repercussions not lacking in interest of their own, this problem is, after all, for the most part only a question of dating which cannot claim to be of supreme importance. There are many less controversial aspects of life and culture in the Mycenaean Age that deserve to be mentioned even in this much curtailed survey. I am thinking for instance of the abundant new material of many kinds that has been brought to light almost within the past decade. Mycenaean pottery offers opportunity for a rewarding investigation, especially in a comparative study dealing with all the principal regions of the country. There are problems too connected with seals and seal impressions that might benefit from a critical collation based so far as possible on pieces of certified provenience from stratified deposits. Similar comparative research on the remains of frescoes recovered in recent years on the Greek mainland will likewise surely lead to conclusions of value.

In a much broader field a good beginning has been made by the expedition working under the direction of Professor Caskey on the island of Kea at an important fortified site. This undertaking should in time throw much new light on the relations between Mycenaean culture and the culture of the neighboring Cyclades, and thus aid substantially in filling a partial lacuna of long standing in archaeological records.

The University of Cincinnati has already contributed something to the increase of knowledge about Mycenaean Greece. Much is still to be learned, and there are abundant opportunities for research and new discoveries in archaeological field work as well as in the storerooms and workrooms by patient scrutiny and analysis of what has already been unearthed. With its splendid new endowment for the purpose of promoting the study of classics "—in the broadest sense of the term . . . the endeavor to make vital and constructive in the civilization of our country the spiritual, intellectual and esthetic inheritance we have received from the Greek and Roman civilizations"— the University of Cincinnati is in a unique position to advance knowledge in this sector that represents one of the early formative stages in the history of the Hellenic people.

Prologue
to Parmenides

BY GIORGIO DE SANTILLANA

Delivered March 26 and 27, 1962

2

PROLOGUE TO
PARMENIDES

I: THE WAY OF CLARITY

T HERE HAVE been as many ways of looking at the Pre-
socratics as there have been intellectual generations and
changes of attitude in modern times. Prodigious amounts
of exact philology and ingenious interpretation have been expended
on them, and yet they remain today as mysterious, perhaps more
mysterious, than they appeared in the Renaissance. For as our own
awareness of history builds up, we cannot help realizing that it is
those ancients who have dealt out all the ideas that Western thought
has played with ever since—so enticingly near to us in one way, in
another remote and incomprehensible beyond retrieve, as they stand
out like statues of Memnon in the wastes of the past, each uttering,
as it would seem, one note and only one, compared to the tumult
and the dialectic of later times.

Of these great ones, the most difficult is Parmenides.

"It is insufficiently known that the philosophy of the Eleatics
still forms an obscure chapter in the history of philosophy." Such
are the opening words of the latest book on Parmenides, by Dr.
J. H. M. M. Loenen, University of Leiden, published in 1959.
I consider this one of the most engaging understatements of the
year. Yes, it may be insufficiently known, let us then proclaim it.
The never-ending tangle of successive interpretations, assisted by
the most refined philological analysis, by ingenious conjectures
and emendations, by all the critical study of the *variae lectiones*,
has only made confusion worse confounded. For each point really
cleared up (a minor point at best) ten new doubts have arisen.
The moment of history defined by Parmenides was described
dramatically by Karl Reinhardt forty years ago: "When from the

shambles of the past, awesome, spectral, the Sphinx of Metaphysics first reared its head."

The Sphinx is still around, and the shambles still very much in evidence.

Part of the trouble is modern. Since the rescuing of the texts by the great philologists of the Nineteenth Century, one school after another has tried to inject its preconceptions into their meaning, according to the way in which they read the history of philosophical ideas.

Part is ancient. And it begins very early. Plato, Aristotle, Eudemus, Theophrastus, Proclus, Simplicius are clearly at odds about what Parmenides may really have meant. But he has suffered mostly from Plato's accolade. "August and terrible in his greatness," as Socrates says of him, he stands there as the founder of the doctrine of Being, on which Plato's metaphysics is founded. But surely, it is a very particular doctrine. No one is going to say that the dialogue entitled *Parmenides* is an historical document of the Eleatic's own thoughts. Plato himself is explicitly apologetic about the liberties that he takes with Parmenides' thought, and speaks playfully of having to commit parricide. But the irresistible effulgence of Platonic thought causes Parmenides to be lost, so to speak, in it. He becomes hardly identifiable as an independent thinker. And indeed the Neoplatonists have completed the work of incorporation, by presenting him as the first step towards a Gnosis of the Divine.

Now it so happens that modern history of philosophy, from Hegel onwards, is mostly written by idealists, who found it natural to preserve the Neo-Platonic scheme, and to present Parmenides as the indispensable link in their intellectual chain, the founder of ontology. A number of such today have extolled him for his "splendid intransigence" towards natural knowledge. And so he has become the banner-bearer of the anti-scientific attitude, however vast the difference may be between our time and reasons, and his.

One should like to ask those bold modernizers: who would imagine Fichte, Hegel, or Heidegger proceeding from cryptic statements on Being and Non-Being to a treatise concerning the mechanism of the planets and the illumination of the moon, or the sterility of mules? For these are subjects in the second part of Parmenides' poem. And if the inattention and the prejudice of commentators had not left us with the pitiful shreds we have of it, no one would have entertained the idea that Parmenides' physics was an insignificant appendix to his doctrine of Truth.

The current interpretation of Parmenides seems to have moved beyond these problems. Carried on in the wake of the Platonic dialogue, armed with the refined apparatus of exact philology, it puts all the stress on the verbal copula *is*, as if this had been at the heart of the epoch-making Eleatic discovery. What sense does it make? Ontological sense, answer the logico-verbalists. But not only in the direction later developed by Plato; Parmenides stands as the originator of logico-verbal Truth, and hence also of sophistic argument. A considerable amount of research has gone into showing the links between Eleatic and Sophistic logic, and that since the times of the ancient pseudo-Aristotelian treatise *De Melisso, Xenophane et Gorgia*. If the tools of reasoning are basically the same, how could there be a basic difference with the Sophists, even if the intentions are admittedly not the same? This seems to be Calogero's view and that of several contemporary authorities.

If the man of Elea had heard this explanation of himself, he might indeed have been, to use his own words, "wondrous hard to convince."

I am going to suggest a very different way of approach. The case has been worked out in a rather substantial essay, as yet unpublished, and the proof cannot be given within the span of a brief lecture. The argument is therefore merely indicated; but in a few key issues, I shall try also to justify my line of reasoning. Let me start from an old and sound remark of John Burnet:

"Does Parmenides refer to the world of sense or the world of ideas; concrete existence or abstract being; matter or spirit? All these questions would have been absolutely meaningless to an early Greek philosopher, and the system of Parmenides is the best touchstone for our understanding of this fundamental historical truth."

These are words of wisdom. It is pointless to use names like idealism and materialism before object and subject, form and con-

tent, matter and spirit have been set up as pairs of well-charac-
terized oppositions.

So we are led back to the neutral ground on which Parmenides
had placed himself, a ground where reason and truth about
nature were one and the same. Only *that* can be which can be
logically; for logic exists "for the sake of what is." Stated thus,
in the original words, we cannot but feel that it comes nearer to
the spirit of scientific rationalism than to any idealistic or materialistic system. But to keep exactly tuned to Parmenides' own key,
we should have to insist on the absence of a higher or lower, or
of a difference between abstract and concrete. It is a *conversio
veri ac entis.* Thought is coextensive with being, νοεῖν and ἐόν are
only two aspects of the same thing, and that thing is also the one
background—what stays forever. It is Anaximander's Unbounded,
Pythagoras' Order, Xenophanes' One, Heraclitus' Fire-Logos: τὸ
θεῖον, the Divine.

When the "ancients," as Aristotle calls them, had meant a
primordial substance or a substratum, they had not thought of
something present only to the discursive mind, but of something
that either meets the eye, or would meet a super-acute eye, if it
were refined enough to perceive it right where it is, *in* things. "If
we could only say what is exactly so," muses Xenophanes, while
Anaxagoras affirms: "Appearances are a sight of the invisible."

With Parmenides instead, and this is undeniable, we have a
complete break with the past and a new departure. So far we must
agree with those who speak of a radical novelty. But what kind
of novelty is it? Let us take an unprejudiced look at the poem—
at least at what was preserved of it.

The Proem

The overture is a grandiose and mythical adventure, which is
enough to show the text as a *griphos* in the archaic sense—unless
we consider it as some do a mere rhetorical exercise, which is hard
to suppose. The poet is taken aloft on a divine chariot, beyond the
Gates of Night and Day, until he reaches the abode of the Goddess of Truth, who undertakes to explain to him the ways that are
open to mortals, that of Truth and that of Opinion. I cannot go

here into the intricacies of her initial argument, nor into her violent
reprehension of the "akrita phyla," the ordinary speculators, who
think that a thing is and is not at the same time, and thus end up
by not knowing whether they are coming or going. I am trying to
look at the formal and mythical element. The first thing that appears is the Hesiodic model, and it would lead us into a fascinating
and most instructive comparison between the two theologies. But
then there is another element, too neglected by the commentators,
that Diels had brought out seventy years ago, when he described
the poem as belonging to the *Epimenideslitteratur*.

This insight, due to Diels' great philological instinct, cuts the
ground from under a lot of purely literary criticism of Parmenides
as "unpoetical." Parmenides is first and last a mythographer of
the "Orphic" kind. When you have to convey a *griphos* your
literary capacities do not stand out to their best advantage, and even
Dante is not at his most felicitous when he has to work out his
vision in Terrestrial Paradise. Such texts are not meant for literary,
but for scriptural understanding. Too little is left of the *Epimenideslitteratur* to establish valid parallels, but given the character of the
poem, which is eminently an "intellectual purification," and the
straight Pythagorean lineage of the author, we might speak of it
as of a *Hieros Logos*, a Sacred Discourse.

"How," says Reinhardt, "can Parmenides be credited with any
kind of unexpressed theology, he who knows no desire except
of knowledge, feels no fetters except of his logic, who is untouched
by either god or sentiment?"

It is strange that Reinhardt, who shows such an attentive understanding of Parmenides' personality, should have lent him these
traits of illuministic arrogance, in view of the master's obvious and
transparent worship of the Female principle. The Pythagoreans
had no sex prejudice, contrary to later times, but Parmenides goes
much further than they did, further than ever Mr. Robert Graves
would dare. His matriarchal absolutism is revealed not only in
his Daemon Lady but in all her attendants and epicleses, Dike,
Ananke, Moira, Themis, the Heliades, even to the "most intelligent" mares. Even when he speaks of the universal constraint that
urges "the female to union with the male, and conversely the male
to the female," he opposes the habitual order of thinking which

brings the courting male first to the mind: also the word *stygeros* applied to birth strikes one as the woman's point of view. It is usually treated in this case as an ordinary epic epithet, and rendered as "painful" (Diels: *weherfüllt*) but the real meaning is "miserable, wretched, abhorred," which is the connotation it has in Hesiod when applied to Doom and Strife, children of Night. As far as the divine figures go, one might find the consistency in sex easier to understand, since they are all fundamentally aspects of the one feminine power; the Heliads, in fact, may have been originally a college of her priestesses, like the daughters of Neleus, and the mares more sacred to her in her frequent aspect of the Mare-Goddess, which appears in several myths, such as that of Demeter and Erichthonius. But in the strictly physical explanations this line of reasoning does not apply; yet there, too, the feminine element is shown to prevail. We discern here something which cannot be mistaken for an allegorical dressing, which is actually the intrinsic and living form, the "entelechy" in the Aristotelian sense, of Parmenides' thought.

The Way of the Gods

The moment of discovery, the way to the gods, has perforce to be mythological, since it involves that the understanding of the "man who knows" has been rightly guided, and raised above the opinions of mankind. But if the revelation itself has nothing mythological about it, this does not mean a break in style and a change into abstract theory: for that "theoria" itself is the Way of Truth, the Way of the Gods. It is thus that the Pythagoreans had understood mathematical discovery. "Follow the god" was their maxim, or, "Follow in the footsteps of the god." In all early philosophical literature understanding and the Way of the Gods are one. There is no other proper object for the higher awareness. We say understanding, and not explanation: for what the wise man is vouchsafed in this way involves a recognition, a fulfillment, and also a renunciation.

And so we are left to face the Daemon Lady in her absolute, singularly non-Olympian power; just as she is un-Olympian in her personality, ignoring purely and simply the constitutional gods of the Greek cult. Proclus informs us that her name is Hypsipyle,

"High Gates" which is strictly a title (cf. Pharaoh, "High House," or the Turkish Sublime Porte). By careful comparison with Hesiod, we can work out her homologues in the Theogony as Themis, Hekate, the Oracle of Night, artfully dispersed by Hesiod, here concentrated in one figure which is also given total cosmic power in the Second Part of the Poem—"The Daemon who steers all things." That the two aspects, the intellectual and the physical, belong to one and the same figure, can hardly be doubted, but has been established conclusively by Rivaud, who identified her as the ancient Aphrodite Urania.[1] It is she that Lucretius invokes as *orbis totius alma Venus*; Lucretius who ignored the gods, and believed only in atoms and the void, but whose consistency yielded to the poetic feeling engendered by the Parmenidean vision:

> *Quae quoniam rerum naturam sola gubernas*
> *Nec sine te quicquam dias in luminis oras*
> *Exoritur. . . .*

These lines are so close to the exact conception of Parmenides that they may well be a paraphrase of some lost lines of this poem; they have certainly nothing to do with Epicurus. Several such lines appear in Lucretius, taken almost bodily from the *veteres docti poetae* he had chosen as his models.

Another almost exact parallel can be found in the Orphic hymns (n. 27 Abel):

> "Holder of the sceptor of famous heaven,
> *Lady of the Many Names, Awful One*
> Who holdest the central throne of the cosmos . . .
> From you has sprung the race of immortals and men"

This is indeed the way the Daemon appears in the Second Part of the poem, steering the whirling world from her high seat on

---

[1] Aphrodite Urania was an archaic Athenian deity, worshipped with the ancient rites of wineless libation. She was associated in the cult with Mnemosyne, the Dawn, the Sun, the Moon and the Nymphs (schol. ad *Oed. Col.* 100). Hence she belongs to the entities described in the second stage of Hesiod's *Theogony* (265-452). Empedocles reminds us that such deities as Aphrodite Urania came before Kronos and Zeus. In Hesiod, it is Theia who bears Sun, Moon, and Dawn, and Dawn in its turn bears the star Eosphoros "and the gleaming stars with which heaven is crowned" (371-382). Aphrodite Urania was in tradition 'the oldest of the Moirai': cf. Parmenides (fr. 8. 37). Hence in the Hesiodic line she would precede even Theia, as the earliest manifestation of Night herself, cf. below.

the Ecliptic Pole (at least if I read Aëtius right, for critics have
put her into all sorts of strange places)—and anyway it cannot be
denied, because Aristotle quotes it, that

"First of all things she created Eros"

But here she is now, and she turns to her disciple in a sudden
movement of intellectual compassion, to teach him about her
works:

"Meet it is that you should learn all things, as well the unshaken heart of well-rounded Truth, as also the opinion of mortals,
in which there is no certain reliance: but this you shall learn too,
how an explanation of things that appear must be considered valid
when it goes through all that we know."

This passage is one of the most controversial among philologists,
and it has been firmly decided by most that she announces a
physical world that can be shown to make no sense (is Parmenides
not the "freezer" of all reality, as Plato remarked once?), to the
point that Diels went so far as to emend a δοκίμως in the text to
square with his preconceptions. But the reading above has been
supported by Wilamowitz, and that ought to be safe enough. Dr.
Loenen is willing to accept it.

The Way of Men

Then, once she has explained the Way of Truth, the Goddess
takes up her earlier promise:

> . . . δόξας δ'ἀπὸ τοῦδε βροτείας
> μάνθανε κόσμον ἐμῶν ἐπέων ἀπατηλὸν ἀκούων.

Now, this is definitely a two-edged proposition. If you begin
by translating the perfectly neutral word *doxa* with *Wahngedanken*,
as Diels does, you have prejudged the issue: she is going to deal
with the "delusions of mortals," and therefore her words are bound
to be "deceptive." But in Presocratic usage, *doxa* means "opinion"
without any pejorative connotation. It means, barring supernal
knowledge, the kind of conclusions a man has been able to reach
and is willing to stand by. So, for example, in Xenophanes. In
Pythagorean language, it is equivalent to "scientific inquiry" pure
and simple. Why should it be here "delusions"? Because of the
ἀπατηλόν in the next line, which is commonly understood as "de-

ceptive." Since the Truth has been set up already, the next thing cannot be but deceit and illusion. What a black-and-white notion. When the goddess in the beginning warns her disciple to keep away from ways of inquiry which make no sense, she calls them such in vivid and explicit language. She wastes no words on irrelevant details. Not so here. Nor, on the other hand, does she offer a *gnosis* which should show up all things physical as sick dreams. That kind of *gnosis* had not yet been invented. She is offering a *diakosmos*, and the poet's song rises to Orphic solemnity as he announces it:

"You shall know the origins of things on high, and all the signs in the sky, and the secret works of the glowing sun's clear torch, and whence they arose. And you shall learn likewise of the wandering deeds of the round-eyed moon, and of her nature. You shall know, too, the heaven that encloses round, whence it arose, and how Necessity took it and bound it to keep the limits of the stars ... ."

There is no hint here of meaninglessness, and no one would have started thinking this way if he had had the full text of the Way of Opinion, instead of the few lamentable shreds transmitted to us by doxographers who shared the idealist preconception of modern historians.

Plutarch, who did share idealist preconceptions but had a refreshing sense of reality, brings back things into proportion in his *Adversus Colotem*:

"Parmenides, being, as he was, an ancient naturalist, and one who in writing sought to deliver his own and not to destroy another's doctrine, he has passed over none of the principal things of nature."

Let us stand then by this: "he was an ancient naturalist," and his doctrines of nature cannot be a mere exposure of the deceit practiced by such people as naturalists in giving a doctrine of nature. Nor is the Goddess of Truth supposed to utter mere deceit. On this point, I am glad to say, Dr. Loenen finds himself in agreement with me. And we notice that the adjective applies not to the words of her statement, but to the "order of her words." We have then to translate ἀπατηλόν as something else than the too pat "deceitful." We find that the word is used for puzzles, riddling truths, for what seems absurd to the listener and yet turns out to be so. A prime example is Heraclitus fr. 56. There is a whole mythological literature of the difficult saying and the "riddling truth" apt to lead men astray. Amlethus—not Shakespeare's Hamlet, but the age-old powerful personage who appears in Saxo Grammaticus—already bewilders men in this way. We might call it his mark. Let us then take those lines to mean: "Henceforward learn the notions of mortals, lending ear to the cunning order of my words." For it is the *order*, κόσμος ἀπατηλός, not the words themselves, which makes the difficulty.

This idea of "cunning" or "tricky" is connected with the next line: "They came to a resolution to name two forms. . . ." It cannot refer to a chance conjecture of some individuals, nor does it refer to the pointless "indiscriminate crowd" against which the poet had been cautioned earlier. The words imply something like a legislative assembly issuing a decree. Caught inside the flux of phenomena, men must work out an acceptable order. One clause however, lends itself to error, that is, we might consider each of those "two forms" separately. This we must not do. We can accept for the present Dr. Loenen's conclusion: "It is clear that Parmenides believes he is bringing something fundamentally new in the *doxa*-part as well, viz. the idea that everything in the world is a combination of 'fire' and 'night'. This is indeed a new idea, at least if 'everything' is really taken very strictly, so that there does not exist a single thing which consists either exclusively of 'light' or exclusively of 'night'." Such a condition makes it very plausible that the Goddess should warn us not to be led astray by the "tricky order of her words."

But *if* the way of Opinion *is* a physics—and it has taken centuries of exegetic blinkering to obscure this obvious fact—then the Way of Truth must make a sense which is correlative to that. We have again to start afresh, looking for a congruence and an integration between both sides of the panel. Indeed, if the discovery of the First Part is simply logical implication, (and surely it is at least that) mankind would have been grateful for a clearer statement. The Way of Truth is, without any doubt, one of the most impressively obscure affirmations in the history of thought. Confronted with the solemn chant of the hexameters, Parmenides' contemporaries must have thought that this man had been granted the sight of things unspeakable, and that he had become intellectually sunstruck. Some, no doubt, must have wondered whether it was the practice to interrupt the ruling deity of the universe at her work, to bespeak the services of "exceeding wise" mares and of a cortege of Daughters of the Sun to carry him aloft, only to come back with a set of oracular tautologies.

Metaphysics, whatever it may be, seems still to lead men astray much more than any physics.

On reading the recent book of Dr. Loenen, which is, as it were, the end point of learned and penetrating decipherment over several decades, I think anyone will be impressed with what little progress that has been achieved in solving the riddle of the Sphinx. Dr. Loenen is sound in his approach: he avoids the extreme position, of idealism and logico-verbalism, he does not suppose like some that Parmenides was hypnotized on the verbal copula *is*, or inventing an empty ontological reason. He has come in fact a good part of the way, in presenting the Eleatic doctrine as an epistemological rationalism, and in allowing the Way of Opinion the status of a valid physical theory. And yet, with all his ingenious comments and solicitations, the Way of Truth does not seem to come to life under his hands. Let the reader rather judge by himself. Here we are dealing with a key point of the Way of Truth, the indivisibility of Being: Fr. 8 insists on it in many ways:

"Nor is it separated, since it is all alike, and there is no more anywhere, to prevent it from being continuous, or lesser, but everything is full of Being. Wherefore it is all continuous, for Being presses on Being. . . . But since the last bound is defined on all sides, like the body of a well-rounded sphere, it is equally poised from the center in all directions, for it is necessary that it should not be greater in one direction and smaller in another. Nor is there Non-Being to prevent it from reaching out to its like, nor is it possible for Being to be more here and less there, because it is all inviolable. For it is equal from everywhere, and fits equally in its limits."

The idea of a homogeneous *plenum* seems here to be passionately insisted on. Some modern commentators have even seen a simile

for the uniform radiance of spiritual light. Yet this is what Dr.
Loenen makes of it:

(pp. 108-110.) ". . . The passage is preceded by the reference
to the *image of a ball or a sphere* (the former seems more probable); this implies that Parmenides here considers being from the
statical point of view of completeness rather than from the dynam-
ical one of the mental process referred to above; another consequence of this is that a spatial aspect naturally presents itself. The
occurrence of this image proves that Parmenides had not yet succeeded in freeing himself entirely from imagination: pure thought
is still hampered by it. But in this passage again it will be clear that
he intends to transcend all spatiality, which accords with my previous remarks on this subject (I 41 and 44, cf. 45). Being is not a
ball, and as a matter of fact Parmenides only says that it is *like* a
ball. The only problem is *what exactly is the point of comparison*
(see I n. 239). Now it is precisely in connection with this ball-image
that he rejects the possibility that the many ideas of being do not
fully coincide, that the uniformity might be broken by a greater
or smaller idea of being, so that they would not cover each other
completely (ll. 44-5). The difference with ll. 23-4 seems to be
that here not only qualitative differences (1. 48, cf. 23ff.) but also
quantitative differences are denied. One might perhaps think that
one idea is greater or smaller than the other, in accordance with
the greater or smaller quantity of concrete things which form the
regular starting-point for thought. This notion, however, is rejected,
and since the ball too is merely an image, one has to assume that
he intends to *exclude fundamentally all spatiality from the idea
of being.* The passage ll. 46ff. is thus clear: 'for there is neither
an (idea of) being which might stop its arriving at identity'
(because there are no quantitative differences), 'nor is it possible
for an (idea of) being to be here and there less than an (idea of)
being' (because there are no qualitative differences), 'since it is
all inviolate; for from every side it is identical with itself, uni-
formly it is within limits.' The last line (49), in which we meet
with the problem of the πείρατα, forms a suitable transition to the
third attribute."

The author seems to find the passage at last clear. I can only
envy him. I have always understood that there is a kind of philo-

sophical language which is only accessible to special philosophers. I trust Dr. Loenen will not take it as a personal remark, which would be far from my intention, when I admit that I could not help being reminded of Voltaire's remark: "Quand celui qui parle ne se comprend plus, on appelle cela de la métaphysique."

Let me cite, rather, certain words written by Klaus Reich, the Marburg historian of philosophy, in his 1954 essay on Parmenides:[2]

"The most modern interpretations, both philosophical and philological, can only fill the reader with concern. One or the other may also drive him to scorn or ridicule. . . . It seems to me that the fault lies largely with the prejudice which attributes to the so-called archaic period a 'structure of thought' different from that of the men of today. Any logical paradox may then appear plausible as the end product of that archaic process, and in fact we must be ready for anything. Empathy is supposed to take the place of clear understanding, as happens in dealing with pathological cases. . . . If a writer today is ready to content himself with that, it is due in my opinion to the insistent trend among philosophers in the last hundred years to equate themselves with literary historians. I fear that this is a way of making the history of philosophy irrelevant to the history of exact sciences, and thus depriving it of what should be its highest distinction."

These are far-reaching remarks, which hold a promise of sound interpretation, and indeed when Reich derives Eleatic Being from an attempt to impose more rigorous conditions on the Anaximandrean Unbounded, one may not agree wholly, and yet accept the cogency of his argument. It is as if the history of ideas were put back upon its feet. Real problems follow upon each other in a way which makes sense to the intellectual imagination. The substrate of all things is found back where it should be—everywhere, rather than nowhere.

I am wondering, with all respect for the learned commentators, whether that shying away from any hint of spatiality is not due to a misunderstanding about the very idea of space—a misunderstanding as old and as hard as the rock of ages. Their main authority is of course Plato, who in the well-known passage (*Parmenides* 150e)

---

[2] Klaus Reich, "Parmenides und die Pythagoreer," *Hermes* No. 82 (1954), 287-294.

rejects any connection of Being with the Great and Small, that is, with magnitude. Whatever is not connected with magnitude, so it has been decided *ab antiquo*, can have nothing to do with space. If we take this for a valid critical statement, we forget the depth of the Platonic preconception. The role of extension in Plato is played by that difficult idea, the Receptacle, that which is at the beginning and is the source of all multiplicity as well as concrete magnitude. It is a kind of principle of dispersion, the nearest thing to non-being: it is thus perforce at the other pole from the idea of Being. Plato's denial, then, powerful though it has been in history, has reasons which are not ours.[3] But do they belong to Parmenides? I have noted Socrates' modest disclaimer in the *Theaetetus*, and Klaus Reich comes to my help in this. Plato, he says, implies more than once that he does not wholly understand what Parmenides was really at, and even his quotations from memory are inexact. The logic of implication is there, the imagination that guided it remains hidden.

In Aristotle we find another kind of authority, and another kind of barrier. While he restores Parmenides to his rank as *physikos*, and does not deny the spatial metaphor, he insists that Being must be unconnected with any kind of *topos*, and hence—as we should say—unspatial. Is this straight interpretation, or is it due to the basic Aristotelian preconception about essences? Dr. Loenen is clearly impressed by the argument, as he supports his own interpretation by appeal to the well-known Zenonian paradox on *topos*. If Zeno thus denies "place," because it would in turn have a place, and so on, does it not follow that Parmenides too denied "place" to his Being? Why surely, we make free to answer, and the farthest thing from Parmenides' mind should have been the ordinary idea of space as a collection of places: an idea which stands out in Aristotle but had a long past of common-sense representation. The idea is in fact so commonsensical that we can bring it out easily in cultivated contemporaries of ours who have had the

---

[3] Dr. Loenen has found out, too, that we must assume such grave misunderstandings in antiquity. He manages to make sense of the impenetrable fr. 16 by throwing overboard Theophrastus' official interpretation, and assumes the passage was not only misread but misplaced from Truth into Opinion. The word πλέον is made to mean not "more," but "full," and a possible meaning is restored.

benefit of a strictly classical education, and on whose horizon Descartes has never dawned, let alone what followed. I tried the experiment once on a distinguished philologist and got in all naïveté a startlingly Aristotelian definition of what space is. Aristotle, it is well known, refuses geometrical abstraction in dealing with physical reality, and his space is nothing but a juxtaposition of qualitatively different loci. The modern idea of space, as I have proved elsewhere, becomes current only about 1400 with the first generation of Renaissance architects. How can the philologist step outside of the circle of ideas if he is unaware of that other world of mathematics?

We are rehearsing here as a scholarly skit what was once a tragedy of misunderstanding at the time of Galileo's contemporaries, the men of the Aristotelian culture who simply could not see what he was driving at. Let me illustrate this tangle with a modern example. We find it in Albertelli's excellent study on the Eleatics, often referred to by Loenen, apropos of Parmenides' sphere of Being. Some authors, says Albertelli, have suggested the possibility of an infinite sphere, but that obviously makes no sense. "To speak of a sphere with infinite radius would be like speaking of a square circle." Now we all deeply respect the mind and personality of Albertelli, the size of his achievement for one who was to die so young in front of a German firing squad: but it is all the more revealing to note this gap between the world of the philologist and that of mathematical ideation. What inner contradiction can anyone find in the concept of an infinite sphere? It is a very natural concept, whose course in time was traced by Dietrich Mahnke, and the *Schriftgelehrten* could well have taken notice of it were it only from the revolutionary influence of Nicholas of Cusa. But the line of mathematical imagination and that of philological critique seem to have faced each other in mutual incomprehension through the centuries.

Metamathematics

Hence, I trust I may be forgiven, if I approach the mysterious text from an entirely new angle—that which Jaeger and Stenzel would have called of mathematical ideation; this is far from implying a denial of the metaphysical content, but it would show us the still unknown underlying intellectual structure, which is meta-mathematical. I suggest then, that we treat the word "Being" throughout as an undefined term, and replace it in the text with X. It is surely good method to posit our ignorance of a dazzling, familiar and yet ununderstood word, by treating it formally as an unknown term, and trying to define it by context. Now, if we keep our mind "washed clear of preconceptions" as Bacon suggested, and try to define X strictly by context, it will be found that there is one, and only one, other concept which can be put in the place of X without engendering nonsense or contradiction, and that concept is pure geometrical space itself, for which the Greeks did not yet have a technical term (it is known that the early *Elements* were essentially two-dimensional). Moreover, as I think I could show, it was built up by the use of what we would call scientific logic, while Plato and Aristotle discuss Being with different—and far from scientific—logical tools. We shall have to come back to this more explicitly.

So, after Parmenides the physicist, there emerges another, and even less known, Parmenides the mathematician. Why is it strange? It is, I suggest, because we tend to forget that the Master of Elea was considered among the foremost mathematicians and astronomers of his own time.

Yet Proclus mentions him as the author of that negative definition which suits geometrical principles, and elsewhere he is referred to as having first classified figures into rectilinear, curvilinear and mixtilinear. This may sound an unexciting type of activity, until you find in Pythagorean theory all the profound implications of the one vs. the other kind of figure. Kepler spends a passionate page on that, in the *Mysterium Cosmographicum*, and we may be sure that Parmenides, the disciple of Ameinias, undertook the question in very much the same spirit as Kepler. These interests are a kind of intellectual signature.

In the field of astronomy, Parmenides is said to have taught the division of the sphere of the earth into regions corresponding to the celestial circles marked by equator and tropics, and indeed, if we are to believe Theophrastus, it is *he* and not Pythagoras who first taught that the earth is round. He is also said by Diogenes Laertius to have identified the morning and the evening star as one and the same planet. These could hardly have been called discoveries in one or the other region of the Mediterranean World, but in a Greece still under the spell of Ionian Physics, they put Parmenides in the forefront of *mathematikoi*. His contemporaries might well have referred to him, as Socrates says of Timaeus, as "the *astronomikotatos* of us all."

Is it the metric song, the mythographic imagery, that have led critics to overlook the scientific background, in favor of the Hesiodic element? It would be again an error of perspective. Images like the gates of Night and Day are defined unequivocally by archaic precedent. Gates, pillars, *nyssai, metae, portae solis,* always lead back to solstices and equinoxes. The literary *genre* is a superficial guide. Hesiod hardly belongs to a well-set *genre* anyway. We shall find:

1. That Hesiod has written a poem called *Astronomia*—Callimachus claims that it was the model for Aratus;[4]

2. That Hesiod's "Shield of Heracles" with its concentric zones (314) is a cosmographical item as much as the Homeric one.[5]

3. Furthermore, we may note that this shield is contained in Hesiod's "Catalogue of Women," a precedent to Parmenides feminized imagery.

Do what we will, whatever the line of descent we prefer, call it Hesiodic epic or *Epimenideslitteratur,* we cannot avoid running into the Royal Art, which bore the seal of the scientific knowledge of the time. It is hardly congruent, then, to have issue from that a writer who derives the whole universe of phenomena as vain illusion, and dispenses instead a world of verbal subtleties.

If we add now to these clues what we have right under our eyes, viz. the astronomy of the Way of Opinion, our conclusion will become bodily evidence. Out of the few mutilated fragments, the same type of commentators which is responsible for its perishing sits now in judgment to pronounce it some kind of cosmological fantasy which cannot be made into a physical system. It is clear that

[4] Pliny *N.H.* 18,213. I transpose "Astrologia" into "Astronomia," because that is what it meant then.
[5] With the significant difference that the Homeric shield was ordered by Thetis, Hesiod's by Zeus (320) and that the latter shield was used by Heracles in his fight against—Mars "in" Cygnus.

even Aëtius, the lone doxographer to whom we owe a partial summary, did not understand what he was writing down. Yet it is enough to presuppose that a pattern of spherical symmetry must be intended, i.e. that the text must make astronomical sense, and it will fall into place, without even need of the emendation suggested by Diels, with the Daemon not in the various impossible places supposed by commentators, but logically seated at a northern pole, and the "crowns" marking an intricate plaited device of tracks over a wide band of heaven. A physics of a rigid geometrical kind, impossibly rigid to be sure, but still in the nature of a kinematic diagram, exactingly precise, with no animation or animism involved. The astronomy is mechanical and geometrical constraints all through, a kind of graphic vision of laws of nature. We have here a perfect example of what I have called the synoptic capacity of archaic astronomy, which is able to grasp the shifting positions of points of light as a complete path on the sphere.

So much I must ask you to take on faith, since I cannot prove it here. But regardless of details which have perforce to remain conjectural, you can verify its main tenets from the only relevant portion of the text that survives: "The narrower (crowns) are filled with pure fire, and those supporting with night, and between these rushes a portion of fire. In the midst of them is the Daemon that steers the course of all things."

Sufficient Reason

Enough evidence has been collected to place Parmenides in the frame of his own concerns, and to dissociate him from the sophistic group who were to occupy the scene two generations later.

The best evidence, in fact, is afforded by his strongest tool of analysis, which depends for the large part, not on the verbal quibbles to be found in Gorgias and Plato's *Parmenides,* but on the fundamental Principle of Symmetry or Indifference, a form of the Principle of Sufficient Reason. This principle states that symmetrical effects, or more generally, that causes which are indistinguishable intrinsically, when considered by themselves, cannot produce distinguishable effects.

At the dawn of scientific philosophy Anaximander applied the principle of symmetry to explain the immobility of the earth. We might paraphrase the argument by saying that a spherically symmetrical system of forces about the earth could cause only a spherically symmetrical motion in it, which excludes the possibility of its moving as a whole in any one particular direction.

We find a somewhat subtler use of it, applied to time, in Parmenides, fr. 8:

"If (Being) came from nothing, what need could have made it arise later or sooner? Therefore it must exist either altogether or not at all."

That is, the points of time have no distinguishing character *per se* that might enable us to pick one and single it out from all the rest; being placed at a given time and with nothing else to refer to, we cannot tell which point of time it is. Therefore, by the Principle of Indifference, the existence of Being must stand in the same relation to all of them; it must either hold at all of them or at none. To speak metaphorically, if Being wanted to come into existence at a definite time, it would have to be able to tell that time absolutely from all the rest, which is impossible.

It is worth noting here that in Aristotle's universe, so lovingly constructed to minimize mathematical symmetry (for all the points are distinguishable), the case of time is the one case where the conditions for the application of the Principle of Indifference are fulfilled, and there he applies the argument in exactly the same way as Parmenides:

"Moreover, why was it destroyed at this particular point of time rather than any other, when up till now it had always existed, or why generated now, when for an infinite time it had not existed?" (*de Caelo* 283 *a*).

In fact the Eternity of the World is one of the few points where he applies classical rationalism. But one must note that his argument takes a secondary place in his exposition.

It is, however, in connection with space that the Principle of Indifference finds its greatest scope, as Parmenides well saw when he made it the fundamental instrument in his logic. Euclidean geometry puts three requirements on its space; first, it must have continuity (in a sense somewhat stronger than the mere absence of gaps between points); second, it must be the same, homogeneous throughout, so that we can move figures freely from place to place without altering their geometrical properties; and finally, it must be isotropic, or the same in all direction, so that figures can be turned around without affecting them. In other words, if you are placed in geometrical space, it must be impossible to tell where you are or in what direction you are looking. In modern terms, we say that Euclidean space is invariant under the continuous three-dimensional translation and rotation groups. In fact, from the last two conditions we can derive the first, because of the continuity of the groups. All this is implied by Euclid's axiom affirming the possibility of superposing any two figures, which is known to date from early times, since geometrical algebra depends on it.

Now it is also true that anything satisfying these three conditions must be isomorphic with and intrinsically indistinguishable from Euclidean space. That is the fundamental reason why, when we find Parmenides stating repeatedly and emphatically that his Being satisfies our three conditions, we conclude that it was in fact the space of the mathematician (and physicist) he had in mind:

a. Continuity.

"Discern steadfastly with your mind what is at hand and present and what is distant and absent together. For Being does not divide from its connection with Being, neither dispersed in arrangement everywhere nor compacted. (fr. 4)

"Nor is it separated, since it is all alike, and there is no more anywhere, to prevent it from being continuous, nor lesser, but everything is full of Being. Wherefore it is all continuous; for Being adjoins Being. (fr. 8)

"Nor was it ever, nor will it be, for it exists now, all together, a single continuum."

The argument from the principle of indifference is that the presence of gaps in space destroys its homogeneity, in distinguishing between the "points" and the places between them. For completeness it requires the Zenonian procedure, of actually constructing such places in infinite number by successive division; but given that, it is compelling. It is hard not to see a direct criticism of the Pythagorean theory of space in this passage.

b. Homogeneity.

". . . In it are very many tokens that Being is uncreated and indestructible, one all through, whole, unmoveable, and without end.

". . . Nor is it separated, since it is all alike . . .

". . . For Being is not permitted to be incomplete; for it is not in want; while if it were, it would miss being all.

". . . Nor is there Not-Being to prevent it from reaching out to its like, nor is it possible for Being to be more here and less there, because it is all inviolable."

The Pythagorean space does not satisfy this requirement either: the diagonal starting out from one corner does not intersect the other: it meets it "between" points. But the diagonal might have started from the other corner.

c. Isotropy.

"But since there is an ultimate bound, it is limited on all sides, like the body of a well-rounded sphere, equally poised from the center in all directions; for it is necessary that it should not be greater in one direction and smaller in another . . .

". . . For it is equal from everywhere, and fits equally in its limits."

In the Pythagorean space there is no isotropy, either; there are preferred directions in the lattice. The course of thought that I have outlined, starting from the problems of the discontinuous, is not a matter of mere inference: it comes clearly to light in frs. 5 and 8 which could hardly be referred to anything except formalized Pythagorean theories of discontinuity:

"Nor is it separated, since it is all alike, and there is no more anywhere, to prevent it from being continuous, nor lesser, but everything is full of Being. Wherefore it is all continuous; for Being adjoins Being."

It is further explicitly confirmed by fr. 4

"Perceive steadfastly with the mind the far and the near together. For Being does not divide in its connexion with Being, neither dispersed in arrangement everywhere, nor brought together."

Logico-verbalists have sweated blood over it. "This mysterious fragment," says Calogero, "of which we still lack a satisfactory interpretation." The most common interpretation, he adds, is the idealistic one, but it is also the most far-fetched. For if we understand, e.g. with Diels, "see how now the far is present to your mind reliably," it is difficult to make sense of the following line: "because Being does not divide from its connexion with Being." Fraenkel, in fact, gives up in despair and suggests that the text must be corrupt. But then, he, Diels, Nestle, and Albertelli understand *νόῳ* as *intellectui* tied up with "far" and "near," which inevitably gives, "what is absent and present to the mind" or some such embarrassing sentence; whereas, omitting prejudice, we have the natural translation *νόῳ = intellectu*, as appears in Burnet and Reinhardt, and suddenly the line makes sense, not only with itself, but with the next one: "Discern steadfastly with your mind the far and the near together; for Being does not divide from its connection with Being . . ." Calogero, reasonably enough, sees that this is the only way, and concludes that what is meant in fact is extension and spatial contiguity, whence he promptly concludes: "It is clear that this aspect, so definitely materialistic, of Parmenidian Being, cannot be but the product of the ontologization of the logical requirement of the absolute indifference of Being; a product all the more characteristic because of the effort and the incongruity from which it issues, of a being in its turn all full of being." Calogero is thus back on his feet again, and the arrested pirouette shows him gracefully holding hands with Gorgias; but Albertelli is left on the ground dizzily protesting, "It makes no sense anyway; for if Being does not divide in its connection from Being, this is no reason for the far to be near."

The difficulty for idealistic interpreters is revealing. We are here at *the* parting of the ways in the history of thought. We perceive the deviation that Aristotle later inflicted on already established terms for his own purposes. His objects of thought are not in nature, they are in an order of discourse constructed on nature. This is how he understands the "unchangeable entities" which are to be the object of understanding and wisdom. It is the discourse which is the ultimate end, for it is supposed to reflect in some way that of the Active Intellect with itself in its eternal process; and that is where the Good is too, which reflects itself down into the articulation of the Discourse. Hence what Aristotle is seeking is not knowledge as we would mean it, but a regularization of the grammatical categories whereby the discourse may flow on in good order, each predicative sentence interlocking with the others in the proper distinction, coordination and context.

But we are here at the point before Plato, where, if the past had to be dropped, the future was still entirely undecided.

Surely, the high abstraction cannot have come in one move to a man thinking in 480 B.C., when everyone before him had been thinking of an organ of the mind that goes by correspondence of similars. Parmenides must have started in his youth from such an assumption, and something of it seems to stick in his ideas about the relation of mind and body. We must not forget that every true naturalistic mind, so long as it was spared the wringer of modern nominalism, has always instinctively assumed what Goethe expressed so well in his own unphilosophical way: "Man knows himself only insofar as he knows the world, of which he can be aware only in himself, as he can be aware of himself only in the world. Each new object, rightly considered, opens up a new organ of perception in us."

Parmenides can no longer understand this in the simple way of imagining a physical super-eye which can see "into the more subtle," the actual grain of things. He has gone beyond it, for he is looking for "that which holds it all together . . . " And this implies no longer visualizing, but an *abstract* representation.

We might say that whereas his predecessors had been projecting symbols of eternity in their element, or life-stuff, or monad, or the like, Parmenides has reached the point where he has to try and project the abstract frame of eternity itself; but such an insight requires a new way of reaching it, a new method; and therein lies his fateful originality. His continuum cannot be visualized as an object; it is of the nature of the mind itself, it is identical to νοεῖν, what the mind does. Hence, says Aristotle, Parmenides is the first to speak of the One "according to reason," and he undeniably prepares the ground for the Platonic abstraction.

This, the conversion point in which Truth and Being become interchangeable, contains in itself all future developments of speculative thought. They are not distinct as yet, and can be confused *in fieri* with dangerous ease. But Hegel is quite right in seeing here the transition from the stage of *Vorstellung* to the stage of *Begriff*. This is the illumination which answers the doubts of Xenophanes.

This concept involves no measures, no magnitude, no places, no "great-and-small." Nothing but relations, all-the-relations-there is. It is that new intellectually dazzling Thing, the three-dimensional extension pure and simple. Whenever the mind meets it, as it were, for the first time, it experiences that metaphysical seizure which manifests itself in ontological declarations. It happened again in the XVIIth century: Henry More, Spinoza, Malebranche, Newton himself, express in several ways this ontological experience born of Cartesian space. Says Henry More in the language of his times:

"It is necessary that, because it is a real attribute, some real subject support this extension. This argumentation is so solid that there is none that could be stronger. . . . When we shall have enumerated those names and titles appropriate to it, this infinite, immobile, extended entity will appear to be not only something real but something Divine (which so certainly is found in nature): this will give us further assurance that it cannot be nothing since that to which so many and so magnificent attributes pertain cannot be nothing. Of this kind are the following, such as: One, Simple, Immobile, Eternal, Complete, Independent, Existing in Itself, Subsisting by Itself, Incorruptible, Necessary, Immense, Uncreated, Uncircumscribed, Incomprehensible, Omnipresent, Incorporeal, All-penetrating, All-embracing, Being by its essence, Actual Being, Pure Act."

Some imp would drive one to remark that many such honorific and capitalized adjectives have been often wasted to confer existence on what turned out to be nothing much. But we must sternly repress it. This is the genuine metaphysical experience that can arise out of space conceived as a substrate of all reality, and Henry More's words, as they refer unbeknownst to that very selfsame Eleatic Being, can give us an idea of what Parmenides experienced in the way of intellectual illumination.

There is no doubt that in using this grid everything falls into place. The enumeration of the properties of Being implacably pressing in on the reader of the poem is in no need of the groping justifications worked out by the critics.[6] Fr. 8 does not need a labored exegesis such as we have found in the work. It comes out conceptually as it does from the literary aspect—a single bloc of affirmation poured from the central idea.

"Being" or "that which is," cannot be real, it is a plenum. It is extended, "like unto a sphere" in its intrinsic symmetry. But if it is by itself a plenum, and all of "real body" (we must put these words between strong quotation marks, but they have to be there, for what the senses add is only phenomenological, Light and Night), it is also indistinguishable from isotropic space. A strange kind of "body" indeed, devoid of all concreteness. It might be more adherent to this stage of ideation not to call it "real body" but "body-of-my-thought"; body of Truth, body of reality; not Being, but "Be-er."

Is this, then, the "Truth"? The poem answers with imperatorial absolutism that it is, for no other way is thinkable. Non-Being is "not to be spoken of," for it is, in the strictest sense, nowhere. Being is the same as to say it is. But from this stratospheric peak of logical immediacy there is no going backward; no, nor forward either, except in mathematical theory. In all directions around this point there is an abyss. We can see why young Socrates brings up his question in the beginning of the *Parmenides*: If this is the only point of Truth, or shall we say the one Idea—do we not have an impassable *chorismos*, a separation, between the world and ideas, so that the living mind cannot cross it to reach the ideas, but neither can the gods from there understand the world? Where can be found a *methexis*? How is that very moment of abstraction guaranteed whereby we found the One?

We can put it in our own words, by asking whether this is really an object of the mind's apprehension, and then which is the relation? Or the mind itself, and then surely the mind can proceed further on its own, but where is the object? We have no organ that can be imagined as grasping Being. This is indeed the first time in which thinking has to mean "being aware" in an explicitly dif-

---

[6] e.g. Loenen p. 100: "A much graver problem (is) the question why Parmenides devotes so many additional lines (up to l. 21) to these two attributes (ἀγένητον καὶ ἀνώλεθρον)."

ferent sense than that of perceiving or imagining through φαντασία. Taken all at once, the gradient is impassable, it frightens young Socrates into suggesting infinite regression (134a).

There is in our language and our civilization a long experience, going from an implicit and half-realized acceptance of a transcendence between knower and known to modern positivistic resignation, which cushions the impact of such thoughts; but to someone living in the fifth century B.C. they well may have been, as is said in Plato, of the kind that will allow a man no peace. Gorgias had shrewdly chosen the subject for his *succès de scandale*.

But—please—let us remember the very real problem which had motivated the quest. Allow me to go back to my *Origins of Scientific Thought* (pp. 96-99):

"The great concern for science had been to find the common substrate of all things, the One that unifies the Many. The Pythagoreans had suggested that the substrate is Numbers, that is: points having position. These points, Limit placed in Unlimit, it had been concluded, were the origin and as it were the substance of things. But here begin the difficulties with a doctrine still eminently poetic and magical. What is the single monad but a repetition of identity? Unlimit had been assigned the role of a field, or filling, but it carried within it all the determination of limit, since it was the field of all positions. The Pythagoreans had thought of the power of Number and Limit in a kind of imaginative intuition, but on the very grounds of arithmogeometry the representation would hardly stand scrutiny, because, clearly, it is Unlimit which is the bearer of Position, and hence of Limit. Any logical thought on the idea of number brings forth a continuum underlying it. The Pythagorean School had taken its dualism without investigating it too deeply. But its mathematicians had to.

"We know what happened to Pythagorean 'number atomism.' In the reduction of geometry to numbers, the expression of all the geometric magnitudes which come up in the theory of proportion necessitated a common unit to measure them all that became smaller and smaller. The universal common measure had to shrink to a smallness indeed beyond measure, and yet it had to remain a unit: an uncertain kind of *actual infinitesimal*. Such is the new monad. But the difficulties of defining the line as a row of pebbles remain, however far we shrink the pebbles. Either each monad is separated from next by a tract of Unlimit, or it is not. Either conclusion leads to sacrificing a part of the doctrine. We can sacrifice the discreteness of units, or we can sacrifice precision. A wrongness will remain. Limit and Unlimit are crowded together at every point.

"It is curious to note that the Pythagorean movement, which had aimed from the beginning at discovering the principle of form in nature, should have wrecked itself on a rock so much like the one the Ionians had struck. To have order, harmony, and form in the world presupposed a formal substratum which should have no form itself, but be the bearer of all form, exactly as the hydrodynamic universe of the Ionians had been a quest for a material substratum which should be sufficiently neutral in its own intrinsic properties to be modifiable into all the kinds of matter in the world.

"It was Parmenides, standing at the confluence of the two traditions, who realized that the two problems were in fact one. The true conception of geometrical space, once formed, is equally well adapted to serve as a substratum for physical form, in view of its rigidity and impassibility, and for matter, if one adopts a view of matter which transforms it into an accidental and contingent property of the space it 'occupies.' That was the course taken by Parmenides, and later by Newton. It is not surprising that he should have ascribed such a master stroke to the inspiration of the deity. As was natural for one trained primarily as a Pythagorean, it was probably their form of the problem, the analysis of the continuum, which led him to his discovery. That continuum fulfills, then, the same role as the Anaximandrean Unbounded[7]—and also as the Pythagorean numbers. It can no longer be visualized as a great Flow with its eddies, or as points of light in space radiating power. There is nothing to visualize in this kind of substrate; what we put there in imagination falls apart into points, and so on without end, until it becomes clear that what we have to comprehend is the texture, which is that of the continuum. 'Grasp firmly with thy mind the near and the far together. . . .' This is truly the 'Be-er' (*Eon*, a

---

[7] I am glad to note that Klaus Reich has come in, as I have noted earlier, to suggest that the logical origin for the One lies in Anaximander's substrate, but seen as bound and packed in the Bonds of Necessity.

grammatical construction very similar to that of 'filler') since it permeates all things and bears their properties. We have not been able to locate the Many in any 'trustworthy' way, and the conclusion is that there are not many separate points of space but only the One. We have moved out of the magic of numbers and entered the realm of pure logical Necessity.

"What Parmenides thought he could do to make his position unassailable was to formalize it so as to force total assent from the start. This was later to be the way of the metaphysician. Spinoza asks us to accept the conception of the All, and to deduce consequences therefrom. Parmenides asks: 'Would you deny that Being is?' We can not know at that point what is the 'Being' he has in mind, hence later ontologists have been tempted again and again to see in it the pure verb *is* of the grammatical copula. The deduction from there can proceed only on the logico-verbal plane. But neither does Descartes, in his *Discourse on Method*, make it clear at the start that his procedure of enumerating and subdividing, by which he hopes to solve all and any difficulty, is described with simple geometrical operations in mind. From all that we have seen, this would seem to be the case with Parmenides.

"In that newly conceived continuum, all of mathematics has its native heath and its abode. To it belong the surfaces, lines, figures, numbers, proportions and relations that the mind can bring forth. The realm of Truth is that of mathematics in its amplest formulation as our time has brought it forth: the domain of all the possibilities of rigorous thought. It is unalterable and unmoving, but the mind moves freely in it, for it is of the mind itself. It contains the life of reason. It *is*, even as reason *is*. Such is the true world beyond sense, whose existence has been revealed to Parmenides by something he felt to be divine inspiration."

There is, of course, for us, the difficulty that it is described as a sphere "resting within its bounds." The difficulty persists in whatever interpretation; in fact, the more "unspatial" the worse. But the statements are quite compatible with a sphere imagined as stretching as far as the mind will go, i.e., of infinite radius, and I am pleased to see that Calogero from the other side comes to agree with me on this. The image of the sphere would then express isotropy ("the same in all directions") as opposite to the uncharacterized Unbounded of Anaximander. And it seems singularly true, thinking of a dense continuum which is "all limit" at every point, that if it lacked a limit it would lack everything.

We should note that Parmenides did not use the already current *peras* for Limit, but the somewhat archaic *peiras*, which indicated "texture" and "design" more than mere "boundary." However it may be, we are following logic into a difficult situation that Parmenides did not have the means to solve. If we have to stand undeviatingly on the principle that the *pampalaioi* did not use reason differently from us, we must still take distance into account. Nor should we try to simplify Parmenides' thought until it meets ours. Or is it ours? More than considerable doubts concerning an infinite kosmos occurred to Kepler and Galileo, for whom yet infinite space was a matter of course. Too few of those doubts came to our Newtonian scientists before they found themselves confronted in our time with Einstein's space and Olbers' Paradox. It is better respectfully to leave Parmenides to stand there bestriding the unknown—*Achille immobile à grands pas.*

Let us see, finally, how the two parts of the poem complement each other.

Men, caught in the flux of time, themselves part of phenomena, cannot set their life in timeless Truth which is beyond them. They must cope with events and "give them a name," it is a solemn legislative act similar to the foundation of a city. The gods of the city, Parmenides' whole theological position implies, are no less relative, yet they should be considered valid gods. We have to build our own world, we are only asked to *know* what its relation is to the "true faith," and then it becomes wholly legitimate. A very Eleatic character of our time, the man who set up again the Continuum as a substrate of reality—I mean Albert Einstein—has stated it concisely: "If it is certain, it is not physics. If it is physics, it is not certain." Let me talk here in modern terms. Metamathematics, the foundation of the Continuum (Leibniz calls it the Labyrinth of the Continuum) is that on which mathematics itself is founded. Seen from there, the world of physics, that which "takes place" in the Continuum, receives its metaphysical justification. These ought to be the proper terms to talk of these things,

since an ethics is engendered therefrom, a clear if one-sided vision
of Freedom and Fate.

The Geometer who lays down a theorem partakes at that moment
of freedom absolute. He does not aim at sharing or persuading;
the Other, and be it his listener, does not exist. Yet he will gen-
erate that same freedom in the Other who shares his truth. And
the ancient paradox is, that man is free in that he knows himself in
the "bonds of Mighty Necessity." That is the way of the gods.
But then he must turn to and assume his burden as man among
men, he must take on his share of the common relativity, he must be
a legislator, a historian, a physicist. He must accept to become a
phenomenon, subject to coming-into-being and passing away, to
what is positively and implacably decreed, the *stygeron*. His absolute claims are as nil. But he will "receive" (*doxa*) as well as give.
The order of his words may be sheer opinion but he will know
the power of prestige and persuasion. "Of these things" says the
Goddess, "I tell you the whole profitable disposition, in order that
no mortal may surpass you in knowledge." His explanation may be
valid, in that it brings coherence. The order that sound opinion
affirms in the flux of reality is a durable good: things have accepted
from man "the seal of a name."

And so at last, man the phenomenon will find himself "at home"
(that so significant Greek expression) in a world of phenomena.

These, in sketchy outline, are the reasons that I suggest for
restoring Parmenides to the world of science without removing him
from metaphysics. There would be much more to say before the
ground can be considered clear. I have concentrated on the specifically geometrical fragments. I have not attempted to establish the
link of Parmenides with Melissus, nor, further, the filiation of
thought which makes of the Eleatics the fountainhead of Sophistic
logic. That a new concern with the possibilities of pure reasoning
runs through this line is undeniable. The word-play of Zeno is
the fateful point when words begin to veer away from the central
concern with the kosmos, and to live a life of their own. Inside the
Eleatic school itself, there is evidence that some very reckless ex-
perimenting went on with the possibilities of the newly discovered
verbal instrument, and here we might find the legitimate source

of Plato's *Parmenides*. But if the enterprise wandered off into
eristics, it also led to Bryson. It was the most adventurous moment
of Greek thought, the freest adventure, and it would seem the
greatest hope. What the men of those generations saw in the promise of the Goddess is surely incommunicable. All true metaphysical
experiences are. By linking the realm of geometry with that of the
"logos that is spoken," Parmenides provided a complex of mean-
ings as rich as that of Herakleitos, but lending itself to rigorous
deduction at all levels. Nothing in modern thought can provide
more than a pale image of that wealth of living meaning: only
Plato can show us what a contemporary could hope of it, and in
that sense, if in that sense only, his exegesis is valid. For us, dealing
with the autopsy of what is no longer an overwhelming truth, the
anatomy of logic shows a clear distinction. The logic of the Eleatics
is so guided by their object of contemplation as to remain scientifi-
cally impeccable; that of their successors is not, and we must assume that the object has changed. On this we rest our case.

We shall get nowhere near Descartes, rather, we shall transform
him into the usual caricature of schoolbooks, so long as we do not
grasp the *Cogito* for what it is, not a thought but the creative act of
the will which discovers at one stroke God, the soul and the real
world. It is the act which equates man to eternity. In the same way,
for the same reason, we shall lose Parmenides into a set of "Bei-
träge" to technical philosophy, if we do not grasp his *diakosmos*.
It is a word more ancient than 'system' and considerably better.
The kosmos is of the essence, and if you talk about it you have to
be a *physikos*. Idealism, ontology, pure logic are at best consequences, roads taken by others with other aims than his. The two
ways of his poem are one whole, needing one another. There is
a way of Necessity which is Freedom, there is a way of Law which
is uncertainty, limitation, choice, decision, what men can *do*. The
kingpin is still archaic Myth, in the figure of the Daemon. The
whole structure breaks asunder if we take that figure as a rhetorical
device, which is also not good method in any case, since Aristotle
would remind us crisply that rhetoric had not yet been invented.
The discursive metaphysics of Plato, that first of the moderns, gives
itself leeway, built as it is on language, but it is no longer that dia-

mond-hard, impregnable thing based on metamathematics. That is why Plato's *Parmenides* is no good witness to the thought of the Master of Elea; and Socrates talking familiarly with Theaetetus is much more to the point when he modestly admits: "I fear we do not understand him any too well."

I hope I may be forgiven, if I borrow for this lecture the title from a poem by W. H. Auden, which to me is one of the few proofs that modern science is not incompatible with poetic expression.

> . . . That sense of famine, central anguish felt
> For goodness wasted at peripheral fault,
> Your shutting up the house and taking prow
> To go into the wilderness to pray,
> Means that I wish to leave and to pass on,
> Select another form, perhaps your son;
> Though he reject you, join opposing team
> Be late or early at another time,
> My treatment will not differ—he will be tipped,
> Found weeping, signed for, made to answer, topped.
> Do not imagine you can abdicate;
> Before you reach the frontier you are caught;
> Others have tried it and will try again
> To finish that which they did not begin . . .

In this case the situation is old: man facing nature's harshness in the same timeless context. The power that Mr. Auden brings forward on the scene for a few crisp pitiless statements is surely not the Queen of Heaven, Lady of Truth and Rigor, who appeared in Parmenides' Proem. But she is the other aspect of the Second Part, the Force of Becoming, the ruler of this world, a surely more necessary presence than Lucretius' *Alma Venus*, for Epicurus would not need her but Darwin does: she is exactly Parmenides' dreadful Daemon Lady, the δαίμων ἣ πάντα κυβερνᾷ, who now "steers" evolutionary change.

Having once been introduced to this far-from-insignificant Lady through the poem of Parmenides, I realized how often I had met her.

In the catechism for Akousmatics, which belongs to the oldest tradition of the Pythagorean school, we find a number of the 'secret names' of things which refer to her: "What are the Bears? They are the Hands of Rhea." "What are the planets? They are the Dogs of Persephone."

The variety of names emphasizes her different aspects. But the hands of Rhea—why they are the very hands of the Daimon of Parmenides, as she keeps the heavens revolving and sends all things to their fate. One sees her turning the celestial sphere by way of those shining handles. So much was clear to me long ago. It was only much later that I learned that those two, the Great and Little Bear, were quite literally the handles of heaven in archaic astronomy. Ursa Major was the key constellation embodying the planets in her seven chief stars; whichever power at a given age held her, held the heavens.[1] She is the Chariot from which Zeus threw Kronos when he succeeded him in the rulership, and it is a relic from far-distant times when we hear that the Norse Kings still held their investiture "from the power of the Bear," although the plumb-line from the Pole to the equinoctial point had long since shifted from the Seven Stars owing to the Precession. Ursa, so to speak, was the great hand on the dial of the year, she was the minute hand while Ursa Minor marked the great hours of the Precession, which stretched each over thousands of years.

Curiously enough, as we all know, the Little Bear was known as Kynosoura, the Tail of the Dog. How many times have we spoken of cynosures without wondering why this bear should become a dog's tail. But the figure of the Dog is elusive and ubiquitous. It has to do not only with Sirius, but also with the pole of the Ecliptic, with which the Little Bear was associated. While Alcor the Fox sits just above zeta of Ursa Major, she who was once Electra the Pleiad before the fall of Troy. . . . I cannot go now into this prodigious saga of dogs, wolves, coyotes, jackals, foxes *and* their twin brothers, which spring at us from all sides of the archaic jungle of heaven. The tale of Reynard the Fox is only a small chapter of it. I hope our distinguished colleague Dr. von Dechend, the indefatigable searcher, will soon give us some bearings to go by in this primeval landscape. It looks, if I may speak out already, like the most intricate and dynamic symbolism ever devised to do justice both to exactly timed phenomena and to a

---

[1] We still have the ritual formulae spoken by Pharaoh when he staked out the foundations of a temple: "I have seized the peg. I take the measuring line. . . . I observe the progressing motion of the stars. My eye is fixed on the Great Bear. I count the Time, I check the clock, I establish the corners of my sanctuary." (Brugsch translation).

great eschatological myth. I cannot even indicate it here. Suffice it
to say that there is good reason why the planets should be the
Hounds of Persephone.

Here are already two different names given to the goddess, but
it has been known since ever that they expressed different attributes
of the archaic earth-and-sky goddess, called also Hera, Artemis and
other names. Still another name we have met with already—
Aphrodite Ourania. From a Pythagorean list of deities we learn
something of her role, and it is there also we learn of the great
importance of the number Five which belongs to her. She was
identified by Rivaud as the same as Parmenides' goddess. There
is a list of attributes many lines long concerning her in Nicomachus.
We find ζωναῖα among others—the Lady of the Girdle—also
κυκλιοῦχος, owner of the circle, and ἀξονεδραία, restored by
Delatte, "Steadfast Axis." This makes a fairly consistent set of
attributes for the ruler of heavenly revolutions. We retain that her
symbol was Five, or the pentagon, whether plain or stellate, the
classic Pentalpha.

Why? Plato will answer us. In the *Timaeus* 53C-55B he tells us
first about the four elements, requiring the construction of four
polyhedra. Then he adds:

"There still remained one construction, the fifth;
and the god used it for the whole, making a pattern
of animal figures thereon (*diazographon*)."

Cornford (*Plato's Cosmology*, p. 219) explains: "Not requiring
a dodecahedron with plane faces for any primary body, the Demiurge 'uses it for the whole,' i.e. for the sphere, to which this figure
approaches most nearly in volume, as Timaeus Locrus remarks."[2]

Plato's brevity is rather puzzling. He has dealt amply with the
construction of the pyramid (tetrahedron), the octahedron, the
icosahedron and the cube; follows the quoted sentence, and off he
goes inquiring into the plurality of worlds.

Two points are clearly omitted: a) why should the dodecahedron
be used as the frame of the whole; b) why should that frame not
be the sphere, whose fitness and nobility (τὸ πρέπον καὶ τὸ συγ-
γενές) has been mentioned already at 33B? We are left with the

[2] Cf. A. E. Taylor: *A Commentary on Plato's Timaeus* (Oxford, 1928), 377,
Timaeus Locrus 98e.

impression that the Demiurge had one figure left over, and that he did not know what to do with it otherwise. This is a little too disingenuous even for a myth.

Plutarch tries to fill the gap with his questionings:

> "... is their opinion true who think that he ascribed a dodecahedron to the globe, when he says that God made use of it in delineating the universe? For upon account of the multitude of its bases and the obtuseness of its angles, avoiding all rectitude, it is flexible, and by circumtension, like globes made of twelve skins, it becomes circular and comprehensive. For it has twenty solid angles, each of which is contained by three obtuse planes, and each of these contains one and the fifth part of a right angle. Now it is made up of twelve equilateral and equiangular quinquangles (or pentagons), each of which consists of thirty of the first scalene triangles. Therefore it seems to resemble both the Zodiac and the year, it being divided into the same number of parts as these."[3]

Taylor comments on this dodecahedron with its 12 regular pentagons:[4] "Timaeus does not describe its construction. (Is it just a touch of Pythagorean 'reserve'?)." He answers himself in a footnote: "Perhaps not. His reason for silence may be that he does not know how to construct a pentagon by placing pairs of similar triangles κατὰ διάμετρον, a thing which, in fact, obviously cannot be done." Considering that Hippasos was excommunicated just because he had revealed "the construction of the sphere with twelve pentagons," and Plato's reverential attitude towards the Pythagoreans, we need "perhaps" not look for such far-fetched reasons.

Like Plutarch, Proclus etc., Taylor refers of course, to the *Phaedo* (110 B 6) which

[3] *Qu. Plat.*, Question 5.1 (1003C).
[4] Taylor, 377, quoting Euclid: *Element.*, XI def. 28: a solid figure composed of 12 equal pentagons with equal sides and equal angles.

"compares the spherical *earth* with
balls made by sewing 12 pieces of leather together.
The pieces of leather would be pentagonal, and, if
leather were inelastic, the ball would be a dodecahedron;
owing to the elasticity of leather it can be inflated
until it is sensibly spherical. Plutarch saw there
an allusion to the twelve zodia of the Zodiac. This
is out of the question as these constellations form
a circular band, but the twelve angular points of the
dodecahedron inscribed in a sphere do not lie on
any such band. Plutarch seems to suppose that the
angular points of a regular solid are all in the
same plane: Presumably he confused the dodecahedron
with a dodecagon in a circle."

I have quoted at some length Taylor's analysis because I feel
it shows how easy it is for coldly critical scholarship, even in such
a great scholar as Taylor, to defeat itself. A certain Pythagorean
reserve is perceived by the philosophical historian; it is hastily
withdrawn in a note suggesting an implausible alternative. In the
next step, finding a difficulty in Plutarch, he goes so far as to
suggest that he confused the dodecahedron with a dodecagon, and
imagined that the angular points of a regular dodecahedron are all
in the same plane. This is pretending to play croquet with fla-
mingoes. Plutarch is not even one of those archaic thinkers of whom
it is rather lightheartedly granted that they lived in a state of perpetual confusion. He was a well-schooled gentleman of Hellenistic
culture, and for all his journalistic temperament, a very serious
scholar indeed. Rather than dismiss his text as nonsense, it would be
better method to keep an open mind about a possible meaning, as
Burnet did. We shall now try again, reverting for a start to that
diazographon, and to what Plutarch adds: "It seems to resemble
both the Zodiac and the year."

And to begin with, let us accept resolutely the idea of a "Pythagorean reserve" on the part of Plato. Once you begin to ponder about
the dodecahedron with its constituents, its symmetries, its almost-
sphericality, you come gradually to understand that *if* mathematical

cosmology was deemed classified information at all, then Hippasos' punishment was deserved, and a needed public example.

Behind that Twelve there is a Five, and again, we shall not pass it over as one of those oddities of the mystical mentality that need not be explained, the more so, as it ties up with another oddment, the Pentagram as emblem of the sect. It was supposed, as you know, to stand for the Tetraktys, which is "the root and source of all being," and why, as Lucian wryly remarked, should the Five stand for a Four which is a Three?

When I wrote a book three years ago about the "Origins of Scientific Thought" and had to deal with the Pythagorean system, I could do no more than state the privileged position of the pentagram, and connect it with certain well-known properties, like the presence of the Golden Section throughout, and its links with musical theory. One could figure out other arithmological reasons, but none of them seemed decisive. I still lacked a satisfactory motive for that particular privileged position. I felt sure that the true reason must ultimately be connected with the heavens and I had not forgotten Nicomachus' allusions, but they looked to me far too 'mystical' to be taken into account. The prudent critical attitude was the Mighty Necessity which restrained me in its bonds.

Last year, as we were looking into the records of quite other civilizations East and West, we fell to thinking about the insistent recurrence of the 8-year cycle in so many inscriptions and seal cylinders. Dr. Hinze set up for us a chart of the heliacal risings of Venus as morning star over the cycle, and lo, here was the image that Venus drew of herself, a fiery pentagram staked out in eight years along the Zodiac. The figure was almost impeccable, rotating only 2.4 degrees at each successive cycle. Of course, the same pentagon will be given by the planet as evening star—in fact, any synodic position we choose will give it with the proper shift of phase. Anyone could have formed it who had let his curiosity run along Pythagorean lines.

Still later, we found that the diagram had been published by Dr. Manfred Knapp in 1934.[5] Knapp had been inspired by the uninhibited Pythagorean imagination of Johann Kepler, and taken

[5] *Pentagramma Veneris*, Basel, 1934, that we traced through being quoted in F. C. Endres, *Die Zahl in Mystik und Glauben der Kulturvölker, Zürich*, 1935.

as his model the famous Keplerian time diagram of the Great Conjunction (Fig. 1), where we see the Fiery Trigon (as it was called)
formed by successive conjunctions of Jupiter and Saturn slowly
shifting on the circle until it closes a complete cycle in 860 years.
He tried the same with Venus, and got the pentagram—that is here
reproduced. (Fig. 2)

Fig. 1

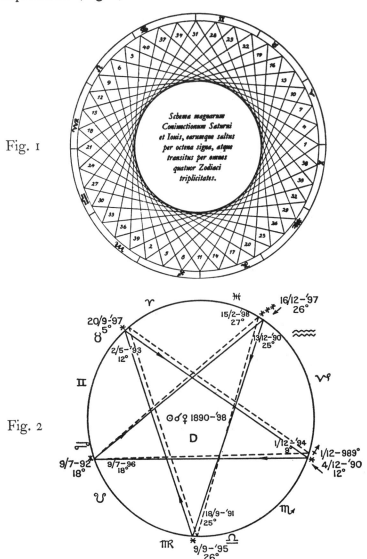

Fig. 2

What ancient soul could have resisted this vision? Here is the portrait of the Daimon, a time image of her motion limned in the skies for such as have eyes to see.

Surely, not modern eyes. Knapp's diagram was ignored—at least I had never heard of it until 1960, nor, apparently, did the professional historians of ancient astronomy, who had so expertly and ingeniously interpreted the numbers of the Babylonians. Perhaps the poet was right: *Ne Babylonios temptaris numeros.* . . . Those numbers take your mind away from the arresting moments of geometric fantasy.

What are numbers in the traditional Pythagorean statement? "Points having position." An oracular word. For what gives them position? Here, I felt, I had found one physical meaning of these strange cosmogonic images which leave us wondering. Those points of light in the darkness which cause other points of light to appear in positions prearranged, according to angles dedicated to the several gods—this was no longer an arbitrary fantasy. For this point of light in heaven, shifting position by itself, causing the pentagram to flash forth in the order of time, *was* the physical image. That image had been known and worshipped for many ages. It had now acquired full significance.

We have too often thought of the Pythagoreans as simpleminded. We liked to picture archaic gentlemen like Eurytos arranging pebbles somewhat after the manner of esthetic stationmasters in our own time, and forgot how even the *psephismata* could go far and wild in inference. The musical theory is very far from simple. The simple spatial arrangement can tell us little. It gives the bare bones. It is time which is of the essence, represented by that key word, *kairos.* Our image of the pentagram in the sky will tell us how position was divinely given by the order of time, and how points having position could be imagined as generating things in their turn. Time, it has been known from ever, brings all things. But time means essentially rhythm.

Pythagorean theory does not start from notions casually associated. It has a strong conceptual structure which gives meaning to the word 'things are numbers'; and however much successive Congresses of the Party may have revised the General Line, as we would say today, the interpretation rests on a firmly held spatio-temporal complex. Time was the preponderant component.

It is to it that we owe the fundamental pattern of our classical physics, based on periodicities. The astronomical model of reality —points without extension in a field of central forces, interacting by oscillation and revolution—has remained central throughout Newtonian mechanics. The continuity of thought is undoubted. Yet, for us moderns, the original complex of thought is very far away. Bergson would remind us that we place rhythm, and the intuition that goes with it, off bounds for our clear awareness, and think in terms of pure amorphous space: "Nous découpons l'espace selon le pointillé de notre action." It is not easy then to fit back into ancient schemes. We see a planet as a point changing positions in the sky, or think of it more abstractly as a track or an orbit. We do not visualize it both synoptically and rhythmically as a five-fold apparition "drawing" a pentagram in its tempo. There is a change in the way of seeing which cuts us off from archaic astronomy.

The space-time complex projects two areas of mathematizable reality, music and the 'dance' of planets. The space factor in either is given by the *sectio canonis* and by positional astronomy, the essential factor remaining rhythm: both projections converge in the Harmony of the Spheres. In the complex, Time is firmly set and normative, it gives the *kairos*; space is transformable, it gives room for mapping and symbolism. In the case of our planet, Five will give the original meaning, expressed in the orbital plane by the pentagram, but that five is expressed no less in the "sphere of twelve pentagons." This figure, too, was known as a cult object long before it could be geometrically constructed, as we know from many specimens found all over Europe. It was the three-dimensional image, the frame whereby that same power enfolded the cosmos.

May we then dissent from A. E. Taylor? Plutarch was not talking nonsense. The time-command of the deity over the zodiacal belt, which gives her the name *zonaia*, becomes distributed over the heavens three-dimensionally according to the symmetry of the dodecahedron, and the whole body will appear *diazographomenon*, 'inscribed all over with figures'.

Once the figure is important, all of its properties are, according to the principle of cosmic inherence.

Let us review some of those properties, beginning with the most obvious, that $12 \times 5 = 60$, the basic unity and unit per se (and the highest 'god' Anu) in Cuneiform texts.

There are 30 edges, 20 solid angles, and "360 elements which are produced when each pentagon is divided into 5 isosceles triangles and each of the latter into 6 scalene triangles."

After numbers, intervals. Consider the 'golden section', says Burnet:[6] in the scholion on Euclid II, 11 (vol. 5., p. 249, Heiberg) we have what appears to be a Pythagorean way of expressing this. This problem, we are told, 'is not to be exhibited by means of pebbles' (οὐ δείκνυται διὰ ψήφων). That golden section, as we know, appears as fundamental in the pentagram. It gives the proportion between the two halves of each leg and the whole. Irrationality is thus the kind of essence that is brought under control in the figure.

We might compare to this 'problem' the immense efforts of harmonic theory to divide the octave, with its 12 half-steps, into equal parts (stumbling block: the fifth) not only in Antiquity, but in the very same manner in China. The golden section gives for the relevant numbers:

5: 3,1   8: 4,9   12: 7,4   13: 8,0

Does it not look as if the very construction of the dodecahedron by pentagrams, revealed by the 'traitor' Hippasos, were meant to give away the whole system? We, as geometric 'spacers,' are naturally fascinated by the regular 'body' without minding the time dimension, although Plato talks enough about time in the *Timaeus* —but even there he does not disclose the moments which really 'count': Timaeus ceases to be communicative after having dealt with those times which are produced by Sun and Moon.

What Taylor considers to be "out of the question" turns out to be the case. He is apparently too rigid for the special kind of abstract imagination which distinguished Pythagorean thought: The dodecahedron is a 'projection' of time-units into space.

There would be more to say, but I think we have a fairly coherent description of this divine figure, whose dodecahedral 'sphere' en-

[6] *Greek Philosophy* (London, 1950), 55.

folds the cosmos, and whose name, as we have stated already, is
Aphrodite Ourania.

She presents herself here not as a person, not as a "Thou," not
even as a force, but as a polyhedron, Pythagorean manner, for she
is not so much a force, as an ordering principle.

Once we have her in our sights, we shall discover easily that in
her various guises she is a lady of intercontinental standing. It is the
figure of the pre-Hellenic, pre-Hesiodic celestial queen of the
Ancient Near East: Ishtar/Dilbat. 'Orbis totius alma Venus' is
indeed the Lady of Many Names: from astrological cuneiform
tablets we know 31 of these names—she may have had many more;
nor was her repertory here and there too different.

If it be felt that I am moving with too much unconcern from one
to the other side of the Mediterranean in the search for "prece-
dents," I should perhaps remind you of a certain historical frame
which has never been in fact denied, but is growing ever clearer in
the light of contemporary research. It was in a sense ignored by
the classical, humanist tradition which took the uniqueness of the
Greeks for granted; it still may make certain Hellenic specialists
unhappy: but since Frazer revealed once and for all to us the submerged mass of the iceberg, many new data have come to show us
the intrinsic links of Greek culture with the Near East, especially
in the time that preceded the Persian invasion. Herodotus, being
a classic, was himself under no classicist delusion; and when today
Neugebauer shows Pythagorean geometry to have sprung directly
from Babylonian algebra, he only redefines something which was
always accepted by the Pythagorean tradition.

As concerns the goddess figures of Greece and the Orient, we
have a morphological test to prove that they are indeed one and the
same personage. I shall submit two famous texts in conjunction,
whose authenticity has never been doubted. The first is from
Pherecydes' *Theogony*, recovered in one of the Grenfell-Hunt
papyri. It concerns the wedding of Zas and Chthonie. Three days
after the marriage, Zas makes a robe, large and fair, and on it he
embroiders Earth and Ogenos. He addresses Chthonie as his wife,
saying: "In my desire that your marriage should exist, I honor
you with this gift." Whence (it is said in another fragment)
"Chthonie acquired the name Ge (Earth) because Zas gives her

88 PROLOGUE TO PARMENIDES

Earth as a (wedding) present." There is no conflict here with
Hesiod, Zas is simply a different (Orphic?) name for Ouranos;
but an important new feature is added. It is the mantle that
Dionysus/Ouranos gave Ariadne, the Mantle of Hypsipyle.

So much for the Greek side.

The other text is a bilingual one, Sumerian and Babylonian,
first published by Thureau-Dangin. We give it in Ebeling's translation:[7] "After Anu, the king, had determined on the exaltation of
Innin, had bestowed on her the temple Eanna, his holy mansion,
he covered her form with the mantle of divine royalty, the splendor
of shining heaven. . . ."

The text is, of course, a thousand years older, but the ceremony
and the characters are the same. Anu is the primeval divine principle
like the Egyptian Atum. He is written in cuneiform with one
wedge=1 or 60. Ishtar/Innin becomes the Heaven-and-Earth
deity by being decked with the starry mantle of cosmic rulership.
Her titles are spelled out solemnly in the New Year's festival,
the so-called Akitu ritual. Although she is wholly celestial, an
awareness of her feral aspects makes the priest sound like an ap-
prehensive visitor in the den of the Lioness:

> My merciful Lady—My Lady, be calm!
> My Lady, who does not become angry, who is calm,
> My Lady, who gives, My Lady, who is so very good,
> The calm lady, who does not become angry, My Lady,
>   who confers gifts. . . .
> Damkianna,[8] mistress of heaven and earth, whose name
>   is My Lady.

This last name, as Deimel and Zimmern have shown, goes with
"Ruler of the Celestial Tiara"—*Zonaia*.

Here we have a case where morphological criteria can overcome
difficulties in the literal meaning. In one case the goddess is
Chthonie, who acquires the title 'Ge' by investiture with the Starry
Mantle. In the second it is Ishtar/Innin, who is Venus beyond

---

[7] *Alt-Orientalische Texte*, p. 252.

[8] Sumerian Dam.gal.nun.na. Deimel: *Pantheon Babylonicum* (Roma, 1914),
700, p. 100ff. est nomen antiquissimum uxoris dei Ea, quod semper manebat in
usu . . . "mater 'magni filii' (=Marduk/Jupiter)." Deimel quotes Zimmern:
"Beachtenswert erscheint . . . dass Damkina als Nin-men-an-na 'Herrin der
himmlischen Tiara' bezeichnet wird."

doubt. The ritual and the conception behind both are certainly the same. We must conclude therefore that in Pherecydes' very specially designed language, Ge becomes a title for Venus, seen here in the role of sky-and-earth goddess, not at all 'chthonic' notwithstanding her earthly title. If we trust this logic, we shall be greatly rewarded when we find that in other related cosmologies, the title of "earth-in-heaven" applies to the celestial band of 47° comprised between the two tropics, which is also called the "inhabited earth" because it is where the planet gods move around. With this our interpretation ought to be secured.

What is it that gives Venus this particularly exalted place in mythology? We could give all sorts of reasons, which come down to this, that Venus and Sirius are the brightest stars in heaven, each in its category, and are accordingly singled out for dominant roles. But what we have seen of the Pentagram might focus our thoughts on the importance of precision.

'Mother Nature' does not spoil her mathematically minded offspring in dispensing dates that 'fit'; but those 5 synodic revolutions of Venus leave only a minute remainder with respect to 8 solar years; the 8-pointed star on countless Mesopotamian seal cylinders, borderstones, etc. means every time Ishtar/Venus, as every Orientalist knows; the Egyptians, laying the accent on the five, have been even more 'Venus-minded'; the five revolutions are hers; after all, *she* draws the pentagram. She has, moreover, a unique distinction in her recurrences. There is a simple observational rule which antedates by far all Greek systems, *viz.* that the heliac phases of the planets stand in constant intervals of time to their station points in heaven, before they start on the retrograde loop. (This becomes obvious in Copernican terms, but in the Ptolemaic scheme it remains far from obvious. Ptolemy formulated thence a rule: that the circular motion on the planetary epicycle must be synchronous with the anomaly with respect to the sun.)

The periodic returns of station points to the same region of heaven were taken *ab antiquo* as primary periods, as Böker and Gundel point out.[9] Ptolemy (*Synt.* I,5) calls them the "simple and unmixed motions" from which the other "partial and varied motions" arise.

[9] Cf. Gundel, RE *20*, 2085.

Now if we concentrate on those primary periods, we shall find a strange variety: Saturn about 59 years, Jupiter 71, Mars 79, Venus 8, and Mercury 46 years. That means:[10] the shortest intervals of time, after which the same planetary positions repeat themselves with respect to the fixed stars and, at the same time, with respect to the Sun (in other words: when synodical and sidereal revolutions 'fit'), are those mentioned years.

Thus Venus turns out to be a model of reliability, the timekeeper as it were of planetary periods. This fact might help us to understand, why this planet became the Celestial Queen, invested again and again with the 'starry mantle'—remember Pherecydes: Zas *presents* Chthonie with the 'Earth'—meaning Earth-in-Heaven, i.e. he gives it continuously 'all the measures of the whole creation' (that verb *didoi* in Pherecydes is a present tense expressing continuous action). Venus seems to have been a kind of pledge, reassuring the earliest astronomers of the reality of invariable order behind the apparent confusion.

We are moving here admittedly over highly speculative terrain. Historians will discount all such clues which do not belong to their familiar orbit of thought, and hold up against them the vast areas of crude ideas and 'primitive' imagery which seem to them to characterize those past millennia.

Yet those other, precise data also exist, and go back to remote antiquity. They might just as well be brought in to characterize a thought which in any case does not resemble ours. It is a risk but a risk worth taking.

Those data are surely not unimportant. It is not unimportant that they should have riveted the attention of lost ages, of those men, as D'Alembert says, who gave us everything except a knowledge of their name and their being. It is difficult for us, who relegate star observations and meridian instruments to a small corner in the scheme of things, to imagine a time when measures of such minute precision entrusted to memory over vast periods occupied such an area of consciousness, as to be held normative for society as a whole.

Beyond the stamping and the screaming and the orgies and the bloody rites that we instinctively associate with primitive ages it is

[10] Cf. Ludendorff: Untersuch.Astr.Maya *10* (=SPAW, Phys.Math.Kl. 1935) p. 83.

well that we should perceive the steady work of rigorous abstractive imagination placing the values where we would least have expected them, deriving norms from precise measurement. As the field of ancient metrology is opening up, we can discern a close-woven texture of measure as playing a much higher role than even in our own world, where we pride ourselves on our capacity to telemeter systems with split-second precision millions of miles away.

Those of our scholars who still presume that the unit of length was casually given by thumbs or feet or the 'average' size (whatever that may mean) of a grain of barley, are not aware that no unit of length or surface or volume could be considered normative unless it was tied up with cosmic invariants, and this implied a time interval marked by the sun, as Karst and Lehmann-Haupt were first to see, more than fifty years ago. More recently, Erich von Hornbostel has shown how in archaic civilizations the space intervals were tied up with time intervals both in astronomy and in music just as was taught by the Pythagoreans. Why otherwise should the same Egyptian word "Maat" indicate both the standard brick and the standard flute length? When our organ builders designate a tone by such words as "16-foot-tone" they use archaic language. The link between the two areas is the normative link.

Alexander J. Ellis, with his precise measurements on music instruments from the Orient, showed in the 'eighties of the last century that scales and intervals can be multiple and seemingly arbitrary, but that one always discovers in them one or the other norm: he was thus able to show the Near-Eastern origin of the Scottish bagpipe scale. In China the tones of the standard Panpipes were checked by inspectors every year at the time of the equinox, when Yin and Yang are supposed to be in proper balance. These inspectors were sent by the "Department of Laws rooted in the Great All." In Egypt and Babylonia the standard measures went back to the authority of Thot and Nabu, the Hermes figures in their Pantheon. It should be expressive enough.

That central concept which is represented by Maat in Egypt, Me in Sumeria, Rta in India, Asha in Iran, and so on, does not so much express a truth-value, as exactness with reference to a norm. The hieroglyph of Maat is the feather, symbol of precise weight in the balance. That feathered precision is everywhere implicit in the accomplishments of what the Greeks called *Mousikē*, a name which far transcends our "music" and is a close equivalent of our "cultured consciousness." Such states of consciousness do not come into being overnight.

When we go back in time—at least for a few millennia—we do not find everywhere, as we would expect, a crude anthropomorphic or theriomorphic representation of the deity. We may run instead into numbers, into a texture of time units projected into space, which bespeaks an astronomical origin. We are reminded then of those strange words of Aristotle at *Metaphysics* 1074b12 (so casually dismissed by Sir David Ross) when he speaks of "ancient heir-looms," λείψανα, of high levels of thought in the past, and that the gods must have originally been the planets. Music and time —the time of celestial periods—were *ab antiquo* a moving image of eternity. This remained as the Pythagorean frame, and was inherited together with its original divine rulership by Parmenides and then by Plato.

After so much that has been said, and too often in vain, about the "Archaic Atmosphere" as a source of the strangest and most nonsensical representations, I trust we have here a beginning of a coherent image. Archaic thought is cosmological first and last, it faces the gravest implications of a cosmos in ways which reverberate into later classic philosophy. The chief implication is a profound awareness that the fabric of the cosmos is not only determined, but overdetermined, and such that none of its agents admit of simple location. Be it simple magic or astrology, forces, gods, or number, planetary powers, Platonic Forms, Aristotelian essences or Stoic substances, none of them admit of simple location, if a cosmos has to be thought of. Physical reality cannot be analytical in the Democritean or Cartesian sense, it cannot be reduced to concreteness even if misplaced. Being is change, motion and rhythm, the irresistible circle of time, the incidence of the *kairos*.

We can best appreciate the originality of Parmenides' thought if we consider that he made of geometry the core of reality in an entirely different way from his predecessors. Geometric space itself, no longer numbers and rhythms in space, but three-dimensional extension pure and absolute, became the substrate, the

Physis, of things. It seems only right that he should have put such an inspired innovation under the sponsorship of the ruling deity of Time, the holder of the Starry Mantle. She assumes then a double aspect, first revealing the Truth which is unshaken and unmoving, necessary, extraneous to change, and showing herself again as the ruler of time and events, the Daimon who steers all things and drives the living to "dreaded birth and begetting."

Greek Historical Studies

BY BENJAMIN D. MERITT

Delivered April 25 and 26, 1962

FOREWORD

I BEG FIRST OF ALL to express my gratitude to the Department of Classics here for allowing me to participate in this series of lectures honoring Louise Taft Semple. She has indeed been a great benefactor to a great University. My wife and I came to know the Semples years ago—I do not like to think how many—and have admired their enthusiastic interest in Classics both here and in Greece. They have contributed vitally, and at times when help was most needed, to research work in which I have myself been engaged. My feelings are not only those of admiration and gratitude, but of warm friendship. This has meant a great deal, over many years.

May I say also just a word in memory of my fellow-worker in early post-graduate days? Allen Brown West, professor in this University, taught me much that I value most about the study of ancient history. We literally burned the midnight oil together, sometimes working in his rooms here in Cincinnati until the early hours of the morning. His death in 1936 was a great loss to scholarship and a grievous personal loss to me. I like to think that some of the things I have to say today and tomorrow would meet with his approval.

And then, more recently, my close association with the study of the Classics here has been kept up in collaboration with Malcolm McGregor, not to mention my other friends of long standing in the department. Your first Semple lecturer was my teacher, and your present chairman of the Classics department, though much younger than I, was a fellow-student with me. You can see by his performance how much better he learned his lesson as we sat at Blegen's feet than did I. For he has carried on the good work, while I have strayed away into the obscure field, not of early archaeology, but of epigraphy.

None the less, I pay my respects to a scholarly succession which has made the department a vitalizing influence in American classical studies, and which now, through the generosity of Louise Taft Semple, has been given the guarantee of a continuously bright and productive future.

BENJAMIN D. MERITT

3

GREEK HISTORICAL
STUDIES

I: BACKGROUND AND OPPORTUNITY

THE study of ancient history moves ahead at an ever changing and ever accelerating pace. Not many generations ago one might have thought that a certain restful calm had settled upon our discipline. Indeed, even in our own time there have been those who have, in some innocence, asked if the record is not now pretty nearly complete. Has not the bulk of the work already been done? How can one find new ore in a terrain that has been mined so carefully and so long?

The naive inquirer is guilty of two fallacies. There is always new ore whenever a new generation interprets the past, and the terrain is much more extensive than he imagines—much of it has not been mined at all.

Let us note briefly the first of these two fallacies. The old saying that "history repeats itself" is usually referred as a matter of chronological record to Thucydides, who in his famous introduction to the history of the Peloponnesian War set forth his reasons for writing. I give the translation of Charles Forster Smith from the Loeb Classical Library: "whoever shall wish to have a clear view of the events which have happened and of those which will some day, in all human probability, happen again in the same or a similar way—for these to adjudge my history profitable will be enough for me." The student must always judge the present in the light of the past, and the present (unlike the past) is ever changing.

Thucydides does not say that the cycle will be repeated exactly, necessarily, but that future generations may find it profitable to know in the perhaps similar circumstances of their own day what once did actually happen in the past. His challenge was that he was writing his history as a possession for all time.

The cycle of time, if it may be so called, is not a treadmill, and Thucydides himself forestalls this modern interpretation of him. He says that from acquaintance of what has happened under certain conditions valid inferences may be drawn about what may occur again, *ceteris paribus*, under similar conditions. Each age must pit itself against the record. As the so-called similar conditions do in fact differ in one way or another, the historian will come to a judgment, valid perhaps if he is wise, but differing perhaps from that of his forebear or his successor. For example, the historian of our present age of increasing socialism and state-control will study the decline and fall of Rome with lessons to be learned different from those of our ancestors who lived when America was young and when private enterprise and the new frontier were closer to our daily lives.

Dionysios of Halikarnassos attributed to Thucydides the dictum that history was philosophy learned by example. There is in Thucydides no passage where this statement actually occurs, but the introduction to his history, already noted, gives a suggestion that historical events may be the source of an inductive philosophy of history. Herbert Sanborn of Vanderbilt calls attention to Lord Bolingbroke's advice to a colleague on the present value of historical study:[1]

> "Your lordship may well be ready at this time, and after much bold censure on my part, to ask me what is the true use of history, in what respect it may serve to make us better and wiser, and what method is to be pursued in the study of it, for attaining these great ends."

Then he quotes Dionysios from memory, and goes on to emphasize the value of example, which history provides, for their own times, in their own generation, where they learn the wisest lessons in virtue not in the abstract but by applying to themselves what they see happen to other men. Bolingbroke reinforces his case with a quotation from Seneca: "The way of precept is long, of example short and effective." The House of Lords in the early eighteenth century knew the classics, and Bolingbroke

[1] *The Classical Bulletin*, XXXI, 1955, p. 65.

himself, who had among his heroes Alkibiades and Petronius, was able to quote freely from them. He was (alas!) subsequently expelled from the House of Lords, though not, it must be said, for this reason.

So, as each generation approaches the study of history it must evaluate the old lessons afresh. It must also look upon them with a new perspective; and here we touch upon the second fallacy. Like the discipline of literary studies in the Greek and Latin classics, the discipline of history over the years became a highly refined tool for the interpretation of ancient texts. Editions were edited, commentaries written, and critical studies made of individual authors. Scholars were analyzing, dissecting, interpreting. As Sir Maurice Bowra put the matter two years ago in his presidential address before the British Academy: "The discipline was good, but its end, which is to recapture as far as we can the living experience of the Greco-Roman world, was not considered of much significance - - - -. The discipline was good, but it was not conducive to the expansion of learning, and those who attempted this were regarded with some suspicion."

All this is now fundamentally changed. The nineteenth century saw the flowering of *Real-Geschichte*. Ancillary disciplines were brought into play. August Boeckh and Theodor Mommsen founded the Greek and Latin epigraphical *Corpora*. Archaeology moved from the societies of the Dilettanti to the professional schools and institutes of Athens and Rome. Excavations were systematically begun, and the results published. The national consciousness and pride of the newly liberated kingdom of Greece led to the founding of the Greek Archaeological Society in 1837, and this was followed in time by the foreign schools of other nations, including our own.

In Rome the pattern was somewhat different. The French Academy was founded more than two hundred years ago, and the national unification of 1861 did not have the critical effect on Roman archaeology that the wars of liberation had on Greece. Rome was Rome, the Eternal City, and it attracted to itself the academies of foreign lands whenever these found the necessary support at home.

But the result has been the same. The ancient historian could no longer confine himself mainly to texts. There were available all the new evidences of coins, inscriptions, sculpture, architecture, papyri, pottery, glassware, and the new knowledge of lands and places where these things were being discovered.

It would be tedious, indeed impossible, to illustrate all the several ways in which these new fields of study, and the discoveries made in them, have added to our knowledge. Let me cite a few examples only. Within this generation the expanding scope of historical study has been probably its most notable phenomenon, and we are beginning to have the interpretative studies that follow in the wake of new discoveries of fact, like Denys Page's *History and the Homeric Iliad*, and Chester Starr's book on *The Origins of Greek Civilization*, written not primarily from the point of view of the archaeologist, though the evidence from pottery weighs very heavily in it, but of the historian.

Moses Hadas of Columbia calls the age of which Starr treats "the one department of Greek Studies which our generation has revolutionized." I think that this limits the field too narrowly. We have witnessed the precision that airplane photography can give to the discovery and description of ancient sites. I once heard the present president of the Archaeological Institute, Jotham Johnson, give a lecture devoted to this topic alone. We have now the new technique of underwater exploration and photography. Those of you who have heard Stanton Waterman give his lecture on "3000 Years under the Sea" will have been impressed by the vast possibilities of an entirely new field of discovery. He has also written a popular account of some of his diving off the shores of Greece and Asia Minor for the *National Geographic Magazine*. We are a long way from the age when to be a Greek professor meant to be absent-minded, cloistered in some ivory tower, surrounded by books. The Greek professor of tomorrow may have to wear fins, do skin-diving, and carry a tank of compressed air. Waterman has a healthy respect for what a diver has to know about the subject of his search, and has proclaimed that as a matter of economy it will be easier to make a skin-diver out of an archaeologist than to teach archaeology to a skin-diver.

The results of these underwater explorations are, in truth, amazing. Wrecks of ancient vessels have been found off a treacherous reef near Boudrum, Turkey. Three of them had complete cargoes of ancient amphoras. The knowledge that such discoveries can give on ancient trade routes and commerce is obvious. The study of the amphoras and of the seal-stamps on their handles is a special branch of historical research in which an American scholar, Virginia Grace, has made herself an acknowledged expert. Her account, published by our School at Athens last year, of "Amphoras and the Ancient Wine Trade" is a model of popular, yet scholarly, presentation. Farther east, Waterman has found a wrecked ship which dates back to about 1500 B.C. with a cargo of bronze weapons and tools and copper ingots. Ingots of exactly the same shape and size are represented in tomb-paintings in Egypt. Obviously, they came from Cyprus, the island of copper. History has been pushed back under water, as already on land, so that the pre-history of yesterday has become the history of today.

It would be presumptuous of me to speak here in Cincinnati of the historical achievements of your own faculty in this once prehistoric field. The names of Korakou, Zygouries, Nemea, Troy, Pylos, Lerna, and now Keos, are eloquent witness to the monumental contributions of Blegen and Caskey and their associates in a field which they have made peculiarly their own, and which has been laid before you by Blegen himself some months ago in the initial lectures of this series in honor of Mrs. Semple. The decipherment of Linear B script by Michael Ventris (with preliminary work by Emmett Bennett and Alice Kober), for which Pylos has given so much of the new evidence, is one of the modern historical miracles.

In the field of papyri, Aristotle's *Constitution of Athens* made a revolution in the study of Athenian history when Sir Frederick Kenyon's first edition appeared on Friday, the thirteenth of January, in 1891. There was nothing unlucky about the date. It was a memorable occasion, and, as the Cambridge historian G. T. Griffith has said, "the tranquil surface of classical studies in the field of the Greek historians was still dancing with the waves" which the discovery created, well into the twentieth century.

Of more prosaic sort, and by way of contrast, I should like to call attention to two substantial advances in the fields of early epigraphy and pottery which have been made during the past year by scholars, one in England and one in America, as the result of long and careful study. As, in the mining of gold, the rare nugget is indeed a thing of value and of beauty, and yet the more systematic washing of the pay dirt must be followed through until all the returns are in, so the rare archaeological discovery is always welcome, but the systematic study of collections and of the results of archaeological exploration has its own reward.

Lilian Jeffery's study of the local scripts of archaic Greece traces back the forms of letters still preserved in inscriptions in all parts of Greece until she is able to conclude that bilingual Greeks from the Aegean islands, established at the eastern end of the Mediterranean in or near Al Mina, who knew both Greek and Semitic, adopted the letters of the local Phoinikians and so gave to Greece its phonetic alphabet.[2] This was spread throughout Greece by traders who carried in various ways back home the new sound values and their acrophonic system of naming the letters. The Greek alphabet began, perhaps, about the middle of the eighth century, somewhere in the Late Geometric period. The history of its origin and transmission is based upon the observation of innumerable local variations, which nevertheless lead back to a common source in time and place.

In the field of pottery, Judith Perlzweig's account of the lamps of the Roman era shows how even the style (and opulence or lack of it) of the humble lamp is mute testimony to the poverty of Athens after the devastation wrought by Sulla in 86 B.C. and to the mild prosperity under Augustus, and to the hard times under Hadrian, which are known from literary sources, until the lamp-maker came once more into his own in the third century.[3] This continuity of development was broken

[2] *The Local Scripts of Archaic Greece*, Oxford, 1961.
[3] *The Athenian Agora*, VII: *Lamps of the Roman Period*, Princeton, 1961.

in the sixth century, and when "once more, in the 10th century, lamps were commonly made in Athens, all connections with the mouldmade lamps of the Attic shops had been lost." The dark age of Athens was past, and the Middle Ages had begun. These new sidelights will stand the historian in good stead when he comes to write again the history of early Greece or of Athens under Roman rule.

One of the many difficult periods in Athenian history has been the third century before Christ, where consecutive literary sources are not available. It is here that the other evidence is sought with especial zeal, so that it may be thrown into the balance to redress the shortcomings in our knowledge. In the very middle of this era, as it happens, small excavations in Attica, with the ever-present finds of coins and with the fortunate discovery of inscriptions, are giving us new light on the Chremonidean War, an episode in the life of Athens which surely must be studied again, and about which we know, in some details, a great deal more than we did when Ferguson wrote his *Hellenistic Athens* and Tarn his *Antigonos Gonatas*.

This war takes its name from the Athenian orator Chremonides who proposed the decree of grand alliance with Sparta and her allies so that together with King Ptolemy II Philadelphos of Egypt they might win their freedom and save "their laws and their ancestral constitutions" from the tyranny of Macedonia.[4]

It was a lucky epigraphical discovery in 1954, in the Athenian Agora, that gave the clue to the date of this Athenian decree in 265/4 B.C.[5] The war was over within four years, and Athens had lost her last real bid for freedom. But the details of what happened within these four years have been hard to come by. Most of what we know comes from Pausanias, who wrote about four hundred years later. But in 1960 a small excavation was carried out by the American School of Classical Studies near Porto Raphti on the east coast of Attica. Remains were discovered there of a Ptolemaic fort, dated by the coinage not earlier than

[4] *Inscriptiones Graecae* (Berlin, 1913), II², 687.
[5] W. B. Dinsmoor, *Hesperia*, XXIII, 1954, pp. 284-316, and B. D. Meritt, *The Athenian Year* (Berkeley and Los Angeles, 1961), p. 233.

267/6 B.C. The fort evidently belonged to a Ptolemaic garrison established as a bridgehead on the coast of Attica. It has been known from Pausanias that Ptolemy sent his general Patroklos to the aid of Athens, and that Patroklos made his main base on the island of Keos (the earlier history of which is now under investigation by Professor Caskey), also that he occupied and fortified a small island near Sounion where the remains of his fort are still to be seen. But it was not known that he dared to match his troops against the Macedonians on land, and it has been supposed that he had no such bridgehead. The American excavations have revealed this army camp, preserved entire, with its barracks, fortifications, and storage rooms. The exact dating of it to the years between 265 and 261 is of significance, in a century where so few definite dates are known.[6]

As it happens, this was not the only Ptolemaic bridgehead in Attica. Apropos of it, Mrs. Eirene Varoucha-Christodoulopoulou has called attention in the columns of the Athenian press (and in the journal of the Greek Archaeological Society) to a chance find of coins of Ptolemy I and Ptolemy II, the latest dating in 265 B.C., along with arrowheads and slingshots and broken pottery of Hellenistic date among ancient ruins of walls, made in 1943 in the suburb of Athens known as Helioupolis, formerly known as Kará, on the western slope of Mt. Hymettos southeast of Athens. This second Ptolemaic fort was quite like the one at Porto Raphti, and Mrs. Varoucha assigns it to Patroklos, who occupied it with a military force of Egyptian troops during the Chremonidean War. There was also a small fort with Ptolemaic slingshots and coins found on the small peninsula of Cape Zoster on the south coast of Attica near Vouliagmeni in 1959. And finally, there is now an inscription from Rhamnous, as yet unpublished, but in the hands of Mr. B. Petrakos, which mentions the archon Peithidemos, in whose year the war started, and which praises a certain Epichares for a number of things he did, among them "for having made provision for adequate shelter for the troops of Patroklos who came to their aid."[7]

[6] See *A.J.A.*, LXV, 1961, p. 191. A full account of the excavation is now published in *Hesperia*, XXXI, 1962, pp. 26-61.
[7] Information from the Athenian daily Ἐλευθερία of January 21, 1961. See also Ἀρχ. Ἐφ., 1953-1954, Part 3 (published 1961), pp. 321-349.

So Patroklos is now known to have had garrisons in at least four different places on the mainland of Attica, one of them within about three miles of Athens. In spite of the failure of Patroklos to relieve the siege of Athens, we are better informed than we were a generation ago about his efforts. The final result we know from Pausanias, who says of Patroklos "he accomplished nothing great toward the saving of Athens." But of such stuff, sometimes, history is made; it must record not only the successes of military effort but also its failures, and if possible something of its strategy and tactics.

I am reminded of a paper that was read last year by Robert Palmer before the American Philosophical Society on "The Kingdom of Corsica and the Science of History." The kingdom of Corsica, an ephemeral by-product of the French Revolution, lasted only two years, from 1794 to 1796. Palmer argued that "in a sense there never really was any Kingdom of Corsica, and there is no science of history. The point lies in the connection between the two negatives. The Kingdom of Corsica was a might-have-been, an attempt that failed. But a historian must take account of might-have-beens. He must show not only what happened, but what might have happened." Raymond Aron, in his *Philosophy of History*,[8] called this "the retrospective calculation of probabilities," which is a scholar's way of designating something non-scientific by a scientific name.[9]

It has taken some time to bring about a harmonious understanding and a mutual respect between the classicist, the historian, and the archaeologist. Fifty years ago the classicist was apt to cast a slur on the "archaeologist's Greek." Now the classicist is much more apt to be an archaeologist himself, and both have become historians. It is significant that some of our best ancient historians have been primarily classicists, like Ferguson at Harvard, and that more and more a close co-operation is bound to exist between the ancient historian, the classicist, and the archaeologist, as here at the University of Cincinnati, where the department of Classics teaches all three disciplines, or,

[8] *Introduction à la philosophie de l'histoire: essai sur les limites de l'objectivité historique* (Paris, 1948), p. 165.
[9] See Robert Palmer, *Proceedings of the American Philosophical Society*, CV, 1961, pp. 354-360.

better said, teaches the all-inclusive discipline, which takes into account the available evidence and source material, from wheresoever derived, for our understanding of ancient life and times.[10]

The American School of Archaeology at Athens is not named the "American Archaeological School," though indeed it is popularly so called, but "The American School of Classical Studies." The same name is used by the School in Rome. This is significant. When Charles Eliot Norton undertook the task of founding the Archaeological Institute of America it was his hope, as he himself said, "that, by the establishment of such a society, the interests of classical scholarship in America might be advanced, and especially that it might lead to the foundation of a school of classical studies in Athens where young scholars might carry on the study of Greek thought and life to the best advantage, and where those who were proposing to become teachers of Greek might gain such acquaintance with the land and such knowledge of its ancient monuments as should give a quality to their teaching unattainable without this experience."[11]

The beginnings of the School were made in 1881, with tentative endorsements from Harvard, Yale, Brown, The Johns Hopkins, and Cornell. The name then suggested was rather cumbersome: "The American School of Classical Studies, Art and Antiquities," but it defined the new horizons of classical study. There has been some legal quibbling about the title, for the articles of incorporation, drawn up and signed in Boston on February 20, 1886, define the school as a corporation, set up under the laws of the Commonwealth of Massachusetts, to be known as "The Trustees of the American School of Classical Studies at Athens." The official seal of the School for many years made no mention of the Trustees, but was changed in 1949 and 1950 to reflect the legally correct title. It was aesthetically not an improvement in the design, and the School had actually been in operation in Athens in rented quarters since 1882. So the old seal was restored in 1951, and indeed has always been used in the School's journal *Hesperia*.

[10] See Chester Starr's account, "Ancient History in Search of a Home," in *The Classical World*, LV, 1961-2, pp. 109-112.

[11] Louis E. Lord, *A History of the American School of Classical Studies at Athens* (Cambridge, Mass., 1947), p. 1.

But this is digression. The important fact is that the purpose of the corporation was "the establishment and maintenance of a School of Classical Studies at Athens, in Greece, for American Students." The articles of incorporation were signed by James Russell Lowell, William W. Goodwin, Charles Eliot Norton, Basil L. Gildersleeve, Theodore D. Woolsey, William M. Sloane, Henry Drisler, Frederic J. de Peyster, Henry G. Marquand, Martin Brimmer, and John Williams White. You will have recognized, in this roster, the distinguished founder of the *American Journal of Philology* and author of *The Syntax of Classical Greek*, the author of that *Greek Grammar* which most of us used as students, and the author of the *First Greek Book* with which many of us began our tentative probing into the mysteries and the beauty of the Greek language. There have been many good beginners' books in Greek since White's time, but those of us who used it long ago have never lost our affection and admiration for it. The significant fact of the School is that classicists were recognizing, by that time, the new fields of exploration and making way for expansion into a broader discipline. New colleges were rapidly enrolled in support, but none without proper scrutiny of its standing. Wesleyan, for example, offered to contribute toward the School, and was accepted by the trustees only when they were assured that Van Benschotten was a sound scholar with a genuine interest in Greece. Moreover, there could be no question, they felt, of the propriety of taking into the ranks, as the record has it, "the oldest Methodist college in the country." Today the School is supported by the contributing membership of eighty-six American and Canadian institutions of higher learning, of all denominations (I am glad to say), and its influence in American classical studies can only be called profound.

On the Latin side a similar influence has been exerted by the Academy in Rome. The Academy was founded initially as a school for architects, and was opened in Rome on November 1, 1894. But before the year was out a proposal had been submitted at joint meetings of the Archaeological Institute of America and the Philological Congress, at Philadelphia, to inaugurate an American School to coöperate with the Academy, and to promote

the study of archaeology (Italic, Etruscan, Roman, early Christian, Mediaeval, Renaissance), inscriptions, palaeography, Latin
literature, and the antiquities of Rome itself. The already successful school at Athens was to be the model, and indeed some of
the same scholars were on the committee of organization. It was
to encourage and assist in original research and exploration. This
is not the place to give even a brief history of the School, which
became an integral part of the Academy in 1913. Suffice it to
say that it has made for itself in Rome the same enviable reputation that the American School in Athens has made in Greece.
Roman historical studies, like those of Greece, have had all the
benefits of the ancillary disciplines, to the inestimable advantage
of the colleges and universities of America where ancient history
is taught, and to the health and welfare of historical studies
generally.

I do not here discuss the other foundations in which the Archaeological Institute has been interested, like the School of
American Research in Santa Fe, which lies outside the range of
our inquiry, or the Schools of Oriental Research in Jerusalem
and Baghdad and the American Research Center in Egypt,
though the latter have made, and will continue to make, their
contribution to classical studies. The time may come when it will
seem desirable to establish also in Turkey a School of Anatolian
Studies, as has been suggested in the last Bulletin (LII, 1961)
of the Institute.

Lay interest in archaeological studies has grown steadily over
the years. The journal *Archaeology* has a subscription list now of
8,197. The latest finds are regularly reported in the *Illustrated
London News*. Our excavations in Sicily, Asia Minor, and
Greece have been featured recently in the columns of the press,
and the discovery of the inscription from Troizen which gives
the decree of Themistokles for Athenian preparation to ward
off the Persian attack of King Xerxes and his barbarians in
480 B.C. has quite justifiably made the front page. The *editio
princeps* of many a Greek inscription is now to be found in the
columns of the daily press of Athens.

Nor is the interest confined to prehistoric and classical Greece.
The continuity of classical studies has been more and more in

our mind's eye. The history of Greece and Rome merged into the Middle Ages in the west and into the Byzantine Empire in the east. The influence of Hellenistic art on Byzantine art has been the theme of the great Byzantinologist Dmitrii Ainalov and his school. The countless churches and monasteries with their mosaics and their frescoes are one of our priceless heritages from the past. And surely Constantinople was one great center and repository of classical learning until the time when the west was once more prepared to pick up the torch from falling hands and carry it forward.

The great Gennadeion Library at the American School in Athens caters to students from many lands who wish to study mediaeval and modern Greece. It is a far cry now from the days when Greek history was taught only from the tyrants to Alexander the Great, and this on the basis of the traditional texts almost alone. Greek history is now taught from no one dares say how early down to modern times. Milman Parry's work with the modern epic and James Notopoulos's recordings of song and story have given us new insight into the poetry of Homer. As Waterman has said about under-water exploration, so we might say about the whole new frontier of Greek history. This is not an end, but merely a beginning, and the field of investigation is as wide as life itself.

This is the great challenge that faces the student of ancient history today, and with the growth of the challenge have grown the ways and means of meeting it: our schools in Athens and Rome, for example; the numerous facilities offered by our universities for original work in the field, like the expeditions organized by Harvard, Yale, Cincinnati, Michigan, Chicago, New York University, Princeton, Pennsylvania, and others, whether sponsored by local "Institutes" or by local departments and museums; the increase in number of research organizations, in which I am happy to say that the Institute for Advanced Study in Princeton has a prominent place,—but one should name, too, among others, Dumbarton Oaks for Mediaeval and Byzantine studies, the new center for Hellenic Studies in Washington, and the Institute for Research in the Humanities at Wisconsin (where Emmett Bennett carries on his work with Linear B).

The Institute in Princeton has achieved a happy fusion of research and exploration, particularly with reference to the history of Athens. The director of the Agora excavations in Athens is a permanent member (with the rank of professor) of the School of Historical Studies at the Institute. The study of the results of the excavations is under his general supervision. Each year scholars engaged in this study, when they need time and leisure to prepare their manuscripts, come as temporary members to the Institute, and are thus enabled to finish their tasks. This work is now in full progress, with meticulous attention paid to the complete and very careful records kept for the excavations during their course throughout the last thirty years. The range is from pre-history to modern times. Indeed, the staff architect, John Travlos, has just finished an architectural history of Athens, a study of the walls and public buildings from the beginning down to the nineteenth century. It is a historical account, based on the evidence of the excavations and such collateral evidence (old and new) as is available.[12] Travlos finds, for example, that an outer defense wall of the city was built in the late fourth century after Christ, about a hundred years after the Herulian invasion of 267 A.D. The excavation has now turned up an inscribed herm (or bust) of Iamblichos, the wealthy Syrian, friend of the sophist Libanios, and frequent visitor to Athens, who is said, in the inscription, to have "made the rampart of the wall by the expenditure of his wealth."[13] One bit of evidence links itself to the rest, and the wall can thus be dated probably sometime after the visits of Iamblichos in 357-362 A.D.

But this anticipates in a measure what I plan to talk about tomorrow. Today I want to emphasize the extent of the opportunity for research work, in many fields, in ancient history, and to indicate how much we owe to the Classical Schools which we have established abroad, and in Athens particularly to the

---

[12] Πολεοδομικὴ Ἐξέλιξις τῶν Ἀθηνῶν (Athens, 1960). A translation into English by R. E. Wycherley is soon to be published by the University of Chicago Press.

[13] Agora Inventory No. I 3542. A full discussion will be published soon in *Hesperia* by A. E. Raubitschek.

American School of Classical Studies and to the excavations of the Athenian Agora.

There is provision made at Rome for the study of music. I think we might do more to encourage an understanding of the folk-music of Greece and the use that is made of Greek themes in the modern classical music of Athens. The symphonies of Kalomires deserve to be known to Americans as they are known to the educated Athenian. The Gennadeion Library could be the focal point for such a study, though the University of Cincinnati, as you probably know and as I am sure Professor Topping will testify, has one of the finest libraries on Modern Greece in the United States, happily now described in a recent catalogue by Miss Kyparissiotis.

Other tasks that await the historian are those of coöperative enterprise. We need somewhere to have the equivalent of the working staffs of the old European academies. The epigraphical *corpora*, for example, should be indexed; I have tried to come to grips with this problem at the Institute for Advanced Study in Princeton, with only partial success. A number of inquiries have come to me even from so far away as Russia about it. The Berlin Academy is not now able to fill the need, and there is no organization in this country as yet able to take up the task. Perhaps a communistic state will manage in the end more easily than we do. But if some benevolent donor would provide a suitable working staff, such things could be done. We need a classical foundation with some of the long-range planning to consolidate our hard-won knowledge into standard books of reference and standard compendia. It would help the historian mightily, whose task is synthesis, and who writes the connected historical narrative of tomorrow. We need to prepare the way for another Mommsen, and Busolt, and Tarn, and I would add, in our own country, among others, the names of Rostovtzeff, and Tenney Frank, and William Scott Ferguson.

But with all that is new, we must not forget or neglect the older discipline. A little more than a year ago John Hough delivered the presidential address to the Classical Association of the Middle West and South under the title *History and Literature*. He rightly pressed the claim that belles-lettres, philosophy, and art have on the historian's attention. We need to prepare the way, too, for another Gilbert Murray, and Basil Gildersleeve, and Paul Shorey.

Some of the historian's problems, and some observations on the use of evidence, will be the theme of my lecture tomorrow, with special reference to the history of Athens.

II: SOME ATHENIAN PROBLEMS

Yesterday we spoke of the receding horizon of the study of ancient history. Today I want to illustrate some ways in which the new evidence, especially in the field of Greek epigraphy, helps to correct old misconceptions and to round out the story which the narrative historian must tell when he hopes to give a valid synthesis.

The idea of this kind of lecture is not new with me by any means. Indeed, the subject has been masterfully treated by that dean of Greek epigraphers, Marcus Niebuhr Tod, in a lecture delivered thirty years ago entitled, somewhat formidably, "The Characteristics and Value of the Evidence derived from Inscriptions."[14] Tod claimed that "there is no part of the Greek world, no period of Greek history, no aspect of Greek thought and activity on which Greek inscriptions have not thrown fresh and valuable light. The debt which we, as students of the ancient world, owe to the epigraphical evidence is so great, and increases so rapidly with the progress of excavation and exploration, of decipherment and interpretation, that to appraise it adequately would demand a survey of the ancient world from the beginning of the classical period to the dawn of the Middle Ages."

So Tod limited himself to selected examples for purposes of illustration, and I shall do the same; but my examples will be different, mainly, from his, and I want to make some observations also on epigraphical method.

First, and of especial interest here, are the Athenian tribute-quota lists. The late Allen Brown West and I began working together on these in 1924. After West's untimely death much of the work was done by his successor here, Malcolm Francis

[14] M. N. Tod, *Sidelights on Greek History* (Oxford, 1932), pp. 11-36.

McGregor. Another collaborator was H. Theodore Wade-Gery, Wykeham Professor of Ancient History at Oxford, and our results have been published, in some measure with the help of the Charles Phelps Taft Memorial Fund of this University.[15]

The records exist on stone in the Epigraphical Museum at Athens, reconstructed out of many fragments. The cities of the Athenian Empire in the fifth century are inscribed, with the amounts of quota as given to the goddess Athena from their annual tribute. The range covered by the lists is from 454 to 406 B.C. We can follow the extent of the Empire, its growth and decline, and something of its management from year to year.

This is all the more welcome, since Thucydides says so little about the financial affairs of the Empire. But even what he does say is interpreted for us by the epigraphical records of the quota. A famous passage in the historian describes the founding of the Delian League, which later became the Empire. This was in 478 B.C., and the problem was defense against possible attack again from Persia. The Greeks, under the leadership of Athens, planned a campaign of reprisal against Xerxes, and the Athenians decided which of the allied cities should furnish money against the barbarian and which ships. A magistracy, called Hellenotamiai, was set up to receive the money, called *phoros*, and the first *phoros*, or tribute, assessed was 460 talents.[16]

No doubt all this was perfectly clear and intelligible to Thucydides and his contemporaries; but moderns have debated whether the 460 talents were in addition to the ships or inclusive of them. Insisting that *phoros* can mean only money (and I think rightly so), some have claimed that the 460 talents did not include the ships. The evidence of the quota-lists is that they did. The money collected in the early years, before many states had tired of service and commuted from ships to cash (Plutarch tells the story in his *Life of Kimon*), can have been only about half the 460 talents. Do we therefore accuse Thucydides of inaccuracy? Not at all. The first assessment made was levied in terms of money, and amounted to 460 talents; the Athenians decided which allies should pay this in service and which in

---

[15] *The Athenian Tribute Lists*, 4 vols. (1939-1953).
[16] Thucydides, I, 96, 1-2.

cash. Furnishing ships had (and this is only natural) a cash value equivalent, and the first tribute assessed was in fact 460 talents. Which cities worked this out in service in the first year was settled by the Athenians, as leaders of the League, and we know that Kimon's policy, right down to the time of his death, was to strengthen the relative position of Athens vis-à-vis her allies by accepting more and more payments in cash in lieu of service and by using this money to build up her own navy. But even in 454, when the quota-lists begin, the amount of money collected each year amounted to less than 400 talents. Some states were still furnishing ships; but the first assessment, the assessment of Aristeides the Just, was held to be the norm right down to the Peloponnesian War, and it included both money and ships.

If we wish to split hairs, the assessment was 460 talents in cash, and Lesbos and Chios were still paying in service rather than in money. The inscriptions leave no rational doubt of the meaning of what Thucydides says. This is one instance in which the epigraphical record gives a clear interpretation of an otherwise ambiguous historical text.

Thucydides again touches on the finances of Athens at the beginning of the Peloponnesian War. I allude to this, because it involves a question of method in historical study which seems to me important. The text of Thucydides exists in two versions: (1) The Athenians had still at that time minted silver of 6000 talents on the acropolis (the maximum had been 9700 from which expenditures had been made for the Propylaia and the other buildings and for Poteidaia),[17] and (2) The Athenians always kept about 6000 talents on the acropolis (most of which were still there, from which expenditures had been made for the Propylaia and the other buildings and for Poteidaia).[18]

The epigraphical evidence shows that a maximum on the acropolis of 9700 talents at any one time is not possible. The argument is somewhat complex, and Wade-Gery, McGregor, and I have dealt with it elsewhere.[19] But the important point

[17] Thucydides, II, 13, 3.
[18] Scholion on Aristophanes, *Plutus*, line 1193.
[19] *Athenian Tribute Lists*, III (1950), pp. 118-132; Meritt, *Hesperia*, XXIII, 1954, pp. 185-231.

here is that the epigraphical evidence decides which version of Thucydides is sound. We are so accustomed to taking the Teubner text, or the Oxford text, as the last word in authority that this sentiment, I know, is shocking to many scholars. For the accepted text has the incorrect version. The correct version comes down to us in a scholion on the *Plutus* of Aristophanes. But this depends on Alexandrian scholarship, just as does the *textus receptus*. The canon established by the Alexandrians has been so authoritative that in papyri or copies of later date there are relatively few significant variants. Yet we have known little about the transmission of historical texts before the establishment of the canon. Obviously, here, at least, two versions of Thucydides were available to the Alexandrians. May it not be true that in pre-Alexandrian times there were other variants, now lost to us? The answer, I think, is in the affirmative.

About six years ago, Eric Turner published a small papyrus fragment from the first book of Thucydides, now in Hamburg and dating from the middle of the third century before Christ.[20] This is by far the oldest testimony we have for the text of Thucydides, and it antedates the Alexandrian canon. There is no iron-clad evidence that the Alexandrians had a "preferred" text of Thucydides, though Bertrand Hemmerdinger argues persuasively that an edited copy prepared by Aristophanes of Byzantion (about 257-180 B.C.) was the basis for the Alexandrian text.[21]

It is remarkable that in this small earlier papyrus of less than eighty words of Greek there are at least eight variants from the *textus receptus*, a percentage of divergence vastly higher than that of post-Alexandrian papyri. There are differences in word-order, in omission, and even in the choice of words. The noun διάνοια, for example, occurs in the papyrus instead of the παρασκευή of the book-texts, a peculiarity which the papyrus shares with a late Paris manuscript (H) not in the tradition of the preferred manuscripts accepted since the editorship of Hude. Recent studies have emphasized, indeed, the need to establish a broader basis for our text of Thucydides, using manuscripts

[20] *J.H.S.*, LXXVI, 1956, pp. 96-98.
[21] *Essai sur l'histoire du texte de Thucydide* (Paris, 1955).

not heretofore used. This is undoubtedly true; we need a new
collation. Hemmerdinger and Kenneth J. Dover (of St. An-
drews) and David Lewis (of Oxford) have accumulated a considerable amount of evidence that there are readings in the Paris
manuscript H that transcend the minuscule archetype and are
independent of B.[22] There is sound text, in other words, not in
our now generally accepted canon. But we need also to know
more about the transmission during the fourth and third centuries before Christ before the tradition of any of our present
manuscripts begins.

We are making some progress. The "off-Broadway" version
of Thucydides, if I may use that term for the scholion on the
Plutus, on the resources of Athens in 431 B.C., was not even
mentioned in the *apparatus criticus* of Powell's Oxford text of
1942. Luschnat has deigned to include it, at least, in the *apparatus criticus* of his edition of Hude's Teubner text of 1954,
and now in the revised edition of that work in 1960, though he
warns "Textum Thucydideum non mutandum esse censeo." In
very truth, all that we urge is to relegate a bad text (non-Thu-
cydidean) to the *apparatus criticus* and to print a good text (Thu-
cydidean) in its place. The scholion will no doubt in time
achieve the status it deserves. In the meantime the historian still
has a problem with the sources, and with early transmission. The
Hamburg papyrus is simply one of the proofs that early copies
were not made with the accuracy we associate today with court-
room stenography.

This question of ancient copying of official documents was
brought to the fore two years ago by Günther Klaffenbach in
Berlin.[23] He comments on the preservation of documents in
ancient public archives, and confirms Adolf Wilhelm's demonstration that only texts of personal or permanent official concern
were cut on stone. You see now my own special stake in the
matter; it takes on also an epigraphic interest. Moreover, the
copies cut on stone "in the majority of cases reproduced the
original decrees only in abbreviated form." The copy cut on

[22] Cf. D. M. Lewis' review of the latest Teubner Thucydides in *J.H.S.*, LXXXI,
1961, p. 172.
[23] "Bemerkungen zum griechischen Urkundenwesen," *Sitzb. Ak. Berlin*, 1960,
No. 6.

stone, and so published for all to see, is to be distinguished from the archival record, recorded on a painted board, a plaque, a tablet (λεύκωμα, δέλτος, σανίς), or even on papyrus. Paper was known and used at Athens, but it was expensive.

The names of those cities in arrears of tribute, according to a decree of 426/5 B.C., were to be inscribed on a panel.[24] And in 448/7 the tribute assessed, and paid, or in arrears, was to be recorded on a whitened plaque.[25] These records did not get onto stone, but were rather part of the archives. Felix Jacoby comments on these Athenian archives earlier in date than the founding of the Metroon in 403 B.C.: "it is obvious," he says, "that the inner administration from 508/7 B.C. onward, and still more the administration of the Empire from 478/7 B.C. onward, could not have been achieved without records (which may be distinguished, as the more general concept, from documents proper), and the records had to be kept somewhere. - - - From the time when Kleisthenes made the Council the supreme executive the archive of the Council was of the greatest importance, and the contents of it were simply transferred to the Metroon in 403/2 B.C."[26]

Let us go a step further. If there was an inscription on stone, there is ample proof that its provisions had equal validity with the "original" in the archives. This is true, even if the text was abbreviated, or even if its wording varied from the original. To us moderns this is astonishing. We demand at law either the original of a document, or a notarized copy, absolutely identical as to wording, orthography, and punctuation, verified, signed, and sealed, with the notary's seal guaranteed by the County Clerk. The Greeks made no such demands. They were interested in content, not in wording or form. In order to understand an ancient inscription we have to disabuse ourselves of the modern point of view, and we must not demand standards of copying so strict as those now required by our custom.

This leads me to speak of a much debated text, the well-known decree of Themistokles, of which a copy on stone was

[24] *Athenian Tribute Lists*, II (1949), p. 52 (D8, line 19).
[25] *Op.cit.*, p. 51 (D7, line 44).
[26] *Atthis*, p. 383 note 27, quoted by Klaffenbach, *op.cit.*, p. 29.

found in Troizen in 1959 by Michael Jameson.[27] The decree was quoted by Plutarch and Aelius Aristides, and there are many other references. Aischines read out the text in one of his orations in the fourth century. And, of course, the story of the defeat of the Persian invaders of Greece in the great naval battle of Salamis in 480 B.C. is legendary. The master strategist was the Athenian general Themistokles.

This decree now gives us the text of Themistokles's proposal before the Athenian Council and Assembly to abandon the city and the countryside and to concentrate all their strength on meeting the Persians at sea. The oracle at Delphi had recommended defense behind a wooden wall; Themistokles persuaded his compatriots that this did not mean to barricade the acropolis but rather to take to their ships—a wooden wall, indeed, from which to defend themselves.

This is the decree:

"Gods
Resolved by the Council and People
Themistokles son of Neokles of Phrearrhoi made the motion

To entrust the city to Athena, Protectress of Athens, and to all the other gods, to defend and to ward off the barbarian for the sake of the land. The Athenians themselves and the foreigners who live in Athens are to send their women and children to Troizen, their guardian being Pittheus the cult-hero of the country.[28] They are to put their old men and movable possessions on Salamis. The treasurers and the priestesses are to remain on the acropolis watching over the property of the gods. All the other Athenians and foreigners of age are to embark on the 200 ships now ready and defend against the barbarian for the sake of their own freedom and that of the rest of the Greeks, along with the Lakedaimonians and Corinthians and Aiginetans and those others who are willing to share the danger - - -."

---

[27] The *editio princeps* is in *Hesperia*, XXIX, 1960, pp. 198-223, 418.

[28] This line cannot be restored with certainty, but it was natural for resident foreigners to have a guardian (*prostates*).

The decree then goes on to give details of how the ships are
to be manned; it gives the qualifications of the trierarchs (they
are to be not over 50 years of age and they must own a house
and land in Athens and be fathers of legitimate children), and
tells how the crews are to be selected by use of the lot from the
citizen registers of each deme and from the register of foreigners
in the hands of the polemarch. Sacrifices are to be made to Zeus
Pankrates, and Athena Nike,[29] and Poseidon the Securer, and
when manned the ships are to be put to sea, 100 to go to Artemision
in Euboia and 100 to cruise off Attica and Salamis. The decree
is a perfect prototype for the historic accounts given by Herodotos and Thucydides and, as Jameson claims, we have here the
"clearest new light on the Persian Wars."

There has been a storm of protest, with learned arguments
that the decree is not genuine, but a forgery. Everyone seems
to feel that he must say something about this text.[30] I have taken
for our brief consideration an article by Christian Habicht as
representative of the detractors and one by Helmut Berve as
most effective for the defense.[31] Since I am myself one of the
defenders, and since Berve and I both express our disagreement
mainly with Habicht, it is inevitable that my arguments should
be much like Berve's, or his like mine. But we have so far not
exchanged ideas with one another, which I should very much
like to do. The fact that we have so often come to the same conclusions gives me confidence that we are both proceeding in the
right direction.

The detractors say flatly that the Themistokles decree dates
from the fourth century, and condemn it for its many anachronisms. What no detractor has comprehended is that the anachronisms do not matter. Themistokles is named, with patronymic and demotic, as the orator. In the early fifth century he
would have been named by *nomen* alone. But we are not dealing with a fifth-century text. We are dealing with a third-cen-

[29] I regard the καί between τῆι 'Αθηνᾶι and τῆι Νίκηι in line 39 as an intrusion; see below.
[30] The bibliography grows almost daily. The record of publication is complete in *S.E.G.*, XVIII, pp. 56, 246-247, down to the time of its going to press.
Further contributions will be noted in following volumes of *S.E.G.*
[31] Habicht, *Hermes*, LXXXIX, 1961, pp. 1-35; Berve, *Sitzb. d. bayerischen
Akad. d. Wissenschaften*, 1961, Heft 3.

tury copy of a fifth-century text, and the addition of patronymic and demotic to the name was pure routine to a mid-fourth-century or third-century copyist. We do not know how many times the text was copied until it came to have the form in which we know it.

It is an alleged anachronism that the acropolis, which the treasurers and the priestesses were to guard, is called "acropolis," not "polis," as should have been the case in a fifth-century decree. This, too, is a matter of no more moment than the name of Themistokles. It is surprising only, when one thinks about it, that this trifle could have been advanced as a serious argument against the genuineness of the decree. Moreover, the acropolis was sometimes called the acropolis, even in the fifth century,[32] and it is almost a necessity that it be called "acropolis" here, for the "polis" (line 4) had just been turned over to Athena.

I have selected certain other alleged anachronisms, and make some comment (though by no means exhaustively) upon them.

The number of marines, ten, allotted to each ship was too low for 480 B.C., and the triremes could not have been assigned by lot to their trierarchs except during the fourth century. As for the number of marines on each ship, only ten, I suggest that any argument about them is in the dark unless we know how many were thought to be available for so large a fleet (200 ships or more) and what the tactics of the impending battle were to be; and with the new ships, all presumably alike, to be assigned to the trierarchs, who now shall say that the lot was not the easiest and quickest way of making the decisions? The magistrates (that is, the generals) would have been busy enough selecting the trierarchs. If they had to use judgment and decide each case separately, weighing pros and cons, to fit each trierarch to a trireme, they might well have given way under the strain, as did the Virginia farmhand, according to the story, who was told to sort a pile of Winchester apples, putting the large apples in one pile, the small apples in another pile, and the medium-sized apples in a third pile. He fell asleep, you

---

[32] *I.G.*, I², 92, lines 36, 42.

will recall, not because the labor itself was hard, but because he was worn out having to make "all them decisions."

The qualification that a trierarch should have legitimate children, it is alleged, must be dated after the law of Perikles about citizenship of 451/0 B.C. But this is not true. In purging the citizenship Perikles did indeed order that the parentage be Athenian on both the mother's and the father's side. But the only provision for legitimacy in the time of Themistokles was that the child be born of an Athenian and his wedded wife. Aristotle assigns this definition to the constitution of Drakon.[33] Aristotle's account of Drakon's constitution has not been free from attack, and Habicht, for example, thinks that this too derives from a post-Periklean source. But it is only fair to point out that legitimacy is not in Drakon's constitution defined so strictly as it was in the law of Perikles. If some post-Periklean forger was using post-Periklean definitions, why did he define legitimacy differently here?

The whole Athenian body could not, it is alleged, have been taken from the muster rolls of the demes because these rolls did not include the lowest property class, the thetes, until much later than 480 B.C. This is not true. Habicht, from whom I take the objection, has labored the point, but he depends largely on an Athenian decree of the late fifth century (*I.G.*, I², 79) which he, and others, have misread and misinterpreted. The decree is lost, but Fourmont's copy of it was used by Boeckh, and then taken over by Kirchhoff and Hiller in the later editions of the *Corpus*. The decree provides that two men shall be elected by the Council from their own number as Treasurers of the money of Apollo. Income which they are to steward comes to them each year from the Knights (two drachmai), from the Hoplites (one drachma), and from the Archers both citizen and alien (three obols). The demarchs are to collect this money from those who are recorded on the citizen registers, and the toxarchs (police captains) are to collect from the archers (that is, the policemen). Habicht claims that the absence of any mention of thetes in the deme registers shows that they were included only after this date. There is here a misinterpretation

[33] Ἀθ. Πολ., 4, 2.

of the inscription. There is no provision that *all* Knights, and *all* Hoplites, are to pay a small annual sum to Apollo. The text gives a regulation about the cult, and from the preserved indications would seem to be concerned with participants in a religious procession or celebration. Knights and Hoplites and Archers draw a fee for their services, and of this fee they pay a quota to Apollo. If they do not pay, the quota is stopped from their wages.

Knights and Hoplites are appropriate enough for a festival procession (some Knights and some Hoplites, not all of them): the Archers must have been policemen to keep order. Their contribution was to be collected and turned over to the treasurers by their police captains. The inscription merely says: "The toxarchs are to collect from the Archers." It makes no distinction between citizen archers and alien archers. Boeckh's idea was that the toxarchs collected only from the alien archers. This may be so, for the demarchs were supposed to collect from the others, whose names were written on their deme muster rolls.

To argue from this text that there were citizens who were not on the muster rolls in the late fifth century is to deny the purpose and effect of the reforms of Kleisthenes. Every Athenian, no matter what his propertied class, belonged to a deme and was liable for military service according to his age group as shown in the deme registers. The inscription does not mention thetes (why should it?); it has nothing to do with them.[34]

It is alleged that Nike could not appear alone, as a goddess, in her own right, as recipient of a sacrifice, in the fifth century;

---

[34] The present restoration in *I.G.*, I², 79, is not epigraphically sound, being in line 5 (with δεμοτῶν) too long by three letters. One could restore παρὰ τῶν ἀστῶν οἱ - - - - ἐγράφεσαν, but this is tautological: if they were demesmen, or citizens, there was no need to specify that they were on the deme register. The primary definition must be that those who were on the deme register were to pay to the demarchs; hence a non-definitive word should be supplied as antecedent of οἱ - - - ἐγράφεσαν. This purpose is served by ἄλλον, contrasting with τοχσο[τῶν] below. The English idiom reverses the order: the toxarchs from the archers, the demarchs from the rest. But the order here suggested is natural to the Greek. I suggest the following restoration for lines 5-7 (στοιχηδόν 39):

ἐκπραττόντον δὲ ͱοι δέμαρ[χοι παρὰ τῶν ἄλλον ͱοἱ]
ἐς τὸ λεχσιαρχικὸν γραμματ[εῖον ἐγράφεσαν, οἱ δ]
[ἐ] τόχσαρχοι παρὰ τῶν τοχσο[τῶν· ἐὰν δέ τινες μὲ ἀπ]

but the stone records a sacrifice to Athena and Nike. One might add that we have only a single literary allusion, in the 54th prooemium of the Demosthenic *Corpus*, that Nike could appear alone in her own right even in the fourth century. There is no epigraphical evidence this early. So the detractors of the decree are in almost as much trouble as the defenders.

My belief is that Athena and Nike should be read as Athena Nike. Once intruded, the "and" might well go undetected in the third century—or even earlier. By a curious coincidence, Jameson's *editio princeps* had an intrusive "and" in the 26th line of the text, an error in copying which escaped the attention of four or five readers of the proofs, and was not caught until David Lewis detected it while studying the published text in his rooms at Oxford. This intrusive "and" provides an excellent illustrative example of what I believe to have happened in the fourth or third century B.C., though I can assure you that it was not left in Jameson's text for this purpose. The three deities who were to receive sacrifices now all have their epithets: Zeus Pankrates, Athena Nike, and Poseidon the Securer.

There is yet another alleged anachronism. The very first clause of the decree provides that the Athenians shall entrust their city to Athena, protectress of Athens: Ἀθηνᾶ Ἀθηνῶν μεδέουσα. This was Athena, the patron goddess, known also by the epithet πολιοῦχος, and in the prose inscriptions of the fifth century called Athena Polias, or simply Athena, or more simply still the Goddess. Whatever the epithet, the cult was officially that of Athena Polias.

Erich Preuner, in 1924, discussed the epithet Ἀθηνῶν μεδέουσα in connection with the boundary stones on Samos, of the fifth century, where the epithet also appears.[35] He emphasized the fact that in various parts of the Ionian (or even Dorian) lands of Asia Minor the verb μεδέων was used with the name of a locality as the epithet of a god or goddess who watched over it. The usage was particularly frequent among the Ionian colonies in the region of the Black Sea. He concluded that when the epithet was used of Athena and Athens it owed

[35] *Ath. Mitt.*, XLIX, 1924, pp. 31-34.

its existence to Athenian colonists (as on Samos) or to the friendly feeling of former Athenian allies. The epithet (aside from the Themistokles decree) is known from only two Athenian decrees, one dealing with an ally (Kolophon) in the mid fifth century[36] and the other praising a former ally (Karpathos) in the early fourth century.[37]

Habicht concludes that the epithet has no place in an Attic decree as early as 480 B.C., that, in fact, its usage presupposes the existence of the Delian Confederacy, and he cites with approval Preuner's "proof" that the appearance of the epithet in the literary versions of the decree shows these versions to be later than Themistokles. The discovery of the Troizen text, according to Habicht, confirms Preuner's thesis "with compelling force."

Good though the argument may seem, it is still worth while to consider it further. The decree for Kolophon is evidence that the Athenians in mid fifth century knew the epithet, perhaps in connection with some shrine or precinct in Kolophon. None the less, the phrase does appear here (apparently; there is some restoration), and it surely appears in the decree for Karpathos of the early fourth century. Perhaps the usage in the fourth century was an attempt to define the temple of Athena Polias in a way that would be clear to the Karpathians. Once more, the question of copying arises, and one could suggest that the decree on Karpathos was *their* copy of an Athenian text which, as passed by the Council and People, had the more familiar (in Athens) Athena Polias.

But this is not necessary. The Athenian decree probably reflects the language of the Eteokarpathian gift, which is itself evidence that an old Athenian locution persisted on Karpathos. It is a well-known phenomenon of artistic and literary history that old usages survive in the provinces that have been outgrown in the mother country. The language of Shakespeare has survived in the mountains of North Carolina, though not in London or Stratford-on-Avon. Middle High German sur-

---

[36] I now believe that the restoration of *I.G.*, I², 14, line 5, is correct; it was rejected in *A.T.L.*, II (1949), p. 68 (D15, line 14).

[37] M. N. Tod, *Greek Historical Inscriptions* (II, 1948), No. 110.

vives in the Yiddish spoken by Jews who were exiled in the fourteenth century. The Pennsylvania Dutch preserve in gravestones, diplomas, and marriage certificates forms of art that they brought with them which no longer exist in Germany.

As a comparandum, a phrase or usage of the early fifth century, carried abroad by colonists—Ἀθηνᾶ Ἀθηνῶν μεδέουσα— may have survived in the overseas domain though not at home, at least in general use. No hard and fast line needs to be drawn. The point to remember is that existence of the epithet in the middle fifth century and in the early fourth century abroad does not prove that it was inappropriate in Athens earlier. The occasion might demand the phrase, and the emotional value of it (which Jameson has stressed) may have led to its use by Themistokles. Von Duhn's interpretation of the epithet, with its epic overtone, as a "solemnis deae invocatio" has, from a purely psychological aspect, much to recommend it.

But there is other, more specific, evidence. I do not introduce this for the first time, for Preuner treated of it, and Jameson alludes to it, and others have dealt with it as well. In brief, Aristophanes, in the *Knights*, has the Paphlagonian (Kleon) boast of his benefactions to the Athenians. He compares himself to Themistokles, to the latter's disadvantage: by Demeter, he had brought more blessings on Athens than had Themistokles (811-812). The whole passage recalls the glories of the Persian Wars, of Marathon and Salamis (781-785). But the opening speech reflects the opening paragraph of the decree of Themistokles (763-764):

"To our Mistress Athena, Protectress of the City, I pray."

With this phrase Aristophanes brought to mind in his Athenian audience (the production was at the Lenaea; there were no strangers present) the famous decree. This is doubly sure, since the usage is not merely abstract, but coupled with his comparison with Themistokles. The words as we have them in Plutarch, and as they appear on the stone from Troizen, were familiar, then, to the Athenians of 424 B.C. Preuner suggested that Aristophanes may have been thinking of the epithet that Athena bore in friendly foreign parts: he notes that they are

spoken by a foreigner (Paphlagon), and that the Ionic form
'Aθηναίη would best suit this interpretation. But Paphlagon
was Kleon, and it is indeed far-fetched to suppose that either
Aristophanes or his audience was thinking of foreign epithets of
Athena. Nor is the Ionic form 'Aθηναίη by any means sure.
The Venetus and Ambrosian manuscripts of Aristophanes have
the Attic form 'Aθηναία. Benjamin Rogers, an unprejudiced
commentator, in his edition of the *Knights*, has indicated the
reference to Themistokles succinctly (p. 107): "Paphlagon,
whom we shall presently find ready to pit himself against
Themistokles, commences his oration by adopting the words of
that statesman - - -."

We have not yet the evidence for pinning down the date at
which the decree of Themistokles was given written form. But
it was known in 424 to a sufficiently large body of Athenian
citizens to give point to the lines of Aristophanes. To compare
the small with the great, one should think of the poems of
Homer. They were known long before they were written down,
but their authenticity is no less sound because of the delay in
committing them to writing. Of course, poetry was more easily
remembered than prose, but the essential facts need not change
even if some verbal usages do. Here, with "Athena, Protectress
of Athens," the verbal usage is so nearly identical that the
alleged anachronism, I think, adduced by the detractors of the
decree did not exist.

It would appear, indeed, that the arguments here exhibited
against the genuineness of the Themistokles decree based on
alleged anachronisms must be held invalid, partly because the
alleged anachronisms are in fact not true, and partly because
the alleged anachronisms in epigraphic usage are only such as
might occur in copying (Greek style) with no change in essential meaning.

There are a number of stylistic arguments against the genuineness of the decree, notably the rhetorical overtone which is
evident from time to time, which, one claims, would be out of
character in a decree of the early fifth century. This is indeed
true of the decrees as we know them, the documents preserved
on stone, which are notoriously bare and unemotional. But let

us remember Klaffenbach's warning of the difference in charac-
ter.between the document on stone and the probable record in
the archives, to say nothing of the words of the orator as spoken
in the Assembly. Even if our decree had been cut on stone in
480 it could hardly have survived the Persian sack, and the
chances are that it was not cut. Why should it be? Wilhelm's
criterion about documents of permanent applicability is valid
here: the decree of Themistokles was of local and temporary
pertinence only, for a specific emergency. We do not know, I
think, when the decree was put into the archives, or in just what
form. Themistokles must have stressed the fact that the fight
impending would be "for their own freedom and for the freedom of all the Hellenes." This phrase, particularly, has
troubled the detractors. But it was indeed a struggle for the
freedom of all, as contemporary evidence, in full emotional
vigor, attests.

Aischylos, writing poetry to be sure, but a contemporary, has
the Persian messenger report to Queen Atossa the shout of the
Greeks as the battle of Salamis was joined:

"Sons of Hellenes, on! Free your fatherland, your children,
your wives,
your fathers' graves, the temples of their gods! Now you
battle for your all!"

$$\text{Νῦν ὑπὲρ πάντων ἀγών}$$

The same sentiment is expressed on the base of the monument
to the men of Marathon, who, "with their foot-soldiers and on
swift-sailing ships, kept all Greece from seeing its day of
slavery."[38]

These sentiments were appropriate to the occasion; they were
also the sort of thing that men remembered. There must be
thousands today who can remember Churchill's stirring words
of 1940: "We shall not flag or fail. We shall go on to the end,
we shall fight in France, we shall fight on the sea and oceans,
we shall fight with growing confidence and growing strength

---

[38] B. D. Meritt, in *The Aegean and the Near East: Studies presented to Hetty
Goldman* (1956), pp. 268-280. An improved text will appear in an early
number of the *American Journal of Philology*.

in the air, we shall defend our Island, whatever the cost may be, we shall fight on the beaches, we shall fight on the landing grounds, we shall fight in the fields and in the streets, we shall fight in the hills; we shall never surrender." The words may not always fall in exactly the same way from each one's remembrance, but the historicity of every version will be sound. The future historian could say, "This was Churchill speaking."

We do not have to attribute the emotional overtones of the decree of Themistokles to political invention in the fourth century; it is surprising, rather, that the decree as we have it retains so little rhetorical flourish.

And yet again, the claim has been made that the phrase "others who are willing to share the danger" is too elaborate for the early fifth century.[39] Habicht, for example, says that this should have been, if genuine, simply "the other allies." But this is not the same thing; it limits the field to the present allies. Themistokles left the way open to new allies, and, anyway, the phrase "who are willing" is guaranteed by Herodotos, for he quotes it (VII, 144: ἅμα Ἑλλήνων τοῖσι βουλομένοισι) from the decree. Are we asked to believe that Herodotos was quoting from a fourth-century forgery?

The authenticity of the decree has been impugned also because of the use in it of the word βάρβαρος to mean the Persian (or the Mede). This, the detractors claim, is a fourth-century phenomenon in Attic epigraphy, following the style set by Herodotos. This is not strictly true, for the detractors make no distinction between βάρβαρος in the singular and βάρβαροι in the plural. The latter frequently means simply non-Greek (cf. Thucydides, I, 3, 3), and as such it appears in both fifth- and fourth-century Attic epigraphy; the former, the singular, in both Herodotos and Thucydides always means the Persian enemy of the Persian Wars. But in the epigraphical references of the early fifth century the enemy is called Μῆδοι, and never βάρβαρος. Why, if the Themistokles decree is genuine, does it not use the epigraphical Μῆδοι instead of the literary βάρβαρος?

---

[39] Thucydides (II, 71, 2) has an echo of this clause of the decree in his fifth-century account of the Plataian address to Archidamos in 429 B.C.: Παυσανίας γὰρ ὁ Κλεομβρότου Λακεδαιμόνιος ἐλευθερώσας τὴν Ἑλλάδα ἀπὸ τῶν Μήδων μετὰ Ἑλλήνων τῶν ἐθελησάντων ξυνάρασθαι τὸν κίνδυνον - - -.

The answer depends again on our conception of the transmission of the text. Perhaps Themistokles did call the Persians Μῆδοι. Possibly he called them βάρβαρος. Possibly he called them βάρβαροι. But when the record of his decree was put into the archives, or possibly at some time when it was re-written in the fifth century, the word (fifth century rather than fourth century) was βάρβαρος. This term was well established in Athens in Thucydides's time. Thucydides even used the word βάρβαρος, in the singular, in reporting the decrees of the early confederacy. The Athenians apportioned, in 478/7 B.C., which of the cities were to furnish money against the barbarian, and which ships. In the terms of the decree βάρβαρος instead of Μῆδοι, if we follow Thucydides, was used of the enemy (I, 96, 1). Whether βάρβαρος or Μῆδοι actually stood in the original, no one doubts the substantive accuracy of the account in Thucydides. A copy of the decree of Themistokles made in the fifth century may have had βάρβαρος in its text, a circumstance which might show, but not inevitably so, that the copy was made later than 480, possibly in mid century, possibly about 424 B.C. when the evidence of the *Knights* shows that the generality of the Athenians knew the decree, but in no sense does the use of current fifth-century wording invalidate the historical accuracy of the record.

These examples suffice to illustrate what I mean by urging care in the use of evidence. We must ask ourselves, when we study the genuineness of the decree, what we mean by genuine. We must get rid of captious criticism, and take into consideration the probable method of its survival. Instead of regarding the Troizen text solely as an inscription, subject only to the laws and conventions of epigraphical research, we must study it in the light of its tradition, first perhaps oral (unwritten, as was epic poetry), then written, but for the archives, not for stone, and possibly recopied (when it absorbs some, at least, of the literary forms of its time), and finally as an epigraphical text. This last, of all three phases, is probably the least important.

An undue emphasis on the purely epigraphical details, which show that a third-century copy is not, word for word, identical with what we expect of an early fifth-century original, has led, for many, to the fixed idea of fourth-century fabrication. But the historian must read the decree, and Herodotos, and Thucydides together. They complement each other, and when one realizes that historical performance sometimes differs from plans and expectation they do not clash. In brief, the strategy of Artemision and Salamis is embodied in the Troizen stele and in Herodotos, VII, 144 (with which must be associated Thucydides, I, 18, 2, and I, 91, 5); the performance of Artemision and Salamis (before the battle) is told in Herodotos, VIII, 40-41 (with which must be associated Thucydides, I, 74). Plan and performance were not always kept in their proper place, even by the ancients. Plutarch's account is a notable example of *contaminatio*, for he makes one story of the decree and of the final flight of the women and children. Modern historians must do better.

It was the judgment of antiquity, voiced especially by Thucydides, that Themistokles was the wisest, most far-sighted, statesman of his time, and the architect of victory in the Persian Wars. The new decree from Troizen validates this claim.

Its authenticity, I am aware, has been woven into a fabric of argument that questions all the decrees of the age of the Persian Wars. I would suggest only at this time that this needs to be weighed again, when there has been time for a better judgment to settle upon the decree of Themistokles itself.

Byzantium and Byzantinism

BY ROMILLY JENKINS

Delivered November 5 and 6, 1962

FOREWORD

Though I had not the privilege of personal acquaintance with the generous benefactor in whose memory this series of lectures is given, I have heard and seen enough of the results achieved through her patronage and munificence to know that her name is immortal: not only here, in Cincinnati, but wherever classical studies, and especially Mediterranean archaeology, are held in reverence. That I should have been invited to lecture on this foundation is an honour which I deeply appreciate; and that I should have been chosen to speak in the same series with Professor Blegen and Professor Meritt is an honour which I should appreciate even more deeply still, were it not for the painful sense of my being wholly unworthy of it. This, obviously, is no mere form of words. The medieval letter-writer, it is true, was required by the laws of the *ars dictaminis* to commence with what was called *captatio benevolentiae*, that is, an expression of self-depreciation designed to forestall adverse criticism of his performance. But never was any *captatio* penned with greater sincerity than mine: and, in the words of Mr. Yates to Sir Thomas Bertram, I—though no longer a 'young' performer—must "bespeak your indulgence."

ROMILLY JENKINS

4

BYZANTIUM AND
BYZANTINISM

I: THE BYZANTINE STATE—ITS
ESSENTIAL QUALITIES

I SHALL TRY in these two lectures to speak of the general characteristics of the medieval empire of East or New Rome, which is in these days, though never in those, commonly called "Byzantine"; and to trace the survival of some of these characteristics in its offspring, the Modern Greek nation, at the time when it was liberated from Turkey in the early nineteenth century; and indeed in Eastern Europe generally. The subject is a very wide one, and, as always in these cases, the lecturer is bound to approach it with diffidence. I hope you will not be expecting me to produce any novel or spectacular information, for this I shall not do. My object is merely to arrange, in as succinct and coherent a fashion as I can, a body of essential knowledge which is already the property of every specialist in the medieval and modern history of the Near East. None the less, I have reason to believe that part at least of what I have to say may still appear novel, and perhaps prove stimulating, to many who have not had the time or inclination to go very deeply into these matters. And this is my excuse for accepting your kind invitation, and for putting before you a survey which it has not by any means been easy to compile.

The study and comprehension of the Byzantine State are of, comparatively speaking, recent date in Western Europe and America. This is due to many causes, among which religious prejudice, incompatibility of manners, a dislike of rigid and dogmatic conservatism, and, most of all, the manifest contrast between the splendours of Ancient Hellenic literature and the meagre fruits of a thousand years of Byzantine writing, may be considered the

chief. A knowledge of Ancient Greek, without which Byzantine
literary and historical studies cannot be intensively pursued, has
in itself proved a deterrent: for few scholars so equipped are disposed to abandon Homer and Sophocles, Thucydides and Plato,
for George of Pisidia, Paul the Silentiary, Procopius of Caesarea
and Michael Psellus. And this difficulty persists even today. Moreover, the erroneous and pejorative approach to Byzantium of the
greatest of eighteenth century historians, Edward Gibbon,[1] despite
his encyclopedic learning and minute accuracy, inspired in his
contemporaries an aversion and disgust for the subject in general.
A similarly contemptuous attitude was evinced, at nearly the same
time, by Voltaire:[2] "There exists another history yet more absurd . . . the history of Byzantium. This worthless history contains nothing but declamations and miracles. It is a disgrace to the
human mind." Gibbon, as is well known, extolled the age of the
Antonine Caesars as one of culture, polite manners and free enquiry: as, in short, that age of the ancient world which seemed
to approach most nearly to his own. The succeeding twelve centuries he regarded as a story of continuous decline from this condition, accelerated from without by successive barbarian inroads
and from within by the tyranny, quarrels and obscurantism of the
Christian religion. Brilliant as his work is, he failed to realise that
in and after the seventh century A.D. a Byzantine state had arisen
which in effect differed profoundly from the Roman empire of
Justinian: a state whose way of life he did not understand, and
whose achievements and triumphs he ignored because they were
not those of the Antonine age. Assuredly there was much, and
that the most obvious and spectacular, which the truly Byzantine
state inherited from the Rome of Augustus, and did its utmost to
preserve unaltered. But behind this imposing, though inevitably
restored, façade the fundamentals of society developed and
changed; and while in all departments—imperial, ceremonial, literary, linguistic—the old terms and nomenclatures survived, the
realities to which they were attached were in continual, if gradual,
mutation. To us, the contrast between old and new is the most

[1] G. Ostrogorsky, *History of the Byzantine State* (Oxford, 1956), 6.
[2] A. A. Vasiliev, *History of the Byzantine Empire* (Madison, 1961), I, 6. Both
these introductions should be studied.

striking feature of any survey; to the Byzantine observer, it did not exist at all.

If we take a view of the medieval Byzantine state at the time of its greatest temporal glory and cultural magnificence, that is, in the tenth and eleventh centuries, after it had emerged from three hundred years of apparently chronic weaknesses brought on by external pressures and internal contradictions, we shall get the best idea of what its inhabitants conceived it to be in theory, and what it was still, to a large extent, in practice. The empire of East Rome—so ran the theory[3]—was nothing less than the continuation, the survival in full vigour, of the Roman empire of Augustus, for which Jupiter had decreed eternal and universal dominion over all the world: "to these seven hills of Rome," as Ovid had proclaimed, "the whole world was one day promised." But to this belief in the natural, pre-ordained supremacy of Rome had for centuries been harnessed a spiritual dynamic no less universal and imprescriptible: the dynamic of Christian dogma. Almighty God, at the very time (and this was of the utmost significance) when the single earthly ruler Augustus had emerged as the temporal Prince of Peace, had sent among men his heavenly counterpart, Jesus Christ, of whose Kingdom there should likewise be no end. During some time these temporal and spiritual manifestations had seemed to be in conflict. But at last, with the coming of the thirteenth Apostle, in the person of Constantine the Great, the two traditions had been fused into a single, perfect theory, at once material and transcendent, which was of overwhelming conviction and potency. God, of Whom Christ in His human form was the manifestation to mankind, ruled as sole Emperor over the Kingdom of Heaven. His Realm was administered in perfect order and harmony by various angelic subordinates—dominions, princedoms, powers, and so on—backed by a standing army, organised in legions, which was invincible by the powers of hell, and which hence secured the greatest of all blessings, universal peace. Christ had, in His own Prayer, expressed His will that the earth should be similarly organised: that is to say, that it should, so far as might

[3] The best summary account of the Byzantine *Weltanschauung* is that of F. Dölger, *Byzanz und die europäische Staatenwelt* (Ettal, 1953), 10-13. This passage should be thoroughly mastered by every intending Byzantinist.

be in this imperfect sphere, be a *mimesis*, or imitation, of the celestial *idea*, of the City laid up in Heaven. In the words of Richard Hooker, who in sixteenth century England expounded a rather similar doctrine: "But now that we may lift up our eyes (as it were) from the footstool to the throne of God, and consider a little the state of heavenly and divine creatures: . . . as in number they are huge, mighty, and royal armies, so likewise in perfection of obedience unto law, such observants they are thereof, that our Saviour Himself did not teach to pray or wish for more than only it might be with us, as with them it is in heaven."

It followed from all this that the Roman empire was the earthly counterpart of the New Jerusalem, and that God's will was only to be done by subscribing to its universality and to the sovereignty of the Roman emperor of the day, who was God's own choice, manifestation and vice-gerent. According as God's purpose was nearer to, or further from, realisation on earth, earthly things were in better or worse case: and this variation between better and worse was conditioned by the spiritual state of God's Chosen or 'Peculiar' People, the Christian Romans. If they abstained from sin, the empire expanded and prospered, the menaces of barbarians receded, and the discords excited by heresy declined. If they did not so abstain, the reverse was the inevitable consequence. It was all delightfully simple, logical, and flattering to the pride of the East Roman Empire.

I have made in three sentences a statement of the bare fundamentals of a creed which would need—indeed, has needed—whole volumes to formulate and illustrate.[4] And I could spend the rest of this lecture in developing some of the theoretical corollaries which depended, always with rigorous logic, from the initial premiss. As it is, I can do no more than mention two or three which are the most important for the general history of Byzantium, and for that of its Near Eastern successors.

The first of these corollaries is what we may call the theory of divinely ordained and achieved perfection: and 'perfection' means, literally, the end of a process. This theory is antagonistic to every-

[4] A good, short bibliography of the subject, compiled by the late H. St L. B. Moss, will appear in the forthcoming re-edition of Volume IV of *Cambridge Medieval History*.

thing which western civilization has stood for since the Renaissance;
or at least since the Reformation. The West believes in progress
by means of practical empiricism. In so far as we believe in per-
fectibility at all, this is to be brought about by experiment and reform. The medieval Byzantine believed the precise opposite of this.
From the moment when the Roman and Christian theories of terrestrial and celestial empire had merged, the world *had achieved*
its final order. This dogma ruled out any idea of future progress,
except towards a more complete fulfillment in practice of what was
already true in theory; and left only the danger of deviationism.
A striking illustration of this is seen in the semantic change of the
word καινοτομέω, which in classical Greek means 'I innovate,' but in
Byzantine Greek, 'I injure.' Since the dogma was divinely ratified,
any fundamental reform was construed, not merely as rebellion, but
also as blasphemy. In the celestial sphere, the great reformer had
been Lucifer, and everyone knew what had happened to him.
Lucifer, now called Satan, was, to be sure, still active among mankind; but the only result of listening to his temptations would be
anarchy, or 'democracy,' a concept which all proper Byzantines held
in the utmost abhorrence. This theory of static perfection was, as we
shall see, bound to be fatal when the outside world began once more
to move forward in knowledge and skill and culture.

In the second place, the political component of this doctrine was
no less perfectly and unquestioningly received by the Byzantines
than was the religious. Fundamental to the thought-world of Byzantium was the conviction of the divinely ordered supremacy of the
East Roman Empire, and hence of the Byzantine's own innate superiority to every other part of mankind. Self-love is a human
weakness which does not generally require any very strong or
rational justification to nurture it. But where it could, as here, be
justified by the most powerful, august and undoubted of sanctions,
its hold naturally became unshakable among the 'Peculiar People',
and it survived all changes of historical fact and all modifications of
political theory. Such was the blinding influence of this doctrine
that the plainest facts of observed history, if they seemed to invalidate it, were either unrecognised or ignored. If the *data* of the
worlds of spirit and sense appeared to conflict, it must obviously be

the latter that were at fault. The faculties of erring mortals could be deceived: God's purpose and decree could not. And it is here that we meet with the fundamental cleavage which, even today, sunders east from west, where the infallibility of dogma clashes with the truth of observed fact. Yet, even in the Byzantine empire itself, on the lower or sensible plane of truth, contradictions with dogma continued at all periods to multiply and increase: and some of the chief of these may now be briefly examined.

In the first place, the universality of the Roman empire under Christ in theory overrode all conceptions of nationhood. The boundaries of the empire were coterminous with those of Orthodox Christianity, and those boundaries were in theory unlimited. The Latin and the Slav, the Helladic and the Armenian, the Syrian and the Teuton, were all equal in subjection beneath the Elect of Christ. The modern tendency to ascribe certain political events of the early Middle (or 'Dark') Ages to the operation of some sort of 'nationalist' feeling, such as we have observed during recent years in Mediterranean, Asiatic and African countries, is probably misconceived.[5] To say, for example, that the eastern and southern provinces of the Roman empire ultimately fared better under the Saracen dominion than they had fared under the Byzantine, is quite different from saying that, in the seventh century A.D., these areas felt a conscious, *nationalistic* resentment against the empire, which manifested itself in religious heresy and caused them virtually to secede to Islam. The *de jure* unity of the world under a single Roman Caesar was at that time universally admitted. The superiority of the Roman conquerors themselves had been axiomatic during the early centuries of their empire, and Roman citizenship had been a much prized privilege; and the tradition of this one-time superiority was still alive in the memory of tenth-century Byzantium.[6] Yet, almost as soon as his contacts with Hellas had begun, the conqueror had bowed his head before the superior genius of the Hellene, frequented the Greek university and learnt to speak the Greek language. After the seventh century the Romans themselves, that is, the race of conquerors from the banks of the Tiber, were

[5] A. H. M. Jones, 'Were the Ancient Heresies National or Social Movements in Disguise?,' *Journal of Theological Studies* 10 (1959), 280-298.
[6] Constantine Porphyrogenitus, *De Administrando Imperio*, ed. Moravcsik (Budapest, 1949), 13/121-122.

gone; and the Ancient Hellenes had long ceased to form a distinct racial element. The bonds which held the Byzantine State together were purely imperial, religious and cultural. The multitudinous races of Asia Minor, which constituted the core and kernel of Byzantine strength, mingled freely with those of Syria, Palestine and Egypt by means of the *lingua franca* of Hellenistic Greek; though Hellenistic civilisation made slow progress in the interior, and though in the Asiatic countryside Mysians, Lykaonians, Galatians, Phrygians and others are known to have preserved their proper dialects at least up to the end of the sixth century.[7] The importation of foreigners into Asia Minor was in all ages catholic and indiscriminate, and for a very good reason: since, owing to continual wars and invasions, the land was chronically starved of hands to till it. If an immigrant subscribed to the Christian God and the Christian emperor, no one troubled himself where the immigrant's father came from, and he was as satisfactory a Roman as any descendant of Brutus or Cassius. Constantinople itself was always polyglot, though the various tongues to be heard in its streets of course differed from age to age. In the twelfth century the grammarian Tzetzes[8] described how he commonly addressed his fellow-citizens in Russian or Alan or Latin (Italian) or Arabic, or even Hebrew. The empire was as indifferent to variations of colour as to those of language. Four hundred years before the time of Tzetzes, we learn of the emperor Theophilus that "he loved foreigners more than did any of his predecessors and collected an enormous company of various speech"; and that he settled his "beloved Ethiopians" in or near Constantinople and forced marriage with them upon the daughters of the citizenry. There are good grounds for believing that Stylianos Zautzes, father-in-law of the emperor Leo VI, was a negro, and his daughter the empress in consequence at least half a negress. But, after the sixth century, the great reservoirs of manpower from which the empire was continually recruited were Slavs from north or south of the Danube, and Armenians. The former were imported in numbers which, even if we allow for

[7] K. Holl, 'Das Fortleben der Volkssprachen in Kleinasien in nachchristlicher Zeit,' *Hermes* 43 (1908), 240-254.
[8] J. Moravcsik, 'Barbarische Sprachreste in der Theogonie des Johannes Tzetzes,' *Byzantinisch-Neugriechische Jahrbücher* 7 (1928-9), 352-365.

some exaggeration in the sources, must have been enormous; the latter, though probably fewer, furnished the finest troops and the ablest administrators to the empire during the seventh to eleventh centuries. The great emperor Basil I, himself an Armenian, encouraged them to immigrate by thousands.[9]

The very conception of a 'nation', an 'ethnos', was alien and odious to Byzantine political thought. An 'ethnos' was a tribe or race of barbarians or heretics, or both, who lived beyond the pale of Christ's Kingdom on Earth, and refused to acknowledge the sway of Christ's anointed emperor, beneath which was neither Greek nor Jew, but the single 'logical flock' of the Good Shepherd and His New Jerusalem.

In such a society as this there should, in theory, have been no social distinctions save those of administrative function, and no feelings of superiority and exclusiveness. Yet, despite theory, there was in all ages at Byzantium an aristocracy of birth (though this was not based on racial stock), and an aristocracy of culture. The aristocracy of birth established itself in landed property and military experience. The pretence was certainly made in some noble families that their lines went back to the early days of senatorial and republican Rome; but by the eighth century this claim could not be substantiated, and was often manifestly false. The majority of the military and landed clans which dominated Asia Minor during the Middle-Byzantine age were in fact of Armenian origin, and their local authority had in most cases not existed before the seventh century. This aristocracy, while it cultivated the military virtues, was grasping and arrogant, and exerted a centrifugal and disruptive tendency on a society which was by definition single and united. Far different was the aristocracy of culture, which was centred in Constantinople itself. We have already noted the chief of the bonds which held together that polyglot and heterogeneous populace: the bond of Christian imperialism, the feeling of 'belonging' to the elect of God. But there was also the bond, equally strong but much more exclusive, of initiation into Hellenistic culture.

Since the establishment of the Hellenistic kingdoms by the successors of Alexander, a Hellenic, that is, a Hellenistic, education

---

[9] *Skazanija o 42 Amorijskikh Muchenikakh* (ed. Vasilievskij-Nikitin; Saint Petersburg, 1905), 27/4-5; *Acta Sanctorum* November, IV, col. 692 D.

had been indispensable to all who sought social or political advancement in the Near East: and the chief element in this education was the acquisition of the Greek language, not as spoken by ordinary folk, but as compiled by rhetoricians out of classical texts. The literary and artistic productions of the Hellenes from the age of Homer to the age of Aristotle were rightly seen as unapproachable by later generations, and were regarded rather as a legacy of pictures or plate, to be studied, imitated, and commented upon, than as a legacy of money which might by prudent investment increase and multiply. What we ourselves regard as the grandest part of the Hellenic literary legacy, poetry, could scarcely be added to, since poetic genius and originality were virtually extinct. The talent for speculation and philosophising survived during some centuries among the Hellenists; and Graeco-Roman philosophers, Neo-Platonists and Christian Fathers preserved much of the subtilty, if little of the originality, of the classical thinkers. The writing of history, among much that was worthless, established a splendid post-classical tradition and proved the most valuable literary bequest of the Hellenistic age to Byzantium. But the most easily acquired, and hence the most eagerly pursued, portion of the legacy was the barren study of words, grammar, syntax, and rhetorical expression. To be able to speak, and especially to write, what was thought to be polite classical Greek, as codified in a thousand school-books and exemplified in ten thousand selected quotations from Hellenic texts—this was that Hellenistic culture which distinguished the elect, whatever might be his racial origin, from the barbarian. This was the *Open Sesame* to the highest and most lucrative employments in the bureaucracy, and even to the imperial cabinet and the imperial chamber.[10]

This devotion to the husk rather than to the kernel of classical letters was not simply a matter of declining taste and abilities. Religious causes were operative also. In a state which was, by its most fundamental postulate, the kingdom and empire of Jesus Christ, Whose earlier followers had waged a long and cruel war against Paganism, an absorbing devotion of educated men to Hellenic or Hellenistic letters was not without its dangers and contradictions. And in fact the contradiction between the pure Word of the Gospel

[10] Cf. F. Dölger, *Paraspora* (Ettal, 1961), 39.

and the pagan lore of Hellas was insoluble: it was always latent and very frequently overt. St. Basil in the fourth century had tried once for all to solve it, in his celebrated pronouncement on the use which should be made by young Christians of classical letters.[11] In this document St. Basil, himself an alumnus of Athens University and a very accomplished Grecian, had laid it down that Greek studies did form a necessary part of primary and higher education; but he had added the caution that only those precepts and examples of classical literature should be received which could be reconciled with the new ethic, and could fortify the faith of a Christian gentleman. This meant in practice that the Christian's education could and should include classical Greek grammar and modes of expression, together with edifying history (especially Roman), and moral essays such as those of Plutarch. The more specifically pagan part of the ancient legacy, such as drama and above all pagan philosophy, was to be eschewed. This edict was followed in general outline, the more readily since the language of imperial administration, an artificial idiom based on later Attic, could be acquired without spiritual danger. But the lines drawn by St. Basil were constantly and inevitably overstepped. Scholars in all ages, and especially in and after the eleventh century, delved deeper and deeper into the treasure-house of Hellenic wisdom, and thus aroused fierce opposition and denunciation from the more pious, or less gifted, party of Christian orthodoxy. This dichotomy in Byzantine thought, both lay and ecclesiastical, was one of the most important features in the age-long strife of parties which we may, for convenience, call 'liberal' and 'conservative', or 'broad' and 'orthodox': a strife which formed so striking an anomaly in the (at first sight) homogeneous and monolithic structure of society. The contradiction was of course not confined to Eastern Christendom: it is repeated in the distress of Dante at seeing the pagan worthies confined in limbo, and in Milton's pathetic rejection of all the poetry of Hellas in exchange for the Songs of Sion. At Byzantium, let it suffice merely to repeat that the second, and more influential, aristocracy was a caste which boasted neither birth nor nationality, but Hellenic culture: and formed what has been called the 'bureaucratic' aristocracy of the

----

[11] Πρὸς τοὺς νέους, ὅπως ἂν ἐξ ἑλληνικῶν ὠφελοῖντο λόγων (*MPG XXXI*, cols. 564-589).

capital and its civil service, supplemented by a small, but always considerable, party of 'broad' and educated churchmen. Even among the party of the orthodox, which was, in its profession, profoundly distrustful of pagan letters, the opposition was more formal than real: and authors ecclesiastical and hagiographic, while clamorously insisting on their apostolic simplicity, continued to write in as educated a fashion as they knew how: so general was the feeling that the acquisition of polite letters was among the *summa bona*, and that their neglect was a sign, not so much of piety, as of boorishness and incompetence.

Hellenistic letters therefore were the strong bond which united in fellowship the educated class of the empire. Every subject of the empire, whatever his racial affinity or social status, was equally a Christian Roman, a member of Christ's flock. To the privileged *élite* alone was given the command—as it seemed to them—of the noblest idiom, and with that idiom of the noblest genius, ever granted to mankind. It cannot be too strongly emphasised that in the greatest epoch of Byzantium, when she still claimed, and still strove with some success to preserve, a world empire, this pride in, and sense of belonging to, the superior culture of Hellas was not in any way connected with a sense of Hellenic nationalism, in the late medieval or modern sense of that word. No Byzantine supposed for a moment that, by writing in Hellenistic euphuisms or by quoting from two dozen classical authors on every page, he was vindicating a lineal descent from the contemporaries of Pericles and Plato. He did indeed use the adjective 'Hellenic' to denote his education; but when he used the noun 'Hellene' he meant a pagan.[12] Hellas was to him the name of a not very important province in his Roman empire, and its inhabitants were 'Helladics', just as the inhabitants of the Armeniac and Anatolic provinces were 'Armeniacs' and 'Anatolics'. The tongue of the 'Hellenízontes', or 'Imitators of Hellas', was that of the Christo-Roman empire: not simply because of the incomparable value of the classical writers, but also because Greek was the language of the Christian scriptures and of the Christian Fathers. It therefore constituted the finest,

[12] See the excellent dissertation of K. Lechner, *Hellenen und Barbaren* (Munich, 1954), *passim*.

and, after the seventh century, the unique, mode of interpreting Roman majesty and Christian faith and righteousness.

A striking example of this monopoly, which, unlike many single examples, does in fact illustrate the general rule, may be found in the greatest dynasty which ever sat on the Byzantine throne, the house of Basil the Macedonian (867-1056). Basil I was the son of an Armenian peasant, and his mother was probably a Slav. His first language was Armenian. To the end of his life he could neither read nor write. He married a lady of probably Scandinavian origin, and had by her two sons called Leo and Alexander. So much convinced was he, like all his contemporaries, of the absolute necessity of Hellenistic culture for a future emperor, that he had these sons educated by the greatest scholar of the age, the ex-patriarch Photius. Both boys became capital Greek scholars, and one of them a learned theologian. Neither, so far as we know, spoke a word of any language but Greek. Leo's son Constantine went further, and became the most notable antiquary and one of the most celebrated historians of Byzantium. Of such was the educated class in the Middle-Byzantine empire. Whether this allegiance to what after all remained a barren discipline was beneficial to the ruling class, may be disputed. Barren it certainly was as regards the advancement of knowledge; yet it is hard to think of any other discipline which could have bound together a hundred racial types into a single cultural and learned tradition.

Thus, in the cultural field, we come across one more social contradiction or dichotomy. On the one hand, the doors to the bureaucratic aristocracy were literally open to the talents. Any clever boy, however lowly his origins, whose parents could get him a primary education, might with industry aspire to the highest posts in the administration. On the other hand, it was always doubted in military circles whether a knowledge of Homeric particles was exactly the best qualification for statesmanship or for the command of armies in the field.

This Hellenistic lore is so constant and prominent a feature of both Byzantine and post-Byzantine epochs that we must try to define rather more closely in what it consisted, and in what way it was related to the Hellenic tradition which it claimed to perpetuate. It had little or nothing in common with what the modern world knows as 'classical studies', that is, the study of the art, writing, and mind of a distinct and chronologically defined civilisation. The Homeric poems were indeed used by Byzantine school-masters, who explained the vocabulary and grammatical peculiarities. But the chief part of a Hellenistic education had from the first been orthographic, that is, the correct usage of the old Attic dialect. The approach to this study in the Middle Ages was more and more the approach to a dead language, since most of the students, even if they had heard Greek at their mother's knee, had heard a Greek which differed as widely from that of Plato as Italian differs from classical Latin.[18] In the hands of every student were the Hellenistic grammars of Apollonius and Herodian, and the Hellenistic treatises on rhetoric of Hermogenes and Aphthonius. Apart from Homer, original Greek texts were scarcely studied; instead, a hundred hand-books of word-lists, quotations, sayings, proverbs and potted biographies were got by heart: and it was mainly from these that the embellishments which characterised the polite style were borrowed. The result was a style artificial, laboured, obscure and repetitious, in which all originality of thought, all freshness of observation were doomed to be submerged. As in political and religious theory, so in the modes and styles of expression, the ultimate of perfection had been attained in a far distant past. The whole duty of the scholar, as of the Christian, was to refer back to and, so far as he could, to preserve unaltered, a canon from which any deviation must be for the worse. To write a simple, straightforward Greek was regarded as a sign of *amathia* or *amousia*, requiring verbose apology and self-exculpation. And an amalgam of the rarest locutions, the most strained constructions, the harshest apostrophes and the most recondite mythological allusions was alone considered worthy of those who thought they were preserving the tradition of Demosthenes and Isocrates.

The place of poetry was supplied by rhetorical exercises in ancient prosody.[14] History-writing did continue at all periods; and here, although the forms of such writing were borrowed from antiquity, the content could not be so. But by far the largest part

[18] Dölger, *op.cit.*, 40.
[14] For a good definition of Byzantine 'poetry,' see N. Tomadakis, Εἰσαγωγὴ εἰς τὴν βυζαντινὴν φιλολογίαν (Athens, 1952), 121-124.

of educated writing was mere literary exercise, in which one author or one century differs from another simply in his or its degree of tastelessness and frigidity. Hagiography alone, the simple lives and adventures of good men told in a language to be understood of the many, forms a striking exception, and often succeeds in combining edification with genuine narrative ability.

This was a sad state of affairs; but one which was inevitable in any society whose chief tenet was that all innovation is evil and betrays an inherited trust. Historians have puzzled their brains, and will doubtless continue to do so, over the causes of the rapid decay of Byzantium after the eleventh century. But they need look no further than this. Byzantium remained static in face of a Europe that by this time was rapidly beginning to advance: in the arts of peace[15] no less than in the arts of war: in a diversity of cultural centres, and in the employment of native vernaculars as means of expression. It is often overlooked that up till that time the education and spiritual climate of the Latin West were strictly parallel with those of the Greek East. There was the same hidebound and slavish devotion to the Roman imperial idea, and to the great literary masters of antiquity. Classical Latin in the West enjoyed the same prestige as Classical Greek in the East. Cicero was as tyrannical a master as Demosthenes; Virgil as Homer. The Latin counterparts of Apollonius and Herodian were the grammarians Priscian and Donatus, and the western commentaries on classical writers supplied those compendia of knowledge which the Greek East drew from Stobaeus or Hesychius. The rhetorical training in epistolography at Byzantium was exactly parallel to the rhetorical *dictamen* of the West.[16]

Up till the twelfth century the cultural balance between East and West had inclined decidedly in favour of the former. The strength and unity of the empire had been able at least to maintain its spiritual inheritance, although unable significantly to increase it. But from the period of the Crusades onwards the advance of Western Europe was such as hopelessly to distance its eastern

---

[15] It is no accident that the great revolution in the principles of animal traction was made in the XIIth century, in the West: see Lefebvre des Noëttes, 'Le système d'attelage du cheval et du boeuf,' *Mélanges Ch. Diehl* I (Paris, 1930) 187-188.

[16] G. Karlsson, *Idéologie et cérémonial dans l'épistolographie byzantine* (Uppsala, 1959).

rival. This is not the place even to summarise the European achievement during the twelfth century, which has been brilliantly done by
a great American historian.[17] Suffice it to say that John of Salis-
bury was already the peer of the foremost Byzantine scholar of
his day, Eustathios of Salonika; that Canterbury Cathedral was
built (1174-84) in the time of the Comneni; and that Dante and
Chaucer were contemporaries of the earlier and later Palaeologans.
We are already in quite different worlds. Up till that time, the
conservatism of Byzantium had been her salvation in a world of
flux and barbarism. After that time, progress, and an element of
revolt, in the West inevitably made ground against immutability.
    For, of necessity, to stand still was to regress, both relatively
and absolutely. In no sphere is this truth more plainly discernible
than in that of language and letters. The literary Greek of the
twelfth century, not to speak of the fourteenth and fifteenth centuries, was far inferior as an organ of communication to the col-
loquial Latin of the West. While the Byzantine strove to preserve
the ancient idiom, he was making the worst of two worlds: for
his style, while it would have made Isocrates stare and gasp, was
also incapable of clearly expressing his meaning. He continued to
criticise literature in terminology which had long since ceased to
be applicable to the language he wrote. He continued to see in
the stylised, two-dimensional art of his epoch that exact natural-
ism which the early critics had extolled in the statues of Myron
and Praxiteles, and the paintings of Apelles and Euphranor. It
was this obsession with continuity which constituted the educated
Byzantine's most obstinate and most pernicious delusion. He could
never see the Hellenic heritage with fresh eyes, and thus could
never understand its true significance and splendour.[18] It must
in fairness be remembered that contrasts between 'ancient' and
'modern,' and divisions of history into periods, are western renaissance concepts, which were scarcely realised before the time of
Petrarch, and scarcely defined before the time of Francis Bacon.
The influence exerted on the West by the rediscovery of classical
Greek culture was the greater simply because it *was* a re-discovery,

[17] C. H. Haskins, *The Renaissance of the Twelfth Century* (Harvard, 1939).
[18] E. Panofsky, *Renaissance and Renascences in Western Art* (Stockholm, 1960),
10 ff., 36 ff. I am grateful to my friend Mr. Cyril Mango for drawing my attention to this excellent and illuminating work.

a revelation of something undreamt of, which it could stand apart from and bring into the focus of historical perspective. To the Byzantine no revelation of this kind was possible. By speaking a version of the same tongue in which the ancient masterpieces had been written, he concluded that he was heir to the whole, and one who, by his very nature, must understand the Greeks of old better than any barbarian.

The history of Byzantium as a rapidly diminishing state in the post-crusading era is in several ways distinct from her history as a—not to say 'the'—imperial power before 1204. The Palaeologans, as Norman Baynes said, 'wear their crown with a difference.' None of the pretensions to political, religious and cultural supremacy was overtly abandoned, since these pretensions were regarded as universal laws ordained by God from the beginning: and God does not change His mind according to changes of observed phenomena in this world of sense and decay. It was and remained His will that His Kingdom on earth would one day be consummated in universal subjection to His vice-gerent who sat on the throne of His earthly Jerusalem. And if this grand consummation seemed to be continually fading into the distance, this was not due to any change in His decree, but merely because that decree was hampered by the sins of His people. But faith and practice were, as in the Byzantine sphere they have always been, perched on the separate horns of an insoluble dilemma. The Palaeologan emperors in general saw clearly enough that without some doctrinal concessions to the Catholic West which would make possible an alliance of the Christian powers, nothing could ultimately save their feeble state from destruction by the infidel. This was the practical horn. But the vast majority of their subjects, both lay and ecclesiastical, regarded any and every concession to the heretic as blasphemy, which, by displeasing God, would accelerate, rather than turn aside or postpone, the downfall of Byzantium. God, they reasoned, had more than enough legions of angels at command with which to annihilate the Ottoman Turks; but He was not likely to employ them in defence of a people who showed themselves unsound on points touching Papal supremacy and the Double Procession of the Holy Ghost. The faithful theorists won the day, as they were bound to do, and Byzantium fell to the invader. But the faith itself did not die: it survived to become the most powerful and intractable element of the Byzantine legacy to eastern Europe.

Yet, in the Palaeologan age (1262-1453), the stubborn pressure of hard facts was not wholly without influence on the fortress of theory.[19] It could not substantially weaken, far less destroy, the citadel; but it did succeed in bringing about some change of emphasis in the distribution of the garrison. The spiritual bastions were reinforced, while the political were, though not abandoned, more thinly manned. Thinking men, who had to devise and do the best they could in an ever deteriorating political and military situation, could not remain blind to the unpleasant fact that the claim of their city to universal sway under the elect of Christ, however much justified in theory, corresponded to very little in practice, and was likely, in the not very distant future, to correspond to nothing at all. It was not only that the glory had departed from the Roman arms, wielded though these might be by Franks or Turcomans or Albanians. It was also that the preponderance in culture, as in commerce, had very unmistakably shifted westwards. There is some evidence that even as early as the twelfth century the Byzantine was beginning to recognise the merits of western scholarship; and the emperor Alexius I is even said to have observed, "Olim sapientia deducta est de oriente in occidentem . . . nunc e contrario de occidente in orientem latinus veniens descendit ad grecos":[20] though I have my doubts of the truth of such a story as early as this. But by the fifteenth century, the superiority of the West was too patent to be disregarded by a practical man. Kydones and Bessarion, even the fanatical Gennadios, had to admit that wisdom now resided among the Franks, and, what was worse, that these knew far more about Hellenic letters than did the Byzantines themselves.[21] If Greeks wished to be educated, they must go to Italy, and endeavour to reclaim from the barbarians their neglected and dissipated inheritance.

What reserves then could be thrown into the breaches opened by declining power and declining cultural prestige? There re-

[19] I. Ševčenko, 'The Decline of Byzantium seen through the Eyes of its Intellectuals,' *Dumbarton Oaks Papers* 15 (1961), 169-186.
[20] *Echos d'Orient* 32 (1933), 24-25.
[21] Lechner, 126-127; Ševčenko, 175 ff.

mained one element, hitherto somewhat slighted, in the glorious heritage of Byzantium to which none but she could lay claim. It was at this time, in the thirteenth and succeeding centuries, that eyes became open to the grandeur of the specifically *Hellenic*—as opposed to the Romano-Hellenistic—legacy, both in its literary remains and in the surviving traces of its material monuments. Byzantine scholarship began to go back to the study and appreciation of original Ancient Greek texts in preference to Hellenistic. And, at last, discerning travellers such as the exiled emperor Theodore Lascaris began, perhaps under impulsion from the west, to gaze and to marvel at the imperishable constructions of ancient Greek architects and engineers. Now, in the creation of all this magnificence Roman imperialism, which had hitherto been the main tradition by which its Byzantine successor had lived, had had no hand, and had, at best, played the part of a preserver only. And the doctrines of Orthodox Christianity, which were the motive power of that imperialism, had of course played no part at all. Hence, in the short space remaining to the independent existence of Byzantium, we observe among educated men traces of a spiritual revolution, which, *pari passu* with that of western Europe, turned away from the concept of Roman universality and back to the pre-Roman civilisation of classical Hellas.

The Ancient Hellenic race itself began to be looked on no longer as dangerous and corrupting heathens, but as a people of eminent genius, before whom even the all-conquering Romans had bowed the knee. Their poetry and thought began to be studied and interpreted in a fashion which, though by no means as promising as that which was burgeoning in the west, yet indicated a more truly humanistic approach to those studies. And this revived appreciation of Hellenic grandeur began among educated men to supply the place of the Roman imperial tradition as the justification of the claim, which could never be forfeited, of Byzantine superiority over all the nations of the world. The Byzantines, it was now claimed, and especially those who lived in the Hellenic homeland, were the legitimate and true-born heirs of Ancient Hellas. They spoke a tongue which, as they maintained, preserved unchanged the accents of Pericles and Leonidas. It was their own forefathers who had written the "Antigone" and the "Clouds," the "Republic" and the "Politics"; and who had reared the temple of Pallas and the theatres of Pergamum. Whereas in former days they had claimed the monopoly of empire and truth, they now insisted upon the monopoly of that learning and culture which had civilised the barbarian and given expression to mankind.

The express Byzantine version of these revised claims to pre-eminence came in the years which immediately preceded the final catastrophe; and came in the writings of the last of the Byzantine theorists, George Gemistus Pletho. In his view, as he expounded it to the emperor Manuel II, two of the three main props which had since the beginning upheld the myth of East Rome had been unsound. Eternal and universal Roman empire had proved an illusion. The Christian religion, which had lent sanction to that claim, was equally delusory. Only the culture and thought of the Greeks—not any longer of Byzantine Hellenists but now of the actual Hellenes, and especially of Plato—could be admitted for truth and trusted as a talisman for future renovation and greatness. Pletho at last overtly formulated the doctrine toward which so many of his fellows had been groping during the past two centuries: the myth of direct descent and heritage from the Hellenes of old.

But this theory was by no means universally or even widely received by the Byzantines in general. And here we touch on the last, and perhaps the most irreconcilable, of those internal contradictions which time allows us to notice today. I do not now speak of a contradiction between faith and historical fact, which is a question I reserve for tomorrow; but the contradiction between two incompatible faiths. The classical myth, though potentially very strong for a future Romantic age, exercised little influence at the end of the Middle Ages, when it was confined to some scholars and antiquaries. The incompatibility is well expressed by Mr. N. B. Tomadakis: "Medieval Hellenism (he says) was a different spiritual world from the Ancient: it rests its soul elsewhere, looks to other ideals of happiness, and consequently cannot express itself in the manner of pagan Hellenism."[22] The claims and creeds of Orthodox Christianity, though these, as Byzantine power declined, became less material and more spiritual, and tended to exalt the pres-

[22] Tomadakis, op.cit., 12, 16-17.

tige of the Patriarch at the expense of the prestige of the Basileus, were still dominant in the breasts of the Byzantine people. It was the medieval rather than the romantic faith that enabled the Ortho-dox Church, with its spendid organisation, to sustain its people through the long night of Turkish occupation, and never allowed it for a moment to doubt the divine purpose that one day it should recover all it had lost to the Frank and the Turk.

What then, in brief recapitulation, were the dominant and per-manent elements in Byzantine and post-Byzantine thought? First and foremost, an unquestioning *faith* in the postulate of exclusive supremacy, both in religious orthodoxy, and in material sover-eignty, and in cultural eminence. Second, and consequentially, an inbred, instinctive hatred of the West of Europe, whose inhabitants were abhorred as heretics and contemned as barbarians. Third, the unwavering belief that the Greek empire of the East, when once its sins and vices had been purged away, would in God's good time be resurrected in all its pristine majesty, before which every knee should bow, and from which the world should once more receive the ineffable blessings of the Pax Romana and the Hellenic culture, which it alone was worthy to interpret and to dispense. Such were the unchanging tenets which dominated the belief and policy of Greece in the nineteenth century, and found expression in the *Grande idée* of imperial restoration. "Do not suppose," said a prominent Greek man of letters to Mr. Senior in 1858, "that we consider this corner of Greece as our country, or Athens as our capital . . . Our country is the vast territory of which Greek is the language and the faith of the Orthodox Church is the religion. Our capital is Constantinople. Our national temple is Santa Sophia, for nine hundred years the glory of Christendom."[23]

What amount of practical, matter-of-fact truth can be marshalled in support of any of these credos we must inquire tomorrow. Let us pause here with the reflexion that, for a true understanding of the Near East—indeed, of Eastern Europe—, the watchword must be, not, as with us, '*magna est veritas*,' but '*magna est* FIDES, *et praevalebit.*'

---

[23] N. W. Senior, *A Diary kept in Turkey and Greece* (London, 1859), 358.

II: BYZANTINISM AND ITS SURVIVAL IN THE NINETEENTH CENTURY

We ended our last lecture with the claim of the learned Gemistus Pletho that the inhabitants of the fifteenth-century Morea—multiracial as other contemporary evidence shows them to have been— were directly descended from the Hellenes of old, a conclusion deduced by him from the twin circumstances of a Greek tongue and a Greek educational tradition surviving among them. This claim was, as we saw, antipathetic to the Christian tradition of Byzantium, and made very little progress, even among educated people, during the earlier centuries of Turkish occupation. The contradiction between Christ and Apollo must always be irreconcilable, even though the Former had been for centuries adopted, and indeed monopolised, by the Greek-speaking empire. None the less, the Hellenic germ had by the end of the Middle Ages been planted in the seed-bed of national mythology; and, watered at length by the refreshing dews of the Romantic age, it put forth a sturdy growth in the nineteenth century. Although it could not be successfully grafted on to the hoary but still vigorous trunk of Byzantinism, it flourished along with it in the same soil of national pride, and constituted a powerful appeal to European generosity and indulgence in favour of the new nation. Its chief nourishers were in fact educated Europeans, who had rediscovered and made capital of the genius of Ancient Hellas, but had remained abysmally ignorant of the medieval history of the Near East. It was Romantic Europe that reassured nineteenth-century Greece of her classical ancestry. Can Greece be blamed for having accepted this assurance?

But my first object today is to examine, not the origins of the myth, but how that myth conflicted with historical fact; and how, in the nineteenth century, as in the Middle Ages, it was the myth that carried all before it. It is one of the few signs of increased sanity in our world today that questions of racial origin can be discussed rationally and dispassionately. Nowadays, especially since the collapse of Nazi Germany, we do not trouble our heads about where people come from, so much as about where they are going to; (we are all of us, to say the truth, a pretty mixed bunch—even, perhaps, *quod dicere nolo*). But, a hundred years ago, this attitude was far from universal. Racial pride was widespread, immense, and acutely sensitive. When a sensible, level-headed historian like Lord Macaulay could seriously describe the English as "the hereditary nobility of mankind," we shall not be surprised at similar nonsense uttered in other, less cultivated countries at the same epoch.

Well, then: as regards the fifteenth, and subsequently the nineteenth, century claim to historical, that is, racial continuity with ancient times in the Greek peninsula: no educated person nowadays would maintain this claim in the realm of sober, historical fact. The failure of the Hellenes to survive as a recognisable racial group in the later Roman empire mattered the less since, after the conquest of Greece by Alexander, its people themselves evinced a striking, and continuously increasing, decline in the creative genius which had characterised them during the past four and a half centuries. They now became, over a wide area of the Mediterranean and the Near East, the interpreters and codifiers of their ancestors. It may well be that the chief reason for this decline lies in the region of biology rather than of politics: I mean, in a final disequilibrium between the two racial stocks, Nordic and Mediterranean, whose harmonious fusion had till then produced so much of glory and nobility, of creative artistry and intellectual majesty.

The history of the Hellenic homeland during the last three centuries before Christ is one of continuous depopulation, and of emigration to the thriving centres of Hellenistic power in Egypt and Asia. The Roman conquest of Hellas accelerated this process to a fearful pace. In the year 146 B.C. the consul Mummius totally destroyed Corinth; and seventy years later, Sulla perpetrated such a massacre among the population of Athens as made the ears of all who heard of it to tingle: one of the most atrocious mass-killings of history, comparable with that perpetrated in Jerusalem by the first Crusaders. In Cicero's time Greece was generally regarded as desolate. Whole districts lay uninhabited. Cicero's friend Sulpicius Rufus gazed with awe on the "corpses of so many cities" of Greece which lay before his eyes.[24] A few decades later, Plu-

---

[24] Cicero, *Ep. ad Fam.*, IV, v, 4: *quae oppida* (Aegina, Megara, Piraeus, Corinth) . . . *nunc prostrata et diruta ante oculos iacent.*

tarch, a reliable witness in an age of accurate observation and statement, declared: "In this general depopulation, brought equally
upon all the world by the past broils and conflicts, Greece has been
the principal sufferer; and now the whole country could scarce
furnish 3,000 infantrymen, or as many as the single city of Megara
sent out to fight at Plataea [sc. in 479 B.C.]."[25] Those who in the
nineteenth century A.D. spilt gallons of ink in discussing word by
word what Byzantine historians of the tenth century meant by
their statements regarding the Hellenic homeland, could have
saved themselves much time and trouble by pondering the implications of this revealing passage. Vigorous efforts were made by
Julius Caesar and Augustus to repopulate some of the western
and southern areas, and settlements of Italians were established
in cities along the Gulf of Lepanto, including Patras and Corinth,
where the strife of tongues was vividly described a century later
by St. Paul. These cities survived in their Italianate form during
some centuries; and it is significant that, in a list of nine early
Christian martyrs recorded at Corinth, four—Victor, Victorinus,
Claudian and Quadratus—bear Latin names. Athens too survived
the depredations of Sulla, and her famous academies were well
attended by foreign students; but an observation of Cnaeus Cal-
purnius Piso, made as early as A.D. 18, shows us of what her
population then consisted. "I do not speak of the Athenians (he
said), for these have been extirpated by a whole series of dis-
asters; but of that hotch-potch of foreigners (*colluvies nationum*)
who allied themselves with Mithridates against Sulla, and with
Antony against the Divine Augustus."[26] The more enterprising
remnant of the Hellenes had departed overseas, first to the east,
where they merged with the more or less hellenized populations
of the Near Eastern littoral, and then westward to Rome: to teach
Greek grammar and rhetoric and geometry to the Roman gentry,
or, as Juvenal maliciously observed, to get money by telling for-
tunes and dancing on a tight-rope.[27]

The history of the Greek peninsula during the earlier centuries
of Byzantine authority is the history of a very sparsely populated

[25] *De def. orac.*, 414 A.
[26] Tacitus, *Annals* 2, 55.
[27] III, 60-125. The whole passage merits study.

countryside dominated by half a dozen imperial garrisons lodged in fortresses which art or nature had rendered impregnable. The Teutonic Herules in the third century, and the Goths of Alaric in the fourth, spread devastation among what there was left to devastate. Alaric occupied the towns of Corinth, Argos and Sparta, and plundered the till then nearly untouched sanctuary of Zeus at Olympia. That he yet further reduced the populace by slaughter and slavery, is undoubted. But he did not expel the imperial forces; and, in his retreat, left no Germanic settlements in his wake. The new population, which was to occupy and permanently to settle in the old homeland, began their invasion not before the sixth century, when the imperial ambitions of Justinian I in Italy and the West had ruinously depleted the forces of Roman resistance to the new invader.

These invaders were land-hungry Slavs, who had, during several decades, gathered in uncountable multitudes across the Danube; and now, under the leadership, first of Turkic Avars, and later of Turkic Bulgars, poured down in torrents over Hellas and Peloponnesus. The historical sources, scanty though they may be, are unanimous that between the last quarter of the sixth and the first quarter of the seventh century (to be more exact, between A.D. 577 and 615) the occupation proceeded apace. Procopius is witness that this was no peaceful occupation. Whatever the Slav invaders found in their path was mercilessly exterminated. There was little resistance in the countryside, since there were but few to make any. The western districts of Hellas and Peloponnesus were the first to be slavised. There is some evidence to show that in the eastern parts of Greece the invaders, lacking siege equipment, and being in search of agricultural and pastural lands, never occupied the citadels of Salonica, or Athens, or Corinth, or Monemvasia, where the Byzantine garrisons, which could be relieved by sea, maintained a tenuous hold. All else was lost. And Isidore of Seville could tersely observe: "At the beginning of the fifth year of Heraclius [that is, A.D. 615] the Slavs took Greece from the Romans."[28] An attempt was made at a Roman re-occupation in the middle of the seventh century, by the emperor Constans II, one of the few

[28] Migne, *Patrologia Latina* LXXXIII, col. 1056 A: *Sclavi Graeciam Romanis tulerunt.*

Byzantine emperors after Justinian whose eyes were turned to the west; but this was without any permanent result. From that time, during more than a century, the terrain was abandoned to the invader. The picture that emerges is one of a loose federation of Slavs under a principal župan, or chieftain, who, in 799, and in the person of one Akamir of Thessaly, was powerful enough to liberate the brother of Leo IV imprisoned in the fortress of Athens, and to make him an emperor in opposition to his sister-in-law, Irene.[29]

Everything outside the fortress was abandoned. The careful and brilliant work of American archaeologists supplements and corroborates, in a striking degree, the literary evidence: both at Athens and at Corinth. At Athens, the archaeological evidence shows that between the third and the sixth centuries A.D. the city below the Acropolis was confined to a walled area of not more than about forty acres in extent. Then, in the last quarter of the sixth century, came the cataclysm. "The evidence of the excavation," says Professor Thompson, "points to wide-spread devastation in the area of the Agora at this time, most likely in the 80's of the sixth century. There can be little doubt that the damage is to be connected with a particularly savage incursion of Slavic peoples. After a short interval, some at least of the buildings were patched up . . . But it was a squatter's existence . . . Coins and pottery indicate a certain amount of habitation down to the second half of the seventh century [that is, to the time of Constans II]. Then ,follows a period of well-nigh complete desolation, until the area was re-occupied as a residential district in the tenth century. But, by this time, to use the words of Archbishop Michael Akominatos, 'the glory of Athens had utterly perished; one could see nothing, not even a faint symbol, by which to recognize the ancient city.' "[30]

It is, we have said, probable that the Athenian acropolis was never wholly abandoned, even during the darkest period of the

[29] The best summary of the literary evidence for the Slavonic occupation is M. Vasmer, *Die Slaven in Griechenland; Abh. d. preuss. Akad. d. Wiss.* 1941, Phil.-Hist. Klasse, Nr. 12 (Berlin, 1941), 11-19; see also G. Ostrogorsky, *History of the Byzantine State* (Oxford, 1956), 84-85 and note 3.

[30] Homer A. Thompson, "Athenian Twilight, A.D. 267-600", *Journal of Roman Studies* 49 (1959), 61-72.

eighth century. The testimony of Theophanes, indeed, that in the year 728 the 'Helladics' and Cyclades set on foot a naval revolt against the iconoclastic policy of the emperor Leo III, proves nothing for Athens at that time, whatever it may imply for Hellas as a whole; and the revolt was, pretty clearly, in the main a mutiny of the great naval province of the *Karavisianoi*, with its several bases in the islands of the Aegean, a mutiny which resulted in a division of this wide authority under two separate commands. But the history of the empress Irene provides more solid evidence. She was born in 752, and the testimony is unanimous that she was of Athenian origin. The very fact that she was chosen to be the consort of the emperor Leo IV by his shrewd father Constantine V proves that Irene's family were 'archons' of note; and that she was rechristened 'Peace,' that is, peace between rival religious factions, shows that as late as 769 the hostility of western garrisons to the prevailing policy in Constantinople had to be taken seriously by the imperial government.

The archaeological evidence from Corinth is nearly the same as that from Athens. There is, Dr. Scranton tells us,[31] some reason to think that Corinth existed as a city up till the second half of the seventh century (that is, once more, up to the time of Constans II), but no evidence at all that she did so during the eighth century. And no significant recovery is discernible before the middle of the ninth, when the byzantinisation of the Slavs of the Morea was vigorously and systematically carried out by the emperor Theophilus.

Meanwhile the Slavonic inundation had spread over the whole of Peloponnesus. As early as the first half of the seventh century they were raiding the Aegean islands and even Crete from eastern, and Southern Italy from western, Peloponnese. In the autumn of the year 722 the pilgrim Willibald, on his way to the Holy Land, put in at 'Manafasia,' that is Monemvasia, on the south-eastern tip of Laconia, which was, as his biographer states, *in Sclavinica terra*.[32] This probably does not mean that the fortress itself was then occupied by Slavs, but that the surrounding terrain, like that sur-

---

[31] R. L. Scranton, *Corinth* XVI (Princeton, 1957), 27-28.
[32] *Acta Sanctorum* July, II, 505 B.

rounding Salonika and Athens and Corinth and Patras, was inhabited by Slavs.

The fact of the matter very plainly is that the Slavs had poured, not only as raiders but also as settlers, into territories—Epiros, Hellas, Peloponnesus—which were virtually swept if not garnished, and that they set up their habitations and became the repopulators of the land. All the historical testimony of any value points to this conclusion; and, were it not that Romantic prejudice amounting to monomania recoiled from it in the nineteenth century, no historian would ever have questioned it for a moment. Writers of tenth-century Byzantium, among whom no such Romantic prejudice existed, and who had the best of reasons for knowing the truth about what lay on their own doorstep, are quite positive on the subject. The text over which there was most throwing about of brains was an apparently unambiguous statement by none other than the emperor Constantine Porphyrogenitus, who lived in the middle of the tenth century. He was one of the most careful and accurate of Byzantine historians, and his care and accuracy are demonstrated over and over again in the most celebrated of his works, the so-called *De Administrando Imperio* and the *De Cerimoniis*. Moreover, as emperor, he had at command all the sources then available for forming a true estimate. Writing, about the year 930, of the Peloponnesus, he states: "But the whole country was slavised (ἐσθλαβώθη) and became barbarous when the Plague Death ravaged all the inhabited world, when Constantine called after the excrement [*i.e.* Constantine V] held the sceptre of the empire of the Romans."[33] This plague, as we know from Theophanes, raged between the years 745 and 747. And it is easy to see why the emperor-historian should have pointed to this moment as marking the total slavisation of Peloponnesus: for the chronicler, describing the plague, tells us: "In the same year [745] the Plague Death . . . spread like fire over *Monemvasia* and Hellas and the off-shore islands." Monemvasia here stands for the byzantine-occupied Peloponnesus: for, until the plague, that fortress was probably still in Byzantine hands. After 747, as the imperial historian states, the whole peninsula was for a time a 'Sklavinia,'

---

[33] Costantino Porfirogenito *De Thematibus*, ed. A. Pertusi (Studi e Testi, 160; Rome, 1952), 91/33-36. Cf. P. Lemerle, *Revue Historique* 211 (1954), 303-304.

an area inhabited by the Slavs. Of less absolute value, but still significant, is the remark of the late tenth-century Epitomator of Strabo's *Geography*: "and now, nearly the whole of Epiros and Hellas and Peloponnese and Macedonia is inhabited by Scythian Slavs."[34]

As has been hinted, endless attempts were made during the nineteenth century, both in Greece and outside it, to controvert or explain away this evidence. The emperor Constantine Porphyrogenitus was stigmatised as ignorant and prejudiced; and his words were twisted in every conceivable way to suggest that he did not mean what he so plainly said. But this was due to the tenour, rather than to the authority, of his text. A hundred statements made by the same authority, which are corroborated by no other evidence at all, are universally and rightly received for truth. Our medieval records do not often provide us with such unequivocal testimony as this; and to reject it was striking proof of the survival in the nineteenth century of a Byzantine faith that could remove mountains.

While such was the devastation and repopulation of the peninsula, the islands of the Aegean, though subject to Slavonic raids from the mainland, were relatively immune. But this immunity did not long continue. In or about the year 827, Spanish Saracens seized the rich island of Crete, and occupied it, despite several attempts on the part of the imperial government to recapture it, during one hundred and thirty-five years. The occupation was thorough. It is known that, on its recovery by Byzantium in 961, no fewer than 400,000 of its inhabitants were massacred or enslaved; and these must all have been Moslems. The island enjoyed a century of prosperity from the slave- and booty-markets set up by the Saracen raiders of the Aegean islands and the coasts of Asia Minor. If we say that these islands were largely desolated during the ninth and early tenth centuries, we are going no further than the written evidence warrants. We need cite but two examples of such evidence. The Life of St. Theodora of Thessalonica,[35] written in the tenth century, states that the large island of Aegina, off

---

[34] *Geographi Graeci Minores*, ed. K. Müller (Paris, 1882), II, 574.
[35] *Des Klerikers Gregorios Bericht ueber . . . Hl. Theodora von Thessalonich*, ed. E. Kurtz; *Zapiski Imp. Akad. Nauk*, viii série, classe hist.-phil., vol. VI, no. 1 (St. Petersburg, 1902), 2/24-26.

the coast of Attica, had at the time of writing fallen into the hands
of the Ishmaelites, "and is now deserted and inglorious." The Life
of St. Theoctista, written at nearly the same time, shows that, a
few years previously, the island of Paros had had one single in-
habitant, the recluse and naked saint herself.[36] No rational person
will deduce from this evidence that the original populations of
these areas, whatever and however small in number these may
have been, must necessarily have been exterminated to the last
man; on the other hand, no rational person will deny that these
populations were reduced to a minimum, and that, at least on the
mainland, they were succeeded by a population of immigrants
overwhelmingly more numerous than they.

The history of medieval Byzantium includes one long period of
recovery, expansion and glory: the period from the ninth to the
eleventh centuries. At the very beginning of this period, one of
the first tasks was the re-occupation and re-settlement of Roman
lands occupied by barbarian invaders: and Macedonia, Hellas and
Peloponnesus naturally came high in the list of priorities. As early
as the year 783 the empress Irene was strong enough to send a
powerful expedition into the Greek peninsula, which penetrated
into Peloponnesus and chastised the Slavs. But their systematic
reduction and civilisation began under the emperor Nicephorus I
(802-811), and was triumphantly carried on in the middle and
later ninth century by the emperors of the Amorian dynasty, and
by their Macedonian successors. The method was thorough, not
to say drastic: and consisted in the forcible settlement of Byzantines, mainly but by no means wholly peasant-soldiers, among the
occupying barbarians, and the gradual Christianisation of the latter. The chronicler Theophanes gives us a very vivid account of
the commencement of these measures by the emperor Nicephorus:
"In this year (A.D. 810) Nicephorus ... gave orders that colonies
of Christians from every province [including, there is reason to
think, Southern Italy] should be planted in Sklavinia, and that
their military holdings should be sold":[37] and he goes on to de-

[36] *Acta Sanctorum* November, IV, 228-229.
[37] Theophanes, ann. 6302 (= A.D. 810). I pass over the dubious evidence of
Arethas and the *Chronicle of Monemvasia*; but if this evidence preserves (as it
well may) a true memory of an influx of South Italian Greek-speakers into
Peloponnesus during this decade (802-811), then the influx is to be connected

scribe, and rancorously to exaggerate, the distress and despair caused among those who were thus forcibly transplanted. This policy was continued in the '30's of the ninth century by the emperor Theophilus, and archaeology has followed the progress and success of that byzantinisation. The disgruntled Slavs twice rose in revolt, but were twice defeated, and either submitted to conquest, or else retreated to nearly inaccessible areas of Laconia.

But the most effective method of bringing foreign populations into the Byzantine fold was of course by means of the spread of Orthodox Christianity. The work of the Christian missionaries is one of the most glorious and lasting Byzantine achievements of that great century: and nearly all of it was among the pagan Slavs. Moravia, Dalmatia, Bulgaria, Kievan Russia, all surrendered to the Roman Christ; and in so doing became politically, as well as spiritually, linked with Byzantium. But in Hellas and Peloponnesus, where a radical reform of ecclesiastical administration and wide-spread missionary endeavour followed the military re-occupation, the success was far more complete. In Slav territories outside the empire, a brilliant and unique stroke of policy allowed the propagation of Orthodox Christianity in the Slav vernacular. In Hellas there could be no question of this. The language of empire was Greek, and language came hand in hand with religious and imperial faith. Almost at once, the Slav dialect began to die away in the lowlands, although in the highlands it was still spoken as late as the fifteenth century.[38] With religion came education, and with education came the pride of tradition which we saw in our last lecture to have been so strong a feature of Byzantine civilisation. After less than a century, we find in Peloponnesus magnates (or 'archontes') of unimpeachably Slav antecedents, who, though sneered at in the Capital for their 'sly, Slav faces,' have at their finger-tips citations from Homer and Euripides, Demosthenes and Plutarch, even Sappho and Theognis; and who boast themselves of their 'Hellenic' origins in the place of their settlement.

Seldom has any evangelisation been more thorough and com-

---

with the same policy of Nicephorus. [On the *Chronicle* see now P. Lemerle in *Rev. Et. Byz.* 21 (1963), 5-49.]

[38] Vasmer, 18.

plete than this. The population, whatever its racial origins, became absolutely Byzantine, in language and religion, in tradition and outlook. And nowhere is this evangelisation more remarkable than in the virtual extinction of the Slav language, and its substitution by the Byzantine Greek.

Yet this, though remarkable, is not surprising: still less unparalleled. We have only to think of the Slavs of Pomerania and Brandenburg and Ruegen, who in the course of time became wholly German-speaking. But the triumph of the English over the Celtic in Ireland is a more valuable instance, since it can be followed by statistical records. The circumstances were in some degree parallel. Byzantine imperial influence, though not always political control, lasted in Greece during about six hundred years. The English exercised a loose control over Ireland from the twelfth to the seventeenth centuries—that is, from the day of Strongbow to the day of Mountjoy—and an absolute control from the seventeenth to the nineteenth centuries. The difficulties of the English were indeed more formidable: since the Irish to the last preserved their sense of nationhood and their Catholic creed, in conscious protest against their heretical conquerors: and, as lately as the third decade of the nineteenth century, four out of the seven million resident Irish were still Celtic-speaking. Yet, seventy years later, only about half a million even understood the language, and not more than one half per cent were monolingually Celtic.[39] The language of the Irish race, on both sides of the Atlantic, is, for better or worse, likely to remain English. And this is a very plain case where identity of language does not imply identity of stock; for if any of you were brave enough to tell a Boston Irishman that his tongue made him kin to Henry Tudor, Oliver Cromwell and William Pitt, you would probably get a very detailed, and very forcible, repudiation.

In the same way the Slavs of Hellas adopted the Greek language, because it was the language of empire. In a state in which every hope of advancement or success—in the civil service and the armed forces, in the church or in society—was contingent on a knowledge of Byzantine Greek, it is not strange that in course

[39] *Encyclopaedia Britannica*, 11th edition, vol. V, 616.

of time this language should have become supreme and well-nigh exclusive.

Along with language, education and religion came also some terms of literary mythology which at length descended into the common usage of the folk. Largely on the basis of the survival of this nomenclature, nineteenth-century folklorists constructed a theory that the distinctive *beliefs* of pagan Hellenism had during two millennia lived on in the body of the people beneath a veneer of Christian culture. Their successors would hardly maintain the same today. Indeed, the very conception of a corpus of folk-belief and folk-poetry nurtured independently in the bosoms of an illiterate but creative 'folk' has long been abandoned as untenable. "Folklorists of the twentieth century," as the Opies tell us, "are reluctantly having to admit that the folk 'had neither part nor lot in the making of folklore,' that the early ballads were the concern of the 'upper classes,' that the dancers on the village green were but imitating those who danced at court, and that the picturesque peasant costumes of today are simply survivals of the fashionable apparel of yesterday."[40] In the same way, it was not due so much to an unbroken folk tradition, reaching back into classical times, as to the Byzantine learned literature of the high Middle Ages, that the Modern Greek called death 'Charos,' a fairy 'neráida,' and a mermaid 'Gorgó.' These names are indeed etymologically connected with classical terms; but the nature and functions of the persons to whom they are applied are seldom if ever those of the classical age, and often, as in the case of the fairy, or 'neráida,' come from the common stock of European folklore.[41]

The dangers of arguing the opposite thesis are patent. We need but consider our own, Anglo-American, heritage. The English word 'fairy,' or more properly 'fay' (for 'faerie' was where the fays *lived*, as 'Jewry' was where the Jews lived), derives from the late Latin feminine substantive 'fata' and the verb 'fatare,' to enchant. It came to us as Old French 'faée,' and was brought to England by the Normans, that is, not earlier than the eleventh century. The Anglo-Saxon word for it is 'aelf.' A type of malicious male fay was called by our common ancestors 'portune,' which is

---

[40] *The Oxford Dictionary of Nursery-Rhymes* (Oxford, 1952), 2-3.
[41] Cf. L. Spence, *The Fairy Tradition in Britain* (London, 1948), 200-206.

a corruption of Latin-French 'neptune.' The Queen of the English fays is Titania, which is Ovid's name for Diana; and even her predecessor Queen Mab probably derives her name from 'Donna(m) Habundia(m),' a late Latin witch. These terms descended into the body of English folk-lore, and there lived on equal terms with 'elf,' Puck and Robin. They cannot be cited to prove a Roman origin for the Anglo-Saxon race; any more than an anecdote of Giraldus Cambrensis proves the Welsh and Irish to be Trojans. Gerald, who lived in the latter part of the twelfth century, came of the great Norman clan of the Fitzgeralds (from which, if I did not know that you held such matters in proper contempt, I would remind you that your own President is also descended). Gerald records[42] that shortly before his time a Welsh youth was abducted by the fays into a fairy paradise. On his return, he was repeatedly interrogated by the Bishop of St. David's, who elicited from him that the fays in question spoke a dialect of Greek: for, when they wanted water, they would say "Ydor ydorum," which was clearly the Greek word 'hudor.' Gerald explains it thus: the Ancient Britons were notoriously descended from the Trojans of old, who, during their captivity after the fall of Troy, no doubt picked up a word or two of Greek from their captors in the time of Clytemnestra. But the fact more probably is that the Greek word here cited was picked up, not by the offspring of Laomedon and Priam in the twelfth century B.C., but by western churchmen in the twelfth century A.D. As Mr. Barfield well puts it: "When . . . the Roman missionaries . . . came [sc. to Anglo-Saxon England] . . . coming, as they did, from a developed civilization, they not only ousted the old Teutonic gods from the language, but brought with them a supply of ready-made Greek and Latin words, many of which—did they but know it—drew their peculiar shades of meaning from a pagan mythology which they held in equal abhorrence." Or, in the words of Professor Grierson: "These Germanic and Celtic vistas faded away, and their place was taken by the history and literature of the Bible, the mythology and literature of Greece and Rome."[43] It was no

[42] Giraldus Cambrensis, *Itinerarium Cambriae*, cap. viii.
[43] O. Barfield, *History in English Words*, new ed. (London, 1962), 92; H. Grierson, *The Background of English Literature* (Peregrine Books, 1962), 22.

doubt the same with the coming of the Orthodox missionaries to Greece in the ninth and tenth centuries.

The story of the Hellenic peninsula during the four centuries between the reign of Nicephorus I and the Fourth Crusade was, apart from the fearful devastation of the eleven-years war with Symeon of Bulgaria (A.D. 913-924), one of relative quiet, striking commercial prosperity and rapid byzantinisation. Not that the population ever became homogeneous; but the presence among it of large numbers of Jews, Armenians and Italians was a sign of settled progress. Agriculture, silk-worms, weaving, purple-fisheries, even armament manufactories, flourished. The people were, by the twelfth century, almost wholly Byzantine in speech, manners, outlook and, of course, in religion. The second medieval period of invasion and racial change in that area took place in the thirteenth to fifteenth centuries. The occupation and exploitation of large districts of it by Franks and Venetians and Catalans were accompanied (especially in the last instance) by wide-spread destruction. But these western elements occupied, rather than settled, their possessions from the Adriatic to Cyprus. The second *racial* change in the populace, a change comparable with the coming of the Slavs in the sixth century, was the coming of the Albanians in the fourteenth.[44]

The origins of this great but enigmatic race are still obscure. It seems probable that they existed in what is still Albania from time immemorial; and it is a pleasing thought that the stout Macedonian levies of Philip and Alexander, who were certainly not Hellenes, were in fact Albanians, or Illyrians. At all events, in a sudden eruption of national energy which took place in the middle and later years of the fourteenth century A.D., the Albanians flowed down from their native, mountainous confines, and spread inexorably southwards and eastwards over land and sea. Their martial qualities were in strong contrast to those of the local inhabitants; and their aid was eagerly solicited by Serbian and Byzantine despots alike. The numerical extent of their migration is astonish-

[44] For the Albanian migration, see J. Ph. Fallmerayer, *Geschichte der Halbinsel Morea* II (Stuttgart and Tübingen, 1836), xxiv-xxxiii, 240-263; *id.*, *Das albanesische Element in Griechenland; Abh. d. K. bay. Akad. d. Wiss.* 8/ii (1857), 417-487, 8/iii, 1-80, 9/i (1860), 1-110. And, more recently, A. E. Vakalopoulos, *Istoria tou neou Ellenismou* (Thessalonike, 1961), 26-34.

ing. They came with their wives and families. The Despot Manuel of the Morea, in 1349, imported them in such numbers as seriously to weaken their homeland. Forty years later, the Despot Theodore admitted ten thousand more. We hear of them in 'swarms' (*smini*). Like their Slavonic predecessors, they came to stay. And everywhere there was, once again, room and to spare. The islands of the Aegean during the fourteenth century experienced the same fate as previously in the ninth to eleventh centuries. The decay of the Byzantine navy left them the prey of Greek, Catalan, Spanish and Turkish pirates. Depopulation was again followed by repopulation, this time by Albanians from the mainland. This process went on steadily during the centuries of Turkish occupation. The kilt of the Albanian was the badge of hardihood and courage. By the end of the eighteenth century, the population of Attica, Salamis, Boeotia, Southern Euboea, Corinthia, Argolis, Poros, Spezzia and Hydra, was predominantly Albanian. But this second wave of settlers differed in some ways markedly from their predecessors. Whether it were that, by the fourteenth century, the forces of Byzantine assimilation were too weak, or that the Albanian preserved a stronger sense of nationhood than the Slav, the fact is that the Albanian showed, during five centuries, a strong reluctance to exchange his dialect for the Greek. Yet, in the struggle for Greek Independence during the early nineteenth century, none was more wholehearted in the cause of Freedom than the Albanians; and the most glorious exploits of the Greek navy in that war were devised and executed by them. The language of the Greek Naval Command might be Albanian; but the sentiments expressed in it were worthy of Pericles or Demosthenes. In the early Kingdom, under Otto of Bavaria, the number of monolingual Albanians in Athens and Attica was still so large that a special judicature had to be maintained in the capital to try in the Albanian tongue the various legal issues that came before it. It was estimated at this time that the monolingually Albanian-speaking part of the population was not less than two hundred thousand, or more than 10% of the total.

Such, in the briefest outline, was the troubled and turbulent history of the Hellenic peninsula during the two millennia which elapsed between the Roman conquest and the nineteenth century

A.D. Two facts predominate: first, the continually shifting character of the racial stocks which inhabited it (and in reviewing this we must not forget that the civilising Byzantines were themselves by definition multiracial); and second, the enormously cohesive force of Byzantinism in that area, which, despite all internal vicissitudes, inculcated and preserved the unity of the Romano-Christian imperial ideal: its claim to universal sovereignty, the exclusive orthodoxy and spiritual supremacy of its church and creed, and the continuity and ineffable superiority of the Hellenic/Hellenistic culture of which it claimed to be at once the guardian and the representative. Empires, however long-lived, have tended to be unpopular, because of the galling claim to superiority assumed by the governors over the governed. The Byzantine empire was, in general, not different. The exasperating pharisaism of the tenth-century Byzantine is surely to be regarded as one of the causes of the hatred with which he was looked on by Bulgarians, Serbs, Croats, South Italians and Franks. Hellas formed an exception to the rule —and it is easy to see why. The steady and successful transfer of language and religion, through centuries of occupation and proselytism, combined with topographical and historical tradition to make of that area no longer an occupied province, but the ancestral domain of a governing *élite*; and, finally, in the fifteenth century, the unique receptacle of all the cultural heritage, religious self-righteousness, and imperial pride of East Rome, as well as the birthplace of the Hellenes, whose children still lived in it.

As we saw last time, the return to classical Hellas was most clearly expressed by Pletho in a memorial to the emperor Manuel II. Now that we have briefly surveyed the historical facts, it is time to cite the actual words of this claim: "We, over whom you rule and have sway, are Hellenes by race, as is evinced by our language and our ancestral education. And for Hellenes there is no more proper and peculiar land to be found than Peloponnesus, together with the part of Europe contiguous, and the islands adjacent to it. For in this land it doth appear that these same Hellenes have always lived, as far as the memory of man reacheth back: none lived here before them, nor have immigrants occupied it and cast out the others, and themselves been cast out in like manner thereafter. No: on the contrary. The Hellenes themselves appear always to have been its possessors, and to have left it never."[45] It would be hard to discover any statement of belief more exactly and absolutely opposed to historical fact.

This 'Hellenic' myth, as we have seen, existed alongside the more popular belief that one day, when the sins of the people were purged away, the Roman empire of the Bosphorus would be restored to the Orthodox Christian and Greek-speaking inhabitants of the Levant. The two beliefs had, at first, little or nothing in common; but it must again be pointed out that both of them were of genuinely Byzantine origin. To the humbler classes in nineteenth-century Greece the 'Hellenes', if they had heard about them at all, were a race of giants in the legendary past: and many of their folk-tales began with the words, "*stis meres ton Ellinon*", or "in the days of the Hellenes", which designated remote and indefinite antiquity.[46] The 'Great Idea', which dominated national thought in the nineteenth century, was a longed-for return to the empire of medieval Byzantium. But the belief in the legitimate descent from the Hellenes was unquestioningly and passionately held by every educated person in Greece who knew of the prestige which that extraordinary folk had for centuries enjoyed in renaissance Europe. These persons did not, it is true, very well understand in what this greatness consisted, since their own education in classical learning hardly went beyond the bounds of grammar and Hellenistic rhetoric. But the asseveration of European scholars, who knew all about Herodotus and Thucydides but nothing at all about Pachymeres and Chalcocondyles, that the inhabitants of Greece were the undoubted descendants of the most gifted race known to history, was not one which was likely to be received by them with any great scepticism or critical scrutiny. The Hellenic homeland, during the eighteenth and nineteenth centuries, was full of European antiquaries, who were proclaiming the discovery of 'pure Hellenic types' amongst the peasantry; though, to be sure, we have no correct notion of what the Ancient Hellenes looked like in their own day, since the graphic and sculptural arts of those times represented mankind in a fashion wholly idealistic. None the less, the

---

[45] Migne, *Patrologia Graeca* CLX, cols. 821 B-824 A.
[46] Rennell Rodd, *Customs and Lore of Modern Greece*, 2nd edition (London, 1892), 172-173.

statements of these travellers strongly fortified the already en-
trenched belief that such a continuity existed.

The disease from which these follies emanated has been termed
by the finest of Modern Greek prose-writers[47] 'progonoplexia': or
'ancestoritis', as we might translate it. Such afflictions are not necessarily and wholly deleterious: and if mankind is to be stripped of
all its delusions, many or most of us would find life quite unbear-
able. But in nineteenth-century Greece these delusions passed all
bounds. "We civilised Europe," was the common cry; and this
was made the excuse for sitting back and waiting for the living
which the World so obviously owed to Hellas.

The return to historical fact, made in the 1830's by a German
historian of genius, was therefore the more confounding. The
proofs that the two dominant racial stocks in nineteenth-century
Greece, along with many other foreign accretions, were Slav and
Albanian, were received in that country with a resentment which it
is nearly impossible to describe without suspicion of hyperbole. The
whole allegation was criminal and blasphemous. If we suppose that
an evangelical Fundamentalist were suddenly to be presented with
irrefutable proof that the Gospel story was fabulous, we shall get
some faint notion of the sense of outrage experienced, not only in
Greece, but also among European Romantics, by the disclosures of
Fallmerayer.

For the person who uttered this fearful blasphemy, and, worse,
substantiated it with a wealth of historical detail, was the German
historian, Jacob Philipp Fallmerayer, who lived from 1790 to 1861.[48]
The world owes an immense debt to the German historians of the
nineteenth century—to Niebuhr and Mommsen, to Von Ranke and
Von Raumer: and of these Fallmerayer was no contemptible rival.
His various works devoted to his thesis are valuable not only in
themselves, but also because the reaction they produced illumi-
nates contemporary European Romanticism. The widely made
allegations, that he was actuated by hatred of Greece, by self-love,
or by ambition to advance opinions wildly untrue and paradoxical,

[47] George Theotokás, *Pnevmatiki Poreia* (Athens, 1961), 67. The whole
article, *ibid.* 67-77, is well worth careful study.
[48] For full bibliography, see H. O. Eberl, *Jakob Ph. Fallmerayers Schriften
in ihrer Bedeutung für die historische Erkenntnis des graeko-slavischen Kultur-
kreises* (Berlin, 1930), 79-83.

may be dismissed at once. When his first volume of *The History of the Peninsula of Morea*, in which he described the Slav inroads into Hellas during the Dark Ages, appeared in 1830, he had never been in either Greece or Turkey. Moreover, his Slav theory, as it touched Greece, was only a small part of a much larger historical conception of Byzantinism as a whole, and of its survival and destiny in Turkey and Russia. It is true that the fanaticism of his opponents and the insults, quite unexpected by him, which he encountered during his visit to Athens in 1833, exacerbated his temper and hurried him into errors and excesses in maintaining his position which were afterwards held, quite erroneously, to have invalidated his whole thesis. But he started out on a purely scholarly pursuit of truth, which was thorough, disinterested, and profoundly original; and which, in essentials, remains of great value today.

However, the resentment which his conclusions excited, above all in Greece and Germany, raised the temperature of the controversy to that of a theological issue. Forty years later the American diplomat Charles Tuckerman, *quem honoris causa nomino*, and who stood intellectually above his English colleague at Athens in much the same degree that Benjamin Franklin stood above General Braddock, tells us that, "At the name of Fallmerayer, I have seen a University man at Athens, whose natural temperament was that of imperturbable calmness, rise from his seat with flashing eyes and excited gesture, and pour forth for a good ten minutes a volley of indignant rodomontade against the memory of the unfortunate Professor, which, if not absolutely conclusive in point of argument, had the effect of adjourning *sine die* any further discussion of the subject."[49] The Greek detractors of Fallmerayer, who were, to say the truth, animated rather by spleen than by scholarship, could be very easily refuted; and Fallmerayer, who had a streak of drollery, spent many pages—far too many, as we can now see—in exposing their absurdities. The statement of an Athenian orator, to whose lecture Fallmerayer was taken, that "it is notorious that from King Ogyges down to the present Minister for War Vlachopoulos the line has gone on unchanged from father to son", is very good fun, but unworthy the notice of a serious historian. But his German op-

[49] C. K. Tuckerman, *The Greeks of To-day*, 2nd edition (New York, 1878), 330.

ponents, especially the equally great historian Karl Hopf,[50] we
another matter; Hopf was able to point to some errors committe
by Fallmerayer in Slavonic philology, and also to expose a vei
unlucky and absurd forgery, concocted by the Director of Atheni;
Antiquities, Kyriakos Pittakis,[51] which had been seized on by Fal
merayer to prove that during four hundred years, from the seven
to eleventh centuries, Athens herself had been an abandoned rui
A historian who could be deceived by such a patent fabricatio
however high the standing of the fabricator, deserved all th
reprobation that Hopf could apply to him. But the careful examine
of Hopf's splendid work will probably conclude that Fallmerayer
main thesis was not materially damaged thereby.[52] Even his theor
of the abandonment of Athens after the earlier Slavonic irruption
based though it might be on false evidence, was more right tha
wrong: and here the testimony of archaeology, as we have seen, ha
in our own day come strikingly to his aid. It is melancholy t
record that Fallmerayer's last years were clouded by a quite un
justified conviction of failure. None of his works satisfied him
none, he thought, had met with acceptance. Posterity judges di
ferently. He made mistakes—who does not? But the main stru
ture was firmly based; and, in an age dominated by Romantic prej
dice, he successfully vindicated the pursuit of objective truth.

He had moreover that dash of intuitive genius which distinguishe
the great from the merely useful historian. His chief study wa
Byzantium and its legacy. He was nearly a century in advance c
his time in distilling the essence of Byzantinism: its theocratic an
monolithic structure, its divinely sanctioned claim to world dom
nation, its instinctive hatred and mistrust of the heretical Wes
Fallmerayer saw that such an outlook, ingrained during centurie
in the character of the East, could not die away with any change c
sovereignty, or even of religion. The Turkish Padishah had beer
in all material respects, the successor of the Byzantine autokrato
and with the same ideals. And, after all, was Islam any more alie

[50] C. Hopf, *Griechenland im Mittelalter und in der Neuzeit* (Separatausgat
aus der Allgemeinen Encyklopädie der Wissenschaften und Künste von Ersc
und Gruber; Leipzig, 1870), 100-119.

[51] Hopf, 112.

[52] Eberl 30, note 1: *die Slaventheorie im ganzen wird hiervon nicht wesentlic
betroffen.*

to Orthodox Christianity than the Iconoclasm promulgated by the
Isaurian and Amorian emperors? But the centre of Byzantinism in
the early nineteenth century had shifted back to the spiritual child
of Orthodox Byzantium—to Holy Russia. Nobody, said Fallmerayer, seemed to realise how far the area of Byzantium reached. To
the north, it extended to the banks of the Sea of Ice, and the heart
of it was no longer south of Thermopylae, but north of the cata-
racts of the Borysthenes.[53] A vast wedge of Slavs, animated by unquestioning faith in their imperial supremacy and pre-ordained
sovereignty, stretched unbroken from Archangel to Cape Taenar-
um. Its avowed object was to subjugate the West to Slavo-Byzan-
tine dictatorship. To this design, nineteenth-century Germany was
the first and most obvious barrier. Italy and Greece, he believed,
stood on either side of this great division: for, just as Greece had
been re-peopled by Slavs, who now spoke Byzantine Greek, so
Italy had at the same epoch been re-peopled by Teutons, who now
spoke Italian.

Thus—by the bye, as it were—he noted the Byzantine inheritance surviving in a relatively small part of the Eastern Block, that
is, in Greece: Greece's claim to be the sole representative of Christianity, its 'Grande idée' reaching back to Near Eastern hegemony,
its fundamental religious kinship with Tsarist Russia, its hatred
of western ideas and influence, its acceptance of western generosity
as "tribute which the heretical and simple-minded West pays, as in
duty bound, to its Greek masters."[54] This was the gold, and
frankincense, and myrrh, for which no gratitude need be expressed,
and, of course, no interest paid.

As we contemplate the Modern Greek state in the middle of the
twentieth century, we are amazed at the progress made by it in the
past fifty years. Greece is in all essentials a western country, and
likely to remain so. Her arts and letters are in a flourishing state.
Her vernacular tongue has triumphed over the fossilised jargon
of Byzantium, and is daily enriched by writers of talent and taste.
She has at length ceased to rest her reputation on the memories of

[53] J. Ph. Fallmerayer, *Fragmente aus dem Orient*, ed. G. M. Thomas (Stuttgart, 1877), 225-226. The whole 'Fragment,' 'Ueber die weltgeschichtliche
Bedeutung der byzantinischen Monarchie im Allgemeinen und der Stadt K/opel
insbesondere,' written in 1842, should be studied.
[54] *Geschichte der Halbinsel Morea* II, xvii.

a remote past, and has staked it, with a full measure of success, on the industry and ability of her living children. "Ancestoritis" is no longer paralysis, but inspiration; and the name of philhellene is proudly borne by men who do not know whether Leonidas ruled in Sparta or Singapore. Most of this progress has been made since 1922, when events, painful in themselves but in the long run salutary, caused Greece finally to turn her back upon Byzantium.

But what are we to say of Fallmerayer's diagnosis of the spirit of Byzantium as it lives on in the Slavonic world? At first sight the modern creed of Eastern Europe seems to be so different from its predecessor that any continuity must be impossible. But a change in the dynamic does not necessarily mean a change in ideals and instincts. A man may cross the Atlantic, under sail, or under steam, or by the power of a jet-engine; but his direction and object remain the same. If the object is domination by Orthodoxy of the heretical west, does it really matter so much whether the divine sanction for this is the *fiat* of Jupiter or Jesus, of Mahomet or Marx? So Fallmerayer himself would, I think, have argued.[55]

These are deep matters, which all of us must ponder. Faith dies harder even than dogma. I would merely suggest this to you. If on reflexion you are disposed to agree with me that implicit belief in the ultimate dominance of a single orthodoxy, propagated by a single Chosen People, is the legacy of Byzantium to her Orthodox daughter, then Byzantine studies in the west have now acquired an urgent and practical significance which far transcends the sphere of abstract scholarship.

[55] See the important note of F. Dölger, *Paraspora*, 8. It is useful to note that one of the shrewdest political observers of the XIXth century, the English Jew Benjamin Disraeli, noted in 1875 (forty years after Fallmerayer had expressed his own opinion), that the Tsar Alexander cared as much for Christians as a cuckoo cares for a thrush, and that "he (the Tsar) and all his court would don the turban to-morrow, if he could only build a Kremlin on the Bosphorus." Cf. H. Pearson, *Disraeli* (New York, 1951), 256.

The
Classical Ideal
in Greek Sculpture

BY BERNARD ASHMOLE

Delivered February 19 and 20, 1963

THE CLASSICAL IDEAL IN
GREEK SCULPTURE

I: ITS FORMATION IN THE SIXTH AND
EARLY FIFTH CENTURIES B.C.

IT IS BOTH an honour and a pleasure to deliver these lectures: an honour to pay tribute to the memory of Mrs. Louise Taft Semple; and a pleasure to do so among friends. I cannot believe that anything I say will be new: the classic ideal is a subject on which, during two thousand years or so, everything possible must have been said. But since the purpose of the Semple Bequest was to bring alive for our use the inheritance of antiquity, it may be that if we study together, first the formation of that ideal, and then the use our forbears made of it, we may come to understand more clearly both its true nature and its potential value to ourselves.

The word 'classic' has a curious history. It is not in origin a subtle word, for it began by meaning "of a class," and then for no apparent reason except careless usage, came to mean "of the first class." To-day it is commonly used in three different ways. First, for the whole of Greek and Roman art. Second, for Greek art from the time of the Persian Wars to the time of Alexander the Great, say 480-330 B.C. Third, for the art of the middle of the fifth century B.C., the period of Pheidias and Polycleitus and of the Parthenon, when a special quality was attained which is widely recognized even if it defies complete analysis. This afternoon I am using the word in this, its most limited sense, to denote that quality in its perfection, about mid fifth century, and I am concerned to show why it came to perfection at that particular moment: but it did not of course spring from nothing, and I want also to discuss what its antecedents were, and how the store of emotion and knowledge which went to its making was gradually built up. This I shall hope to do by taking a succession of sculptures, made in various parts of Greece, and covering a period of about a century and a half before the Parthenon, and shall try to indicate the origin and development of various elements that persisted.

Rhys Carpenter, in his stimulating book on Greek sculpture, lays stress on the importance of seeing it as a "discipline to which the artist submitted, a craft in which he served his apprenticeship, and a technique in which flights of fancy had no place," and he speaks of it as "an anonymous product of an impersonal craft."[1] That is an important aspect. But there is another equally so, and it is this: the craft of sculpture, like every other craft, was started by one man (even if one man in several places and centuries) and it cannot exist independently of the series of men who practise it. Moreover, any advance, whether technical or artistic, is, ultimately, the act of a single person.

In other words, the whole development of Greek sculpture, aided though it was by what Carpenter aptly calls "cumulative wisdom and gathered experience," was the result of a series of these individual acts; and it is some of these which I should like you to consider. We cannot be sure that in the examples I am showing we have pinned down the first occurrence of these features: all we can say is that by the time this statue or that was made they had been invented. The pieces of sculpture I shall show are mostly quite familiar, but I want you to try and look at them as if you had never seen them before, and to try to put yourself into the sculptor's place, to understand his state of mind and to discover his intentions.

We begin about 600 B.C., a generation or so after the Greeks first started carving sculpture on a large scale in marble, with a familiar piece of Athenian sculpture in New York (figs. 1, 2). Why and how was it produced? The sculptor had been commissioned to make an image of a god or a man, and the Greek ideal of a god being a perfect man, the statues are at this date usually indistinguishable. Three main elements go to its making. The idea of man in the sculptor's mind; his training in his craft; and his material.

[1] *Greek Sculpture* (University of Chicago Press 1960). The first quotation is from the cover of the book: the second from the Foreword (p. v.).

The three are not independent of one another. The training has included traditional formulae for laying out the design of the human body, and this is bound up in the sculptor's mind with his observation of living men and his consciousness of his own body. His training has included carving in marble, and this material—marble from the Cyclades—is of a wonderfully uniform structure, and a month or two after quarrying becomes exceedingly hard. It "abets his skill," as the modern poet puts it, "and sternly aids the artist's will."[2] It is, then, from the struggle of the sculptor, armed with the craft he has learnt, to express his idea of man in this resistant but not perverse material, that the work of art is born.

Now we know that the Greeks originally learnt the craft of sculpture in Egypt, where statues were made according to a fixed system of measurements, and it has been shown that this particular statue keeps closely to the Egyptian system.[3] It is, in a sense, irrelevant that centuries of tradition lay behind what the Egyptian was teaching his Greek pupil. (As it happens it was not Egyptian art at its best, just as it was not Greek art at its best which inspired the sculptors of the Italian Renascence.) For what is important is not what the Greek borrowed from the Egyptian, but how he transformed what he borrowed. And in fact it is clear that Greek sculptors soon modified the Egyptian system of measurements: but some system they continued to use, we may be sure, even if only as a practical aid to carving a block of marble into a statue: so that the idea of a scheme of interrelated measurements, which was to come to the fore at the height of the classical period, was not a new idea but an old one, even if it carried in the later period a new and deeper significance.

The marble would be quarried in a roughly rectangular block. That would then be dressed smooth, and by means of squared diagrams the measured design of front view, side views and back view would be laid out on the four main faces of the block. The sculptor then proceeded, within those main limits, to shape the individual members and areas according to his ability; using both mem-

---

[2] Oliver St. John Gogarty, "The Image-Maker" (*Oxford Book of Modern Verse*, 170).

[3] E. Iversen, "The Egyptian Origin of the Archaic Greek Canon" *Mitt. des deutschen arch. Instituts* Abteil. Kairo 15 (1957) p. 134.

ory and observation, and tending to observe more closely, and to render with greater care, those parts that are not easily remembered.

Some books on Greek art contrive to convey the impression that exact imitation of the human body was the main aim of Greek sculptors, and that step by step, at long last, they successfully attained it. This is so near the truth as to be dangerously misleading. It is true that knowledge of the surface-forms and structure of the body steadily increased, but it was always in subordination to the main idea. Visual phenomena were filtered through minds that saw things primarily in terms of pattern: in archaic times comparatively simple patterns; later, more complex and less obvious: minds which were adept at grasping the underlying design of natural form, and disregarding accidentals.

This particular composition, which we call for convenience the kouros type, lasted for more than a century, and at the end of that time could contain no longer the knowledge that had been accumulated, not so much of the surface-forms as of the way the body worked. The type then vanishes, but it gives place to another, equally though not so obviously artificial, in which all the old knowledge is incorporated.

It was this concentration on a limited number of types, each presenting a comparatively narrow set of problems, which enabled the Greeks to establish standards of such enduring authority.

The head from the Dipylon (fig. 3) is broken from a statue which must have been similar but superior to that we have just seen. It is a large head: the statue from which it comes must have been about eight feet high.

Havard Thomas, the first professor of sculpture at the Slade School of Art in London, once set his first-year students the task of modelling an egg in clay. When they had finished, the eggs were cast in plaster, and each student was allowed to put in any further work he thought necessary on his own egg. Finally, when all were ready, Thomas brought in and exhibited a real egg, and demonstrated to them how far superior in subtlety and in formal quality nature's product was to their own. If that apparently simple task had problems, think what infinitely more complex ones are presented by the task of rendering the human head—and body—in a satisfactory form on this scale in marble.

At this period the statue is not being pointed off from a model, however small, but carved direct from guide-lines marked on the surface of the block. No question here of a second chance. If the point bruises too deeply, or more than a few strokes go astray, the whole block is ruined. Hence, partly, the boldness of the main forms: the grand design of the brows with their sweeping grooves above the eyes, and the almost horizontal lower lids. But hence also some of the unwillingness to adventure far into subsidiary modelling, and the fondness for working certain parts not by percussion (or only in the early stages by percussion) but by abrasion, probably by rubbing with slivers of emery, of which an abundant supply existed in the Cyclades.

Naturally the sculptor does not succeed in producing a statue which provides satisfactory views from all round. There are some awkward transitions between the various aspects, between front and sides and back. The features tend to cluster on the front of the face: that groove above the eyes stops the moment it touches the cheek, because the design of it was laid out on the front face of the block and was being worked in primarily from the front. The cheek itself is one vast, almost flat, area, and the little diagonal groove on the neck is more like a scar than an indication of the great sterno-cleido-mastoid muscle (fig. 5). Nor is the ear an organic part of the head: set too high, and not apparently giving any access to the interior, it might almost be an attachment to the hair or the hair-band.

But because the sculptor preferred not to tackle—or not to create for himself—some of the major difficulties, do not underestimate his feeling for depth of form or his ability to render certain difficult passages with understanding and skill. Look at the eye, and see how the solidity of the eyeball and its relationship to the opening lids is realized (fig. 6). This cannot have been in the flat diagram from which he was working: it was his own feeling which brought it alive.

Carving marble by the mallet and point is slow work. But the impossibility of hastiness is a blessing—one rarely enjoyed in our own world of largely aimless hurry. Shaping marble by abrasion is slower still, and it forces the sculptor to explore, not only by eye but constantly, by touch, every part of the surface, however minute;

it gives him a special understanding of the forms, and his work a special character.

With what a feeling of relief, after wrestling with such problems, must the sculptor have turned to the hair (fig. 4). No sculptor, ancient or modern, has tried to imitate the hairs of the head individually: there is bound to be patterning of some kind. The archaic sculptor tended to see most forms in terms of pattern: here he is forced to do so, and has hit on the secret of that wonderful geometric form the hexagon—so much more exciting and so much more accommodating than the octagon—and has created, as it were, a honeycomb on a monumental scale. Nor must we forget the knot, a perfect reef-knot and the value which it and the ribbon, including the outcurving ends, possess in containing and defining the form.

Even so early as this, then, Attic sculpture already exhibited some of those essential qualities—monumentality of design and a capacity for understanding form—which were to serve it well in the classical period.

We now jump forward sixty years or so, still in Attica, to one of those statues of women set up on the Acropolis at Athens which we call for convenience Korai (girls) because we do not know exactly whom they were intended to represent (fig. 7). Although this looks, and is, more advanced than the last, it is in the same unbroken tradition. Reckoning, as we commonly do, three generations to a century, this would be two generations later than the last. But that does not necessarily represent the true facts. This sculptor could easily have been a pupil of the maker of the other. For instance, my father was born in 1850 and could, if he had been a sculptor, have made a statue by 1870; whilst I, if I were a sculptor, should still have the strength to carve one now, more than ninety years afterwards. In thinking about the relationship to each other of the ancient statues which happen to have survived, it is important to remember this overlapping of generations, and that sculptors do not produce just one or two statues and then die off (unless they are unlucky) but may have a working life of as much as fifty years. Thus a single artistic impulse from one powerful sculptor may, through his pupils, cover almost a century without undergoing any fundamental change of trend.

Certainly in this statue there is no loss of monumentality, although the whole thing is lighter and livelier. The main lines of design are still simple and grand, and they are made easier of attainment by the forms which the dress naturally assumes. It is a woollen peplos worn over an undergarment. This peplos, a rectangle of cloth, has its upper quarter, or third, folded over, is fastened on the shoulders, hangs weightily (because it is double) from there to the waist: at the waist it is girt, and thence it falls again straight to the ankles. The body is thus encased in a kind of cylinder which changes diameter, with a strong horizontal accent, at the waist, and allows a muted expression of the forms beneath. Even in a photograph it is possible to see the great advance towards the equal understanding of the various elements, and the ability to express them with equal force.

It is the same in the head (fig. 8). The oval of the face approaches very nearly a geometric form, as does all great sculpture. The brows still have that noble sweep, and the existence of the invisible part of the eyeball is adequately suggested, whilst the cheekbones and jawbones seem both to originate and to underlie the delicate contours of the cheeks. The mouth does not quite partake of this sculptural unity, and is not quite harmonized with its surrounding parts. Of this its so-called "archaic smile" might be called a symptom.

The archaic smile has been explained in various ways. It has been suggested, for instance, that the statue smiles because its sculptor is unable to make it do otherwise. That cannot quite be so, because early archaic heads are often grim and straight-lipped. Or again, it has been said that the statues smile because the attitude to life of archaic man was gay and self-confident. If that were so the people who appear in contemporary vase-paintings would also smile: but they do not. Yet there is some truth in both these explanations. The smile is there because the sculptor naturally wants to give this important feature a lively expression, but it is exaggerated because he does not succeed in setting the lips sufficiently deeply into the face, and in bringing them into correct relationship with their surroundings. The smile is therefore largely in two dimensions, whereas the subtlety of a real smile depends on its being in three.

The defect, if defect it is, is inherent in the sculptor's whole approach. He likes to have as much in view as possible, and tends to carve all the features too near the front plane of his block of marble. Therefore no feature will be at a depth corresponding to that in nature: all will be spread out too much on the surface, and will be distorted. An extreme example may perhaps make this easier to grasp. In a map of the world, on Mercator's Projection, the object is to display in two dimensions everything on the surface of a globe, and as a result the shapes of all the land-masses and areas of sea have to be distorted.

Especially in mainland Greece was there this tendency to think in terms of a frontal viewpoint only, to make the front view dominant, and to bring the other aspects of the statue somehow into conjunction with it. This arises partly from the method of carving the four faces of a rectangular block, but partly also from an attitude of mind, which thinks of the elements of a composition as separate. So in Greek temples: which consist of a front, two sides and a back, with nothing to lead the eye from one to the other. There is, I think, a third factor; and that is the atmosphere of Greece, which presents objects as a series of planes with crisp shadows and sharply defined edges; whereas in a less clear atmosphere the form of solids is expressed by gentle gradations of shadow which assist an observer to appreciate their rotundity.

It is often implied that Greek archaic sculpture developed everywhere in the same way and at the same speed. This cannot have been so. Although the general movement may have been similar, the positions from which the various schools of sculpture started were different: so were the speed and vigour of their advance. It would be a mistake to imagine that only Athenian sculptors contributed to the classical achievement of the fifth century. We can trace (not with certainty and not in detail, for there are many gaps in our evidence) elements that derive from eastern Greece and from the Cyclades. This head (fig. 9) is from an Ionian city, Ephesus. The eastern Greeks, whether because of their ancestry, or their prosperity and rather easier outlook on things, or because of their oriental neighbours with old traditions of sculpture—whatever the reason or reasons, the eastern Greeks do seem to have a softer, less linear style, do seem to have thought more in the round and to have concerned themselves more with continuity of modelling, with producing a flowing surface in which the planes melt gently into each other over the whole of the work.

A certain fashion in women's dress became popular in the later sixth century; and a favourite scheme for a statue, which came, like the dress itself, from Ionia, is that in which the upper part of the body is covered by a system of folds formed by the cloak, whilst the lower part of the dress (the underdress, the chiton) is held to one side by one hand, usually the left. At the same time the leg on that side steps forward slightly. The result is a group of almost vertical folds hanging below the left hand, and a series of shallow folds radiating out from the hand across the front of the legs. It is to this general type that the next few pieces belong.

We have now looked at several sculptures from Athens and one from Ionia. From sculptors of another area, the Cyclades, comes a deepened feeling for and understanding of weight and volume. This statue (fig. 10), though found on the Acropolis at Athens, is probably Cycladic, for it is closely related to a series found on Delos. This is not the involuntary unconscious massiveness of very early works, but a deliberate and studied voluminosity. The body itself gives a strong impression of fleshiness and solidity: the draperies seem to weigh the body down, and instead of being, as often in archaic statues, undifferentiated from the figure, have an existence and a decided character of their own.

Alongside these new major attainments there continued the steady refinement of knowledge already mastered and the ceaseless study of form and structure. A fragmentary statue, still in the sixth century, dedicated in Athens but not necessarily made there, provides a good example of this (fig. 11). The lower part of the dress is held to one side by the left hand: the action stretches this across the legs in front and creates on its left side a rich complex of tubular folds. These are most elaborate, deeply cut and subtle in section. But at the back (fig. 12), where the folds are shallower, the sections are more subtle still, and more varied. These at the back of the left calf—to take just one area—do not lie flat in a row like the slats of a Venetian blind. There is one form—a form in nature—that they are more like, and that is a succession of those shallow wavelets formed when water from breakers further out is running up a broad sandy beach. Each fold, as it nears the edge, first sinks slightly, and then rises in a delicately rounded lip which falls on to the fold beneath it. This is the sculptor's explanation of what is happening when drapery falls: the folds in nature are not as orderly as that, so he reduces them to order and eliminates anything which interferes with his explanation. It is patterning, if you like to call it that, but it is alive and satisfying because it is based on a carefully-observed natural form.

This extreme sensitiveness of observation can be seen in the second fragment of this statue—a foot (one of the most beautiful ever carved) and the drapery above it (fig. 13). The lowest folds in front fade imperceptibly into the inert area—inert because the stuff is neither stretched nor bunched—which lies over the foot. This is surprisingly early to find such an attempt at differentiating material that is under strain and material that is simply lying still: but it is an important element in the classical ideal, where so much depends on repose.

These are the means by which sculpture advances. Discoveries of this kind were made by the acute observation of some single sculptor and put on record by him in his work. Some of them no doubt passed unrecognized and thus failed to survive: others were seen, adopted, exploited, by succeeding sculptors, and used as stepping-stones to the next advance.

In order to see, not only what happened, but when it happened, it is not a bad thing to look at a dated piece. This statue of Iris or Nike (fig. 14) was set up on the Acropolis at Athens with a dedication on behalf of Callimachus, the Polemarch who was killed at the Battle of Marathon. It can therefore be dated after 490; but before 480, when it was destroyed by the Persians. The central section is restored and restored wrongly—there is a good deal too much of it—so that the whole composition can hardly be appreciated, but I want to draw your attention to two features. One is the great beauty of the neck (fig. 15). The articulation of the body with the neck and head always presents something of a difficulty to archaic sculptors: and the neck is therefore apt to be conveniently masked by locks of hair, and those parts which do show, to be empty of modelling, or uncoordinated with the rest of the composition. Here the hair, as befits a goddess who takes a good deal of exercise in the open air, is knotted back, and the neck is therefore exposed. The sculptor has studied it and rendered it with a wonderful balance of nature and style.

But when you look at this detail of the upper part of the arm (fig. 16), you see that even this outstanding sculptor is not particularly interested in the way the folds radiate from these buttons on the sleeve: that is to say not interested enough to study and render them in a new way consistent with his own advanced rendering of the neck: he simply adopts the old archaic convention, by now stereotyped and outworn. This inconsistency is characteristic of much archaic work, and even of much of what we call early classical: the charioteer of Delphi, for example, is a bundle of inconsistencies. Of the full classical, consistency is the hallmark.

This is another of those statues of korai from the Acropolis at Athens, possibly the last dedicated there before the Persians sacked it in 480 (fig. 17). At the height of the archaic period statues were beings who, reflecting, as all works of art must do, the minds of their makers, like their makers looked out at the world with lively interest. They now begin to look inwards at themselves. And this new self-examination, though at first it evidently gives rise to thoughts of sombre tone, deepens the illusion that the statue is a person, a sentient being. No longer the archaic smile; but the same causes which exaggerated the archaic smile now exaggerate this other mood. The lips are too shallow, too much on the front plane of the face, and therefore appear to curve more strongly downwards than they would if they were more fully three-dimensional (fig. 20).

It has been suggested that this sharp change is due to influence from the Peloponnese. But works of art are not made by influences: they are made by people, though one must not underestimate the importance of the schools of sculpture in forming and perpetuating style, in transmitting the knowledge of technique, and in keeping up the general standard of achievement. The change is not only in the expression of the face: it pervades the whole statue. The figure is robust, and is realised more fully in three dimensions: it is articulated beneath the drapery; the parts are now consistent with each other and with the whole. So with the feet (fig. 19). The basic proportions are rather square—which again is very much in keeping with this sculptor's temperament—and they are carved with a controlled and patient literalness which tries to express their strength and their solidity, which disdains to produce any prettiness of effect; which shirks no detail, but never over-states it.

With the details of the drapery it is different (fig. 18). Here it is clear again that archaic conventions are losing their meaning. The scheme is the old one, with the drapery stretched across the legs by being held in the left hand. The sculptor is, however, far more interested in the structure and the modelling of the legs, and his folds of drapery are little more than a linear pattern drawn diagonally across the surface. Look at the emphasis on the modelling of the kneecap and shin-bone beneath. The archaic patterns are painstakingly executed, but their relationship to the natural forms of drapery is not the same as the relationship of the body to a real body. This is the last of archaic drapery: it has ceased to be an adequate medium for what is now in the minds of the sculptors.

If one lives in England, the best way to gain some idea of the classical spirit at its first appearance is to look at this detail, the back—the front is defaced—of one of the fragmentary figures from Xanthos in the British Museum, probably a work of some sculptor from one of the Aegean islands about 470 B.C. (fig. 21).

Looking at this I do not think one can fail to experience a feeling of calm. It seems to arise from the complete mastery with which this part of the statue is designed and carved, without ostentation, without struggle, without the brilliance of much archaic work, and yet conveying an impression of finality—that it ought to be just so and no different. Apparently quite simple, but within its limits perfect. Simplicity is a word that can often be applied to classical sculpture, but it is a word that must be used with caution, and a quality that can be misunderstood. There is a simplicity that comes from having nothing to express. But there is another kind of simplicity, which is the result of thought and discipline, thought to discern what is essential, and discipline to reject what may be superficially attractive but adds nothing to the main purpose.

This is the front view of a companion figure which is in a better state of preservation (fig. 22). And the upper part here has much the same quality of effortless mastery that we saw in the back of the last. But even this statue, where parts are in their way perfect, seems to lack that harmony of every part which is the mark of the full classical. The dress is now the peplos again: that simple rectangle of cloth, folded down at the top. The wearer then folds it vertically in two, steps inside and pins it on both shoulders. The

action here is the archaic one, becoming a little old-fashioned by
now, of holding out a fold of the lower part of the dress. If one
looks at this statue in the British Museum, and studies the way in
which this motive is brought into relation with the upper part not
only in front but at the back, it is clear that they are not quite integrated with each other; it is not a perfect harmony yet.

These 'peplos-figures' were favourites at this time. Here is one
on a metope of the temple of Zeus at Olympia, about 460 B.C.,
immediately before what we may agree to regard as the climax
of pure classical art (fig. 24). The same dress rather more starkly
drawn than in the statue: and that is appropriate to its position
high on the building.

The last of the labours of Heracles was to obtain the golden
apples which grew in the Gardens of the Hesperides—the last because these apples were symbols of that immortality which he was
about to attain. The garden lay near the place where the giant
Atlas stood supporting the sky on his shoulders, presumably therefore in North Africa, where, under the same name, the mountains
of Atlas still appear to perform the same function. He alone knew
its exact whereabouts, and he agreed to fetch the apples if in the
meantime Heracles would carry the burden of the sky. Here he
has returned and stands, on the right, with the apples in his hands.
Heracles, in the middle, holds up the sky. A double cushion not
only distributes the weight; it also gives him the extra height he
needs between the giant and the Goddess Athena. Athena is not
simply helping Heracles to bear the weight. She is doing something much more important and something which she, as daughter
of Zeus, God of the Sky, is alone competent to do, namely take
the whole of the weight for a moment so that Heracles can be
released to take the apples and to relinquish the burden. It is a
naïve idea, and the scene could easily be comic were it not for
the intentness of the actors. It is rendered in the literal, painstaking
controlled way that is characteristic of the early classical. There is
no evasion, no question of just hinting at the action: the whole thing
is shown, and the composition of strong verticals imparts a monumental, almost architectural quality to the scene.

Perhaps it is easiest to detect the artistic change by looking
at the head of Atlas (fig. 23). It has become a unity: the broad

simple forms, modelled with great subtlety, flow into one another with smooth transitions, so that one no longer has the feeling that the features are conceived and carved separately. It was once unkindly said that you couldn't imagine a Greek statue making an intelligent remark. It is, in fact, difficult to imagine a Greek statue speaking at all. You cannot here. But this shows merely that Greek sculptors have not simply imitated human beings, but have created a world on a plane different from the human, in which the actions, like the forms, are generalised and sublimated. Even the material seems to be neither marble nor flesh but some sublime third substance. And not only do the forms make a unity in themselves, they are now coming to be used in expressing the spirit, in this particular figure the spirit of the ancient god of the mountain, remote, immovably calm.

To turn now to the nude (fig. 25). In this, the personification of a river-god from the corner of the Eastern pediment of the same temple, one can see the efforts which are being made to understand the working of the human body; the effects of movement; the appearance of the different substances of which it is made up, their relative hardness and tension, and their reaction to each other; efforts to understand these things, when understood to render them without irrelevancies, and to incorporate them in a logical scheme. These intense efforts at understanding essentials, at expressing them, and at bringing them under control so that they may fit into the main formal pattern, sometimes result, as here, in a certain starkness: though you must remember that in a figure to be seen, as this was, from a distance of fifty feet or more, the emphasis may well have been more effective than gentler modelling would have been, and the main lines of the design clearer.

And here, twenty-five years later, we have a neat parallel to the last, another river-god, in the Western pediment of the Parthenon (fig. 26). The contrast is remarkable, for here, although the knowledge of the structure and forms of the body is certainly no less, and probably greater, it is far less obviously displayed. The sculptor has a new aim, to depict a being of a particular kind who will display his peculiar nature in the forms of his body. That must be the meaning of the flowing lines of the modelling and of the flowing drapery.

The pedimental figures of the Parthenon differ greatly from one another not only in style, but also in intention. For instance, in this figure (fig. 27) the modelling is more definite and robust, and whatever identification we propose (Professor Carpenter's latest suggestion is Ares[4]) it must not disagree either with the design or with the character of the modelling. What gives this figure its extraordinary life? It is not only that the forms of the surface of the body have been studied, but the causes of those forms. It is not so much that a knowledge of the anatomical structure of muscle and bone has been acquired, but a knowledge of the working of that structure, as it affects the outer surface. Wherever there is tension or relaxation the effect of each is shown, in its essentials, and in its essentials only.

But that which gives it its monumental quality, its quality of permanence, is its design. To this the knowledge of anatomy and movement is subordinate. In the design has been embodied the sculptor's conception of the character of his subject. It is this conception which dominates everything, and uses the knowledge of the human body and the mastery of marble technique simply as the means of expression.

So again with these figures, which are so familiar that it is almost impossible to look at them with new eyes (fig. 28). They differ from other figures in the pediment because a different idea is to be expressed. Despite the powerful basic design, all the forms, both of body and drapery, are devoted to the expression of softness and languor. This poetic approach is not without its dangers, and it is possible that the tendency of sculptors of the next generation to exploit this style until there was little left but its mannerisms, may be the reason for the attitude of Plato to the art of his day. He seems to have been worried by the increasing deceptiveness of art, and by the apparent victory of illusion over formal design. Formal design, which could be recognized as such, suggested something which was subject to a mathematical law, which could be analysed, and which could therefore be fitted into a philosophical scheme. But in some of the sculpture of Plato's time, and perhaps even in these statues made earlier, with which he must have been familiar, the underlying geometry of the structure, although it is more pervasive than a casual glance would suggest, is somewhat obscured

[4] *Greek Sculpture* p. 137.

by the display of surface-forms. But it seems to me that in fact these sculptors of the Parthenon were nearer to Plato's own theory of ideas than he realised. Look carefully at one last piece from the East pediment, the head of one of the horses of Selene (fig. 29). Here there is a full understanding of the functions of the bone, the muscle, and the flesh, and of their respective appearances, that is, their effect on the surface-forms. This understanding allows all irrelevancies to be omitted, enables the selection of essentials to be made. And these essentials are then used to serve the artist's main purpose, which is to express the spirit, the idea (using it for a moment in the Platonic sense) of a horse. In other words the idea is the master. Technical skill is stimulated—made more acute and sensitive—by that idea, because the man whose mind contains the idea is the owner of the hands by which it is to be expressed. Last comes the material, a marble capable of reproducing the boldest concepts and the gentlest refinements on them. This is his means of expression. This is what he will give to the world. This is all he can give, a piece of marble cut into certain shapes; and anything that is written or said about it, whether by its maker or anyone else, can only be directed to the fuller understanding of the thing itself.

The idea is master: and you feel that the production of a work of art has now become a fully conscious intellectual process, understood and controlled. That is classical art.

Perhaps it is of some help in assessing the new elements if we look back at a little masterpiece of about a century before (fig. 31). Here the archaic sculptor is concerned mainly with the beauty of the external forms and with the patterns he can make of them. His misunderstanding of them, for instance, on the forehead, shows that he does not realise fully that the forms are dictated by the functions. Still less has he reached the stage where that knowledge can become the instrument by which he expresses, as it were from the inside, the essential nature of the horse. Nevertheless it is a delightful animal, seen with sympathy through the eyes of a man. And that is perhaps why it has a slightly human look.

We are fortunate in that, at the back of the horse of Selene (fig. 30), the sculptor has not carried the surface detail quite so far, but has let us see the main architecture of his design in its bare essentials. And this is a warning that even where elsewhere in these pedimental sculptures, for instance in the draped figures we were lately looking at (fig. 28), the eye is apt to be misled by the great elaboration of detail into thinking that there is little to it but the accurate copying of natural forms, there is in fact always, in the sculptor's mind, the fully conscious realisation that each part is a certain shape because it works in a certain way. Above all there is the underlying grandeur and strength of the main design, into which this knowledge has been absorbed.

These figures were set in the gables of the Parthenon, a building in which an elaborate system of measurements was incorporated. Where the forms can be analysed, as for instance the profile of the capital of the column, they are found to be designed on a mathematical formula, and there is little doubt that most of the so-called 'refinements' are not merely practical expedients, but have a theoretical basis. Archaic architecture, in its fuller curves and stronger accents, may have a more obvious emotional force: when you stand in front of the Parthenon you are conscious not only of its emotional but also of its intellectual content. It is in fact a manifestation of the classical ideal, the aim of which is not only the creation of perfect beauty, but its creation by a process in which reasoning plays a full part.

Theory was in the air, and not only at Athens. In Argos, at this moment, Polycleitus was devising his ideal statue. I wonder whether he, like Plato later, was disturbed by the increasing facility with which the appearance of nature could be imitated, and wanted to prove that art was not mere reproduction but had principles of its own. Whatever the motive, he made his statue and wrote out his theory in a book. Both were called the Canon (the measuring rod— the standard of proportions): both have perished. But of the statue, the Doryphoros, we have many copies, and although we cannot trust details they agree in the main lines of the composition. This is the copy from the palaestra at Pompeii, almost perfectly preserved. The spear is restored, and you must think away the support for the legs, unnecessary in a bronze (fig. 32).

Attempts have been made, both in ancient and in modern times, to deduce the scheme of proportions embodied in the statue; but all have failed. Certain comparatively simple relationships of rhythm are evident. For instance the cross-relationship of the limbs, in which the left arm and right leg are in action and the right arm and left leg relaxed. There is also the rhythm of the planes, which alternate down the length of the composition: that of the thighs echoes that of the head: that of the lower legs the torso. But all else escapes us. However, in our present enquiry the importance of the statue is that it was constructed on the theory which comes very close to being the classic ideal itself: beauty made rational through an intellectual system of proportions, where the parts are all related, each to the other and to the whole. Polycleitus contributed greatly to perpetuating that ideal, and even to stereotyping it, because subsequent sculptors are known to have referred constantly both to the statue and to the book of instructions.

The statue from Pompeii, being almost perfect in preservation, gave a very fair idea of the complete figure. This replica, the Pourtales torso, gives a better idea of what its quality in detail may have been (fig. 33). I am not certain how small a fragment of the Doryphoros one could identify, and I would not go so far as to say that the whole statue is implicit in each part: but whatever the system Polycleitus invented, it is a fact that his style is extraordinarily distinctive, and harmonious; harmonious, in the literal sense, that all the parts seem, as we know them to have been in fact, interrelated. The effect of tension and relaxation on the various parts is fully understood, the modulations of the surface (just as in the almost contemporary statues of the Parthenon) logically follow from the movement; and they are consciously given by the sculptor just the same degree of emphasis throughout. A perfect balance is the aim, without the over-statement or under-statement of any single feature.

This (fig. 34) is one of the copies of the head, in bronze, the same material as the original statue, and more detailed than the statue from Pompeii, where the hair especially has not been carried to a very careful finish. We must admit that this is not very exciting, and I have no doubt myself that the copyist has just blunted the edge of the work. That is the trouble with the fully-developed classical: it is on the verge of platitude. The line between a great truth and a truism is very fine. The one saying of Polycleitus that has come down to us is that the work was most difficult when it came to the subtler touches: ὅταν ἐν ὄνυχι ὁ πηλὸς γίνηται. Sad that those subtler touches are just what the copyist has failed to reproduce.

This is the back of the same head (fig. 35). In a statue where the sculptor set out to show that the relationship of the parts to each other should be paramount, it was essential that the hair should be given a strong and conscious element of pattern, for only in that way could it be recognized as subject to the system pervading the whole statue. This was not difficult for a Greek sculptor, with the archaic tradition of strong pattern behind him. His own patterning, although no longer archaic, is distinctive. One can recognize a fragment of the hair of this statue, even if it is only a couple of inches across.

The Doryphoros was not of course intended to be merely an ideal statue, an ideal physical body; it was also an ideal human being, master of himself, standard of nature. It was not an accident that about this time Protagoras was saying precisely that. Neither was it accidental that the Doryphoros of Polycleitus and the Parthenon were created within a few years of each other. For each is a manifestation of the same belief in a standard of beauty, truth, goodness—whichever one likes to call it—the existence and nature of which could be inferred by reason. The intention of the classical sculptor was to capture and make permanent that beauty which of its very nature is so fleeting. But this, you might say, is the intention of every artist at every period. The classical artist had a further aim: it was to rationalise the work of art, and explain its permanence, by showing that it partook of this absolute standard. This perfect orderliness, this harmony, where each part is designed to fit exactly into the general scheme, partakes of the divine because it is thus in relationship with the universe. The idea is still familiar to us, or at least it was familiar in the seventeenth century:—

"Man is all symmetrie,
Full of proportions, one limbe to another,
And all to all the world besides.
Each part may call the farthest, brother:
For head with foot hath private amitie,
And both with moons and tides."[5]

[5] George Herbert (1593-1633) "Man." Cf. Guthrie, *Twentieth century approaches to Plato* (Semple Lectures 1963) pp. 24-8.

II: THE LATE EIGHTEENTH AND EARLY
NINETEENTH CENTURIES A.D.

I have been re-reading lately the report of the Select Committee of the House of Commons, appointed in 1816, to inquire whether it was expedient that Lord Elgin's collection of marbles should be purchased by the British Government. There is nothing quite equal to this as a document in the history of taste at that time; and for an understanding of the impact of pure classical art on the late eighteenth and early nineteenth century it is vital.[6]

In the England of those days two main streams of opinion can be seen, the one—Roman—flowing from the Grand Tour, the great private collectors of ancient marbles and the Society of Dilettanti; the other from the initiative of Stuart and Revett (each of them both architect and painter) in surveying and recording the antiquities of Greece. These two streams intermingle; for instance, the Society of Dilettanti assisted the publication of Stuart's *Antiquities of Athens* after his death, and some of the same artists were employed by both: but they do not merge until well on into the nineteenth century, until in fact Lord Elgin in 1831 was invited to become a member of the Dilettanti; although it is true that he declined the invitation with crushing dignity.

The opposition of these two—the long established Roman and the newly discovered Greek—which in 1800 had been latent for about half a century, came into the open first with the arrival of the Elgin Marbles in England from 1802 to 1812, and then with the appointment of the Select Committee to consider their purchase four years afterwards. I shall return to the Select Committee later on, but first I should like to examine with you what is mentioned during its sittings as an agreed fact—the improvement of taste that had taken place in the previous fifty years.

It must be remembered that the original masterpieces of classical sculpture had faded, if not from human consciousness, then from general human appreciation, for close on a thousand years, not perhaps from the very day when in A.D. 385 the colossal statue

---

[6] The best study of Lord Elgin, containing much that is relevant to the subject of this lecture, is by A. Hamilton Smith in *J.H.S.* XXXVI (1916).

of Serapis at Alexandria—a formidable rival to Christ—was destroyed under the edict of Theodosius, but certainly not long afterwards. That thousand years would bring us to 1400, when the Renaissance in Italy was well under way; but it was to be several centuries more before any but a handful of the inhabitants of Western Europe, in Italy or elsewhere, set eyes on any single work of pure classical Greek art.

In these days of sumptuous picture-books and universal travel, it is difficult to put oneself into the state of mind of people who had seen and heard of such things—if at all—only through vague and discursive travellers' tales, and misleading illustrations engraved on wood, steel or copper. But we must make an effort to do so if we are to understand the authority with which a small group of works of ancient sculpture in Italy came to be endowed, a group so small that it could be counted on the fingers of one hand: the Laocoon, the Apollo Belvedere, the torso Belvedere—these were the cream of the Papal collection—and sometimes one or two others. It was the Grand Tour which gave them such immense prestige, for this enabled a small and privileged band to gain first-hand knowledge of the marbles of Rome; and in sculpture these were the accepted masterpieces.

The Society of Dilettanti began as a dining-club in 1734, with the aim of 'encouraging at home a taste for those objects which had contributed so much to their entertainment abroad'; one of the conditions for membership being that of having travelled to Italy. Exactly thirty years later, having accumulated a considerable sum of money, they discussed various schemes for applying it to some purpose which might promote taste and do honour to the Society, eventually deciding that 'a person or persons properly qualified should be sent, with sufficient appointments, to certain parts of the East, to collect information relative to the former state of those countries and particularly to procure exact descriptions of the ruins of such monuments of antiquity as are yet to be seen in those parts.'

The five folio volumes of *Antiquities of Ionia* were the result of this scheme—a very mixed bag, but containing important records of buildings in Greece and Asia Minor, of which several have since perished.

In 1748, that is, after the foundation of the Dilettanti, but before it had promoted its foreign expeditions, Stuart and Revett's great project was put forward. Their prospectus is worth quoting at length, for it gives an accurate picture of the state of knowledge in Europe at the time—familiarity with the Roman monuments, almost complete ignorance of the Greek. The prospectus was sent out from Rome, where both were studying.

Rome, 1748. Proposals for publishing an accurate description of the Antiquities of Athens, etc. by James Stuart, and Nicholas Revett.

"There is perhaps no part of Europe, which more deservedly claims the attention and excites the curiosity of polite Literature, than the Territory of Attica, and Athens its capital city: whether we reflect on the Figure it makes in History, on account of the excellent Men it produced in every Art, both of War and Peace; or whether we consider the Antiquities which are said to be still remaining there, Monuments of the good sense and elevated genius of the Athenians, and the most perfect Models of what is excellent in Sculpture and Architecture."

"Many Authors have mentioned these remains of Athenian Art as works of great magnificence and most exquisite taste; but their descriptions are so confused, and their measures, when they have given any, are so insufficient, that the most expert Architect could not, from all the books that have been published on this subject, form a distinct Idea of any one Building these Authors have described. Their writings seem rather calculated to rouse our Admiration, than to satisfy our curiosity or improve our Taste."

"Rome, who borrowed her Arts, and frequently her Artificers, from Greece, was adorned with magnificent Structures and excellent Sculptures; a considerable number of which have been published, in the Collections of Desgodetz, Palladio, Serlio, Santo Bartoli, and other ingenious Men; and altho' many of the Originals which they have copied are since destroyed, yet the memory, and even the form of them, nay the Arts which produced them, seem secure from perishing; since the industry of those excellent artists, has dispersed Representations of them through all the polite Nations of Europe."

"But *Athens*, the Mother of elegance and politeness, whose magnificence scarce yielded to that of Rome, and who for the beauties of a correct style must be allowed to surpass her; has been almost entirely neglected. So that, unless exact copies of them be speedily made, all her beauteous Fabricks, her Temples, her Theatres, her Palaces, now in ruins, will drop into Oblivion; and Posterity will have to reproach us, that we have not left them a tolerable Idea of what was so excellent, and so much deserved our attention; but that we have suffered the perfection of an Art to perish, when it was perhaps in our power to have retrieved it."

"The reason indeed, why those antiquities have hitherto been thus neglected, is obvious. Greece, since the revival of the Arts, has been in the possession of Barbarians; and Artists capable of such a Work, have been able to satisfy their passion, whether it was for Fame or Profit, without risking themselves among such professed enemies to the Arts as the Turks are. The ignorance and jealousy of that uncultivated people may, perhaps, render an undertaking of this sort, still somewhat dangerous."

Next come the detailed proposals:—

"We propose that each of the Antiquities which are to compose this Work, shall be treated in the following manner. First a View of it will be given, faithfully exhibiting the present Appearance of that particular building and of the circumjacent Country; to this will follow, Architectural Plans and Elevations, in which will be expressed the measure of every Moulding, as well as the general disposition and ordinance of the whole Building; and lastly will be given, exact delineations of the Statues and Bassorelievos with which those Buildings are decorated. These Sculptures we imagine will be extremely curious, as well on account of their workmanship, as of the subjects they represent. To these we propose adding some Maps and Charts, shewing the general situation and connection of the whole work. All this perhaps may be conveniently distributed into three folio volumes after the following manner."

And then the lay-out of each volume is carefully shown.

This then was the state of affairs, and it is to these two projects *Antiquities of Ionia* and *Antiquities of Athens*, that the improvement of taste mentioned in the proceedings of the Elgin Committee is largely to be ascribed.

But how far had they in fact succeeded in placing the remains of antiquity accurately before their public? To answer those questions is one of the purposes of this lecture. The second is to describe the reception and the effect on taste of such of those antiquities as were brought away from Greece.

Stuart and Revett's programme is almost flawless. But the human span of life is not long enough for such an undertaking. Illness, death and incompetent editors delayed the work and distorted its purpose. The true programme was never carried through. But apart from that, it can be said as a general criticism of Stuart and Revett's *Antiquities of Athens* as well as of the Dilettanti Society's *Antiquities of Ionia*, that the reproductions of architecture are much more successful than those of sculpture. The reason is simple. Architecture can be expressed in measurements, and in drawings which depend almost entirely on measurements—drawings, therefore, which can be accurately reproduced by a good engraver. Sculpture cannot. The peculiar excellence of a Greek original sculpture, its superiority over any copy, is apt to evaporate either at the hands of the draughtsman, or, if it survives him, at those of the engraver. And a larger part of my theme is precisely this:—the sometimes almost successful efforts of the draughtsman to reproduce the sculptures, and the failure of the engraver to transmit them through the next stage, which allows them to be reproduced in a book. It is partly that engraving is a less flexible medium than pencil or pen-and-wash, partly that the engravers had been trained to think of ancient sculpture as being like the pieces they knew in the English private collections, or, through plaster-casts, in the collections at Rome; that is, Roman copies of lost Greek originals, often restored and worked over by Italian restorers to make them look classical— in other words smooth and academic. And remember that until the arrival of Greek originals in Western Europe, the public had no other trustworthy source of knowledge, no realisation that they were being, albeit unintentionally, deceived.

Perhaps the most vivid way of pointing the contrast between the established grandeur of Rome and the obscurity of Greece would be to place one of Piranesi's grandiose etchings, in which half the monuments of ancient Rome are manipulated, regardless of scale, into a vast composition of almost nightmarish fantasy—to place that alongside the precise and entirely factual drawings by Stuart and Revett of a single monument of Athens. But more to our purpose at the moment is this etching of 1753 by William Hogarth, the painter, in his *Analysis of Beauty* (fig. 36). It was made in order to demonstrate a theory of beauty which does not here concern us, but the etching does conveniently show all the accepted masterpieces together—the Laocoon, the torso Belvedere, the Apollo Belvedere, the Venus dei Medici and the Hercules Farnese.

When that was being etched, Stuart and Revett were already in Athens (fig. 37). Here they are, dressed discreetly in the costume commonly worn by infidels resident among the Turks, in order to be inconspicuous, and are seen introducing two visitors (in ordinary European dress) to the monument of Philopappos. This monument of Roman date stands, as you know, on a prominent little hill to the south west of the Acropolis, and because it is high and isolated has always attracted a good deal of attention. The text accompanying the picture fulfills the promise in the Prospectus: "First a View of it will be given, faithfully exhibiting the present appearance of that particular building and of the circumjacent country." This is how it runs:—

"On the foreground Mr. Revett and myself are introduced with our friends Mr. James Dawkins and Mr. Robert Wood; the last of whom is occupied in copying the inscription on the pilaster. Our Janizary is making coffee which we drank here; the boy, sitting down with his hand in a basket, attends with our cups and saucers. A goatherd with his goats and dogs are also represented. In the distance is seen part of the gulph of Athens, anciently the sinus Saronicus; on the nearest shore is seen the harbour of Phalerus, and to the right of it Munychia; the Pireus lies still farther to the right so as not to be brought into this view. The mountain seen over Munychia is part of Salamis, and the lower ridge on the left is part of Aegina; at the greatest distance is a mountain in the Peloponnese, not far from Argos."

An example of Stuart and Revett at their best is the publication of the little monument of Lysicrates, erected to commemorate a victory in a dramatic contest in 335 B.C. (fig. 38). The monument still stands in Athens, but it has suffered a good deal since their day by damage and weather. Lord Elgin took casts of the frieze, which runs all the way round it; and these are in the British Museum: they and Stuart's engravings are thus of capital importance. Stuart and Revett devoted to this little monument no less than nine folio plates for the architecture and seventeen for the sculpture. The architecture loses little in the engravings (fig. 39). Indeed in some of them, such as this, the engraving has a brilliance of its own which makes it at least the equal of the original drawing. You will see that the most precise measurements in English feet and inches and decimal parts of an inch are given against every detail. We know that a specially engraved brass measuring-rod had to be sent out from London, and the interesting thing is that there is still a difficulty in obtaining accurate measuring instruments for architectural work of this fineness, even with all the modern materials. Professor Caskey has reminded me that F. C. Penrose, the man who first recorded the refinements of the Parthenon, did so with a measuring-rod made of plastic—a natural plastic, wood, so far unsurpassed by man.

They were equally conscientious with the sculpture. An unpublished study by Stuart for two figures of the frieze of the monument is an excellent example of the laborious way in which they were set out, with numerous co-ordinates (fig. 40). It also goes some way towards explaining the length of time required to bring a volume to press.

And here is the engraving of those figures as they finally appeared in Stuart and Revett's book (fig. 41). The original figures are quite small (about 9 inches high) and rather weathered: the engravings reproduce them at about three-quarter scale. It would be difficult to do better than this except with a first-rate photograph.

The story of the frieze is that of Dionysus and the pirates. The legend, as we have it in one of the Homeric Hymns, was that Dionysus was walking on the shore one day when he was sighted by a pirate ship, which, since he was a handsome youth, bore down and carried him off for a slave. However, when he was on board miracles began to happen—the decks ran wine, the mast sprouted into a vine, wild beasts appeared, and the satyrs, attendants of Dionysus, attacked the pirates, who took panic and finally leaped into the sea, where they were changed into dolphins. This is one of them being bitten on the shoulder by a snake and at the same time attacked by a satyr with a flaming torch.

Stuart and Revett's *Antiquities of Athens* had an immense vogue. The buildings were copied for all sorts of purposes—the monument of Lysicrates was to be reproduced as a garden temple for an English nobleman's country seat; the Tower of the Winds became an astronomical observatory in Oxford. And so on. The engravings of sculpture were equally popular. Excerpts from them were retranslated into low relief in marble or plaster and inserted liberally in the Adam and near-Adam houses of the early nineteenth century. There must still be in existence hundreds of mantelpieces bearing one or another of these figures as central panels or medallions. In short, the prestige of the work was universal.

In the Metropolitan Museum, New York, there is this portrait (fig. 42) of the architect John Haviland, who from 1823 to 1829 designed and built the Penitentiary at Philadelphia, famous throughout the Western world as the first and best model prison. In the background is a drawing of the Penitentiary, which is a castellated Gothic edifice, still standing to-day; a plan of it curls out from behind a book on which the architect's hand rests: the book is not a work on Gothic architecture or castles, not a treatise on the penal code: it is Stuart's *Athens*.

Not all the results in Stuart and Revett are as happy as those we have just seen. Things went much awry after Stuart's illness and his death in 1788. Revett was not his equal as a draughtsman, and although in William Pars, who was then employed, they had a man of the first rank, he was not always fortunate in his engravers. The following pictures illustrate the fate which befell the accurate and sensitive drawings made by him. The second metope from the South-west corner of the Parthenon shows a Greek fighting a centaur (fig. 44). It is better composed than executed: the foreleg and the tail are rather poorly done, but the action is vigorous, and as the Greek tries to kill the centaur there is an important focus where his left hand, reaching round behind, grips the centaur's beard and tugs it downwards, whilst the centaur tries to free himself. Here is the beautiful pen-and-wash drawing of it by Pars (fig. 45). A brief note on the architecture in the right lower corner shows that Pars had detected one of the refinements of the building: "N.B. The centre of the second column is not under the juncture of the second and third piece of architrave but is placed nearer to the angular column." Then there is also a preliminary study for the head of the centaur. The main drawing is perhaps slightly less sensitive than the original, but there are not many people who could do it better. Look at the action of that left hand: the draughtsman has caught it well. And notice the digitations of this muscle on the ribs of the Lapith, the modelling of his knee and the shape of the horse-body of the centaur. The parts not shown were obscured by weeds and shrubs which had taken root on the building, and which are faintly indicated.

That drawing was engraved for publication in volume IV of Stuart and Revett in 1816 (fig. 46). The loss is obvious, and the nature of the loss is clear. First, the medium of engraving on steel cannot reproduce the fine gradations of modelling suggested by the wash. Second, all changes that have been made are in the direction of conventionality. All the emphasis is on breadth of treatment—in a word, it is more academic, which suggests that the engraver's hand was unconsciously directed by his training in some academic school of draughtsmanship where casts of the so-called antique, in other words Roman copies, were studied.

As for the particular points:—the digitations of the muscle have been entirely omitted: the modelling of the knee is unconvincing: the action of the hand gripping the beard is enfeebled: and the proportions and modelling of the horse-body have deteriorated: it is longer and fatter and more tubular than it should be.

Finally—and a very depressing end it is—we have this (fig. 47), in the new edition of Stuart and Revett published in 1825. By this time the marbles were in public possession and could have been studied and re-drawn. But no, the publisher must needs re-engrave the old engraving of Pars' original drawing, herbage and all. And what a travesty it is. The dotted lines, last resort of a feeble engraver, the failure to differentiate body from drapery, the complete loss of the action of that hand—there is nothing that is not deplorable. I suppose one can say that the composition remains—certainly little else.

There was another kind of difficulty, not without its analogies to-day, the awkward conditions under which drawings were made on the Acropolis. William Pars was an enterprising sort of person, and, as his companion, Chandler the epigraphist, says:—"He executed the work with diligence, fidelity, and courage. His post was generally on the architrave of the colonnade, many feet from the ground, where he was exposed to gusts of wind, and to accidents in passing to and fro. Several of the Turks murmured, and some threatened, because he overlooked their houses; obliging them to confine or remove the women, to prevent their being seen from that exalted station." This delicate water-colour, drawn by Pars in 1766, and now in the British Museum (fig. 43), must have been made from some such position, though not from the Parthenon itself, since it shows the East front of it from outside. The ladies are in their garden, and have not yet been confined or removed.

Pars managed to climb high up on the Parthenon, but even when aloft it may well be not so easy to see the sculptures, still less draw them, as anyone who has balanced on that marble ledge nearly fifty feet from the ground can testify. Pars drew the whole of the West frieze, and we still possess the originals of those drawings. Take just one of the slabs (fig. 48). This is from Lord Elgin's cast in the British Museum; the original, in a much more damaged state, being still on the building to-day. It is not one of the most successful slabs, since the action of the legs of the bearded man does not seem physically possible, unless his foot was set on a rock which was depicted only in paint and has disappeared. There is also some doubt as to exactly what is happening: it is thought that the boy on the left is tying a band on his own hair rather than putting a bit in a horse's mouth. That is surely right: putting a bit in a horse's mouth is a difficult enough process, even when you look at what you are doing. Here is Pars' first drawing of it, in pencil (fig. 49). Part of it has been over-drawn in ink, perhaps as a preparation for sending it to be engraved. If you notice the foreshortening, for instance of the boy's head on the right, you will see that the draughtsman was looking down on the slab from an angle, and not straight at it. He was probably perched on top of the ceiling-beams of the colonnade.

When this slab was engraved for the 1816 volume of Stuart and Revett the engraving (fig. 50) was evidently taken from another drawing by Pars, which I suspect may have been made from Elgin's cast, which by then was in London. Now the view is if anything a little from below. It is a good example of how Pars' style suffers at the engraver's hands. If the original marble did not still exist we should certainly think that it had been classical in the old-fashioned sense, namely somewhat cold and academic. But, as everyone knows, this method of drawing, or engraving, sculpture, in pure line, with no shading, is one of the most difficult. It is virtually impossible to reproduce all the modelling.

However that may be, one can say at least that it is a great improvement on what the British public had before that, the etchings made by Richard Dalton about 1750 (fig. 51). Dalton was a draughtsman who later became librarian and keeper of pictures to George III. One of the troubles with Dalton was that he never quite mastered the anatomy of a horse's jaw, and his horses therefore always have the oddest expressions. The difficulty of the boy's action has been neatly eliminated by making him turn his head the other way: and this irresistibly suggests that he is giving the horse a dainty of some kind. The gestures, too, owe more to Richard Dalton than they do to Pheidias, although he no doubt thought they were in the best classical tradition. It is only fair to add that Dalton was probably drawing these from the ground, looking up at a steep angle. And there is one thing that should be put on record to Dalton's credit: he visited Turkey, and was the first to recognize that the sculptures built into the castle of St. Peter at Budrum were the remains of the Mausoleum of Halicarnassus.[7]

There is a curious example of how the later volumes of Stuart and Revett suffered from incompetent though well-meaning editors. The publishers of Vol. II of Stuart and Revett in 1787 had already used Pars' drawing of the West pediment of the Parthenon, and this is the engraving that they had published (fig. 52). Though not a first-class engraving, and not nearly as subtle as the beautiful pencil drawing from which it was made, it gives a very fair idea of the figure of the river-god in the corner, the Cephisus

[7] These too he drew and published. His original drawings, on which the etchings were based, were acquired by the Greek and Roman Department of the British Museum in 1955 (registration: 1955. 4-21).

or Ilissus now in the British Museum. However, the editors of Vol. IV, which appeared in 1816, had what seems the praiseworthy idea of reproducing a set of drawings (what are now called the Carrey drawings) which had been made as long ago as 1683, four years before the explosion of the Turkish powder-magazine which wrecked the Parthenon. These drawings were apparently unknown throughout the eighteenth century, and were then re-discovered in the Bibliothèque Nationale. In 1814 "Mr. Taylor, the publisher of Vol. IV of Stuart and Revett" (I quote from that volume) "procured a sight of the original drawings, which are in red chalk; and by the liberality of the Superintendent of that noble institution (i.e. the Bibliothèque Nationale) was allowed to have copies of them, which were made of the same size as the originals, with the most scrupulous exactness, by an eminent French artist." If you look at the figure in the corner you will see that the scrupulous exactness of the eminent French artist has fought a losing battle with his imagination (fig. 53). The editors publish the plate without comment, and make no attempt to reconcile the discrepancy, although the Elgin Marbles, including this figure, were already accessible in England.

Despite such misunderstandings and failings, the antiquities of Greece were becoming more widely known. The old guard of the Dilettanti, led by the great collector and connoisseur Payne Knight (fig. 54), still proclaimed that the masterpieces of the Papal collection in Rome represented the highest that had ever been achieved by ancient sculptors; but there were many others who were now coming to believe that the marbles newly brought from Greece showed that Greek sculpture was in fact a very different thing from what it had always been supposed to be: that it was not generalised, cold and remote, but fresh and living.

With the arrival of Lord Elgin's marbles in England the two factions arrayed themselves for battle: with the appointment of the Select Committee of the House of Commons in 1816, to inquire whether they should be purchased for the nation, the action was finally joined.

The terms of reference of the Select Committee were four. Number one and two related to the authority under which the marbles had been removed; number four to the value, and number three, which concerns us, to the merits of the marbles as works of sculpture, and the importance of making them public property for the purpose of promoting the study of the Fine Arts.

As to their artistic merit, a set of questions was prepared, designed to discover especially the witnesses' opinions on the River-god of the West pediment (fig. 26) and the so-called Theseus of the East pediment (sometimes called 'Hercules' in the *Proceedings*) (fig. 27), as compared with the Apollo Belvedere, the torso Belvedere and the Laocoon (fig. 36).[8]

As you might expect, the practical sculptors and painters came out of the examination by the Select Committee very well; Westmacott especially. Flaxman admired the marbles from the Parthenon, but was staunch in his loyalty to the Apollo Belvedere, and although admitting that it was not a Greek original but a Roman copy, and giving excellent reasons (what one could rightly call archaeological reasons, for instance that the drapery must have been designed for a bronze) for believing it a copy, still held to his opinion that it was superior. He was asked "Does the Apollo Belvedere partake more of ideal beauty than the Theseus?" To which he replied "In my mind it does decidedly: I have not the least question of it."

Question. "Supposing the state of the Theseus to be perfect, would you value it more as a work of art than the Apollo?"

Flaxman. "No: I should value the Apollo for the ideal beauty before any male statue I know."

In this, though he may not have known it, and might have been embarrassed if he had, Flaxman had the support of the not very good but undoubtedly very amusing young lady Harriette Wilson, who saw the Apollo in Paris, whither it had been brought by Napoleon. "We visited the Louvre" she writes "and there I saw many fine statues; but I have forgotten all about every one of them except the Apollo Belvedere, and that I shall remember for ever: not for its beauty; but for the appearance of life, fire, and animation which never can be described nor imagined by anyone who has not seen it. The quivering lips—the throat! Surely there was life and pulsation about that statue. It is said that a fair lady once sat by the

---

[8] In Hogarth's etching, reproduced in fig. 36, the Apollo Belvedere is on the right, the torso Belvedere in the middle foreground, and the Laocoon in the middle background.

Apollo, whom she could not warm, till she went raving mad and in that state died. I really think that, if they had not come to divert my attention, I should have been in danger of following her example."[9] The danger was not, I think, great: Miss Wilson had a strong instinct of self-preservation. But she also had an instinct for what was in fashion, and her remarks are of interest in showing how fashionable such sentiments were.

One other witness had strong opinions about the marbles; the architect William Wilkins. He was asked:— "Are you of the opinion, that the study of these originals would not be more useful to architects, than drawings and casts?" *Wilkins.* "I am not aware that any artist would obtain much more information than what might be conveyed from drawings." *Question.* "The Committee wish to have your general opinion as to the merit of the sculpture of the Elgin Marbles compared with any other Collection in the Country?" *Wilkins.* "The sculpture of the Parthenon has very many degrees of merit; some are extremely fine, while others are very middling; those of the Tympanum are by far the best. The next in order are the metopes; some parts of the frieze are extremely indifferent indeed. I think a very mistaken notion prevails, that they are the works of Pheidias, and it is that which has given them a value in the eyes of a great many people; if you divest them of that recommendation, I think that they lose the greater part of their charm." Wilkins had doubtless been brought up on that equivocal doctrine that architecture is the mistress of the arts. So that when he was asked "Do you think the value of this Collection very considerable, as laying the foundation of a school of the fine arts in general?" he replied "in one point of view I think that they are valuable, as architectural sculpture; that where a sculptor should be called upon to ornament an architectural building, they would afford a very fine school of study; but that considering them as detached and insulated subjects, I do not think them fit models for imitation. I mean taking the detached figures two or three together; but taking the whole together, the general effect is beautiful, as they add to the architecture." He was evidently determined not to let down the profession.

[9] *Memoirs* (P. Davies 1929) p. 531.

But on the whole the evidence of the witnesses, as well as the findings of the Committee, accord with the conclusions we should reach to-day, who have more comparative material at our disposal and far greater knowledge of the general history of ancient art. The Committee not only recognized the excellence of the marbles, but were able to say where their excellence lay. This is part of their findings:— "It is surprising to observe in the best of these marbles in how great a degree the close imitation of nature is combined with grandeur of style; while the exact details of the former in no degree detract from the effect and predominance of the latter."

Most telling, and most touching, was the opinion of Canova. However little his work may appeal to us now, he was then re- garded as the leading sculptor in Europe, and he certainly repre- sents the highest a sculptor can reach who deliberately bases his style on collections of Roman copies as restored and worked over by seventeenth and eighteenth century Italians. He at once realised the difference between such things and the marbles from Greece. "Oh! that I had but to begin again," he exclaimed, "to unlearn all that I have learned—I now at once see what ought to form the real school of sculpture."

At the inquiry, as everyone had expected, Payne Knight was hostile. When asked "In what class of art do you place the first works in the Elgin collection," he replied "I think of things extant, I should put them in the second rank, some of them: they are very unequal: the *finest* I should put in the second rank." *Question.* "Do you think that none of them rank in the first class of art?" *Payne Knight.* "Not with the Laocoon and the Apollo and these which have been placed in the first rank of art; at the same time I must observe, that their state of preservation is such that I cannot form a very accurate notion; their surface is gone mostly."

Lord Aberdeen (fig. 55) was a disciple of Payne Knight. He was also a professional diplomat. He was asked a similar ques- tion:—"In what class of art does your Lordship place the best of the marbles that have been brought home by Lord Elgin?", to which he replied "In the highest class of art. By this term, how- ever, I beg to be understood only as expressing a very high degree of excellence, and not as in strict language comparing them with the most perfect specimens of the art on the Continent."

Outside, there were people far more hostile than Payne Knight and Wilkins, but on quite different grounds. A cartoon by Cruikshank (fig. 56), of that very year 1816, shows Lord Castlereagh, the Foreign Minister, made to look as much like a sly cheapjack as possible, offering marbles to John Bull:— "Here's a bargain for you, Johnny," he says, "Only £35,000. I have bought them on purpose for you. Never think of bread when you can have stones so wondrous cheap." To this John Bull replies "I don't think somehow that these here stones are perfect and had rather not buy them at present—Trade is very bad and provision very dear and my family can't eat stones. Besides they say it will cost £40,000 to build a place to put them in. As the Turks gave them to our Ambassador in his official capacity for little or nothing, and solely out of compliment to the British Nation, I think he should not charge an enormous price for packing and carriage." Meanwhile the children scream "Don't buy them, Daddy. We don't want them stones, give us bread, give us bread, give us bread." Since the cartoonist is out to create as much prejudice as possible, the marbles shown naturally bear no relation to the Elgin Marbles, but are derived from one of the old-fashioned collections, livened with a good deal of fantasy: a rather decrepit Hercules, an extensively mutilated Venus, and a fragment which I think must be intended for a famous piece in the Bessborough Collection, the middle part of a replica of the Capitoline Venus, perfectly preserved. This used to be kept by its owner, either from modesty or reverence, under a cheese-cloth, and that is perhaps the explanation of the little piece of stuff here shown on top of it.

The marbles were purchased for the nation in 1816. The painting by A. Archer (fig. 57) whom you see at work on the right, is dated 1819, and shows officials of the British Museum, and others, in the temporary Elgin Room where the marbles were housed until 1831. Joseph Planta, the Principal Librarian and Director of the Museum, is talking with Benjamin West, the President of the Royal Academy, who is expounding his opinions with a dignified gesture. West, born in Philadelphia, achieved immense success in Italy and England; he was one of the four painters who proposed the foundation of the Royal Academy, and its President for 28 years. West had already been invited by Lord Elgin, who shared the widespread belief that contemporary art could be improved by direct imitation of the marbles, to make sketches of them "with a view of pointing out" (these are Elgin's words) "how far either individually or in groups they may be worthy of being imitated in painting." Using them in this way, West made compositions of "a battle of the centaurs: Theseus and Hercules triumphing over the Amazons: the marriage of Theseus and Hippolyta: Theseus, Ariadne and the Minotaur: Neptune and Amphitrite, Triton et cetera: Alexander and Bucephalus." It is not surprising to find him explaining that, in order to do this "I have ventured to unite figures of my own invention with those of Pheidias, but as I have endeavoured to preserve, with the best force of my abilities, the style of Pheidias, I flatter myself the union will not be deemed incongruous or presumptuous." And he adds with truth, "For what I have done, my lord, I had the example of Raphael and most of the Italian masters of the greatest celebrity." It just happened that he was not a Raphael.

Above Joseph Planta in the picture is Taylor Coombe, the first Keeper of the Department of Antiquities, who was sent by the British Government to Malta in an attempt, described below, to purchase another famous series of ancient sculptures. By the ankle of 'Theseus' is John Thomas Smith, the Under-Librarian of the Museum: he was the author of an amusing book on the sculptor Nollekens and his times, and a master of that superior kind of wit which you still find in the editorials of some weekly journals. "It has often of late years" he wrote "given me pleasure to observe that the same class of persons, who in my boyish days would admire a bleeding-heart-cherry painted upon a Pontipool tea-board, or a Tradescant-strawberry upon a Dutch table, now attentively look, and for a long time too, with the most awful respect at the majestic fragments of the Greek sculptor's art, so gloriously displayed in the Elgin Gallery."

On the left is Benjamin Robert Haydon, perhaps the first person in England to appreciate the quality of the marbles and the way in which they differed from the hitherto accepted standards of ancient sculpture. He describes in his autobiography the way in which he studied and drew hour after hour from the marbles, when, on their first arrival, they were in an unheated penthouse in Park Lane.

His comments on them are well worth reading, both as aesthetic judgements, and as illustrating the attitude of other artists and connoisseurs. But above all it was he who, in his enthusiasm, brought his friend—a poet—the poet John Keats, to see the marbles.

Haydon went to Paris in 1814, after Napoleon had been sent to Elba, and there he had an opportunity—as Harriette Wilson did— of seeing many of the works of art which had been brought by Napoleon as trophies from Italy and elsewhere. They included the famous bronze horses from an ancient chariot-group which now adorn the front of St. Mark's at Venice, and which in Haydon's day were supposed to be by Lysippus. This is an etching by him of the head of one of these chariot-horses set alongside the head of the horse of Selene from the East pediment of the Parthenon (fig. 58). Underneath are his comments:—

"Head of one of the horses always considered to be by Lysippus— now at Venice. It is astonishing that the great principles of Nature should have been so nearly lost in the time between Phidias and Lysippus. Compare these two heads. The Elgin head is all truth, the other all manner. In the Lysippus head the great characteristicks of Nature are violated for the sake of artificial effect, in the former head the great and inherent characteristicks of Nature are elevated without violation—in as much as the Elgin horses head differs from and is superior to the head by Lysippus, so do the rest of the Elgin Marbles differ from and are superior to all other Statues of this, and every subsequent age."

B. R. Haydon. 1817.

Another important series of ancient marbles was known to the Elgin Committee. They had been excavated by Cockerell, the architect, his English friend Foster, and two German friends. The party had gone to the island of Aegina primarily to study the architecture of the temple we now know as that of Athena Aphaia, had started digging, and had come upon a series of seventeen statues and other fragments of statues from the pediments of the temple, which are still the most important group of Greek archaic architectural sculptures in existence. This mezzotint of the excavations is by the painter J. M. W. Turner (fig. 59). It shows a most amusing and surely deliberately humorous contrast between the

quick and the dead—the group of lively busy excavators gesticu-
lating over their plans, and the uncompromisingly stiff limbs of the
group of statues.

The Aeginetan marbles found the blind spot of the Select Committee, and it was the blind spot of European taste as a whole.
Classical Greek sculpture had long been known through the collections in Rome, and now through Elgin's work in Greece. But
archaic Greek sculpture was known little and esteemed less. The
Select Committee considered them 'valuable in point of remote
antiquity and curious in that respect, but of no distinguished merit
as specimens of sculpture, their style being what is usually called
Etruscan, and older than the age of Pheidias.' This remark about
their being Etruscan in style must be due either to Strabo, the
ancient geographer, having said that certain Etruscan reliefs were
like early Greek statues, or to a recognition of their similarity to
the figures on Greek vases, which, since they were mainly found in
Etruscan tombs, were, in the eighteenth century, still generally
believed to be Etruscan.

The British Government was unlucky over the marbles from
Aegina. Whilst they were still in Greece, their value was estimated
at £6,000, and the British Government offered this sum for them
on condition that they should first be brought to England and
examined. The offer was refused. Later, the marbles were to be put
up to auction, and the Government sent Taylor Coombe, Keeper
of Antiquities at the British Museum (who, you remember, appeared in Archer's painting) to go out to Malta and bid for them,
up to £8,000. Taylor Coombe waited in Malta, but the days went
by and no one appeared on behalf of the owners to proceed with
the auction. It then came out that the marbles had already been
sold, on Zante, to the Crown Prince of Bavaria; and that is how
they come to be in Munich.[10] Thorwaldsen, the Danish sculptor,
was commissioned to restore them, and he did so, as one has to do
when restoring in marble, by cutting off the stumps of the limbs
to a sharp flat surface, and then joining on the new pieces, which
were carved in imitation of the archaic style. Thorwaldsen went
further than this and pitted the surface of the restorations all over
to imitate weathering, so that it is occasionally quite difficult to

---

[10] A clear account of this in Cockerell, *The Temples of Jupiter Panhellenius
at Aegina and of Apollo Epicurius at Bassae* (1860) p. ix.

detect what is restored from what is ancient. But to-day anyone looking at a number of the marbles would guess at once that there was something wrong. Many of the attitudes and gestures do not look right, and some are obviously quite absurd (fig. 60). In this dying man (fig. 61) from the corner of the East pediment, the restorations, although considerable, and in some respects incorrect, are not offensive. The head is well preserved (fig. 62). This is an exceptionally sensitive piece of sculpture, and you can see from this detail that what looks at first sight like the so-called archaic smile, is in fact a spasm of pain, the nostril being drawn up as it is in life, and the lips parted showing the teeth—a most acute observation. It is a good example of how little the true character of archaic sculpture was understood in those days when the classical was the fashion, that a leading sculptor could make an exact replica of that head and set it on the body of a warrior who was completely unhurt.[11] This series of major restorations was a disaster, and has certainly created for many people an entirely false impression of archaic Greek art.

How difficult it was in those days, except by means of plaster-casts, to make sculpture accurately known to the public, can be seen by the efforts to reproduce this, one of the archers from the East pediment, perhaps the most admired of the seventeen figures that have survived (fig. 63).

Cockerell made a number of accurate and delicate pencil studies of the marbles, and these are preserved in the Greek and Roman Department of the British Museum. They are indeed more than studies: they are carefully finished drawings made from several points of view. There is possibly a slight tendency to classicize—to make the heads look less archaic than they are—but on the whole they are remarkably faithful. This drawing of that archer is a fair specimen (fig. 64), and I am sure you will agree that it gives a very tolerable idea of the style of the original.

Now look what happens in the publication, Cockerell's own book published in 1860 when he was an old man. It is illustrated mainly by engravings, but there is one remarkable plate consisting of a large photographic print pasted in, which reproduces a series of etchings made and published by him as long before as 1819 in the

---

[11] The two may be seen together in Rodenwaldt, *Die Kunst der Antike* (1927) pls. 174-5.

Quarterly Journal of Science, Literature and the Arts. Four of these etchings are here shown (fig. 65). Partly because etching is not a suitable medium, they are far less successful than the pencil drawings in preserving the Aeginetan style, even though they are on the whole better than the professional engravings in the same book, which vary much in quality. It is a pity that Cockerell did not have his series of pencil drawings reproduced by lithograph. Indeed, by this time he might have been able to obtain direct photographs of the marbles for reproduction by lithograph, as C. T. Newton was doing in the contemporary publication of his discoveries at Halicarnassus and elsewhere.

It had been intended that Volume V of *Antiquities of Athens*, which eventually appeared in 1830, long after both Stuart and Revett were dead, should contain new engravings of the sculptures of the Parthenon; but when it was found that the Trustees of the British Museum were contemplating a separate complete publication of them, the plan was changed, the title became *Antiquities of Athens and other places in Greece, Sicily &c.*, and the contents consisted of separate articles on various subjects. In its miscellaneous scope it foreshadows in quite an interesting way the modern archaeological journal, except that it is in imperial folio, a size which to-day no ordinary bookshelf will accommodate. Cockerell's contribution was a study of the great temple of Zeus at Acragas (Girgenti) in Sicily (fig. 66), which had been sketchily excavated in 1804 by the King of Naples, and on which Cockerell had worked in 1812. It was the largest or second largest temple of the Greek world, and its fame lived through the Middle Ages because of the survival of three of the great supporting figures—Telamones, Atlantes or Titans as they are variously called—which remained standing until the fourteenth century or, to be exact, until December 9th, 1301, when they collapsed. There is still doubt where these figures (perhaps twenty in all) were placed in the building, some people believing that they were outside, some that they formed an attic storey above the colonnade and inside the main chamber of the temple. "The colossal members of these Titans" says Cockerell "scattered about the ground, are viewed with astonishment: the head alone is three feet ten inches high and three feet wide: the chest is upwards of six feet across, and the whole height would not have been less than twenty-five feet."

Cockerell designed a grandiose frontispiece for this volume to incorporate one of these figures. The way in which he went about it is significant. These great statues are archaic in style, as he himself says:— "The sculpture resembles the archaic manner observed in the Aeginetan statues and those works commonly called Etruscan." Moreover, as we know, he could draw archaic sculpture with accuracy. But the pull of the classical was too great, and his preliminary study is really a classical, not an archaic figure (fig. 67).[12]

The second of his studies for the frontispiece is this delightful water-colour sketch in which he has assembled other elements for the design, with the gigantic figure vaguely indicated behind (fig. 68). There is a shepherd in local costume, two figures to give scale to the enormous capital, vegetation, architectural members, and fragments of later sculpture found on the site.

And here is the final result, the frontispiece—an etching—as it appeared in the book (fig. 69). Curious how the superimposing on a classical figure of the archaic smile has the effect of creating, not a statue, but a living being—a somewhat sinister being—rather like one of the genies from the Arabian Nights. In the four earlier volumes of *Antiquities of Athens* there had been only two frontispieces—quite simple—one a portrait of Stuart after his death, the other a portrait of Revett. This imaginative composition is, then, something of an innovation. Or is it? Is it not simply the last flicker of the eighteenth-century spirit, the last challenge to Piranesi, the last glimpse of classical antiquity through the eyes of romance? After this all illustrations in archaeological works will be strictly utilitarian. Even here archaeological details are not neglected. The correct structure of the colossal figure is shown (it is composed of twelve courses alternately solid and divided by a vertical joint, down to the legs), and the method of hoisting the great blocks of stone for building the temple: the U-shaped cuttings for the lashings were used because the stone was too soft for the ordinary lewis-hole.

[12] This is perhaps not quite a fair statement. Cockerell made several full-length studies for the figure which are less classical than the one I illustrate; measured drawings showing the masonry jointing of the figure, and some exquisite studies for the restored head, which is bearded, and conceived in an archaic style based on the Aeginetan. These, and the other Cockerell drawings and papers in the Greek and Roman Department of the British Museum, deserve more attention than they have so far received. See C. A. Hutton, *J.H.S.* xxix (1909) p. 53.

Cockerell was invited by the British Museum to supervise the new publication of the Elgin Marbles, and this is how he speaks of them:— "Thus a large portion of these invaluable works is preserved to the arts: their renown in the ancient world, and the sensation which their recovery has made in the most enlightened of the modern schools, hold out every hope that they may ultimately be the means of reviving that pure taste which since the age of Pericles has never in the same degree recovered its dominion." Alas, neither Cockerell nor all those others who about this time expressed similar sentiments, realised that good taste is the enemy of great art. Taste is useful in a critic, and useful in preserving a decent standard of general artistic achievement; but it cannot produce masterpieces. The important thing for an artist in studying ancient sculpture is not what he borrows but what he does with what he borrows, just as it was with the earliest Greek sculptors learning their art in Egypt. The benefits of the study of ancient sculpture are not to be seen in Thorwaldsen, who is at his best when he forgets to be Greek, or in Flaxman, or in any other neo-classical sculptor or painter. They are not to be seen at all, because precisely where they have done most good they have been assimilated and transmuted. I suspect that the only great work of art directly inspired by the Elgin Marbles was not a piece of sculpture at all: and even then its inspiration (which took two years to mature) came only in part from the marbles, and in part from second-rate Roman vases. I mean of course Keats' "Ode on a Grecian Urn," which he first recited to Haydon as they strolled through the Kilburn meadows.

ILLUSTRATIONS

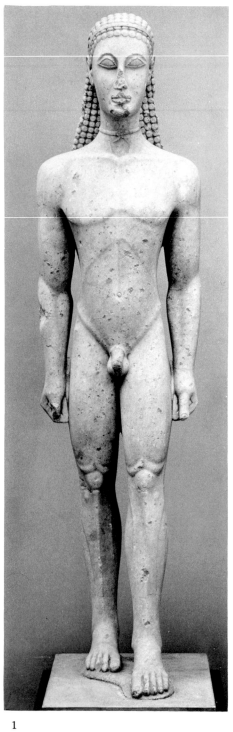

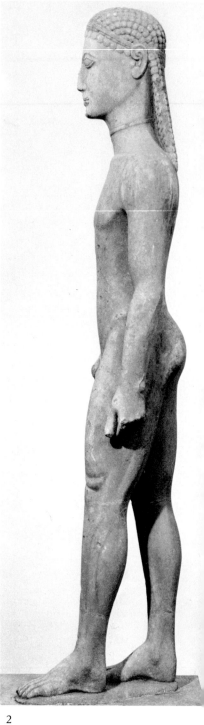

1   2

3

4

5

6

7

8

9

10

12

14

15

16

17

18

9

20

21

22

23

24

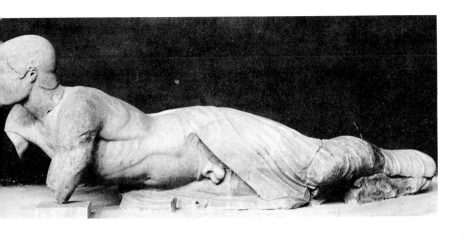

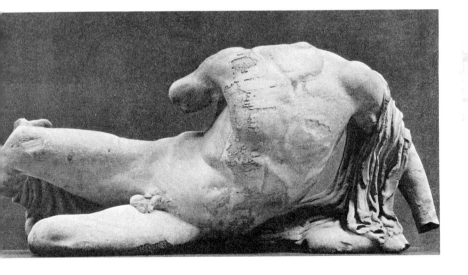

27

28

30

31

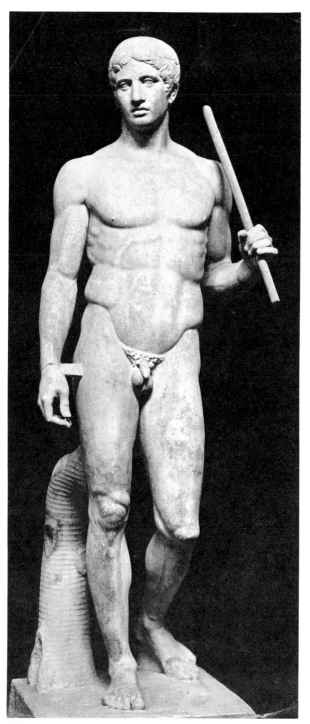

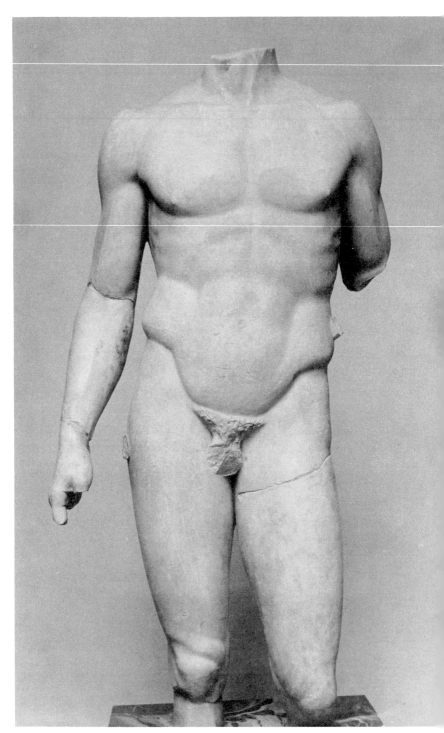

33

34

35

36

37

38

Fig:2.

P. Roche sculp.

42

43

44

46

47

50

51

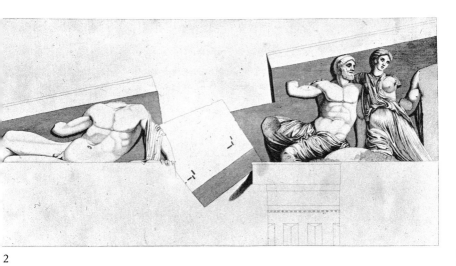

2

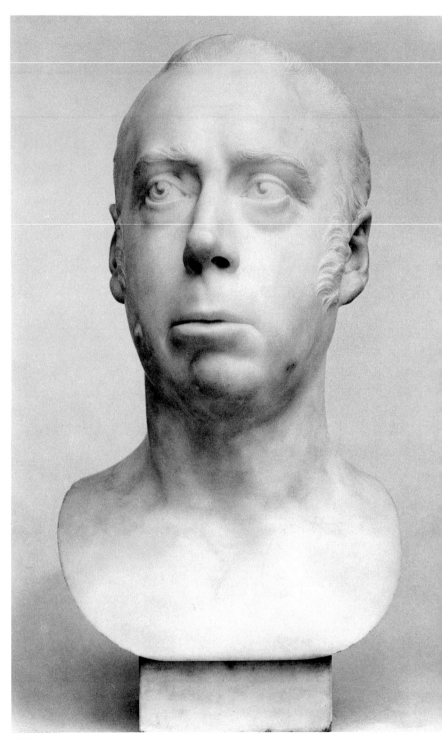

54

55

The Elgin Marbles! or John Bull buying Stones at the time his numerous Family want Bread!!

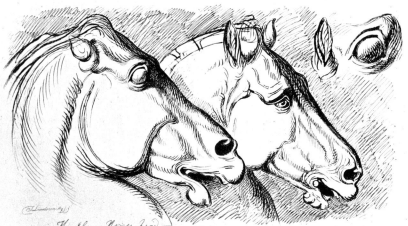

The Elgin Horses head —

Head of one of the Horses always considered to be by Lysippus - now at Venice -

It is astonishing that the great principles of Nature should have been so nearly lost in the time between Phidias & Lysippus — Compare these two heads — The Elgin head is all truth, the other all manner — In the Lysippus head the great characteristics of Nature are violated for the sake of an artificial effect, in the former head the great and inherent characteristics of Nature are elevated without violation - in as much as the Elgin Horses head differs from, and is superior to the head by Lysippus so do the rest of the Elgin Marbles differ from and are superior to all other statues of this, and every subsequent age —

B. R. Haydon 1857 -

60

61

62

64

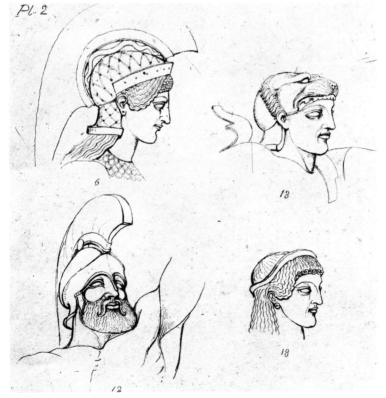

65

66

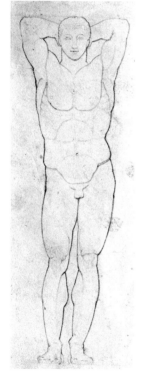

67

68

SIGET·AGRIGENTV·MIRABILIS·AVLA·GIGANTVM·

69

ILLUSTRATIONS

ILLUSTRATIONS

(The references in parentheses are to the sources of the illustrations.)

1, 2. Statue of a young man. New York. Richter, *Kouroi* (2nd ed.) no. 1, p. 41. (Metropolitan Museum)

3, 4, 5. Head from the Dipylon, Athens. Richter, *op.cit.* no. 6, p. 46. (*Ath.Mitt.* LII, 1927)

6. The same (B. Ashmole)

7. Statue of a girl from the Acropolis: no. 679. Payne & Young, *Archaic Marble Sculpture from the Acropolis* (2nd ed.), p. 69, pl. 29, 2. (Mr. G. Mackworth Young)

8. Head of the same. *id.* pl. 32. (Mr. G. Mackworth Young)

9. Head from Ephesus. British Museum no. B.89. Pryce, *B.M.Cat. Sculpt.* I, i. p. 50. (B. Ashmole)

10. Statue of a girl from the Acropolis: no. 594. Payne & Young *op.cit.* p. 70, pl. 48. (Mr. G. Mackworth Young)

11, 12, 13. Fragments of statue of a girl from the Acropolis: nos. 453 & 136. Payne & Young, *op.cit.* p. 70, pls. 43, 8, 4: 44, 3. (Mr. G. Mackworth Young)

14, 15, 16. Statue of Iris from the Acropolis: no. 690. Payne & Young, *op.cit.* p. 74, pl. 120 (B. Ashmole)

17, 18, 19, 20. Statue dedicated by Euthydikos on the Acropolis: no. 686. Payne & Young, *op.cit.* p. 72, pls. 85, 87-8 (Mr. G. Mackworth Young)

21. Statue of a girl from Xanthos. British Museum, no. B. 317. Pryce, *op.cit.* p. 148, pl. 32. (British Museum)

22. Statue of a girl from Xanthos. British Museum, no. B.318. Pryce, *op.cit.* p. 148, pl. 33. (British Museum)

23. Head of Atlas from the metope fig. 24. (Bildarchiv Foto Marburg)

24. Metope, Heracles and Atlas, Temple of Zeus at Olympia. (Bildarchiv Foto Marburg)

25. The River-god Cladeos, East Pediment, Temple of Zeus at Olympia. (German Archaeological Institute)

26. River-god, West Pediment of the Parthenon. (British Museum)

27. Seated figure, East Pediment of the Parthenon. (British Museum)

28. Seated figures, East Pediment of the Parthenon. (British Museum)

29. Horse of Selene, East Pediment of the Parthenon. (British Museum)

30. The same. (B. Ashmole)
31. Head of a horse, New York. D. von Bothmer, *Ancient Art from N.Y. Private Collections*, p. 26, no. 107. (Mr. Walter Cummings Baker)
32. Statue of doryphoros from the palaestra at Pompeii. Naples, no. 146 (Alinari)
33. Torso of doryphoros, Berlin. (Blümel, *Cat. Skulpt.*, Vol. IV no. K 151, pl. 35)
34. Head of a bronze herm from Herculaneum. Naples, no. 854. (Alinari)
35. Back of the same (From a cast, Berlin Museum)
36. Engraving, W. Hogarth, *Analysis of Beauty* (1753).
37. Monument of Philopappos (Stuart & Revett, *Antiquities of Athens*, Vol. III (1794) ch. V pl. I.)
38, 39. Monument of Lysicrates (Stuart & Revett, *op.cit.* Vol. I. (1762) ch. IV, pl. III & VI.)
40. Pen-and-ink study, probably by James Stuart. (G. & R. Dept. British Museum)
41. Engraving, Stuart & Revett, *op.cit.*, Vol. I, ch. IV, pl. XVIII.
42. Portrait of John Haviland by John Neagle. (A. Gardner, *Metrop. Mus. Bulletin*, Dec. 1955 p. 103)
43. Water-colour drawing of the Parthenon by William Pars. (G. & R. Dept. British Museum)
44. Metope from S. side of Parthenon, no. 2(305). (British Museum)
45. Drawing of 44 by William Pars. British Museum (G. & R. Dept. British Museum)
46. Engraving of 45 (Stuart & Revett, *op.cit.*, Vol. II (1787) ch. 1, pl. XII)
47. Engraving of same metope. *Antiquities of Athens*, new edn. by W. Kinnard (1825), Vol. II, ch. I, pl. IV, fig. 3.
48. Slab from West frieze of the Parthenon; Lord Elgin's cast. (British Museum)
49. Drawing of the same slab by William Pars. (G. & R. Dept. British Museum)
50. Engraving of the same slab (Stuart & Revett, *op.cit.* Vol. IV (1816), ch. IV, pl. XVI)
51. Etching by Richard Dalton of the same slab. *Views of Sicily Greece, Asia Minor, Egypt* (1751), unnumbered plate.
52. Engraving from a drawing by W. Pars of the river-god (fig. 26) West pediment of Parthenon. Stuart & Revett, *op.cit.* Vol. II ch. I, pl. IX.

53. Engraving of the same sculpture, Stuart & Revett, *op.cit.* Vol. IV, ch. IV, pl. I.
54. Marble bust of Richard Payne Knight, by John Bacon the Younger (British Museum)
55. Painting of George Hamilton Gordon, Fourth Earl of Aberdeen, by John Partridge (National Portrait Gallery, London)
56. Cartoon by George Cruikshank (G. & R. Dept., British Museum)
57. Painting by A. Archer. A. H. Smith J.H.S. XXXVI (1916) pp. 352ff. fig. 16 (British Museum)
58. Etching by B. R. Haydon. (G. & R. Dept. British Museum)
59. Engraving from a drawing by J. M. W. Turner (C. R. Cockerell, *The Temples of Jupiter Panhellenius at Aegina and of Apollo Epicurius at Bassae* (1860): text-vignette after p. 18)
60. Warrior from the East pediment of the temple at Aegina. Munich. (Ackermann's *Kunstverlag*)
61. Dying warrior from the East pediment at Aegina. Munich. (*do.*)
62. Head of the same (from a cast).
63. Archer from the East pediment of the temple at Aegina (from a cast).
64. Pencil drawing by C. R. Cockerell of the same. (G. & R. Dept., British Museum)
65. Etchings by C. R. Cockerell of figures from Aegina. (*Quarterly Journal of Science, Literature and the Arts*, 1819)
66. Remains of the temple of Zeus at Acragas.
67. Study by C. R. Cockerell for a title-page (G. & R. Dept., British Museum)
68. Sketch by C. R. Cockerell for the same (G. & R. Dept., British Museum)
69. Title-page of *Antiquities of Athens and other places in Greece, Sicily &c.* (1830)

Twentieth Century

Approaches

to Plato

BY W. K. C. GUTHRIE

Delivered March 28 and April 1, 1963

6

TWENTIETH CENTURY APPROACHES
TO PLATO

I: THE THEOLOGIAN, THE PHILOSOPHER, THE SCIENTIST, THE SOCIOLOGIST

YOUR AIM in these lectures, if I understand it aright, is to get a scholar from each of the main branches of classical studies to give his audience an insight into the present state of his subject, the possibilities for future developments, and some evidence that the field is not one for professional classical scholars only, but has something to offer to all thoughtful people. It was entirely appropriate that the series should have been opened by Professor Blegen, not only because of his close personal connexion with Cincinnati and with Mrs. Semple, but also because it is in archaeology that the most spectacular discoveries are being made, and within archaeology no one in recent years has opened up more exciting vistas than Professor Blegen himself. My wife and I visited Pylos for the first time last summer, and we are still congratulating ourselves on our good fortune in that, although the season's work was over, Professor Blegen happened to come to Pylos from Athens during our stay. The privilege of his company on the spot was something which we shall long remember.

The student of Greek philosophy cannot hope to offer anything comparable in the way of newly-discovered material. What he can claim is that his subject is of perennial interest, offering such richness and variety that every age has found something different in the Greek thinkers to stimulate or help it in its own particular concerns. This claim I want to substantiate briefly in a single outstanding instance: Plato, the greatest and richest of them all.

A Greek commentator of the sixth century A.D. tells a pleasing story about Plato.[1] Shortly before his death he dreamed that he had turned into a swan. Men were trying to snare him, but flying from tree to tree he mocked their trouble and none could catch him. His friend Simmias, when he heard the dream, said that all

[1] Anonymous, Προλεγόμενα τῆς Πλάτωνος φιλοσοφίας, 1, p. 4 Westerink.

men would try to grasp Plato's meaning but none would succeed. Everyone would expound him according to his own leanings, be he theologian or scientist or anything else. This was because, as with Homer, the beauty of his style made him accessible to all, from whatever angle they approached him.

The prophecy has come true, just as the remark about Plato's literary gifts was true. One does not need to be any sort of specialist to appreciate the humour and drama of the *Protagoras* or to be moved by the last words of the *Apology* or *Phaedo*. That must never be forgotten, though for reasons of time I shall concentrate on other things. Nor can I embark on the vast subject of the history of Platonism. I shall only draw your attention to some of the different things which different people have found in Plato in recent times. I hope it will be enough to convince you that the hold which he has over men's minds is by no means a thing of the distant past.

To carry on the language of his dream, here are a few of the huntsmen's cries as they chase their elusive prey. First the religious man, a philosophic Christian, the late Dr. Inge: 'He was a poet and prophet. . . . The true Platonist is he who sees the invisible, and knows that the visible is its true shadow.' On the other hand a modern analytic philosopher like Professor Ayer claims to include him among the great philosophers 'whose work is predominantly analytic.'[2] The physicist Heisenberg, who holds that a knowledge of Greek natural philosophy is almost essential to progress in modern physics, argues that among the Greeks it is Plato who comes nearest to the elementary particles of modern atomic science, and that visual models of atoms which he saw illustrated in his youth could have benefitted from a study of the *Timaeus*.[3] Plato's most powerful critic, Professor Popper, calls him 'one of the first social scientists and undoubtedly by far the most influential,'[4] and the advocate of a pernicious political totalitarian-

[2] W. R. Inge, *Plotinus*, i. (London, 1918), 74; A. J. Ayer, *Language, Truth and Logic*, 2nd ed. (London, 1946; and later reprints), 54.

[3] W. Heisenberg has discussed this topic in many places: one may mention *Philosophical Problems of Nuclear Science* (London, 1952), 30-34, 57; *The Physicist's Conception of Nature* (London, 1958), 60 f.; *On Modern Physics* (1961, a symposium with Born, Schrödinger and Auger), 5 f., 18 f. I have not seen his "Platons Vorstellungen von den kleinsten Bausteinen der Materie und die Elementarteilchen der modernen Physik," *Umkreis der Kunst: Eine Festschrift f. Emil Preetorius*, ed. Fritz Hollwich (Wiesbaden, 1954), 137-40.

[4] K. R. Popper, *The Open Society and its Enemies*, 3rd ed. (London, 1957), 35.

ism. Others too—educationalists, psychologists, aesthetic philosophers—have found much in Plato to interest them, but we may
confine ourselves to these four. Who is this creature—surely chi-
mera rather than swan—who can be claimed as religious visionary,
linguistic analyst, ancestor of the modern physicist, and dangerous
social and political theorist? I shall try to show that none of these
pictures is wholly false, and then in my second lecture to suggest
how each falls into its appropriate place, primary or subordinate,
in what was for Plato, at least in intention, an integral view of
reality and of man's place within it.

From the time of Clement and Origen, and even more strongly
after St. Augustine, there have always been Christian philosophers
who sought in Plato a rational basis for their faith. In doing so,
and relying sometimes on the Neoplatonists rather than Plato
himself, they may often have produced a distorted version. Yet
there was much in Plato to support what they learned from the
New Testament. His god was the craftsman who created the world.
Even before the Christian era men had begun to identify him with
the Creator in the Hebrew scriptures.[5] Since Plato called him mind
or reason he could be assimilated to the Logos of St. John. The
natural world, being ordered by reason, was the outcome of a grand
design, a doctrine which might seem consistent with the Christian
view that history is the unfolding of a divine purpose. Plato taught
that men are fallen spirits undergoing in this life punishment for
sin, and that life eternal awaited them in another world. In his
Phaedo the body with its lusts is represented as a hindrance to the
soul's salvation, as flesh wars against spirit in St. Paul. In Plato
man's chief end is to become like God—'perfect', the Christian
might say, 'even as your Father in Heaven is perfect'—and the
impulse to this perfection is called love. The pursuit of righteousness
is central, and the greatest of Plato's dialogues are pervaded by an
intense moral earnestness. Above all, his philosophy is rooted in
the division between temporal and eternal. As for the Christian,
this world is a place 'where moth and rust doth corrupt'. Imperfec-
tion and transience go together, and only in the invisible world can
perfect goodness and unending, unchanging existence be found.
    Yet the Christian must look in vain for some essentials of his

[5] See K. Reinhardt, *Posidonios* (Munich, 1921), 16.

creed. The Incarnation, the idea that God could voluntarily take human form and sacrifice himself for the redemption of the human race, is wholly alien to Plato. In Platonism the movement is all upward, of the longing soul aspiring to higher things. Plato would never say 'Herein is love, not that we loved him but that he loved us', and with that goes the whole doctrine of divine Grace. We should also look in vain in Plato for anything corresponding to the resurrection of the body. If we interpret this, as St. Paul's words probably entitle us to do, to mean something like the persistence in eternity of individual personality, it is probably true to say that this is something in which neither Plato nor any other Greek religious teacher was deeply interested. For him, as for the Orphic and Pythagorean thinkers to whom he owed so much, individuality was the consequence of incarceration in a body and was a curse, because it meant separation from the divine to which the soul was naturally akin. When the cycle of incarnations was completed, and the soul fully purified, its reward would be the utter loss of self, and absorption in the one divine being. This is the goal of mysticism, which has tempted many, be they Christians, Moslems or others, but it is not the teaching of Christ or Paul.

Besides missing much that he believes, the Christian will find in Plato positive doctrines which he cannot accept. The power of the supreme deity is limited, for he does not create from nothing. He exercises the power of reason on a pre-existing material which is to some extent recalcitrant. He does indeed succeed in imposing a marvellous degree of order and design, so that the cosmos is the best of all possible worlds; but there remains an irreducible minimum of brute unreason in it. Although the major cosmic events recur with unfailing regularity—the majestic wheeling of the heavenly bodies ensures that 'seedtime and harvest, and summer and winter, and day and night shall not cease'—yet minor aberrations, with their attendant evils, cannot be prevented. It is an attractive explanation of the imperfections of the natural world, but one which is not open to those for whom the creator is omnipotent.

The divine craftsman of Plato works not only on a given material, but to a given pattern. There is a world of Forms, the perfect and eternal archetypes of which everything in the natural world is a temporary and imperfect copy. Only they deserve the name of true being, whereas all that occurs in our world must be counted as 'becoming'; and becoming is defined as an intermediate state between being and not-being. The Forms exist independently of the creative god. He looks towards them as an ideal to which, being good himself, he makes the visible world conform as far as possible. Christian Platonists, it is true, have reconciled this with their own beliefs by reducing the Forms to thoughts in the mind of God. But for Plato they are the *objects* of his thought, not created by it any more than the stars are created by the mind of an astronomer who studies them. There is one all-embracing Form, called the 'living creature itself' because it is the model of the universe and that is a divine and living thing (again hardly a tenet for a Christian); and it contains as parts of itself the Forms of all the living creatures (including for Plato the sun and stars) which in physical shape are found within the universe. This deification of the world and the heavenly bodies gave rise to a number of later schemes embodying a hierarchy of emanations and descents of being from the One to the many, which were hardly a part of orthodox Christianity. Origen thought that the heavenly bodies had souls, and also followed Plato in believing that the world was a place of punishment for sins committed by souls before birth; but even he could not admit into Christianity one of the most characteristic of Plato's doctrines—reincarnation. The perennial attempt to reconcile Platonism and Christianity has marvellously enriched the Christian philosophy, but it has also produced a varied and interesting crop of heresies.

To the modern linguistic philosopher much in past philosophy was a form of linguistic analysis, even though those who practised it mistakenly thought they were doing something else. 'Plato indeed', it is said, 'constructed a metaphysical theory; but he constructed it on a basis of linguistic analysis. What he was engaged upon was a classificatory analysis of the meaning of certain types of propositions.'[6]
There is much to support this view. Plato, it is true, points a contrast between invisible and immutable patterns in Heaven and a natural world deprived of all stability, permanence and even existence; and this is hardly the doctrine for a modern philosopher. But the train of reasoning which led him to this remarkable view of reality had its roots in the campaign of Socrates to get men to

[6] F. Coplestone, *Contemporary Philosophy* (London, 1956), 2.

tell him what they meant by the words they used. Since the ultimate aim of Socrates was moral reform, his chief interest had been in ethical terms like justice, goodness, courage. His conviction was that in order to establish universally recognized moral standards, it was necessary to analyse the various current notions of the virtues and reach an agreed definition of each. When asked for such a definition, most men replied by citing a string of instances of the sort of thing to which they habitually applied the term. Socrates would then insist that a knowledge of justice was not evinced by the mere enumeration of actions as different from one another as paying a bill and sentencing a murderer to death. These actions must be analysed in order to show what was the common element in them which entitled them to be called just. This to his way of thinking was the form or essence of justice, and no one could claim to know what was meant by the word unless he could isolate and identify it. Knowledge before Socrates's time had been commonly thought of as 'knowledge how'—knowing how things behaved or how to behave oneself. Socrates set philosophy off on a fateful path by insisting that you cannot know *how* a thing works without first knowing *what* it is, nor how to behave without knowing what good behaviour is. If we have not grasped the essence of justice, we shall have no standard by which to judge whether one way of acting is more just than another. Hence Aristotle's laconic summing-up, that Socrates must be credited with two things: inductive argument and general definition.

His method was criticized in the fifth century B.C., as it would be today, by empiricists who refused to believe in the existence of anything corresponding to a universal concept like justice. Such notions differ in different civilisations, different countries, even between different individuals. To try to define them is futile. Some would say today that it is also misleading, because any single definition of an ethical term must inevitably be what Mr. C. L. Stevenson christened a 'persuasive definition,' an attempt to compel assent to a particular moral attitude. According to Stevenson, the analysis is not genuine analysis: 'these very definitions', he writes, 'involved the same persuasion; and in a way that veiled and confused it by making it appear to be purely intellectual analysis.'[7] Socrates of course agreed that different people had different ideas of justice.

[7] *Ethics and Language* (Oxford, 1944), 266.

That was exactly what he complained of. Until they could be brought to agree on the point there could be no stable morality, and in any case it was unhelpful to use the same word without meaning the same thing. The result is at once a failure of communication or linguistic breakdown, and a moral instability. His search for definitions thus had an ulterior aim, but he was none the less convinced that there was a correct answer to his questions and that what he sought was the truth. It must be realised however that his achievement was primarily negative and destructive. He sincerely believed that he did not himself know the answers. What shocked him was the assumption of others that they did. The immediate task was to convince them of their ignorance, after which he and they might together seek the truth. All the weight of his argument was on the refutation of uncritically held opinions.

To Plato it seemed that there were deeper issues at stake. Socrates was right to demand that men who claimed that A, B and C were just actions, or D, E and F were just men, should analyse these statements in order to discover the x that was common to the subjects of all of them: the justice which must be in each one if they are all to be credited with the same attribute. But this raised in his mind a further question. (In all probability it had already been raised by others, and was a current criticism of Socrates which had to be answered after his death.) Is there such a thing as absolute justice, apart from individual just actions? We cannot claim that any of these is justice itself, but only that they exemplify justice in an imperfect or approximate form. What and where is justice—or courage, or virtue—itself? If it does not exist, there is no point in trying to define it.

It does exist, he said; and since it is not fully manifested within its instances in the natural world, it must exist outside them. This was the genesis of the doctrine of transcendent forms. How all-inclusive it was is uncertain, and Plato himself probably wavered; but both from his own dialogues and from Aristotle's criticisms, we may conclude that it was extended from forms of moral qualities to those of natural species like man and horse. Individual men and horses owed the semblance of being which they possessed to imitation of, or participation in, the being of 'man himself' or 'horse itself', a fully existing, transcendent substance. Hence the modern condemnation of Plato as one who tried to solve logical problems by postulating metaphysical entities. As Professor Ryle has put it:[8] 'Whatever its sublimity and inspiration-value, the theory of Forms had been from the start, *inter alia*, a doctrine intended to solve certain puzzles of a purely logical nature. How can several things be called by one name or be of one sort or character?'

However that may be, the Forms once they were there took on in Plato's maturity an exalted status before which the perceptible world faded into an altogether minor importance. Plato's language about them is religious rather than philosophical, strongly tinged with emotion. The Form of the Good is the cause of existence as well as intelligibility, itself beyond being. The Form of beauty is 'beauty itself, pure, unalloyed . . . the divine beauty single and alone'.[9] This is the triumphant middle period of the *Phaedo*, *Republic*, *Symposium* and *Phaedrus*. It mattered nothing that the relationship between Forms and particulars (on which of course the solution of the supposed logical problem wholly depended) could only be referred to in what Aristotle was later to dismiss contemptuously as 'poetic metaphors'. Particulars copied the Forms as patterns, or alternatively they 'partook of' them in some mysterious way. In the *Republic* the vision of the Forms is represented as the culmination of a long and arduous intellectual training, but in the *Symposium* the apprehension of true beauty, identical with goodness, is compared to the sudden revelation which was the climax of the rites of initiation into the mysteries; and the mysteries into which the philosopher is initiated are called the mysteries of Love. If all this started as an attempt to solve purely logical puzzles, it has come a long way. In the *Phaedrus*, the disembodied souls ride round the outer rim of heaven in the company of the gods and are there vouchsafed a glimpse of the eternal Forms; and one does not need a journey to heaven nor divine companions to investigate the nature of general terms or abstract principles. The modern logician would certainly disclaim such aids.

Nevertheless as time went on the religious fervour faded, and the

[8] *Mind*, 1939, 315. Contrast Kneale, *Development of Logic* (New York, 1962), 14: 'Plato would probably have been averse to logical investigation carried out for its own sake without the further aim of establishing moral or mathematical truth. . . . While his dialogues contain much logical material, none of them is purely logical in content.'
[9] *Rep.* 509 b, *Symp.* 212 e.

logical difficulties began to make themselves felt. In the *Parmenides* the awkward consequences of saying that particulars copy Forms, or share in their being, are squarely faced—and left unanswered. But the Socrates who puts forward these notions is represented as an eager youth, full of his new ideas but untrained in dialectic. He is helpless before the wise and elderly Parmenides, who however, after apparently tearing the doctrine to shreds, only draws the moral that Socrates must acquire more skill in reasoning in order to defend it better; for, he says, without it a man will have nothing on which to fix his thought and will completely destroy the significance of all discourse. One may conclude that in spite of the objections (which were evidently current in the Academy, and are in fact repeated by Aristotle), the theory of transcendent Forms had at all costs to be maintained. This is borne out by its reappearance in the *Philebus*, which all would agree (and the *Timaeus* which most would agree) to have been written after the *Parmenides*, and also by Aristotle, whose criticisms of the Platonic Forms are all founded on the supposition of their independent substantial existence. Other late dialogues besides the *Parmenides*—notably the *Theaetetus* and *Sophist*—are also critical in tone. They deal with such questions as the nature of knowledge, the possibility of false statement and negation, and the confusion between statements of identity and statements of predication. So much we must concede to the modern linguistic analyst who claims Plato in his ancestry.

If, then, Plato saw unanswerable objections to the theory of substantial Forms as an explanation, or legitimation, of the use of general terms, and if he became more interested in linguistic analysis and made considerable progress in it, why did he not abandon the theory? Most critics give him credit for intellectual honesty, and all agree that his mind was one of the most powerful of all time. For Professor Ryle the only possible conclusion from this is that after writing the *Parmenides* he did abandon what to most people is the central doctrine of Platonism, but I do not think the evidence bears this out.

There is, I believe, another explanation, namely that Plato's conception of knowledge was different from that of the modern critics I have mentioned. They see the doctrine of independent, substantial forms as designed to explain how a number of particulars can be called by the same general name. Plato would not have put it like that. His aim was to uphold the possibility of knowledge. If knowledge was not even in theory attainable, the destructive arguments of Socrates were reduced to the level of sophistry; but Socrates gave his life for his faith that, although neither he nor any others had attained it, knowledge might one day yield itself to a group of fellow-searchers sufficiently persevering and sufficiently open-minded in the quest. A modern philosopher might agree, but he would not mean by knowledge the same as Plato did. If, he would say, we mean by knowledge something absolutely certain and indubitable, then it is indeed unobtainable, outside the purely intellectual and analytic spheres of mathematics or logic. We may observe and draw inferences from our observations, or we may start with a hypothesis and proceed to test it; but whereas empirical tests and observations can prove our hypotheses and inferences wrong, no amount of evidence can ever conclusively confirm them.

This would not do for Plato. Knowledge is only knowledge if it is certain, and this implies that its objects are permanent and stable. We must first, he says in the *Timaeus*,[10] distinguish between what is always real and not subject to process, and what is always in process of becoming and never real. The former is unchanging and is apprehensible by thought with a reasoned account; the latter is at the mercy of conjecture and unreasoning sensation, for it comes and goes but never truly is. The natural world is a perpetual flux, perceptible but not fully intelligible. Therefore the objects of knowledge must be sought outside it. That is why he made Parmenides say that to abandon transcendent forms was to destroy the significance of all discourse. That is why Sir David Ross can write[11] that it is in the *Theaetetus* (where the Forms are never mentioned) that Plato most fully states the grounds on which his theory rests, because it argues that knowledge is different from sensation. Though, he says, its subject is not metaphysical but epistemological, 'it furnishes the strongest argument Plato gives anywhere for the foundation of his metaphysical theory.' The truth is that for Plato epistemology and metaphysics are inseparable. Knowledge cannot be considered in isolation from its objects, with which it is correlative. In his own words: 'When the

[10] 27 d - 28 a.
[11] *Plato's Theory of Ideas* (London, 1951), 103.

mind's gaze is fixed upon an object irradiated by truth and reality, it gains understanding and knowledge and is manifestly in possession of intelligence. But when it looks towards that twilight world of things that come into existence and pass away, its sight is dim and it has only opinions which shift to and fro, and now it seems like a thing that has no intelligence."[12] It was Plato's inquiry into the nature of knowledge—his epistemology if you like—which made him the ally of the Christian in setting an invisible and eternal world over against the temporal and visible.

What arouses the physicist's interest is a particular part of one dialogue, the *Timaeus*, in which Plato attempts an account of the origin and structure of the physical world. He adopts in general the theory of Empedocles that all visible bodies are made from four elements: earth, water, air and fire. The choice may be unfortunate, but it is the details of the theory that excite. For Plato these simple physical bodies are not, as Empedocles taught, the ultimate constituents of matter, permanent and irreducible. Each of them consists of minimum particles in the shape of one of the regular solids, which for this reason were later known as the Platonic figures: fire is composed of tetrahedra or three-sided pyramids, air of octahedra, water of icosahedra, and earth of cubes. Now the surfaces of the first three are equilateral triangles, and that of the cube can be divided into two right-angled isosceles triangles. These latter, and the right-angled scalene which is half an equilateral triangle, Plato takes as the simplest forms of plane figure. The chemical transformation of one element into another is possible because the particles of three of the elements are composed of identical surfaces, so that, if they should be broken up, the surfaces can re-combine in different ways to form any other of the regular solids so constructed. When the heat of a fire dries up a puddle of water, the small, sharp, mobile fire-pyramids have pierced the icosahedra of water and split them into their component triangles, and in Plato's own words,[13] 'When water is divided into parts by fire, it can give rise to one particle of fire and two of air by combination.' In this case the twenty faces of each water-particle are regrouped as two octahedra and one pyramid.

[12] *Rep.* 508 d.
[13] 56 d.

Even this is not the end of the analysis. The particles of each element have the same shape, but they exist in different sizes, related to each other in strict mathematical proportion, because composed of a different number of identical triangles. This accounts for the different sub-forms of each main element, for the element 'water' in fact stands for all liquids, and 'air' for all gases or vapours. Thus water, oil, wine, acid have the same atomic shape but different atomic size.

These geometrical shapes are imposed by the controlling Reason on what Plato calls the Receptacle of becoming, a mysterious conception, as he admits himself. It is 'of a nature invisible and characterless, all-receiving, partaking in some very puzzling way of the intelligible and very hard to apprehend.'[14] Now he calls it space, and again he compares it to a plastic material or matrix. It is not empty space, for it is full of random and disorderly motion, a field of undisciplined energy. This it is which is reduced to order by the imposition upon it of geometrical figures which cause it to appear now fiery, now watery, now airy and now earthy.

With this scheme Plato opposed the theory of the classical atomists, Leucippus and Democritus. According to them all forms of matter were reducible to tiny, solid, unbreakable particles of irregular shapes moving at random in infinite void. Their coalescence to form a perceptible universe was the result of purely chance collision and entanglements. Blind natural necessity, not reason, was the primary cause of everything. The motive behind Plato's more complex scheme was to present the universe as the work, not of chance, but of a designing intelligence; and the Pythagoreans had taught him to look for the evidence of reason in mathematical, and particularly geometrical, form.

Physicists and historians of science as recent as Singer and Sir James Jeans spoke of the influence of Plato as disastrous and a degradation of knowledge. But now these strictures have changed to a chorus of praise. By adopting a geometrical theory of the world, says Popper, he provided Newton and Einstein with their tools and transformed the 'calamity' of Greek atomism into a momentous achievement. The final answer of physics, according to Heisenberg, will be nearer the *Timaeus* than to Democritus: the elementary particles of modern physics since the quantum theory

[14] 51 a-b.

are more closely related to the Platonic bodies than to the atoms. Again he writes: 'The triangles themselves are no longer matter, for they have no spatial dimensions. Therefore, in Plato, at the lowest limit of the series of material structures, there is really no longer anything material, but a mathematical form if you like, an intellectual construct.' Plato's scheme expresses the conviction that 'the rational order of surrounding nature must have its basis in the mathematical nucleus of the laws of nature. . . . But in the last resort the whole of mathematical natural science is based on such a conviction.' 'Newton', said Whitehead, 'would have been surprised at the modern quantum theory and the dissolution of quanta into vibrations: Plato would have expected it.'[15]

The atoms of Democritus were, as their name indicates, unsplittable, like the atoms of the classical physics of the nineteenth century. Plato's are more like modern elementary particles in that they can be broken up by the bombardment of particles of a different kind and recombine in different formations. One scholar has even seen in the different sizes of the same polyhedron, producing different kinds of the same element, a forerunner of the isotopes of to-day. There is also Heisenberg's famous 'uncertainty principle', that below a certain statistical level there is an inherent indeterminacy in events, not simply an indeterminacy in our own powers of predicting them. An anticipation of this has been seen in Plato's view that the principle of strict mathematical order is valid only down to the level of the elementary triangles: below that level the indeterminate and irregular energy of the 'receptacle of becoming' defies the efforts of the regulating cause.[16]

Not all philosophers of science accept the principle of ultimate uncertainty. As an opponent has trenchantly put it: 'Uncertainty of exact prediction, yes; indeterminacy of existence, no.'[17] There is controversy here in which the classical scholar can take no part. What is interesting to him is to find the modern antagonists stating it in terms of the ancients, the one side claiming Plato as their philosophical ancestor, the others Democritus, to whom Erwin Schrödinger looked back as actually the originator of the theory of

---

[15] Popper in *Brit. Journ. for Philos. of Sci.* 1952; Heisenberg, *On Mod. Phys.* 18 f., 6; *Philos. Problems of Nuclear Sci.* (London, 1952), 57; A. N. Whitehead, *Process and Reality* (New York, 1929), 145.

[16] For this paragraph cf. P. Friedländer, *Plato* i (New York, 1958), 251.

[17] A. Landé, "The Case Against Quantum Duality," *Philos. of Sci.*, 1962, 1-6.

discontinuous quanta.[18] In its widest significance, as Heisenberg has seen, the controversy raised by modern atomic physics and particularly by the quantum theory is the old one of idealism versus materialism; and this battle was first fought on Greek soil between the atomists and Plato.[19]

As a student of scientific method, Professor Popper is entirely on Plato's side when he adopts a geometrical theory of the world. But he parts company with him when he transfers this theory from macrocosm to microcosm, arguing in favour of geometrical relationships in the structure not only of the universe but of human society. This he does explicitly in the *Gorgias*, where his Socrates, rebuking an opponent who upholds a life of unbridled greed and ambition, attributes his fault to ignorance of the 'great power exercised by geometrical equality both among gods and among men.'[20]

Geometrical equality is not numerical equality: it is a matter of preserving a relationship of due proportion or ratio. Its introduction as a principle of social or political organization is not favourable to democracy in the sense of a simple counting of heads. To say that all men were created equal was for Plato not a self-evident truth, but a manifest falsehood. They differed in many respects, but for the purposes of living together in a state might be grouped in three classes: the wise and philosophic, the combative and ambitious, and the materially minded whose interest was in wealth and comfort. In a well-ordered country the first should rule, the second should be entrusted with defence, and the third with the production and exchange of material commodities.

What shocks the modern reader is that Plato when he wrote the *Republic* felt it necessary for the welfare and safety of his community to freeze and perpetuate these distinctions in a rigid system of social classes. Should an artisan or merchant—or a body of these relying on their numbers—try to break into the sphere of defence, or one of the military caste usurp the functions of a ruler, this would be fatal to the community and must be counted criminal. He does, it is true, allow that a man with the qualities proper to one class might accidentally be born into another, and proposes

<hr/>

[18] *Science and Humanism* (Cambridge, 1951), 54.
[19] *On Mod. Phys.* 6. Also interesting in this connexion is N. R. Hanson's article, 'The Dematerialisation of Matter,' *Philosophy of Science*, 1962, 26-38.
[20] 508 a.

that there should be machinery for official transfer in such cases; but in his opinion they would be rare, for he was a firm believer in eugenics, and breeding is to be confined within each class, and at least in the higher classes, only to the best within that class.

The modern attacks on Plato go back to the days of the Fascist and Nazi regimes, and have intensified since their defeat in the Second World War. In the *Journal of Education* for 1945 two Germans[21] cited passages from the *Republic* to prove that, in Plato's view, 'the main purpose of the state (i.e. the legal and civic administration) is to preserve the purity of the race and to organize the people for war'. It was certainly frightening to read in this article that the officially declared aim of the Nazi Party had been 'to govern as Guardians in the highest Platonic sense'. Plato was quoted as saying that a nation must inevitably expand at the expense of others, that non-Greeks are natural enemies to the Greek, that fighting-men should be bred like horses or dogs, inferior children inhumanly disposed of, and the people governed by lies.

Others were not slow to leap to the defence. Texts were met with counter-texts as in old-fashioned religious controversies. Did not Plato say at *Republic* 373 e: 'We have discovered the origin of war in desires which are the most fruitful source of evils both to individuals and states'? The fate of inferior children was not to be exposure (though this was current practice in Greece), but only relegation to a lower class. If Plato 'despised democratic ideals', this refers to contemporary democracy, a system in which offices were filled by lot without regard to capability. Modern democracy, it was claimed, embodies 'a thoroughly Platonic notion', in favouring the *carrière ouverte aux talents*. Joad agreed that Plato's system resembles Fascism in taking a pessimistic view of human nature, and in advocating an authoritarian state in which the best make the laws and the many achieve the happiness and virtue of which they are capable by obeying. But it differs, he said, in two respects. The criterion for choice of the best is knowledge or wisdom. Goodness and beauty exist, and a few men may by education be brought to apprehend them. In Fascism the self-elected rulers treat power itself as a good. Secondly, the end of government is the well-

[21] Neurath and Lauwerys, "Plato's 'Republic' and German Education," *Journ. of Ed.*, 1945, 57-9. Replies (referred to in the text) will be found later in the same volume.

being of the community as a whole. Justice is defined as the discovery and contented performance by each man of the work for which he is most naturally fitted. Only a few are capable of wisdom: the others will be both more happily and more properly employed in other pursuits. It is not true, said Joad, that Plato regards the ordinary man as a means: his welfare is an end, though an end of inferior value.

The controversy shows no signs of abating.[22] Plato's attackers do not always agree among themselves, particularly in their attitudes to Socrates. To some, Socrates is the hero of democracy and freedom of thought, whose ideals Plato betrayed. To others Socrates himself led the intellectual assault on the democratic way of life. Professor Popper's main indictment of Plato is that he tried to arrest political development at a theoretically perfect stage which was essentially that of the closed, early tribal society. To this the best answer possible has probably been made by Hackforth in a review.[23] It 'fails', he says, 'to appreciate the seriousness of Plato's conviction, inherited from Socrates, that government is a science, and a science which can only be mastered by a few persons of exceptional powers. . . . It is surely this conviction that dominates the *Republic*, not any hankering after a tribal society. . . . To say that "Platonic wisdom is acquired largely for the sake of establishing a permanent political class rule" seems to me a precise inversion of the truth: rule is placed in the hands of one class (or rather set of persons, for "class" is a misleading word) because only a few were capable of Platonic wisdom.'

Plato's aim is certainly not the aggrandisement or wealth or happiness of his ruling class in any accepted sense. They are chosen in the first place for their lack of acquisitive and ambitious instincts. After an ordinary education up to the age of 18, followed by two years of military service, they study mathematics and astronomy for 10 years as a preparation for 5 years of philosophy. This gives unity and coherence to their knowledge, and enables them to judge all earthly existence and value in the light of the perfect Forms. They are then sent back into the world and tested by fifteen years of subordinate office. Those who survive all this must from the age

[22] The best book on the subject is R. Levinson, *In Defense of Plato* (Harvard University Press, 1953), where a full bibliography will be found.
[23] *Classical Review*, 1947, 55.

of 50 take their turn to govern, though their taste will be all for philosophic pursuits. Their life is one of extreme austerity, in communal barracks on rations provided by the State, debarred from family life, personal property and the use of money. Whatever the Nazi Party may have said, Hermann Goering would hardly have qualified for rulership in the Platonic State.

II: THE HISTORIAN

IF I devote this lecture to what I call the historical approach to Plato, and acknowledge it as my own, I am not thereby claiming any peculiar merit for it. Scientists, philosophers and sociologists, each bringing some special knowledge to bear on his text, may well have a special insight denied to classical scholars, and what they see may be more fruitful for the advance of knowledge. Moreover, it would be naïve to claim that any interpretation can remain uninfluenced by our own conscious or unconscious attitude. An atheistic scholar will never see quite the same things in Plato as a Christian. Nevertheless there is such a thing as the scholar's approach, and it deserves a hearing with the others. It is not an older or out of date approach. 'The restoration of the study of Greek philosophy', it has been said by a scholar well qualified to know, 'was a task reserved for the nineteenth century';[1] and the twentieth has seen notable advances. For instance, it was only in the latter years of the last century and the first half of this one that stylometric tests (on the frequency of verbal formulae, use of particles and so forth) enabled any but highly subjective criteria to be applied to the relative dating of the dialogues. Only now is the use of computers enabling these methods to be applied comprehensively and with precision. Yet the order of composition of the dialogues is an indispensable foundation for the study of Plato's development.

For all its technical competence, the nineteenth century itself prepared the way, one might say, for the modern attacks on Plato by an uncritical adulation of his philosophy. Bewitched by his talk of the true, the good and the beautiful, idealistic and liberal-minded Englishmen ignored much in his political and social programme and wrote of him as if he were a great Victorian liberal himself. A reaction was only to be expected, and was made inevitable by the harsh experience of our own time. Every teacher of classics or philosophy will confirm the dictum of the American scholar Bernard Levinson that 'to-day friendship for Plato is to

---

[1] J. L. Stocks, *Aristotelianism* (Boston, 1925), 142.

be found chiefly among those scholars (and their friends and disciples) whose vision of him antedated the rise of Nazism'.[2]

But Plato too had been spared the horrors of modern totalitarianism, and can hardly be blamed for that. If he is used to bolster it up, then certainly it is our duty to point out that his practical politics are largely irrelevant to the conditions of to-day. But for one thing Plato designed them for an entirely different historical situation, and for another it is a matter for investigation whether, so far as the *Republic* is concerned, he himself did not have other ends in view than the practical organization of a community.

What follows is intended to be complementary to what I said last time. I shall try to show, without too much repetition, how the various sides of Plato, which were then displayed separately, fall into place as parts of a general, and largely unitary, philosophical outlook which was definitely of his own time.

The facts of Plato's life have often been told. Brilliant and well-connected, he seemed marked out for a political career; but when in his early twenties, at the end of the Peloponnesian War, power fell into the hands of the oligarchic party which included relatives of his own, their violent and unscrupulous conduct made him hold back. Soon afterwards they were replaced by a democracy, which however put to death his older friend Socrates whom he regarded as 'the wisest and most righteous man then living'. He hesitated again, the political situation deteriorated, and he finally gave up all idea of active politics at home and took to writing and later to education in the school which he founded himself. At the age of forty he visited the Western Greeks of South Italy and Sicily. This had two results. First, he made friends with Dion, brother-in-law of the tyrant of Syracuse Dionysius I, who was attracted to Plato's ideas and thought that together they might reform the luxurious habits of the Syracusans and the autocracy of its rule. The immediate result was Plato's expulsion, but when the tyrant's young son succeeded to power Dion persuaded Plato to return. The story of Plato's attempt to make a philosopher-king out of the young Dionysius is a chequered one, and it ended in disaster.

The second result of Plato's visits to the West was that he gained the friendship of leaders of the Pythagorean school, especially

---

[2] *In Defense of Plato*, 445.

248 TWENTIETH CENTURY APPROACHES TO PLATO

Archytas of Tarentum, democratic leader and outstanding mathematician; and it was probably this which determined the direction in which he modified the simple philosophy of Socrates.

The lifetime of Socrates was characterized in antiquity, from Aristotle onwards, as the period when questions of human life and conduct replaced the study of natural philosophy as the chief concern of thinking men. Guidance in practical life had been largely the province of the poets, never backward in giving the moral and political instruction that was expected of them; but this was a matter of *ad hoc* precept or proverbial maxims rather than the establishment of ethical principles on a philosophical basis. Philosophy had begun elsewhere, in an attempt to satisfy man's curiosity about the nature and origin of the world he lives in, and to substitute rational for mythical explanations of it. To the first philosophers in the sixth century, it seemed that the manifold phenomena in nature must all be manifestations or permutations of a single basic stuff. Simplification is the constant aim of science, and it was natural that the earliest scientific philosophers in their blissful ignorance should go for the simplest hypothesis of all. Even a scientific book written in 1960 bears the title 'Towards a Unified Cosmology', and starts by examining the concept of unification in physics.[3]

This monism was challenged in the early fifth century by a man of exceptionally powerful intellect who was the first to employ a solely deductive logic, Parmenides. He argued that on the monistic hypothesis—reality is one—a manifold world could never come into being, for it was contrary to reason to suppose that one could ever become many. If unity is to be accepted, then its consequences must not be shirked: the world of plurality, motion and change, that is, everything that in our everyday experience we take to be real, is illusion. At that early stage of thought his arguments seemed unanswerable.

Heraclitus, writing probably a little before Parmenides, saw the world as a tension of opposite forces. Stability and permanence were only apparent. They were the temporary result of an evenly balanced struggle, in which each side was putting forth its utmost powers but neither had gained the mastery. War was the law of life. Rest meant death. One could not say of any two contraries, such

[3] The author is R. O. Kapp.

as harmony and disharmony, health and sickness, that one was good
and the other bad. No contrary could exist without its contrary.
This he expressed in paradoxical form as the *identity* of contraries:
health and disease, surfeit and famine, day and night, even good
and evil were one and the same. They were the same because
parts of the same continuum, as hot and cold; or because relative
to the experiencing subject, as salt water is healthy for fish, lethal
for man; or again because only appreciated in relation to each
other. 'It is', he said, 'disease that makes health pleasant, hunger
satiety, weariness rest.' Movement and change are never-ending
and are to be welcomed. He symbolized this by calling the world an
ever-living fire, in measures kindled and in measures extinguished.
The phrase 'in measures' is important. There is indeed a law of
measure inherent in all these things which ensures that none shall
overstep its limits and gain permanent mastery over the rest. The
balance and tension, on which the world depends, will always be
preserved. Something like this seems to be the function of the
divine Logos, 'in accordance with which', he says, 'all things come
to pass.'

At that stage of thought there were two ways in which the
dilemma of Parmenides could be solved. One was to abandon the
hypothesis of ultimate unity. If there is more than one basic reality,
then what we speak of as change does really occur—it is not mere
illusion—but it does not imply the change or coming-into-being
of anything real. So Empedocles explained the phenomenal world
by positing four ultimate elements—earth, water, air and fire—
which produced all its variety by combination in different proportions. The other pluralistic systems—those of Anaxagoras and the
atomists Leucippus and Democritus—sought solutions on similar
lines. The second way was by denying the reality of change and
motion; that is, by making a distinction between becoming and
being and saying that the world of becoming is not fully existent.
This, as we have seen, was the way of Plato. He was the first to
advance logic from the primitively uncompromising position of
Parmenides, for whose powers he nevertheless retained a profound
respect

There was also active, from the sixth century to Plato's lifetime
in the fourth, the Pythagorean school. Aristotle, Plato's most
original, gifted and (to his own regret) rebellious pupil, explained

the genesis of his master's thought in the following way. At the beginning of his *Metaphysics*, he conducts a brief, and admittedly slanted, review of his predecessors, with the avowed aim of discovering how far they anticipated his own fourfold scheme of causation: material, formal, efficient and final. The early monists, in his eyes, employed the material cause only: they reckoned to explain the world simply by saying that it came from water, or air, or indeed fire, for here he somewhat insensitively classes Heraclitus with them. Parmenides he leaves out of the account as one whose over-abstract reasoning has no bearing on the philosophy of nature. He then gives his own version of the Pythagorean or Italian school. They saw the explanation of the world in mathematical, and especially geometrical order, that is, ultimately, in harmonious numerical arrangement. They are therefore classified as philosophers of form rather than matter. Immediately after the Italian school he introduces Plato in these words:[4]

'After the aforesaid philosophies came the system of Plato, which in most respects followed the Italians, but had certain features of its own as well. In his youth he became familiar with Cratylus and the Heraclitean view that all perceptible things were in a state of flux and knowledge about them was impossible. This view he retained in his later years, but when Socrates abandoned the natural world for the study of moral questions, seeking in them for the universal and fixing the mind for the first time on the task of definition, Plato accepted his teaching. For reasons like these he was led to conclude that the objects of Socrates's study were not sensible things but something different; for it seemed to him that the common definition could not apply to any of the sensible things, since they are always changing. Things of this other sort he called Forms, and said that sensible things exist apart from them and are called after them, for things with the same name exist by participation in the Forms. "Participation" was only a change of name. The Pythagoreans had said that things exist by their resemblance to numbers, and Plato changed the word to "participation". But what was meant by participation in, or resemblance to, the Forms they left an open question.'

Even allowing for an element of exaggeration at the end, we may take it from Aristotle that Plato's philosophy was based on Pythago-

[4] *Metaph*. A, ch. 6, *ad init*.

reanism with modifications introduced by his reflection on the Heraclitean view of the world and his association with Socrates. This is consistent with what we find in the dialogues.

Earlier literature displayed a strong strain of scepticism about the possibility of certain knowledge for men. The poets liked to contrast the ignorance of mortals with the certainty which the gods claimed as their sole prerogative. That was why a poet needed the Muses: 'For ye', sang Homer, 'are goddesses and know everything'. Among philosophers Alcmaeon and Xenophanes took the same line. Certainty is for the gods. Men can only conjecture, though some opinions may be closer to truth than others. Heraclitus asserted the truth of his message only by assuming the mantle of a prophet and claiming access to a divine Logos outside himself.[5] The contrast between unshakable truth and wavering opinion was explicitly drawn by Parmenides. He in fact reached his 'truth' by a rigid chain of deductive argument, but in the manner of his time represented it as a revelation from a goddess: the whole proof of the unity and changelessness of being is put into her mouth.

Though Aristotle does not mention it, Plato's dialogues show that he was deeply influenced by Parmenides. Parmenides had taught the necessity for a correlation of knowledge and opinion with their respective objects, knowledge being directed to changeless being and opinion to the shadow-world of change and becoming. He as well as Heraclitus would be in Plato's mind as he listened to Socrates declaring that only knowledge could make men good, and plying his unfortunate acquaintances with questions designed to make them admit the necessity of defining the essential nature of the virtues they claimed to uphold. The opposite view, to which most people to-day would subscribe, was maintained by the contemporary Sophists: namely that moral qualities have no essential nature but are matters of convention and agreement. The Sophists offered ambitious young citizens what they particularly wanted in that age of democratic opportunity, practical guidance in the successful conduct of life, and especially of political life. As for truth, there was no truth behind appearances, and appearances were entirely relative to the experiencing subject, different to different men, and to the same man at different times. In the latter part of

---

[5] On this topic cf. B. Snell, *The Discovery of the Mind* (London, 1953), ch. 7: Human knowledge and divine knowledge among the early Greeks.

the fifth century this was reinforced by the physical doctrines of atomism, for the atoms themselves had no sensible qualities: sight, taste, touch, hearing, all were the result of interaction between the arrangement of atoms in the object and that in the perceiving subject.

There was then a powerful current of opinion ready to declare that Socrates's questions: 'What is justice?', 'What is courage?', were misguided. For several reasons Plato opposed it: his belief that a good life demanded adherence to permanent standards, valid independently of *ad hoc* decisions and temporary expediency; a passionate conviction of the possibility of knowledge, which for reasons in part historical seemed to demand the existence of stable, unchanging objects; and finally a deep personal attachment to Socrates and determination to defend his memory.

If Socrates's questions were not pseudo-questions, then it appeared that the virtues must be existing things, apart from their imperfect exemplification in human action; and we know that that is the answer that Plato gave with his doctrine of transcendent Forms. It faced him with two further questions: could any evidence be adduced for the existence of perfect and changeless entities outside the world of sensible experience, and if there were such entities, how could we know them, since they are *ex hypothesi* beyond experience?

The answers to both these questions were provided by the Pythagorean philosophy to which he was so strongly attracted. That is why he made it the basis of the magnificent philosophical structure which his own genius erected on the ideas of his predecessors. According to tradition, the Pythagorean world-view sprang from a discovery of its founder in the sphere of musical theory. In the Greek lyre, four strings were tuned at fixed intervals which were regarded as the primary elements of any scale, whereas the tuning of the remainder varied according to the type of scale required. The fixed intervals were octave, fifth and fourth, and what Pythagoras discovered was that this basic framework depended on certain definite ratios between the first four integers: 1:2 gives the octave, 3:2 the fifth, and 4:3 the fourth. Thus *kosmos*—order and beauty—was, it seemed, imposed on the indefinite range of sound by the numbers 1 to 4. There was undoubtedly an element of primitive number-mysticism in Pythagorean thought, but it is understandable also that new intellectual horizons seemed to be opened up by this revelation of an independent order, a numerical organization within the nature of sound itself. What Pythagoras was seeking, for reasons in part religious, was not the basic matter of the universe, nor the process of its evolution, so much as an explanation of the order and regularity which it displayed in the wheeling of the stars, the rising and setting of the sun, the alternation of day and night, summer and winter. It is hardly surprising that he and his followers, generalising his musical discovery, claimed that the whole of nature was constructed on a mathematical plan. This was for them 'the ideal element in nature', which as a modern physicist has put it, 'consists in the fact that mathematical laws, which are laws of our own thought, really hold in nature.'[6]

Here in this ideal element Plato found the evidence that he sought. The changeless world of mathematics, which the Pythagoreans had revealed behind the changing world of phenomena, made easier his belief in the changeless world of moral and other Forms. The statement that the angles of a triangle are together equal to 180 degrees is true, yet it is not precisely true of any triangle drawn by human agency or seen in a triangular piece of material. These only approximate to the truth, as a just action approximates to the ideal Form of justice. Pythagorean mathematics made it antecedently possible to believe that truth exists beyond the sensible world, exemplified by the rational structure of number existing behind the melody that delights the ear.

The reason which we should give to-day for this independence of mathematical truth is that the mathematician's statements are only analytical. They simply make explicit the logical consequences of defining a triangle in the way we do. They reveal more of what was in our minds, but do not refer to a different order of external reality. This explanation would not have appealed to Plato. What impressed him was the timeless truth of this kind of statement, and the fact that the shapes of earthly things could never, as it were, live up to it completely. It must be the same, he reasoned, with ideas like justice and beauty. We could not compare two actions in point of justice if we had not the conception of an absolute standard of reference. Whence have we this standard? Not, in Plato's view, merely from observing human actions, for

[6] C. F. von Weizsäcker, *The World View of Physics* (London, 1952), 21.

he held that acquaintance with the imperfect can never of itself give knowledge of the perfect. Somewhere, somehow, the perfect Forms must exist.

But how have we acquired knowledge of them? It is no wonder that most of us can only appreciate a part of Plato's many-sided genius, for to answer this question is to remind ourselves that he was not only an ethical and political theorizer, not only a gifted mathematical and logical philosopher, but also a profoundly religious spirit who allowed his religious instincts to provide the culmination of his philosophical system. Pythagoras was also a religious philosopher, who taught that the soul was immortal and suffered many reincarnations. This Plato accepted in all seriousness and adapted to be an integral part of his theory of knowledge. Soul is alien to body and in its pure being akin to the gods; but early Greek mythology had its own story of the Fall, and the punishment for original sin was the cycle of incarnations. The body is for the soul as a prison, or a tomb which holds it away from its true life. Socrates had taught Plato to think of the soul as essentially the mind, whose faculties (he now believed) are dulled, and its power of cognition impaired, by the body with its material needs and gross appetites. In its original state as a divine essence it had a clear and direct vision of the eternal Forms. Between incarnations it may see them again, with more or less clarity of apprehension depending on its attitude to the body in this life. If it has indulged the body by giving way to the lower appetites, something of the body's pollution will still cling to it and impair its faculties after death.

The answer to our question, then, is that the soul became acquainted with the Forms before it entered bodily life. To see things which are all imperfect—whether moral actions, triangles, or instances of physical beauty—could not of itself implant in our minds the knowledge of perfection nor a standard by which to judge them; but given that the vision preceded, they can assist us to recover it. The experience of birth and bodily life has made the soul forgetful, and what the imperfect copies can do is to remind it of what it once knew.

The acquisition of knowledge in this life is thus explained by the fact that it is the recollection of knowledge once possessed. The Pythagorean roots of this doctrine make their appearance when Plato, at its first introduction in the Meno, illustrates it by a mathematical example. An untaught boy is brought to solve a geometrical problem involving the so-called theorem of Pythagoras, though Socrates claims that he has not told him anything but only asked him questions, thereby eliciting knowledge that must have been there all the time. This, incidentally, shows how Socrates also put Plato on the track; for it is surely historical when Plato makes Socrates say in the *Theaetetus* that his mother was a midwife and he practises the same art—only on minds, not bodies; he assists the delivery of ideas with which his interlocutors are pregnant.

The choice of a mathematical example was of course particularly suitable. In mathematics the spontaneous grasp of the subject, as it is unmistakably in itself, is most easily distinguished from what is merely taken over from outside. No one can be taught mathematics as he can be taught historical facts like the course of the Second Punic War. Everyone must achieve comprehension for himself. When he does so, as a German scholar has recently put it, the surprising fact comes to light that he discovers precisely what everyone else must discover.[7] Here is an admitted phenomenon to throw light on how it is possible, by making a common effort over a question, to arrive at an agreed conclusion—in other words, to justify the Socratic method.

Basic and all-pervading in Pythagorean thought was the notion of harmony (in Greek *harmonia*). It means primarily the joining or fitting of things together in an appropriate way, but its particular application to music was established at latest by the early fifth century B.C., and was prominent in Pythagoreanism. This was only natural if, as is most probable, the Pythagorean view of nature was based on a discovery in the mathematics of music, and it is exemplified in the picturesque theory of the harmony of the spheres. Aristotle attests the universal application of *harmonia* in Pythagorean philosophy. 'Since,' he writes,[8] 'the nature of everything else seemed to be entirely assimilated to numbers, and numbers to be primary throughout the world of nature, they assumed the elements of number to be the elements of all that exists, and the whole universe to be a *harmonia* and a number.'

To be a harmony meant that all its parts were organized in the correct order and proportion for the best performance of its func-

---

[7] See N. Hartmann, *Kleine Schriften* II (Berlin, 1957), 57.
[8] *Metaph.* 985 b 32.

tion. It is astonishing how much of the pure milk of Pythagorean-ism was still current thought in the England of Elizabeth I and appears in Shakespeare, notably in Ulysses's speech on degree from Troilus and Cressida:

> The heavens themselves, the planets, and this centre
> Observe degree, priority and place,
> Insistence course proportion season form
> Office and custom, all in line of order.

Ulysses's purpose, you will remember, is to draw the analogy between macrocosm and microcosm, to argue that just as the stability of the world depends on due proportion, priority and order, so the preservation of proportion, order and degree is necessary in human society also. The close connexion between macrocosm and microcosm, based on the idea of the kinship of all nature, was taken very seriously in antiquity, and these two inherited ideas—the importance of harmony and the identity between cosmic and human law—lie at the root of much in Plato's social and political philosophy, including those parts of it which seem most distasteful today: its schematic and authoritarian character, its lack of realism and empiricism. We have seen that for him human nature fell into three broad classes, and that this suggested the necessity of a tripartite division of functions in society to ensure its well-being. When he is explaining how the virtue both of an individual soul and of a community lies in a proper relation between their parts—appetitive, passionate and rational—he expresses himself in Pythagorean fashion by saying that only thus will the strong, the weak and those in between 'sing together through the whole octave'. He sees this goodness as a harmony. The man who possesses it he calls 'well-tuned', and it is achieved 'by bringing three parts into accord, exactly like the fixed intervals in a scale—highest, lowest and middle'.[9] Behind the musical framework is the mathematical, the discovery of the ratios determining the intervals. We can now see a little more into the background of Plato's remark in the *Gorgias* about the tremendous power of geometrical equality both in heaven and among men.

This union of macrocosm and microcosm in the bonds of one and the same law of *harmonia* is most fully worked out in the grand

---

[9] *Republic* 432 a, 443 d.

synthesis of the *Timaeus*. God, being good and free from jealousy, wished everything to be as like himself as possible. Seeing then that the visible realm was in disorderly motion, and holding order to be better than disorder, he imposed order upon it as far as the nature of its material would allow. We saw in my first lecture how this order was put into effect by imposing different geometrical shapes on the formless matrix of becoming. Absolute perfection is only possible in the invisible, incorporeal realm of the unchanging Forms, which he therefore took as his model. The universe itself is, by the providence of God, a living creature with a rational soul, and of the world-soul Plato gives a highly symbolical account. Its two functions as imparting on the one hand the power of motion, and on the other the power of cognition and thought, are interwoven in a way which for us is difficult to appreciate, depending as it does on an explanation of the mental processes of perception and thought as analogous to circular motion on the physical level. The structure of the world-soul is a harmony worked out in fantastic detail on both its musical and its mathematical sides.[10] It animates the stars as they circle round the celestial equator and the planets moving obliquely to it in the ecliptic. These circles are also called the circles of the Same and the Other, symbolizing the power of reason to discriminate between one thing and another and determine their relations.

Human souls consist of the remnants left over from the making of the world-soul, the same ingredients but of inferior quality. They are further damaged by being forced into bodies. Consequently the circles in our own minds cannot always run true, and our thinking is often at fault. The human mind is an inferior derivative from the cosmic mind. We speak of Plato attributing human faculties to the cosmos, and wonder perhaps how he could do it. But for him it was the other way round. The cosmos imparts its

---

[10] *Timaeus* 36 b ff. It represents a diatonic scale of four octaves plus a major sixth. Musically this is arbitrary. It is the mathematical ratios that are of primary importance. The ratio between bottom and top notes is 27:1, reached by taking the first even and the first odd numbers (2 and 3; for the Pythagoreans the unit was outside the number series), and forming two geometrical progressions by multiplying them by themselves until their cubes are reached. The significance of this, in the strange mathematico-physico-psychical amalgam of Pythagoreanism, is that the cube is the first solid number, and the soul in its cognitive aspect must be able to deal with three-dimensional bodies.

psychical faculties to us, in so far as our less perfectly formed bodily frames are capable of receiving them.

Obviously the *Timaeus* contains a conscious admixture of myth and symbol. But the close relationship between macrocosm and microcosm, man and the universe, was for Plato true and essential. It led him to the following train of thought. The cosmic order is divine, man potentially shares this divine order and must reproduce it as far as possible, becoming *kosmios*, orderly, in his own soul. The way to reproduce the divine order is by knowing it, for he followed earlier thinkers like Empedocles in holding that like is known by like. This is the supreme purpose of philosophy. 'Familiarity with the divine and orderly makes the philosopher divine and orderly so far as a man may be.' That statement from the *Republic* is put more concretely in the *Timaeus*: 'The motions akin to the divine part in us are the thoughts and revolutions of the universe; these therefore every man should follow. . . . By learning to know the harmonies and revolutions of the world, he should bring the intelligent part . . . into the likeness of that which intelligence discerns, and thereby win the fulfilment of the best life set by the gods before mankind both for this present time and for the time to come.'[11] All Plato's philosophy is directed by this aim. This is that 'fullest possible assimilation to God' which he commends to his hearers in the *Theaetetus*, one of the later dialogues which wins most admiration from the present-day philosopher for its critical acumen. Recognition of this aim brings home the point which some of Plato's modern critics are apt to ignore, that for him any study of the nature of knowledge must take account of its objects at the same time.

The purpose of the *Republic* is not so much to give the blueprint for a political organization as to show how the life of an individual and of a community can reproduce, so far as mortal creations may, the harmony of the divine universe, because that is the way to a full and happy life. For the reasons given, only those can attain it who are capable of the arduous intellectual discipline of the philosopher, but if society itself is harmoniously constructed, even those of the most limited capacity will live the best life possible for them. The explicit aim of the whole work is the discovery of justice or goodness in the individual, and to this the sketch of a social

[11] *Republic* 500 c, *Timaeus* 90 c - d.

order is subordinate. The community first suggested by Socrates is designed for an extremely simple and frugal life, and it is only when Glaucon protests that its citizens will live like pigs that Socrates gives in and agrees to describe what he calls a city suffering from inflammation. His own, he says, is the true and healthy community, but it may be no bad thing to look at the other, for it will let them see both justice and injustice in contrast. It is this second city, explicitly denied the title of true and healthy, that occupies the main part of the discussion and is usually known as Plato's ideal state. It is to make the best of this, and of faulty human nature as it is, that Plato introduces his threefold division of society with its philosopher-kings and army of toughened warriors living off the labor of the others.

The microcosm-macrocosm analogy has had a long history; that is, the idea that each man in himself, and every social and political order, reproduces, or ought ideally to reproduce, the harmonious order of the universe. It pervaded the Middle Ages, was an accepted part of the Renaissance world-view, and reappears to-day in sometimes surprising places. The last words of a small book by Bertrand Russell on *The Problems of Philosophy*, published in 1912, are that philosophy is to be studied 'above all because, through the greatness of the universe which philosophy contemplates, the mind also is rendered great, and becomes capable of that union with the universe which constitutes its highest good'.

In briefly surveying the contributions of earlier thinkers to Plato's philosophy, I have mentioned the early monists, Heraclitus and Parmenides, but have concentrated on Socrates and the Pythagoreans. His relations with the Pythagoreans are disputed. His ancient enemies accused him of direct plagiarism, putting about a story that he had bought three books by the Pythagorean Philolaus and published their contents as his own. Recent criticism has gone in the opposite direction. It has tended to play down or deny the Pythagorean contribution, sometimes, I think, out of a misguided partisanship, a feeling that Plato's originality is being disparaged. I believe that it provides an essential clue. It shows us on what was based the essential unity of his thought, which we mistakenly divide into logical, metaphysical, scientific or political compartments. Awareness of this unity can only heighten our appreciation of the genius which achieved it.

260 TWENTIETH CENTURY APPROACHES TO PLATO

The aim of the historian is to understand Plato in the context of his own time and problems. Those who approach him with problems of their own—philosophical, scientific or political—are each true to something in Plato, but as they pursue their diverse aims his own may be neglected or obscured. His primary purpose was not logical, scientific or political. It was rather the provision of a metaphysical basis for the moral life, adequate to counteract both the actual decline of morals in his day and the prevailingly sceptical and relativist attitude to knowledge which gave it, as he thought, a spurious intellectual respectability. His theory of knowledge provided, in the transcendent Forms, the objective standards which he required. His cosmology, reaching its climax in the *Timaeus* and the tenth book of the *Laws*, is constructed under the guiding idea of demonstrating that mind is prior to body. This meant, for him, that the antithesis between nature and law, which the Sophists insisted on, was a false one. Nature, being the work of mind, is governed by law. It followed that the Sophists' slogan, 'follow nature', really implied something very different from what they intended. In all this Plato saw himself as only carrying to completion the unfinished work of Socrates.

On the question of attaining a full understanding of his thought, he has said the last word himself. 'There is not', he wrote in the Seventh Letter, 'nor could there ever be a treatise of mine concerning the things I care about most deeply; for this is nothing that can be set down like other subjects of instruction. Rather it is something that from much conversation about the matter itself, and from a life lived together, suddenly, like a light kindled from a leaping flame, is born in the soul and thenceforth feeds on itself.'

None of us can catch our swan. The most we can hope for is to pick up a few of the feathers he has dropped. Perhaps even that may be enough to make us agree with the man who said: 'Wherever I go in my mind, I always meet Plato—on his way back.'

Ammianus Marcellinus, Soldier-Historian of the Late Roman Empire

BY HENRY T. ROWELL

Delivered February 17 and 18, 1964

FOREWORD

Near the beginning of my teaching career, I had the great privilege of becoming acquainted personally with Professor and Mrs. William Tunstall Semple. Although circumstances did not permit me ever to know them as well as I should have liked to, I was always moved, wherever we met, by the warmth of their friendliness and their unfeigned interest in a young scholar who was then only entering into a field which they had already long cultivated with generosity and wisdom. All students of Greco-Roman antiquity are deeply indebted to the Semples and their countless benefactions are too well known to need enumeration here. But I should feel myself ungrateful if I did not make clear that to the great honor of being invited to deliver these lectures, which I deeply appreciate, there is joined a happy and admiring memory of Louise Taft Semple, in whose honor they were established. I hope that the pages which follow may not be entirely unworthy of her.

I wish to thank all members of the Classics Department of the University of Cincinnati and their wives for their truly Salian hospitality. No reception could have been more cordial or more enjoyed. I also wish to express my gratitude to the Editorial Committee for allowing me to rewrite and expand these lectures so that what was originally designed for oral delivery within fixed periods of time might, where the need occurred, be recast in a form more suitable for reading.

HENRY T. ROWELL

AMMIANUS MARCELLINUS,
SOLDIER-HISTORIAN
OF THE LATE ROMAN EMPIRE

I: THE BACKGROUND

THE Roman Historian Ammianus Marcellinus has had a rather unusual literary afterlife. Although the *editio princeps* of his *History* was published in Rome as early as 1474,[1] it was not until the first half of the seventeenth century that the text began to be equipped with running commentaries. The first of these was produced by the Hamburg scholar Friedrich Lindenbrog (Lindenbrogius) in 1609.[2] In the Preface to the text of his edition, he makes three observations, the gist of which has been repeated time and again until today.[3] They concern Ammianus' value as a historian, his lack of popularity and his style.

After some generalities on the pleasure and usefulness of history, Lindenbrog urges the reader to choose writers who can form the mind with precepts of wisdom and lessons drawn from important events, in preference to those who delight the ear, but are empty of substance. He places Ammianus among the former, as a serious

---

[1] Edited by Angelus Sabinus and printed by Sachsel and Golsch.

[2] *Observationes in Ammianum Marcellinum et in eundem Collectanea Variarum Lectionum* (Hamburgi apud Hludovicum Frobenium, MDCIX). This commentary was published separately as a supplement to the text: *Ammiani Marcellini Rerum Gestarum qui de XXXI supersunt libri XVIII. Ad fidem MS et veterum Codd. recensiti et Observationibus illustrati. Ex Bibliotheca Fr. Lindenbrogi* (Hamburgi, Ex Bibliopolio Frobeniano, MDCIX).

[3] The preface and notes of Lindenbrog's edition together with those of the editions of the brothers de Valois and Gronovius are reprinted in *Ammiani Marcellini quae supersunt. Cum notis Frid. Lindenbrogii, Henr. et Hadr. Valesiorum et Iac. Gronovii quibus Thom. Reinesii quasdam et suas adiecit Io. Augustin. Wagner. Editionem absolvit Car. Gottlob Aug. Erfurdt* (Lipsiae, MDCCCVIII, in libraria Weidmannia). References to the prefaces of these older editions, which are now difficult to find, are made to Volume I of this edition, cited henceforth as Wagner-Erfurdt. Lindenbrog's Preface here appears on pp. cxxiii-cxxv.

author of discriminating talent (*ingenii elegantis*) and is therefore surprised and indignant that he is not more widely read. Among Ammianus' virtues as a historian, Lindenbrog praises his breadth, immediate and intimate knowledge of his own times, careful observation, good judgment and many-sided learning—the last, not without criticism of its often untimely use. As to Ammianus' style, Lindenbrog considers it hard and rough (*durus et asper*), if compared with the Augustan Age, and accounts for its military flavor by Ammianus' Greek origin and career in the Roman army; yet, as roses and lilies sometimes grow in a briar patch, so in Ammianus do certain blossoms of urbane elegance shine forth, which could vie with the Latinity of Livy; where Ammianus is obscure, we should attribute the obscurity to our own ignorance; and were he to come to life again, he would not recognize himself, so woefully has he been interpolated in the course of time. So Lindenbrog on Ammianus, some three hundred and fifty years ago.

Praise for Ammianus' qualities as a historian is now a commonplace. It has been bestowed upon him most lavishly by those who have been most familiar with his entire work: his commentators and the modern historians who have depended on him as a primary source. Henri de Valois (Henricus Valesius), whose great commentary followed that of Lindenbrog in 1636, has this to say: "And Marcellinus, indeed, not only in the contents of his work but also in selection and arrangement, is second to none in judgment and reliability. In fact, in his accounts of battles and sieges he surpasses many by far."[4] Edward Gibbon, in reaching a point where Ammianus could no longer serve him as a source, takes leave of him, "not without the most sincere regret," calling him "an accurate and faithful guide, who has composed the history of his own times, without indulging the prejudices and passions which usually affect the mind of a contemporary."[5] Theodor Mommsen, after demonstrating the thinness of Ammianus' geographical digressions and interpreting them as an attempt to parade an encyclopaedic learning which he did not possess, cannot help concluding his discussion with these words: "an honorable, frank and high thinking man and a keen, yet affectionate, judge of the human

---

[4] Wagner-Erfurdt, pp. lxxviii-lxxix.
[5] *The Decline and Fall of the Roman Empire*, III, p. 122, Bury; I, p. 947, The Modern Library.

heart, better qualified to see through baseness at court than to go deeply into the individuality of foreign peoples."[6] Curt Wachsmuth emphasizes Ammianus' reliability as a source, his professional knowledge of military affairs, his impartiality and strong sense of justice, which caused him to rebuke every baseness fearlessly, and his tolerance toward the Christians. He calls him "a born historian," whose depictions of character are not inferior to those of Tacitus in their profound knowledge of mankind.[7] From T. R. Glover's chapter on Ammianus we can quote the following sentence: "One cannot read him through without the growing conviction of his absolute truthfulness and a growing admiration of his power, and the two together present the Roman Empire to the mind exactly as it was."[8] Finally, in one of the few recent books on Ammianus, E. A. Thompson expresses the opinion that his work as a historical document is quite as valuable as those of Sallust, Livy and Tacitus.[9]

This list of encomia could easily be prolonged, but to do so, would be an exercise in diminishing returns; for with normal differences in emphasis, other critics have praised, almost without exception, the same historical virtues in Ammianus which we have already found noted. To summarize the most important briefly, they are impartiality, devotion to truth and justice, reliability in the account of historical events, tolerance in religious matters and moral candor. Ernst Stein had them in mind, when he described Ammianus as "the greatest literary genius that, in my opinion, the world has seen between Tacitus and Dante."[10]

Coming now to the matter of neglect, Thompson doubts "if it would be an exaggeration to say that for every reader of his (Ammianus') work nowadays there are a thousand readers of Sallust, Livy or Tacitus."[11] The assumed figures are startling; but they are a vigorous expression, at least, of their author's conviction that Ammianus is being sadly neglected at the present time. Linden-

[6] *Hermes*, XVI (1881), pp. 635-636.
[7] *Einleitung in das studium der alten Geschichte* (Leipzig, 1895), p. 684; cf. p. 677.
[8] *Life and Letters in the Fourth Century* (Cambridge, 1901), pp. 45-46.
[9] *The Historical Work of Ammianus Marcellinus* (Cambridge, 1947), p. xi.
[10] *Geschichte des spätrömischen Reiches*, I (Wien, 1928), p. 33; French edition, *Histoire du Bas-Empire*, I (Bruxelles, 1959), p. 215.
[11] *Op. cit.*, p. xi.

brog, as we have seen, also complained that Ammianus was not more widely read. He was undoubtedly aware of what had already been done by his own time to diffuse and elucidate the other Roman historians; for example, that, whereas about eleven editions of Ammianus had been printed before 1609, of which some were incomplete and others did no more than reproduce the text of an earlier edition, there existed some twenty-five editions of the *Opera Omnia* of Tacitus, to say nothing of separate editions of particular works. As to commentaries, he would have known that only two years before he gave the public its first complete commentary on Ammianus, Iustus Lipsius' commentary on Tacitus had appeared in its seventh edition (first edition, 1576). We can follow this direction profitably for a moment in attempting to obtain a clearer view of Ammianus' lack of popularity. For interest, both popular and scholarly, is the fundamental cause of the production of the commentaries, books and articles which are written to make a writer and his work more intelligible and a quantitative and qualitative ratio exists between the two.

Let us begin, then, with the commentaries. We have already mentioned those of Lindenbrog (1609) and Henri de Valois (1636). The latter was reissued by Henri's brother Adrien (Hadrianus) in 1681. To the contents of Henri's edition, Adrien added the notes of Lindenbrog, the first detailed biography of Ammianus by Claude Chifflet, first published in 1618,[12] and additional notes which Henri had compiled between the publication of his work in 1636 and his death in 1676. Adrien also contributed some material of his own: a new preface[13] and index, an essay *De Hebdomo* and occasional observations on textual matters.

This was the first Variorum edition of Ammianus and on it we must still largely depend for a comprehensive commentary on all the extant books of the *History*. Gronovius' edition of 1693 adds very little to it except a cantankerous preface.[14] The only extensive explanatory notes on the whole work, since those of Henri de Valois, were produced by Johann Wagner and published in his Variorum edition of 1808 as additions to those of Lindenbrog and

---

[12] As the second part of his *De numismate antiquo liber posthumus* (Lovanii, typis C. Coenesteynii). It is reprinted in Wagner-Erfurdt, pp. lxxxv-cxiv.

[13] *Ibid.*, pp. xxxv-lxxii.   [14] *Ibid.*, pp. i-xxxiv.

Henri.[15] They do not supplant them. Since Wagner, only one scholar has attempted a thorough explanation of the text, founded on the scholarly knowledge of our own times. He is Peter de Jonge who published excellent commentaries on Books XIV and XV between 1935 and 1953.[16] Books XVI through XXXI still await a comparable treatment.

When we turn to general works on Ammianus, we are somewhat better off, although our situation could hardly be described as satisfactory. The first and only full length book which undertakes to explore Ammianus' life and work in every particular was published in 1889 by the Abbé Jean Gimazane.[17] In its opening pages, the author expresses his opinion of Ammianus' position as a writer: "un auteur de deuxième ou même de troisième ordre." Nevertheless, this does not prevent him from devoting 432 pages to his subject. As we read on, it becomes increasingly clear that Gimazane's classification of Ammianus as an author is strongly influenced by his low opinion of Ammianus' style. This is not the moment to discuss the validity of Buffon's famous aphorism on style and man. Here it may be noted simply that Gimazane is less willing than the large majority of his fellow critics to consider Ammianus' style and virtues as a historian separately.

Yet, Gimazane's is still the best general book that we have on Ammianus. It contains the most complete presentation of the evidence and the most detailed discussion of the problems which it raises. If a number of his conclusions seem obvious, this is because they have by now become commonplaces which are repeated in all the manuals. It contains insights and speculations which are not found elsewhere. If the good Abbé seems a bit naïve or fanciful upon occasion, not a few of his observations on the dramatic and moral elements of the contents and the structure of the narrative conspicuously hit the mark.

The monographs of Büdinger and Dautremer, which followed

[15] See note 3 above.
[16] *Sprachlicher und historischer Kommentar zu Ammianus Marcellinus*, XIV, 1-7 (1935), 8-11 (1939); *Philological and Historical Commentary on Ammianus Marcellinus*, XV, 1-5 (1948), 6-13 (1953) (J. B. Walters, Groningen).
[17] *Étude sur le quatrième siècle. Ammien Marcellin, Sa vie et son oeuvre* (Toulouse, 1889).

Gimazane's book within a decade,[18] do not add anything particularly
memorable to what was already known. In fact, it was not until
1923 that a valuable new contribution was made to our understanding of Ammianus. In that year, Wilhelm Ensslin published his
monograph *Zur Geschichtschreibung und Weltanschauung des
Ammianus Marcellinus*.[19] The most original part of this work is
devoted to Ammianus' mental and emotional attitude to the principal institutions and social factors of his own period. In the *History*, the evidence of personal judgment and feeling is abundant
and Ensslin sifts it thoroughly. We learn what Ammianus thought
and felt about the imperial power, the senate and the Germaniza-
tion of Empire and army, what he considered an ideal education
and a proper moral code and where he stood in the midst of the
multitudinous facets of paganism and Christianity which composed
the religious atmosphere of the times. The organization of the
material by rubrics is convenient. But the failure at the end to pull
the parts together into a whole which would give us a total image
of Ammianus' character and mentality is disappointing.

Finally, we must mention E. A. Thompson's *The Historical
Work of Ammianus Marcellinus*, published in 1947.[20] It is an uneven book which is more a series of separate articles—some were
previously published in learned journals—than an integrated whole.
There are chapters on specific matters, such as Ammianus' treatment
of the Caesar Gallus and the military commander Ursicinus, and
others on wider subjects, such as the sources of the *History* as a
whole or the historical circumstances which determined the time of
publication of the later books. Thompson reaches many controversial conclusions; but even where another scholar will disagree,
he will find the treatment stimulating. To general readers who are
at home in the English language alone, it is a boon to have, at last,
not only a competent discussion in English, but one which is also
up-to-date. But if they are approaching Ammianus for the first time,
they would do well to read the last chapter, "Ammianus as an
Historian," directly after the first, "Biography." A book on Am-

[18] M. Büdinger, "Ammianus Marcellinus und die Eigenart seines Geschichts-
werkes," *Denkschr. Ak. Wien*, XLIV, 5 (1896); L. Dautremer, *Ammien Marcellin.
Étude d'histoire litteraire* (Lille, 1899).
[19] *Klio, Beiheft* XVI (1923), Heft III.
[20] See note 9 above.

mianus of the breadth and learning of Syme's *Tacitus* is still to be
written.

In 1889 when Gimazane published his book on Ammianus, he
could cite seventeen articles or dissertations regarding his work. So
far as this bibliography can be verified, it seems to be a reasonably
complete record of the state of specialized Ammianean studies toward the end of the last century. Their number seems unbelievably
small when it is compared with the number of items of the same
kind which a complete or nearly complete bibliography of Livy or
Tacitus would have contained at that time. Since then, there has
been a considerable increase in the yearly production of articles on
Ammianus; but their numerical ratio to those on the earlier great
Roman historians has not changed appreciably.

Thompson attributes this neglect of Ammianus to the fact that
he is stylistically inferior to his Roman predecessors and to the deplorable state of the manuscript tradition.[21] We have seen what
Lindenbrog thought of his style. Henri de Valois also felt that it
had a military character.[22] But the implied criticism of Chifflet is
much more typical of an age which had very firm ideas about good
Latin. Speaking of Ammianus' familiarity with Cicero, he exclaims,
"if only he had imitated his style!"[23] Later he makes his criticism
more specific: Ammianus comes out poorly, when compared to Livy
and Tacitus; his Latin is so frequently forced and uneasy that anyone could guess that it was not his native language, even if he had
not told us so himself; the narrative sometimes flows and sometimes falls into a jolting style which is rough and involved; the
meaning is often obscure; the reader is distracted by transpositions,
broken thoughts and confused exposition.[24] In other words, Chifflet
makes it clear that Ammianus is a most "unclassical" author, who
could not be read, even less imitated, for the virtues of his style.

Nor have later critics been more indulgent. His style is disparaged as excessively rhetorical, unbearably bombastic, tortured,
harsh, incorrect and even barbarous.[25] The same adjectives appear

[21] *Op. cit.*, p. xi.   [22] Wagner-Erfurdt, p. lxxix.
[23] *Ibid.*, p. lxxxvii.   [24] *Ibid.*, pp. cvi f.
[25] The estimates of Norden and von Gutschmid, whom he cites, are typical; *Die
Antike Kunstprosa* II[4] (Berlin, 1923), pp. 646 ff. Extensive reading has produced
only one paragraph in praise of Ammianus' style. It is Joseph Vogt's "Ammianus
Marcellinus als erzählender Geschichtsschreiber der Spätzeit," *Abh. Ak. Mainz*,
1963, 8, p. 804. The present writer agrees completely with Vogt's views.

repeatedly, for a vigorous attack on Ammianus' style has become as much a part of the evaluation of his work as abundant praise for his virtues as a historian. One sometimes wonders how so much good could be expressed so badly.

It hardly need be observed that the style of Ammianus did not commend itself to generations in which the *ars* of an ancient writer was at least as important as his *res* and to the functions of instructing and delighting, which he was supposed to perform, that of serving as a stylistic *exemplum* was added. Least of all did Ammianus possess those exemplary qualities which gain an ancient writer a place in a classical curriculum at any level of instruction. How he wrote, undoubtedly explains a great deal of the neglect which he suffered in the past.

The reverse of the medal is that the peculiarities of Ammianus' style have elicited a considerable number of studies of it. Most of these are concerned with illustrating a specific point of usage, often of small intrinsic importance, through the industrious collection and classification of pertinent instances. A notable exception is the work of H. Hagendahl on Ammianus' *color poeticus, variatio* and *abundantia*.[26] It provides foundation stones for the kind of complete and satisfactory stylistic evaluation which we can hope to obtain, when quite a bit more has been learned about the way in which the various writers of the fourth century came to terms, both psychologically and artistically, with a literary heritage in which they could easily lose their distinctive or personal traits. In the meantime, a modest step forward might be taken in ceasing to accept the well-worn view that the peculiarities of Ammianus' Latin are due to his upbringing in a Greek-speaking part of the Empire.[27]

In connection with the existing literary tradition, it can be mentioned here that Ammianus' "imitations" of earlier authors have been diligently collected. Investigation, however, has not gone beyond this first elementary stage. Why Ammianus repeats or reflects the words of another author at a specific place in his text raises questions regarding his immediate intention, the way in which it is implemented, the effect of the reminiscence on the reader who is

---

[26] *Studia Ammianea* (diss. Uppsala, 1921=*Uppsala Universitets Årsskrift*, 1921); *Eranos* XXII (1924), pp. 161 ff.

[27] Cf. G. B. A. Fletcher, *J.R.S.* XXXIX (1949), p. 203.

familiar with the original context, its purely stylistic function, etc. All these questions remain unanswered. Even less do we know about any principles or patterns underlying Ammianus' imitative procedure.

This brings us to one of the greatest failures of Ammianean scholarship: the failure to study and explain the *History* as a great work of literature. For regardless of its Latinity, it is a wonderfully effective piece of writing, the greater part of which by far, moves us deeply, engrosses our interest and makes us feel vividly that we are participating in the vast drama which Ammianus unfolds before our eyes. How does he achieve this effect? What are the structural qualities of the parts and the whole? What are the devices, the patterns, the silences which are peculiarly Ammianus' own and which we should recognize as parts of his literary seal? How does he compare as a narrator of events to his great predecessors? What is the color, not of his style, but of his entire work? In these matters, where style and contents, literary virtues and historical excellence are intertwined and work together in determining the complexion of the whole, the preliminary work has hardly been begun.

To turn now to the manuscript tradition, it does not seem that its corrupt state has contributed appreciably to the neglect of Ammianus. Since the second printed edition of 1517, a readable text has always been available.[28] We can safely assume that the general reader has been principally interested, at any period, in a Latin text which made sense and did not bother to ask himself whether a certain sentence, phrase or word was contained in a manuscript, and, if so, which one, or had its origin in the ingenious mind of some editor as a restoration or emendation. The beautifully printed Bipontine edition of 1786, for example, in which there is not the slightest indication that the smoothly flowing text does not reproduce the words of Ammianus transmitted in their original purity,

[28] Sabinus, the first editor, who used a manuscript which terminated at the end of Book XXVI, probably the *Reginensis* (*Vat. Reg. Lat.* 1994), indicated the lacunae and other flaws. Petrus Castellus, the editor of the second edition, Bologna 1517, pretended to have filled out, corrected and improved the text with the help of better manuscripts. In fact, he produced a readable edition by introducing his own restorations and readings into the text of Sabinus. On these early editions, see C. U. Clark, *The Text Tradition of Ammianus Marcellinus* (diss. Yale, published by the author, New Haven, 1904), pp. 8 ff.

must have delighted any layman. As time progressed, editors and scholars discovered and put to use new manuscripts in an effort to produce a text which would be closer to the more reliable representatives of the tradition. In Gardthausen's Teubner edition of 1874-75, scholars could believe that they had an edition, at last, which met the criteria of modern textual criticism. A year later, Heinrich Nissen published the Marburg fragments and with them a new set of textual problems were born.[29] Charles Upson Clark not only did a great deal to solve them,[30] but also made good use of the newly acquired information in producing his masterly edition.[31] Based on a thorough examination of the manuscripts and an exhaustive knowledge of the work of previous editors, it permits the reader through two critical apparatuses to see clearly where he stands vis-à-vis the countless difficulties which bedevil his reading and what has already been done to overcome them. It is not likely that this text will be superseded for a long time. All the more, then, one could wish that Clark had been less uncompromising in letting the accentual clausulae determine his punctuation. There are too many places where this procedure tortures the meaning unnecessarily.

An unhappy result of the distressing condition of the manuscript tradition and the relatively late interest in Ammianus' text is the effect which they have had on those afflicted with the *cacoethes emendandi*. Ranging far beyond their legitimate preserve of the *cruces*, *loci desperati* and *lectiones corruptae*, they have treated any word or phrase which they considered subject to improvement as fair game. The golden period of the gratuitous emendation has found its afterglow in the copious "Notes on Ammianus," which constitute a disproportionate part of Ammianean studies.

There is another important reason for Ammianus' neglect, which must be mentioned, before we turn to our main discussion. Interest in the late Empire has lagged far behind that in other periods of ancient history among the ancient historians. The first great scien-

[29] *Ammiani Marcellini fragmenta Marburgensia* (Berlin, 1876).

[30] *Text Tradition*, pp. 15 ff. On the relation between the *Fuldensis* (V) and *Hersfeldensis* (M), see, most recently, R. P. Robinson, "Philological Studies in Honor of Walter Miller," *The University of Missouri Studies*, XI (1936), 3, pp. 118 ff.

[31] Vol. I (Berlin, 1910); Vol. II (Berlin, 1915); both volumes were reprinted in 1963.

tific history of the late Empire by Otto Seeck began to be published in 1897,[32] eighty-six and forty-three years, respectively, after the appearance of the first volumes of the *Roman Histories* of Niebuhr and Mommsen. It is instructive to compare the notes in Seeck's "Anhänge" to his six volumes of text (1897-1921) with those contained in the volume of original and supplementary notes to the 1959 French edition of Stein's *History*, which covers the same period.[33] The comparison makes clear how great a pioneer Seeck was, who invaded a vast field in which he largely had to make his own preliminary studies, and how widely studies devoted to all aspects of the late Empire have expanded during the last three decades. It was to be expected that Ammianus, as the principal source of an important part of the period, would share in the vicissitudes of interest through which it passed.

So much, then, for the scholarly background. It should have shown that, if we go adventuring in these lectures off the well-beaten classical track, we have good reason to do so. The fact that Ammianus is not well known will be our excuse for treating some matters which could be taken for granted in a discussion of a Livy or a Tacitus. The rest of this first chapter will be devoted to presenting Ammianus' career and the scope and genesis of his work. In the second, we shall try to reveal particularly how the soldier in him colored his view of the world in which he lived and the way in which he recorded it for posterity.

———

Let us begin with the *History* itself. It ends with the following words (XXXI, 16, 9):

These events from the principate of the emperor Nerva to the death of Valens, I, a former soldier and a Greek, have set forth to the measure of my ability, without ever (I believe) consciously venturing to debase through silence or through falsehood a work whose aim was the truth. The rest may be written by abler men, who are in the prime of life and learning. But if they chose to undertake such a task, I advise them to forge their tongues to the loftier style (Rolfe).[34]

---

[32] *Geschichte des Untergangs der antiken Welt*, I (Berlin, 1897).

[33] Ernest Stein, *Histoire du Bas-Empire*, édition française par Jean-Remy Palanque, I, texte, II, notes et cartes (Bruxelles, 1959).

[34] (Rolfe), after a passage of translation, indicates that it was taken from the

The eighteen books which have come down to us in their entirety carry the numbers XIV through XXXI in our manuscripts. It is universally assumed today that they are the last books of the single history, extending from the accession of Nerva in 96 A.D. to the death of Valens in 378, which Ammianus appears to mention in the passage which we have just quoted. If this assumption is correct, we have a curiously unbalanced work. Book XIV, the first extant book, begins with the events of the winter of 353-354 and Book XXXI, which is clearly the last, ends with the aftermath of the Roman defeat at Adrianople in 378. Consequently, the eighteen books which we possess cover about twenty-five years, whereas the thirteen books which have been lost must have contained the history of more than two centuries and a half.

Accepting this hypothetical distribution of the contents, scholars have speculated about the place where the character of the narrative changed from a very succinct account to the kind of detailed exposition which we find in the surviving books. Points of time which are historically appropriate as initiating or ending eras have come readily to mind: the ascent of Diocletian and the establishment of the Tetrarchy or the beginning of the reign of Constantine or its end. It has seemed reasonable to some to believe that our extant books begin where they do, because the detailed narrative began with Book XIV and this narrative alone was found worth preserving, so that the more epitomizing parts, which preceded it, was discarded.

But, Book XIV gives no indication of being the beginning of a *maius opus*. It contains no special introduction, such as the one to Book XXVI in which Ammianus justifies the continuation of his *History* after the death of Jovian into more recent times. Rather, the mention in the first sentence of Book XIV of the end of the war against Magnentius ties it closely to the preceding book in which the war itself must have been described. Nor is there any break by reigns. Gallus, with whom Book XIV is largely concerned, had been Caesar for over a year and a half at the time the book begins and the reign of Constantius still had some eight years to run. If

---

translation of Ammianus by John C. Rolfe in *The Loeb Classical Library* (Vols. I and II, 1956; III, 1952).

there were a change from succinct to detailed narrative, it should have occurred between two books, both earlier than Book XIV.

But do we need to postulate a work of such disparate parts? When Ammianus speaks of "these events (*haec*), from the principate of Nerva to the death of Valens," it is quite natural to assume that they were all contained in the work of which we have the epilogue at the end of Book XXXI. But his words do not exclude the hypothesis that he wrote two works, one of which was the continuation of the other. This was just what Tacitus did, in reverse chronological order, with the *Histories* and the *Annals*. We do not know whether Tacitus himself or someone after him put the two works together in the edition of thirty books which is attested by the subscriptions in the second Medicean and Saint Jerome. Jerome states simply that Tacitus wrote the lives of the Caesars after Augustus to the death of Domitian in thirty volumes.[35] The second Medicean numbers the last books of the *Annals* and the first books of the *Histories* consecutively, so that our present Book I of the *Histories* is *Liber* XVII of the manuscript.[36] Although Jerome cites Tacitus only once in the passage with which we are concerned, in view of his encyclopaedic knowledge of Roman literature,[37] it is difficult to believe that he was not aware that the "Lives of the Caesars" in thirty volumes was a combination of two different works. Tertullian had an edition of the *Histories* in which the books had their own numbers, that is, the numbers which we give them today.[38] It is also likely, as Revilo P. Oliver has shown, that the thirty-book edition to which Jerome refers, had a double numbering; e.g., *Liber* XVIII, *Historiarum* II.[39] Nevertheless, Jerome speaks as if the thirty-book edition were a single work—and, indeed, it did cover an unbroken period of time. Could not Ammianus, then, have spoken of his account of the events from the accession of Nerva to the death of Valens, recorded in two dif-

[35] *Comm. ad Zach.*, III, 14=Migne, *P.L.XXV*, col. 1522.
[36] Syme reargues the case for a division into eighteen books of *Annals* and twelve books of *Histories; Tacitus*, pp. 211 ff.; Appendix 35, pp. 686 f. But see Revilo P. Oliver, *T.A.P.A.*, LXXXII (1951), pp. 232 ff., esp. 258 ff., who does justice to the evidence of St. Jerome and the second Medicean.
[37] See H. Hagendahl, "Latin Fathers and the Classics," *Studia Graeca et Latina Gothoburgensia*, VII (1958), pp. 90 ff.
[38] *Apol.* XVI, 2; *Ad nat.*, I, 11, 3.
[39] *Op. cit.*, p. 260.

ferent works, of which one was a continuation of the other, as if it were a single piece of narrative?

That Ammianus might have done so is no proof, of course, that he did. If we had no further evidence, we should have to let the matter drop here as a piece of inconclusive speculation. But there is further evidence and it was collected and correctly analyzed over eighty years ago by Hugo Michael.[40] It is usually said that his views have long since been refuted by Ludwig Jeep.[41] But in fact, Jeep did not even mention the crucial point.

With the beginning of Book XV, Ammianus looks back on the preceding part of his work and forward to what is yet to be written. These are his words in this connection (XV, 1, 1):

> So far as I could investigate the truth, I have, after putting the various events in clear order, related what I myself was allowed to witness in the course of my life, or to learn by meticulous questioning of those directly concerned. The rest, which the text to follow will disclose, we shall set forth to the best of our ability with still greater accuracy, feeling no fear of critics of the prolixity of our work, as they consider it; for conciseness is to be praised only when it breaks off ill-timed discursiveness, without detracting at all from an understanding of the course of events (Rolfe).

The most important words in the Latin original are those referring to his sources of information for the events of the earlier books: *ea quae videre licuit per aetatem, vel perplexe interrogando versatos in medio scire.* In view of the common construction of *licere* with *per*, in which the noun governed by *per* is the agent which permits or inhibits the action contained in the infinitive following *licere*, it would be better to translate *ea quae videre licuit per aetatem* as "those things which my age permitted me to see." As for *perplexe interrogando*, "meticulous questioning" is an excellent translation. Thus, if we accept this statement at face value— and there is no good reason why we should not do so—the first fourteen books of Ammianus' *History* were based partly on personal experience and partly on the personal experience of others,

---

[40] *Die Verlorenen Bücher des Ammianus Marcellinus* (Breslau, 1880).
[41] *Rh. Mus.*, XLIII (1888), pp. 60 ff.

on whose knowledge Ammianus could draw. We shall shortly discuss how far back these sources of information will allow us to go. Here it will be sufficient to point out that participators whom Ammianus could have questioned could hardly have seen and remembered anything earlier than the accession of Diocletian and, consequently, that Ammianus would have had to depend on written records for the period from 96 to 284. But he does not mention written sources in the passage which we are scrutinizing and the reasonable conclusion is that he did not need them in writing the first fourteen books. Certainly, there is nothing in the extant fourteenth book, except the chapter on the eastern provinces (8)—Ammianus admittedly used literary sources in composing his geographical digressions—that could not have been learned from personal experience or the experience of others.

In the second place, there are many references in the extant books to events which took place not long before the winter of 353-354, where Book XIV begins. The most important of these for our present purpose is the mention of the campaign of Constans in Britain in 343 (XX, 1, 1). In connection with it, Ammianus described the tides of the ocean and the site of Britain to the best of his ability (*pro captu virium*; XXVII, 8, 4). If we may judge from the geographical digressions in the extant books, Ammianus' description of Britain was contained in a chapter which far exceeded the limits of the kind of epitomizing narrative which is usually assumed for the earlier books. On this occasion, Ammianus also said something about the secret agents in Britain called the *arcani* (XXVIII, 3, 8), which also points to a detailed narrative.

Now, Ammianus must have observed some uniformity in the treatment of the major parts of his work. If he treated Constans' British campaign in detail then we can assume that he treated the years between 343 and 353-354 in the same way. This assumption is confirmed by certain details which Ammianus recalls having given in describing the siege of Singara in 344 (XVIII, 9, 3) and the death of Constans in 350 (XV, 5, 16). On the other hand, we can assume just as reasonably that Ammianus had already begun his detailed narrative before he reached Constans' British campaign and that he began it at a point of time clearly defined by a change in historical circumstances.

Let us return now to the beginning of Book XV. The passage regarding the books to come reads as follows in the original: *residua quae secuturus aperiet textus, pro virium captu limatius absolvemus nihil obtrectatores longi (ut putant) operis formidantes.* Rolfe translates *limatius* as "with still greater accuracy." Perhaps, in view of the use of the same word in XV, 13, 2, "in a more painstaking fashion" might have retained more of the original flavor. But more important is the implication that the books to come will contain more details and constitute a longer work.

Now it is perfectly clear from the beginning of Book XXVI that Books XXVI through XXXI were written as a separate section of the *History*. Ammianus was fully aware of the dangers involved in discussing persons and events that became closer progressively to the time of composition. He ought, he says, to have drawn back from things more widely known in order to avoid the dangers involved in the truth and the strictures of critics who would deplore the omission of trivialities with which they happened to be familiar; nevertheless, with scorn for common ignorance, he will continue his narrative.

These last six books do not seem to have been part of the original plan of composition at the time when the preface of Book XV was written. Ammianus was almost certainly thinking of the future books in terms of events connected with his hero Julian, of which he knew the details through personal participation, for example, the Persian campaign, or through reliable report. Of these things he could write *limatius*. With the advent of Valentinian and Valens in 364 to 378, the narrative becomes more succinct than ever before, each of the six books covering about two and a half years on an average. Thus we can conclude that when Ammianus wrote the preface to Book XV, he intended to extend his *History* to the death of Jovian early in 364, whose reign had written the epilogue to Julian's Persian campaign.

The period from the beginning of 355 to February, 364, or a little more than nine full years, is covered in the eleven books, XV through XXV. Thus, on an average, each book covers about four-fifths of a year. Book XIV, however, begins in the fall of 353, before the troops are settled in their winter quarters and ends with the assassination of Gallus in November, 354. If we assume that about the same period of time, a year or a little more than a year, was assigned to the first thirteen books, then we are brought back to the vicinity of 337, when Constantine died and a new era began with the accession of his sons.

Finally, we may observe here that Ammianus in his geographical digressions repeats only information that is connected with events before 337. For example, he will not describe Mesopotamia or Britain again because he has already described them in connection with the Persian wars (of Constantius) and the campaign of Constans respectively (XIV, 7, 21; XXVII, 8, 4). Yet, he will describe a country, and in detail too, like Egypt, which he has already described at length (*late*) under the reigns of Hadrian and Septimius Severus (XXII, 15, 1). It appears that he was avoiding undue repetition within the *History* of thirty-one books, but was willing to elaborate themes already treated in a different work.

It has been impossible to do more in this general representation than to touch upon the high points of the evidence. For the moment, let the writer say that he has not only been thoroughly convinced by Michael's arguments of the existence of two works, one on the period from the accession of Nerva to the death of Constantine, the other continuing the history of the Empire to the death of Valens, but also reached the same conclusion through independent investigation.

At the beginning of Book XV, Ammianus states that there were certain things in the first fourteen books which his age permitted him to see. This implies that there were other things that he could not see, because he was too young. Accepting the conclusion that the thirty-one book *History* began with the events following the death of Constantine in 337, let us examine how this statement accords with other data concerning his age.

Ammianus refers to himself as an *adulescens* in 357 (XVI, 10, 21). The Latin term is generally as indefinite as our "young man." But there is one place in which we can pin down Ammianus' use of it. He calls Julian an *adulescens primaevus* in 356, when the latter was twenty-four years old (XVI, 1, 5). A little later in the same book, he refers to Julian again as *etiam tum adultum* ("recently arrived at maturity"; XVI, 5, 8). In the passage in which Ammianus refers to himself as an *adulescens*, he states that the older members of Ursicinus' staff were promoted to commands of troops (almost certainly as tribunes), whereas the *adulescentes*, including himself, remained with their general as staff officers. For the moment, it will be safe to assume that Ammianus was in his twenties in 357.

He first appears in the pages of his *History* in 354 at Nisibis in Mesopotamia, where he had already been attached to the staff of Ursicinus, the commander-in-chief of the cavalry in the East (*magister equitum per Orientem*) by the Emperor's orders (XIV, 9, 1). The way in which he speaks of his duty in Nisibis lets us infer that he already had the rank of *protector domesticus*, with which he appears a few years later (XV, 5, 22). The protectors formed at this time a pool of officers in which membership was obtained as a reward for meritorious service in the field or through influence at court.[42] Flavius Abinnaeus is a perfect example of a soldier who slowly worked himself up to the grade of protector. It was awarded to him by the Emperors Constans and Constantius around 341 after thirty-three years of loyal service.[43] The fact that Ammianus became a protector while still an *adulescens* precludes a tour of duty as a common soldier. Being of good birth (XIX, 8, 6) and having enjoyed a liberal education, he must have been directly commissioned from civilian life like other young gentlemen, for example, Herculanus, the son of a commander-in-chief of the cavalry (XIV, 10, 2). Some of the protectors were assigned to duty with the Emperors or Caesars, wherever they might be; others were assigned to the staffs of army commanders or sent out on special missions. A tour of duty as a protector was the normal stepping-stone to the command of troops in the field.

If we pause to ask ourselves who recommended Ammianus for a commission among the protectors, his own general, Ursicinus, comes first to mind. This brings us to Antioch on the Orontes. Although we are not told specifically that Ammianus was born there, he seems to have spent most of his life in Antioch, when he was not on duty elsewhere, before he moved to Rome. Libanius calls

---

[42] *Cod. Theod.*, VI, 24, 3.
[43] H. I. Bell and others, *The Abinnaeus Archive* (Oxford, 1962), no. 1, p. 34; cf. pp. 8 f.

him a citizen of the city in his later years[44] and we can assume that he was a native of it.

Now Ursicinus had held his command in the East since 349 (XVIII, 6, 2). He owned a house in Antioch, where he must have resided when he was not in the field (XVIII, 4, 3). While there, he would have had ample opportunity to become acquainted with the young Ammianus and to have discerned in him the potential qualities of a loyal and effective staff officer and companion. For Ammianus' duties were to be those of today's aide-de-camp, who accompanies his chief everywhere. Then as now, a commanding general's wishes in regard to appointments to his personal staff with appropriate rank must have been honored. The order was issued, of course, by imperial headquarters, for the Emperor alone could appoint protectors.

In the last analysis, Ursicinus' recommendation of Ammianus remains a matter of speculation. But its consideration has brought up a chronological datum of some importance. It is quite unlikely that Ammianus entered the army before Ursicinus assumed his command in the East in 349. Let us say that he did so at the age of nineteen, the earliest age for recruits at that period,[45] and that he did so between 349, when he first could have joined Ursicinus, and 354, when he was already a member of his staff. This gives us a date of birth between 330 and 335. Thus he would have been between twenty-two and twenty-seven years old when he called himself an *adulescens* in 357. This accords well with his statement at the beginning of Book XV that there were matters in the part of the *History* which extended from 337 to 355, which he could not have known because of his youth.

Ammianus traveled widely with his chief: to Milan, Cologne, Gaul and back to the eastern frontier within the years 354-357; then, in 359, to Thrace as far as the river Hebrus, followed by a return to Mesopotamia. In the same year, he was sent out on a mission to Corduene to explore the Persian line of march. After a period of fighting against the Persians, during which he was separated from Ursicinus, he seems to have rejoined him in Melitina in lesser Armenia and followed him to Antioch (XIX, 8, 12).

[44] *Ep.* 983, dated by Seeck, *Die Briefe des Libanius*, p. 463, at the end of 392.
[45] *Cod. Theod.*, VII, 13, 1.

Ursicinus was summoned to the court of Constantius at Constantinople in 360 to take up the post of commander of the infantry (XX, 2, 1). Although Ammianus would normally have accompanied his chief on this journey, he gives no indication that he did so. In view of his mention of his own presence in Ursicinus' other movements, we can conclude that he remained in Antioch. Through no fault of Ursicinus, the Roman stronghold of Amida on the Tigris had fallen to the Persian King, Sapor, in the campaign of 359. How the enemies of the Roman general at court began a chain of events that culminated in the discharge of Ursicinus and his retirement to private life will be explained in the next lecture.

After Ammianus' return to Antioch in 359, he does not appear again in his own *History* until he joins Julian's expedition against the Persians at Cercusium in 363 (XXIII, 5, 7). It is generally assumed that he left the army in 359 and rejoined it in 363 either by volunteering or being reenrolled by Julian's orders. As a member of Ursicinus' staff, Ammianus' career would naturally have suffered some eclipse because of the discharge of his chief. A top commander would not have been inclined to request the assignment to his staff of an officer who had been closely identified with another commander who had incurred the Emperor's wrath and been forcibly retired. Nor would those in charge of assignments at court have been eager to place such an officer in a post where he could have shone brightly.

Perhaps Ammianus saw no future for himself in the army at this point and requested to be honorably discharged. Since he would have had only eleven years of service in 360, it is doubtful whether his request would have been considered under normal circumstances. But the suspicious and testy Constantius may have welcomed the opportunity to get rid of a person who had been so close to Ursicinus and granted his wish.

What seems more likely is that Ammianus remained in the army with his rank of protector after the disbandment of Ursicinus' staff, but was not reassigned or, if reassigned, was given some obscure or trivial form of duty in a military bureau at Antioch. As we have said above, the protectors formed a pool of officers, who were available for various assignments. We know from the career of Abinnaeus that a protector might enjoy a period of non-assignment.[46] Yet three years of sitting around would seem an excessive waste of manpower, even for an army. So, unless Ammianus obtained a discharge, he probably obtained another post.

With regard to Ammianus' military service in Julian's Persian campaign, it does not matter very much whether he was recalled to the service from civilian life—even the highest veteran officers were subject to recall by an Emperor (XXVI, 7, 4)—volunteered to reenlist or, being still in the army, received a new assignment. Of greater moment are his personal relations with the Emperor Julian: when were the seeds sown of his profound admiration for Julian? How long before the Persian campaign had he been able to estimate the character of the man who was destined to become heroic in his eyes?

Ammianus was with Ursicinus in Rheims, when Julian arrived there in 356 (XVI, 2, 8). They remained in Gaul, where Julian was also, until the fall of 357, when Constantius called Ursicinus and his staff back to Sirmium (XVI, 10, 21).

The conjecture that Ammianus may have met Julian, while with Ursicinus in Gaul, and made a favorable and perhaps memorable impression on the young Caesar and future Augustus, is not as far fetched as some would believe. To speak of Ammianus as a subaltern or junior officer who never would have seen the Emperor, to say nothing of a Caesar, except at a distance, hardly does justice to the position of the *protectores* vis-à-vis the Emperor. They possessed the envied privilege of the "adoration of the purple," that is, the right to enter the Emperor's presence and to kiss the hem of the imperial garment. If the rigid, aloof and pompous Constantius Augustus granted this privilege, all the more, can we imagine the emotional, friendly and unceremonious Caesar Julian permitting a senior general to present to him the *protectores* on his staff. Could an intelligent young Greek have failed to interest him, especially one from Antioch, the city of Libanius, whose lectures Julian had had smuggled to him in Nicomedeia? To the young Caesar, a philosophical student recently torn from the intellectual embrace of his beloved Athens to face the wild barbarian in devastated Gaul, nothing could have been sweeter than

[46] *The Abinnaeus Archive*, no. 1, p. 35, l. 10: *data vacatione*, incorrectly translated on p. 11 as "released from service in the field-army."

conversing in his own tongue with a contemporary who shared his
interests and, in his way, was as extraordinary as himself. But, it is
said, Ammianus would not have failed to mention this meeting or
meetings in his *History*. The objection shows a curious lack of comprehension of what Ammianus considered worth recording as a
historical event and of his delicacy—*pudor* would be a better
word—in regard to a relationship which could be only ephemerally
personal.

Ammianus joined Julian's expedition against the Persians in 363
at Cercusium, whether enrolled at his own request or by imperial
order. He participated in the victorious advance to Ctesiphon, and
the terrible, humiliating retreat under Jovian.[47] From his memory
and his notes he later composed an account of the expedition which
belongs among the greatest chapters of military history. After his
return to Antioch, there is no indication that he remained with the
army. Julian may have promised to dismiss him after his expedition and Jovian kept the word of his predecessor.

He very probably remained in his native Antioch from the end
of 363 until he left for Rome, except when traveling abroad. He
visited Methone in the southern part of Messenia in Greece sometime after the tidal wave of July 21, 366 (XXVI, 10, 19) and it
is in this period that we can place his visit to Egypt. He was at
Antioch in the winter of 370-371 and speaks with horror as an eye-
witness of the abominable trials of persons charged with treason
or the practice of magic arts (XXIX, 2, 1-20). Much of his time
in this period of his life must have been spent in doing the voluminous reading which is reflected throughout his historical works.

There can be no doubt that Ammianus spent the last part of his
life in Rome. A letter sent to him by Libanius at the end of 392
speaks of his presence there.[48] Curiously enough, only once in the
extant part of his *History* does Ammianus indicate positively that
he had ever been to Rome. This occurs in a passage concerned with
a certain senator, not named, who had bought his acquittal when
tried on the charge of having had one of his slaves taught magic
arts. The trial was held during the urban prefecture of Apronianus

[47] The most recent and best analysis of Ammianus' account of this campaign is
by L. Dilleman, *Syria*, XXXVIII (1961), pp. 87 ff. It demonstrates Ammianus'
independence of written sources in dealing with events in which he participated.
[48] See note 44 above.

in 364 (XXVI, 3, 4-5). Ammianus severely criticises the same man for making no effort to erase the stain on his character and flaunting his wealth and freedom "even now" (*nunc usque*) in Rome. From the description of his ostentation and the words "even now," it is obvious that Ammianus saw the person in Rome with his own eyes. But how many years after the bought acquittal this took place we are not told.

There are, of course, several passages in which Ammianus speaks of the Roman scene in such a way that we can conclude that he was describing what he had witnessed. The two vivid descriptions of the Roman nobility and common people (XIV, 6, 7-25; XXVIII, 4, 6-34) are certainly the product of direct observation and it has been suggested, not without plausibility, that Ammianus was among the educated foreigners whose expulsion from the city in 383 is described by him with indignation (XIV, 6, 9). The same passage contains a description of other indignities visited upon strangers by members of the Roman nobility (XIV, 6, 12-15) and it would seem that, when he wrote Book XIV, Ammianus was still rankling from the shabby treatment to which he had been subjected on arriving in Rome. Perhaps, he gradually won some degree of social acceptance. At any rate, when he excoriates the vice of the nobility in Book XXVIII (4, 6-27), he dwells less on their insulting attitude toward strangers. It has been assumed that Ammianus became acquainted with some members of the great Roman families and that his personal likes and dislikes are reflected in his estimate of their characters and actions. This would be difficult to prove.

Ammianus, in his last book, speaks of seeing the whitening bones of the men who died in one of the engagements in Thrace between the Romans and the Goths in 378 (XXXI, 6, 16). Consequently, he visited the field of battle fairly soon after the war was over. It terminated with the defeat of the Romans at Adrianople and the death of the Emperor Valens in the same year, the last major event to be described in the *History*. Thus, it has been assumed, and probably rightly, that Ammianus made his visit to Thrace on his way to take up residence in Rome soon after 378. This accords nicely with the hypothesis that he was one of the educated strangers who were expelled from the city in 383 or 384.

Let us say, then, that Ammianus was in Rome for at least thirteen years (379-392) and assume that during this period he devoted his working hours to the creation of his historical works. In a great and highly civilized city such as Antioch, he would have had no difficulty in finding books, on which he could draw for the history of the Empire during the second and third centuries, and in making the acquaintance of older people, who could give him first-hand information on more recent events. In other words, we can assume that he arrived in Rome equipped with copious notes and, possibly, with parts of his text already drafted. In fact there is no reason why the account of events from the accession of Nerva to the death of Constantine which preceded the history of the thirty-one books should not have been brought close to completion in Antioch between the years 364 and 378.

Of course, in speaking of the composition of the account of the earlier period, we are restricted to the realm of possibility by lack of evidence. But some of the books which we have of the thirty-one book *History* contain indications of the time when they were written. Something has been made of the fact that Ammianus describes the Serapaeum at Alexandria in Book XXII (16, 10) as standing undamaged, whereas it was destroyed in 391. The description, however, is part of a lengthy digression on Egypt, comprising mostly things which Ammianus had seen with his own eyes (XXII, 15, 1). He may have drawn it up at the time of his visit, very probably before he came to Rome, and failed to rectify the bit about the Serapaeum when news of its destruction later reached him.

More cogent are Ammianus' references to two men who later, that is, after the period when his *History* terminates, held high magistracies. In Book XXI (10, 6), under the year 363, Ammianus mentions Aurelius Victor, "Prefect of the City, a long time thereafter." Victor was City Prefect in 389. Again in Book XXVI (5, 14), in referring to events of 365, Ammianus mentions Neoterius, "afterwards a consul." His consulship fell in the year 390. Hence, Book XXI was apparently written in or after 389 and Book XXVI in or after 390. But here again, the references to the later magistracies of these men might have been inserted, to do them honor, in the text before its final publication. One thing, nevertheless, is certain: Book XXVI could not have reached the form in which it has been transmitted to us before 390, when Neoterius was consul.

Now Maenchen-Helfen has argued very persuasively that Saint Jerome was familiar with the last book, XXXI, of Ammianus' *History* and drew on it for parts of his description of the Huns in his *Adversus Iovinianum*, which was written in Bethlehem in 393.[49] The same scholar has also shown that the cursory mention of Theodosius the Great in Book XXIX (6, 15) as "afterwards a most distinguished Emperor" (*princeps postea perspectissimus*) fits in well with the political situation soon after 392, when Eugenius had been proclaimed Emperor and no one knew what Theodosius planned to do.[50] Thus it is likely that Ammianus published the last books of his *History* at the end of 392 or the beginning of 393. At that time he would have been between the ages of fifty-seven and sixty-two.

[49] *A. J. P.*, LXXVI (1955), pp. 384 ff.
[50] *Ibid.*, p. 399.

II: THE OLD SOLDIER

As we have already seen, Ammianus in the epilogue to his *History* refers to himself as "a former soldier and a Greek." Since this is the final image of himself which he leaves in the reader's mind, we can assume that he selected its elements carefully, as the characteristics by which he particularly wished to be remembered. This self-description may also have been intended to justify or explain certain properties of the *History* proper, by recalling the kind of man who had been its author.

Now, at the time when Ammianus called himself a Greek, he was a Roman, a *Romanus* or 'Ρωμαῖος, in the wide sense which the word had acquired by this period.[51] All inhabitants of the Empire were then *Romani*, regardless of origin, and formed a single group or nation in contradistinction to the barbarian tribes beyond the frontiers. This profound consciousness of being a distinct whole is nowhere better exemplified than in the coinage of the new word *Romania*,[52] which first appears in documents of the first half of the fourth century. Formed from *Romanus* by analogy to *Gallia*, *Britannia*, etc., it originally meant the territory occupied by the *Romani* and then, by extension, the way of life or civilization within it. Its first meaning, insofar as space alone is concerned, was covered by the older terms *imperium Romanum* and *orbis Romanus*. But they did not sufficiently make clear that the territory was inhabited by a group, all members of which were bound together by a common way of life—great as the differences were within it—and a feeling of superiority to the world beyond the borders. These people were *Romani* and their land was *Romania*. Surrounding it was *barbaries*, except where *Romania* marched with the Persian Empire or the buffer kingdom of Armenia.

No one was more aware of the concept of *Romania* than Ammianus, whose *History* is truly a history of the Empire viewed as a whole, in which the great task is its defense from the forces which would destroy it from without. We shall return to this later. What

[51] On the *Romani*, see Gaston Paris, *Romania*, I (1872), pp. 1-12.

[52] On *Romania, ibid.,* pp. 12-22; J. Zeiller, R. E. L., VII (1929), pp. 194-198; Ernst Robert Curtius, *Europäische Literatur und Lateinisches Mittelalter* (Bern, 1948), pp. 38-43.

we must now ascertain is what Ammianus meant to convey by calling himself a Greek.

When Ammianus speaks of himself as a Greek in other parts of
his *History*, he does so less directly and only in connection with the
Greek language. The phrase "as we Greeks say," or its equivalent,
occurs frequently when a word is given in its Greek form (e.g.
XVIII, 6, 22; XXII, 8, 33; XXIII, 4, 10; 6, 20). But surely, in
declaring himself a Greek in the epilogue, he must have meant
more than that the Greek language was his native tongue or that
he came from a Greek-speaking part of the Empire. The reader
already knew the one from the references given above and the other
could be deduced from the *History* as a whole, even if he did not
expressly mention his Antiochene origin in one of the lost books.
The admonition to younger writers at the end of the epilogue to
"forge their tongues to a loftier style" (*procudere linguas ad maiores
stilos*), if they intend to continue his account, does not imply in any
way that Ammianus did not attain sufficient stylistic elevation, because he was writing in a foreign tongue. Rather, Ammianus seems
to suggest that the events which occurred after the time at which
he terminated his *History* were of greater magnitude and, hence,
would require an even greater style. Perhaps this was a subtle
compliment to Theodosius who acceded to the purple shortly after
the chronological point where the *History* finishes.

But be that as it may, we may naturally assume that the *Graecus*
in Ammianus referred to his entire παιδεία including, of course, his
linguistic background. We know of one quality, at least, which
Ammianus considered typically Greek. It was painstaking thoroughness. Ammianus attributes it to the historian Timagenes as a Greek
(XV, 9, 2) and possessed it himself abundantly. He might also
have attributed to his Greek background the vast curiosity and
voluminous reading, on which he founded his polymathic digressions, and the importance which he attached to a person's education
as a fundamental element of his character.

But the most interesting connotations of *Graecus* are brought out
by its juxtaposition to *miles*. At the time of Ammianus, the phrase
"a former soldier and a Greek," was virtually a contradiction in
terms. Ammianus himself provides the most detailed information
which we have concerning the personnel of the Roman army during

the years covered by the extant books of his *History*. The relative
scarcity in his pages of officers with Greek names is striking, even
in a period when the army was rapidly becoming germanized.
Ammianus mentions as an exceptional circumstance (*quod his
temporibus raro contingit*) that the companies of Goths beyond the
Taurus were all commanded by Roman officers in 378 (XXXI, 16,
8). Nor can we assume that a Greek officer, that is, an officer from
the Hellenized social strata of the oriental provinces, ever lay
hidden under a Latin name, as was often true of officers of Germanic origin. A Greek name did not need to be civilized.

But in the army a fine Greek education might not be duly appreciated. Ammianus describes an unusual incident which took place
during one of Julian's Gallic campaigns. By a miscalculation on the
part of the Caesar, some of the soldiers under his command were
reduced to starvation. Exasperated by hunger and long arrears in
pay, they assailed Julian with insults, calling him an "Asiatic Greekling (*Asianus Graeculus*), a deceitful fellow and a wise-looking
fool" (XVII, 9, 3). The "Greekling" not only implied that Julian
had all the faults associated with the opprobrious term in the
soldiers' minds—deceit was one of them and it was emphasized
by being mentioned separately—but expressed contempt for the
very attributes which had allowed them to call Julian a Greek at
all. For Julian was no more a Greek by blood, if we may use the
term, than his cousin, the Emperor Constantius. He was a Greek
by education and whole-hearted devotion to all things Greek, especially in the intellectual life. He even affected the outer appearance
of the professional philosopher; hence, the soldiers' "wise-looking
fool." The same contempt for Julian's Greek learning was expressed by his detractors at court in a more sophisticated way. They
called him "a Greek bookworm" (*litterio Graecus*; XVII, 11, 1).

Now, one of the things that Ammianus admired the most about
Julian was precisely that he combined profound intellectual inter-
ests with outstanding military ability. In his first encomium of
Julian, he writes as follows (XVI, 1, 5):

Yet they (the beginnings of his surprising ability) ought to be
preferred to his many admirable later achievements, for the
reason that while still in early youth, educated like Erechtheus

in Minerva's retreat, and drawn from the peaceful shades of the Academy, not from a soldier's tent, to the dust of battle, he vanquished Germany, subdued the meanders of the freezing Rhine, here shed the blood of kings breathing cruel threats and there loaded their arms with chains (Rolfe).

Julian's career had shown conclusively that a "Greek" education or way of life could be combined with brilliant military service. Ammianus, the Greek, brought to his military career the same kind of background as Julian. He, too, must have heard himself called *Graeculus* to his face or behind his back by those who believed that a Greek intellectual had no business doing the man's work of a soldier. But it would never have occurred to him to disavow this side of his nature. In fact, it was with pride that he proclaimed that the Greek and the soldier were both in himself, the two sides of his nature which made him write the kind of history which he wrote.

Let us say, then, that it was the Greek, that is, the educated intellectual, in Ammianus that moved him to undertake the writing of history and gave him the means of expressing himself in a style which won the admiration of his contemporaries. To the Greek let us also charge the voluminous reading caused by a thirst for every kind of knowledge. This book learning appears not only in the digressions, but also in the moralizing *exempla*, drawn from an apparently inexhaustible supply, with which Ammianus spoils the climax of many a superb piece of narrative. We have seen that Ammianus considered thoroughness a Greek quality. It is probably not accidental that in the epilogue his characterization of himself as a Greek is directly followed by his profession that he has never intentionally corrupted the truth. Perhaps we should rather see in his veneration of the truth the reliability of an officer's word.

And now, what of the soldier? Let us observe, first of all, that he uses the generic term, *miles*, not that of his rank, *protector*. He does not want the reader, at the end of his work, to remember him particularly as an officer; in fact, the use of his military title here would have subtracted from the contrast to *Graecus*, also a generic term. He is clearly emphasizing in *miles* the profession of soldiering or the character of being a soldier. He uses the term in somewhat the same way when he calls his revered chief Ursicinus, who at the time was *magister equitum per Orientem* "a warrior, indeed, and soldier always and a leader of soldiers" (*bellicosus sane milesque semper et militum ductor*; XIV, 9, 1). This was something more than being a general.

We can wish that Ammianus had told us more about his military career. But the apparent reason that he did not do so merits our attention. In speaking of himself in a non-military capacity, Ammianus may use the first person plural or the first person singular or even both within the same sentence (XV, 1, 1). No basis for his choice can be discerned except, possibly, rhythm. On the other hand, in relating his career as a soldier he never uses the first person except when he is, so to speak, under his own command or is otherwise detached from a military group.

To be more precise, as long as he is a member of Ursicinus' staff, he identifies himself with Ursicinus or the other members of the staff or both. Even at his first appearance, when he tells us that he has been attached to Ursicinus by imperial command, he uses *nos*, reflecting his position as one of a number of staff officers (XIV, 9, 1). It is only when he informs us that he was one of the ten protectors chosen by Ursicinus to accompany him on his mission to Silvanus that we find him using *ego*. He does not speak of himself in the first person singular again until Ursicinus orders him to go off by himself to save a child, abandoned near Nisibis in the war of 359 (XVIII, 6, 10 ff.). While away from his group, he describes his actions in the first person; on rejoining it, he becomes one of them again and indicates it by shifting to "we." He follows this pattern throughout the war of 359 down to his return to Antioch: on his mission to Corduene (XVIII, 6, 21) and in his escape from Amida (XIX, 8, 5-7), when he is on his own, he is "I." When he is a subaltern in an organized unit, he is "we."

It would not be farfetched to see in this attitude something more than a reflection of Ammianus' natural modesty. As a staff officer, he had the duty to subject himself entirely to the orders of his commander, on whom, of course, all the responsibility rested for the success or failure of a given decision or action. Particularly in a staff was solidarity and coordination of effort under one man's direction indispensable. When sent on a special mission, Ammianus to a certain extent became his own commander and could take the credit or blame for what he did. He then stepped out from staff anonymity and became *ego*.

As for Julian's Mesopotamian campaign, in the account of which Ammianus never speaks of himself in the first person singular, the enterprise was so huge that his own part in it may well have seemed to him to belong to those minor details (*minutiae*) which he was inclined not to record (XXIII, 1, 1; XXVI, 1, 1). In this drama the Emperor himself played the main role, assisted by his army commanders. Men below the rank of tribune are mentioned by name only in connection with some outstanding gallant action; for example, the soldier Exsuperius, who was the first to leap out of the mine at the siege of Maiozamalcha (XXIV, 4, 23).

How did Ammianus acquit himself under arms? During the fighting in Mesopotamia in 359, Ammianus was a member of a small troop of cavalry, which was constantly outnumbered by the enemy forces which it encountered. The action consisted of swift motion and flight in a continuous effort to escape capture or annihilation. Ammianus can not be blamed for not making a suicidal stand, when his own commander, the veteran general Ursicinus, considered the avoidance of an engagement the best strategy. In a desperate situation, Ammianus could scorn life and fight valiantly (XVIII, 8, 9). That he came out of the battle on the banks of the Tigris alive and managed to reach safety within the walls of Amida, after being completely surrounded by the Persians, is to his credit.

Ammianus has been criticised for abandoning Amida at a time when many of the Roman soldiers were still fighting (XIX, 8, 5). Before describing his escape with two other soldiers, he states simply that all hope of defense or flight had been cut off and that soldiers and civilians without regard to sex were being butchered like sheep. It is difficult to see what the Roman cause, already in a hopeless state, would have gained by the death or capture of Ammianus. Surely, if Ammianus had considered it shameful or cowardly to use his superior knowledge of the town and the surrounding country to escape at this time, he would not have recorded the event with such conspicuous candor. Nor would he elsewhere have expressed his scorn for cowards so openly. The action of the Illyrian horsemen who, out of fear of the enemy, withdrew from the roads which they should have guarded is called "a frightful disgrace which ought to be buried in complete silence" (*atrox et silentio omni dedecus obruendum*; XVIII, 8, 2).

The reverse of the medal is Ammianus' respect for the experienced officer; for he knew well that there is no substitute for experience in the formation of the effective commander. He counts it as one of the virtues of the Emperor Constantius that he put in charge of troops only men who had been "hardened in the dust of battle" (*non nisi pulvere bellico indurati praeficiebantur armatis*; XXI, 16, 3). In Ammianus, an officer is often introduced with a reference to his past experience under arms. To command troops is a serious business. Ammianus' scorn for a certain Hyperechius, whom the pretender Procopius put in command of some auxiliary troops for friendship's sake, is unbounded. The man had originally been an orderly in charge of his commander's food and drink. His adversary, a professional soldier, disdained to overcome so despicable a fellow in battle and ordered the auxiliaries to bind their own leader (XXVI, 8, 5). They obeyed the command of a true officer. One need not wonder what Ammianus would have thought of the Egyptian soldier who wrote home to his mother, "I thank Serapis and Good Fortune that while all are toiling all day at cutting stone, I as a *principalis* (non-commissioned officer) am moving around doing nothing."[53]

The Emperor, of course, was the commander-in-chief of the army and had been so since the time of Augustus. Ammianus, like everyone else in the Empire, knew this. But he knew also that the pressure on the frontiers no longer allowed the Emperor to abstain from direct participation in the defense of the Empire. Ammianus expected the Emperor to be the first soldier, as well as the Commander-in-Chief, and to find in the successful fulfillment of his soldier's role the highest achievement of his office. The words with which Ammianus has the Emperor Valentinian I, a veteran soldier, address his son Gratian, on raising him to the dignity of Augustus in 367, are a true reflection of his thought on the Soldier-Emperor (XXVII, 6, 12-13):

"Behold, my dear Gratian, you now wear, as we have all hoped, the imperial robes, bestowed upon you under favourable

[53] *Michigan Papyri*, VIII (1951), 465.

auspices by my will and that of our fellow-soldiers. Therefore prepare yourself, considering the weight of your urgent duties, to be the colleague of your father and your uncle and accustom yourself fearlessly to make your way with the infantry over the ice of the Danube and the Rhine, to keep your place close beside your soldiers, to give your life's blood, with all thoughtfulness, for those under your command, and to think nothing alien to your duty, which affects the interests of the Roman empire. This will suffice for the present by way of admonition; for the future I shall not cease to advise you. Now for the rest I turn to you, great defenders of our country, whom I beg and implore with firm affection to watch over your emperor, not yet grown up, thus entrusted to your loyalty" (Rolfe).

No speech could define more succinctly the duty of the Emperor as a soldier and the mutual dependence between him and his troops.

Again, in his brilliant obituary of Julian (XXV, 4), Ammianus examines him in the light of four principal virtues: moderation (*temperantia*), wisdom (*prudentia*), justice (*iustitia*) and courage (*fortitudo*). Julian's courage is discussed together with his military skill and his *auctoritas*, two of the four outer manifestations of virtue—the others being good fortune and generosity—which Ammianus enumerates after the principal virtues. It is significant that this section on Julian as a soldier is longer than any of those which treat of his other virtues (XXV, 4, 10).

Much of what Ammianus says is based on his personal experience, when he was serving under Julian in the Persian campaign. In fact he illustrates Julian's bravery in hand to hand fighting by an incident from this war (XXV, 4, 10=XXIV, 4, 4). Apart from Julian's courage, Ammianus mentions his skill in besieging cities and fortresses under dangerous conditions, his tactical ability, his wise choice of camp sites in regard to safety and health, and his prudence in taking defensive measures. After the mention of these military qualities, we come to the crucial point: Julian's relations with his men. They illustrate his *auctoritas*. He was warmly loved, while being feared, for he was his men's companion in dangers and toil; in the midst of battle, he would punish the cowardly; as Caesar, he had controlled his men without pay and could quell a mutiny by threatening to return to private life; his Gallic troops, accustomed to the frosts of the Rhine, marched across the Roman world to follow Julian through torrid Assyria to the borders of the Medes. This is praise indeed: of a soldier by a soldier.

This concept of the Emperor as primarily a soldier leading his troops in person in the protection of the frontiers or on campaigns into enemy territory was clearly held by one who believed that the crucial task which confronted the Empire was its defense against foreign enemies. As a soldier and traveler, Ammianus had seen with his own eyes or ascertained from reliable witnesses the devastation and carnage caused by invaders from all sides. He gives us a vivid description of the pitiful state of Gaul, after Constantius' long neglect had permitted large parts of it to be pillaged and bled by the barbarians (XV, 4, 2). This is only one of many accounts of barbarian brutality which make us sympathetic with Ammianus' view that the Romans were justified in using any kind of duplicity or treachery in order to fight the barbarians successfully (XXVIII, 5, 7). Ammianus frequently compares them to wild beasts. He had good reason to do so.

It is all the more remarkable, then, that Ammianus' profound aversion to the barbarians who were threatening to destroy Romania and its civilization did not distort his historical vision in favor of the Romans, when they were unquestionably in the wrong. Of the calamities suffered by parts of the Empire at the hands of the barbarians, none was more hideous than the devastation of Thrace by the Goths in 378. Ammianus gives us a terrifying account of the entire disaster in the last book of his *History*. It is just here, where the fury of the barbarians seems to admit of no attenuating circumstances, that we find a forthright exposition of the culpability of the Romans.

The facts, according to Ammianus, were these. The Goths, fleeing before the Huns and Halani, begged the Emperor Valens to be allowed to cross the Danube and settle in Thrace. The court flatterers urged Valens to seize this opportunity to strengthen his army (with Gothic recruits) and to enrich his treasury (by letting the provinces contribute gold instead of recruits). The Emperor not only granted permission for the Goths to settle in Thrace, but had them ferried across the Danube. "Great pains were taken that no destroyer of the Empire should be left behind" (XXXI, 4, 5).

The presence of the Goths in Roman territory called for Roman leaders of skill and integrity. But the two military commanders were utterly corrupt. "Their deceitful greed was the source of all ensuing woes" (XXXI, 4, 10). They starved the Goths, "who were still blameless," by selling them food at impossible prices and even traded dogs, that they had gathered from far and wide, against human beings, one dog for one slave (this seemed as abominable to Ammianus as it seems to us). Furthermore, one of the Roman generals, who feared a Gothic rebellion, invited two of the Gothic chiefs to a banquet and, while they were being entertained, put to death all the members of their guard of honor who had accompanied them to the general's quarters (XXXI, 5, 4 ff.). This was the final outrage which compelled the Goths to take up arms and begin their devastation.

Whatever the Goths did later—and they were completely ruthless in their savagery—Ammianus knew well where the initial blame lay: with Valens, for allowing the Goths to enter Roman territory *en masse* and with the Roman generals who had treated them unscrupulously. To these two fatal errors Ammianus could add a third, which occurred after the fighting had begun. It was the refusal of Valens, again badly advised by his courtiers, to await the reenforcements of Gratian, before risking a decisive battle, for fear that he would have to share with another the credit for a victory that was almost already won (XXXI, 12, 4 ff.). Ammianus was well aware of the magnitude of the final calamity to which these errors led. He calls the Roman losses at the battle of Adrianople irreparable (*numquam pensabilia damna*; XXXI, 13, 11) and states that only at Cannae was there a comparable slaughter (XXXI, 13, 19). In making the Romans take the blame for setting in motion the tragic course of events and thus freeing the hated barbarians from charges of original aggression or provocation, Ammianus indeed honored the truth which he professed.

It will be instructive now to consider Ammianus' attitude toward his fellow officers of barbarian origin. Let us begin with Silvanus about whom we have relatively abundant information because he

ended his life as a usurper of the purple.[54] His father, Bonitus, a
Frank, fought valiantly on the side of Constantine in the civil war
against Licinius. Silvanus was born in Gaul and received a Roman
education. He evidently joined Magnentius after the assassination
of Constans, but brought his cavalry over to Constantius before the
battle of Mursa. He was rewarded by being appointed *magister
peditum*. At the beginning of 355, he was sent to Gaul to curb the
depredations of the barbarians. We shall have occasion later to
speak of his assumption of the purple and his death, which resulted from it.

Here was a man born within the territory of the Empire and
educated in the Roman way. We can naturally assume that there
was nothing Frankish about him, except, possibly, some physical
traits; and our assumption is corroborated by the fact that the free
Franks outside the Empire no longer considered him one of their
own. When Silvanus in Gaul discovered that his enemies at court
were plotting against him and feared that he might be condemned
to death without a hearing by the Emperor, he considered entrust-
ing himself to "barbarian loyalty" (*barbaricae fidei*; XV, 5, 16).
He was dissuaded from doing so by another officer of Germanic
blood who told him that the Franks, from whom he, Silvanus,
descended (*unde oriebatur*) would kill him or betray him for a
reward.

This reference of Ammianus to Silvanus' Frankish origin does
not, certainly, reflect unfavorably on his character. If anything the
context shows how thoroughly Silvanus had been romanized. But
if the Franks in the service of the Empire had become Romans in
the eyes of the barbarian Franks beyond the frontier, they still felt
a certain solidarity due to common origin. Malarichus, a Frank,
was commander of the gentiles (a part of the palace guard composed of foreigners) at the court of Constantius. Discovering that
the plot to ruin Silvanus had been enlarged to include himself,
who had attempted to defend Silvanus, he lamented his own lot
and that of his fellow countryman Silvanus (*popularis Silvani*; XV,
5, 11). Consequently, he called the Franks together in a meeting
of protest, "of whom there was a flourishing number in the palace

---

[54] The information on Silvanus has been collected by Seeck, *R.-E.*, IIIA, col.
125, n. 4.

at that time" (*quorum ea tempestate in palatio multitudo florebat*; XV, 5, 11). Ammianus was probably not too pleased by this national clique, especially at court, where it could and did bring its influence to bear upon the Emperor. But he is again fair enough to let us see that, if it had not been for the honesty and bravery of the Franks, who dared compel the Emperor to make a formal investigation of the forged evidence against Silvanus, the whole shabby plot against him would never have been disclosed. Even so, the disclosure came too late to prevent his rebellion.

It is in speaking of Silvanus' father, Bonitus, that Ammianus betrays his suspicion—and dislike—of the Frank in the Roman service. In considering the death of Silvanus, "a general of no mean merits" (*dux haut exilium meritorum*; XV, 5, 32) whose death had ultimately been caused by the false accusations of his enemies, Ammianus recalls not only his services to Constantius, but those of Bonitus to Constantine: "he (Silvanus) could also set forth (as a claim to Constantius' gratitude) the brave deeds of his father Bonitus, a Frank indeed, but one who often fought fiercely on the side of Constantine against the followers of Licinius" (*patris quoque Boniti praetenderet fortia facta, Franci quidem, sed pro Constantini partibus in bello civili acriter contra Licinianos saepe versati*; XV, 5, 33). "A Frank indeed, but" one who had redeemed himself by becoming a member of the Roman army, and the right Roman army at that. It is not difficult to guess that Bonitus had been born among the free Franks outside the Empire and had entered the Roman army either in accordance with a treaty between Rome and his own tribe, whereby the latter was obligated to furnish the Empire with a stated number of potential soldiers, or by volunteering. In the eyes of Ammianus, his origin was not far enough behind him to be forgotten, although he had made compensation for it.

There are several occasions where we should have expected Ammianus to express some bitter criticism of soldiers of barbarian origin. A notable occasion was offered by three Roman officers of barbarian origin, who, during a campaign of Constantius against the Alamanni, were suspected of betraying a Roman plan to take the enemy by surprise to their fellow countrymen (*populares suos*), thus allowing them to escape (XIV, 10, 7-8). This would have been an opportune place to speak of the unreliability of such soldiers.

Ammianus merely states that the suspicion (of having so acted) stained the reputation of—and he names three officers and gives the rank of each. The only thrust is his observation, following their identification, that these officers were highly respected at that time, as men who were carrying the entire state in their right hands. On the other hand, a tribune called Hariobaudes, who could be most useful to Julian as an envoy and a spy, because he had a thorough knowledge of the language of the Alamanni—obviously, he had learned it at his mother's knee—is characterized as a man "of recognized loyalty and bravery" (XVIII, 2, 2). Nor is he the only soldier of barbarian background whom Ammianus praises.

The fact seems to be that Ammianus is caught in the great dichotomy of his period. He has a profound realization, acquired through his military experience, that the Empire must be protected by a strong and valiant army, under the leadership of the Emperor, against attacks by foreign enemies. Yet, he must have realized that it was the Germanic element in the army that enabled it to resist with some success the onslaughts of the very peoples from which it descended. Ammianus could hate for their destruction and scorn for their ignorance the Germanic enemies of Romania; but he himself had chosen to enter the organ of the Roman state, in which men of barbarian ancestry were concentrated, because they could, with their peculiar talents for warfare, best serve the state in it. The organ was the army and all men in it became Romans, if they had not been Romans before. And because an army is always something of a closed corporation, in which ranks are instinctively joined against outsiders, whereas in the field mutual confidence and loyalty are indispensable for success or even survival, Ammianus had to have a very different attitude to the descendants of the hated foreigners who were his fellow soldiers.

Ammianus must have had mixed emotions on many occasions and felt quite strongly certain animosities which he barely reveals to us with a subtly colored or ironically turned phrase. On the whole, his professed devotion to the truth is well exemplified in his treatment of his fellow officers, regardless of their origin. What may tempt him into distortion is loyalty to someone whom he profoundly admires and who, in his opinion, has suffered a serious injury.

Arbitio was a soldier who rose from the ranks to one of the great cavalry commands (XVI, 6, 1). He was one of the two men appointed by the Emperor Constantius to investigate the fall of the Roman fortress Amida to the Persians. They closed their eyes to the evidence to avoid placing the blame where it properly belonged: on the incompetent Sabinianus, who had been largely responsible for the disaster; for he had a powerful patron at court in the chamberlain Eusebius. Ursicinus, who had been compelled to stand by helplessly and watch the fortress capitulate, because of Sabinianus' poltroonery, expressed his resentment at this procedure in terms which were critical of the Emperor himself. His words, with malicious additions, were reported to Constantius, who flew into a rage and, without permitting an investigation or explanation, relieved Ursicinus of his command and sent him into retirement (XX, 2). This is the last time in the *History* that we hear of him.

Ammianus never forgave Arbitio for his part in Ursicinus' downfall. He paints his character in the darkest colors, taxing him with duplicity, injustice and cruelty in civil life (XV, 2, 4; 3, 2) and indecision and cowardice on the battlefield (XV, 4, 7; 4, 10). It is difficult to believe that the Emperor Julian would have appointed such a man to the high court which he established, when he came to power, to try those who had committed criminal acts against himself and his brother Gallus (XXII, 3, 1), especially, since Arbitio had been a loyal supporter of Julian's predecessor Constantius and had even been sent ahead with troops to engage Julian's forces, when civil war had broken out between the two (XXI, 13, 16). Ammianus goes so far as to intimate that Julian was either timid or did not know what was appropriate, when he appointed the "shifty and arrogant" Arbitio to preside over the investigations (XXII, 3, 9). When we last see Arbitio in the pages of Ammianus he has refused to join the side of the usurper Procopius and his prestige is still so great, as an ex-consul and an ex-general, that he is able to win over to the side of the legitimate Emperor Jovian a considerable part of Procopius' forces (XXVI, 8, 13; 9, 4). Ammianus cannot, for reasons which we shall soon set forth, breathe a word of unfavorable criticism about Arbitio's last appearance.

It would seem that Ammianus' opinion of Arbitio was clouded

by his loyalty to his old chief, Ursicinus. But there are other facets
to the discharge of Ursicinus by Constantius which deserve our attention. Ammianus states that Ursicinus was attacked by false accusations (*appetitum calumniis*; XX, 2, 5), which indeed was the
case. He mentions the unfairness of the report, the malicious additions to Ursicinus' words of resentment and the Emperor's excessive wrath. We might have expected him to leave the matter
there in order to put Ursicinus' behavior in the most favorable
light. But he doesn't. Instead, he gives us Ursicinus' words *ver-
batim* (XX, 2, 4): "When he (the Emperor) is pulled about at
the will of his eunuchs, not he himself, in personal command, with
the strength of his entire army, will be able to keep Mesopotamia
from being lopped off, piece by piece, next spring." These are hard
words. They impugn the Emperor's choice of intimate advisors, his
capacity to make independent decisions and, above all, his military
ability. The amount of truth in them, which is considerable, is not
the question. They showed an intolerable disrespect for the *maiestas*
of the Emperor and should never have been uttered by anyone,
least of all by a high military officer in the Emperor's service. Ammianus could have concealed these words or softened their impro-
priety in an innocuous paraphrase. His love of the truth did not let
him do so. He feels that Ursicinus was unjustly dismissed; but he
lets us see how Ursicinus contributed to his own downfall. Nor does
he recall the general's advancing years (he had served under Constantine; XV, 5, 19) and his long and honorable service to Emperor and Empire as circumstances which should have made Constantius pause for reflection. We must decide for ourselves if the
anger was "excessive" which made the Emperor act impetuously.

And this brings us to the Emperor again. We have already seen
that Ammianus expected him to carry out his chief task in person:
the defense of the Empire. In this task and in every other, the
soldier was bound to the legitimately reigning Emperor in a very
personal way by the military oath, the *sacramentum militare*. We
can obtain a fair idea of this oath at the time of Ammianus if we
remove the Christian elements from the oath recorded by Vegetius
(II, 5) under Valentinian III (425-455), when the army had already been Christianized. Omitting, therefore, the Trinity, by
which the later soldier swore, we find that Ammianus—and every

other soldier—would have sworn by the majesty of the Emperor to carry out his orders promptly and never to desert or to refuse to die for the Roman state.

This oath seems to have been sworn only once, at induction, and to have been binding throughout the soldier's military career. To be honorably discharged was to be honorably relieved of the oath (*honeste sacramento solutus*, XXX, 7, 3); to be cashiered was to be stripped of it (*sacramento exutus*, XXVIII, 2, 9). The oath was not renewed, even when a new Augustus was proclaimed. There is no mention of an oath in connection with the accession to the throne of Jovian and Valentinian I, both chosen by the army, or of Valens or Gratian, both raised to the dignity of Augustus by Valentinian.

That the military oath fastened the soldier's allegiance to the Emperor as an institution, regardless of his personal feelings toward the person of an individual Emperor as sovereign or commanding general, is made even clearer by the course which usurpers pursued to assure themselves the loyalty of their military supporters. When Julian finally decided to accept the title of Augustus, thrust on him by the troops in Paris, he ordered all the soldiers present to swear an oath of loyalty to him and they swore formally under grim execrations, placing their own swords symbolically at their own throats, that they would suffer anything for him to the point of laying down their lives (XXI, 5, 10). The same kind of oath was sworn before the usurper Procopius by the troops that had defected to him (XXVI, 7, 9). Both these oaths had a personal quality in that the soldiers swore allegiance to an individual by name rather than to the complex of powers and ideas embodied in the person who had legitimately ascended the throne. The rebellious soldiers were already bound to the then existing Emperors, Constantius and Jovian, respectively, by the oaths which they had taken by the "Emperor's majesty" to observe the "Emperor's orders," regardless of the personality of the sovereign under whom they had entered the service; and in breaking this oath, continuity was broken and a new allegiance had to be affirmed, and this time specifically, to emphasize the break. The overriding practical consideration, of course, was the desire of the newly acclaimed Augusti to obtain the sworn allegiance of the forces which supported them.

Ammianus had a very strong feeling for imperial legitimacy which established the person whom the soldiers would serve and obey. It is nowhere more conspicuous than in the part played by Ammianus himself in the overthrow of Silvanus and his attitude toward the whole affair. The story is told in detail (XV, 5) and we shall simply summarize its most pertinent parts.

We have already mentioned Silvanus' Frankish origin and his high command. He was forced to assume the purple at Cologne in the fall of 355 in order to protect his own life, which had been placed in jeopardy by a conspiracy of his enemies at court. When news of the usurpation reached the Emperor Constantius, he sent Ursicinus, Ammianus' chief, with a small staff, of which Ammianus was a member, to Cologne with orders to bring Silvanus back to the court at Milan to be destroyed. The mission was one of duplicity from the start. Ursicinus was to pretend that the news of Silvanus' elevation had not yet reached Constantius, and he carried with him an imperial letter ordering Silvanus to receive him as his successor and to return to the court in possession of his rank and honors.

On arriving at Cologne, Ursicinus found that Silvanus had not been idle. He had by then raised a strong army that was impatient to invade Italy in support of his cause. The opportunity had long passed of persuading him peacefully to obey the Emperor's wishes. Deception, in pretending to support the usurper, and flattery, in order to put him off his guard, were the weapons to which Ursicinus resorted. He was generously entertained and won the confidence of Silvanus, who saw in him a person, like himself, who had labored long and hard in the service of the state without ever being granted the highest honor of the consulship, which less worthy men had enjoyed. Now he, Silvanus, was being summoned on charges of treason, whereas Ursicinus, taken from his command in the east, was being handed over to the hatred of his enemies at court. Under the guise of this friendship, Ursicinus and his staff managed to bribe two companies of Silvanus' troops. They dragged him from a building where he had taken refuge on the way to a Christian service and butchered him with repeated blows of their swords.

In his brief obituary of Silvanus (XV, 5, 32-33), Ammianus

makes it quite clear that he considered Silvanus an able general, who, fearful of the false accusations in which he had been trapped by a hostile clique, had gone to the extremity of self-protection (usurpation) in order to save his own life. Moreover, Ammianus states that Silvanus and his father had a rightful claim on the Emperor's gratitude for services rendered. But, regardless of these mitigating circumstances, Ammianus' fundamental attitude is apparent throughout his account: there cannot be any possible excuse for high treason and any means at all are justified in cutting it down: abuse of hospitality, feigned friendship, bribery and brutal assassination. Ursicinus and his staff, including Ammianus, were involved in every aspect of this wretched drama except the last; this they left to the troops they had bribed. Ammianus tells us of the difficulty of the enterprise; but nowhere does he express repugnance of the means he was compelled to use to carry it out. He was not a devious or hypocritical man himself. He was not cruel, and time and again he cries out against the torture and execution of those falsely accused of treason. But he had seen Silvanus wearing the purple which was not his to wear. His guilt was established and he had to be destroyed.

We can discern this strong feeling for legitimacy, embodied in the military oath, in Ammianus' treatment of Julian's ascent to the rank of Augustus. Julian had much to commend him. The blood of Constantine ran in his veins and he had been appointed Caesar by the Emperor Constantius with due formality. Yet, only Constantius, while he was alive, could make Julian an Augustus in a way which satisfied tradition. Thus we see a net of circumstances compelling Julian against his will to assume the rank. Not only the errors and uncompromising arrogance of Constantius and the stubbornly loyal insistence of Julian's troops moved the reluctant Caesar; but someone in the form of the state's tutelary spirit (*genius publicus*) appeared to him in his sleep, telling him that he had long wished to raise his rank and that if he were dismissed again, he would depart forever (XX, 5, 10).

Ammianus knew that Julian had many compelling reasons to rebel. But we feel that he is worried about the question of legitimacy and that he was as elated as Julian himself when the death of Constantius ended the threat of civil war and allowed Julian to become Augustus at the request of the highest dignitaries of the court (XXI, 15, 4-5). It is a credit to Ammianus' honesty that he terms mere rumor the report that Constantius had designated Julian his heir. The envoys from the court, who were charged with informing Julian of Constantius' death, told him that Constantius, in his last words, had appointed him the successor to his power (XXII, 2, 1). This smoothed the path of succession.

A legitimate Emperor deserves the protection of all. In speaking of investigations of high treason, Ammianus says that no sensible man will find fault with them. For the safety of all depends on the safety of a legitimate prince, who is the champion and defender of all good men, and, consequently, his safety must be guarded by the concerted effort of all (XIX, 12, 17). For this reason, Ammianus continues, no one charged with treason is exempt from being interrogated under torture. But it does not befit an Emperor to exult immoderately in these sad cases, for fear that his subject seem to be ruled by license (*licentia*) rather than by power (*potestate*).

Here is a reflection of Ammianus' basic concept of the office of the Emperor. The power inherent in that office is absolute and unlimited. But he who holds it has an obligation to practice restraint in wielding it. A flagrant injustice committed by the Emperor Valens draws the following reflection from Ammianus (XXIX, 2, 18):

O noble system of wisdom, by heaven's gift bestowed upon the fortunate, thou who has often ennobled even sinful natures! How much wouldst thou have corrected in those dark days, if it had been permitted Valens to learn through you that royal power—as the philosophers declare—is nothing else than the care for others' welfare; that it is the duty of a good ruler to restrain his power, to resist unbounded desire and implacable anger, and to know—as the dictator Caesar used to say—that the recollection of cruelty is a wretched support for old age. And therefore, if he is going to pass judgment affecting the life and breath of a human being, who forms a part of the world and completes the number of living things, he ought to hesitate long and greatly and not be carried away by headlong passion to a point where what is done cannot be undone (Rolfe).

This restrained and thoughtful use of power is what Ammianus calls a *civile iustumque imperium*. The adjective *civile* and the adverb *civiliter* appear often in the pages of the history with political connotations. At one place, Ammianus even speaks of "civil Emperors." The context is interesting. Ammianus is criticising the vainglory of Constantius and his susceptibility to flattery. He finds these faults particularly reprehensible in a man who declared that he toiled diligently to form his life and character "on the model of civil Emperors" (*ad aemulationem civilium principum*; XV, 1, 3). These "civil Emperors" had known how to practice restraint, in accordance with justice and virtue.

But the last thing that Ammianus would have wanted a "civil" Emperor to do was to behave like an ordinary citizen. For Ammianus, the inner virtues should be wed to an outer dignity in the person of the Emperor which emphasized his remoteness. He criticises Julian's love of popularity which led him to delight in the applause of the mob and to converse with unworthy persons. When Julian dashed out of the Senate house in Constantinople, where he was sitting in judgment, to greet his old teacher, the philosopher Maximus, Ammianus tartly observes that the Emperor forgot who he was and seemed to be seeking after empty glory through this act of unseasonable ostentation (XXII, 7, 3). When Julian went on foot to the inauguration of the consuls for 362, Ammianus tells us that some praised this action, whereas others criticised it as affected and base. It is not difficult to conjecture what the historian thought of it himself (XXII, 7, 1).

In the obituary of Constantius, the first of his virtues to be mentioned is that he guarded "everywhere the buskin of imperial authority (*imperatoriae auctoritatis cothurnum*) and scorned popularity with a lofty mind" (XXI, 16, 1). The Emperor is playing a noble role and must not speak or act out of character. Ammianus gives us a memorable portrait of Constantius playing that role on his first visit to Rome in 357 (XVI, 10, 4-17). He entered the city in triumphal procession escorted by resplendent troops with the banners called dragons hissing and lashing their tails in the wind.

The Emperor sat alone on a golden carriage, blazing with precious
stones from which a shifting light seemed to emanate. The hills
echoed with the shouts of Augustus, but he never moved, except to
bend down his short body when he passed through high gates. He
kept his neck rigid and his gaze fixed ahead of him. He moved his
face neither to the right nor the left. When a wheel jolted, he did
not stir. Nor was he seen to spit, to wipe or rub his mouth or nose
or to move his hand.

This respect for the imperial dignity was extended to other members of the imperial household. Ammianus deplores the cruelty of
the Caesar Gallus, the half brother of Julian, whom Constantius
had placed in charge of the eastern part of the Empire. His unspeakable transgressions and outrages to justice were reported to the
Emperor Constantius. The latter's problem was to destroy Gallus
without causing a civil war. The prefect Domitianus was dispatched
to Antioch with instructions to woo Gallus away from the East. On
Domitianus' arrival in Antioch, he scornfully failed to pay a ceremonial call on the Caesar as, Ammianus says, it became him to do
(XIV, 7, 10). Gallus had been acting monstrously—Ammianus'
bitter account of his deeds makes this abundantly clear—but as long
as he was Caesar he had the right to the respect which was due to
his position. And when he was finally lured to Pola, in Istria,
stripped of power and beheaded like a guilty thief, Ammianus has
this to say (XIV, 11, 24): "His own cruel acts crushed Gallus, and
the two men whose flattering perjuries had led him into the lethal
trap, although he was guilty, died a painful death, not long thereafter." This to Ammianus was divine justice. To murder a Caesar,
even on the Emperor's orders, and even when he deserved his fate,
in an unworthy manner could not be countenanced by Heaven.

To turn now from the person and office of the Emperor to the
common soldier, Ammianus has been accused of feeling contempt
for the latter. This view does not accord very well with Ammianus'
statement that the only flaw in Valentinian, as a military disci-
plinarian, was his propensity to punish the slight infractions of the
common soldiers, while overlooking the serious transgressions of
the higher officers (XXX, 9, 1). At least, Ammianus felt that military justice should not be meted out according to rank. He gives
us a vivid description of the demoralization and vices of the

soldiers at the time of Julian's accession (XXII, 4, 6-7). But although much of it is undoubtedly true, we must bear in mind that this picture of the low state of military discipline is presented as a counterpart to that of the corruption and luxury which prevailed in the court. It was Julian's task to correct both.

Ammianus tells us, with obvious approval, of the way in which Julian improved the Roman military situation in Thrace. First of all he appointed veteran commanders, who had already proved their worth. Then, he rebuilt the fortifications and saw to it that the troops on the Danube which had acquitted themselves bravely should not lack arms, uniforms, pay or rations (XXII, 7, 7). Julian knew, as did Ammianus, that the kind of leadership, equipment and treatment which a soldier received largely determined his behavior in the garrison and his performance on the battlefield. Neglected troops were poor troops and of little use in peace or war.

Ammianus' statement that he will not set down the reasons why common soldiers were punished before the standards has been taken as a reflection of his scorn for the rank and file (XXVI, 1, 1). But in this passage, he is giving an example of the kind of unimportant event, the description of which does not accord with his principles of historical writing. He also refuses to report what an Emperor said at dinner.

We have already touched upon the way in which Ammianus effaces himself as a member of a staff. In the same way he is likely to see the common soldiers in terms of the military units to which they belong. The squadrons of Illyrian horsemen who display their cowardice in Mesopotamia are a disgrace (XVIII, 8, 2); the soldiers of the Gallic legions at the siege of Amida are praised for their courage and fighting spirit (XIX, 6). So valiantly did they acquit themselves that the Emperor ordered statues of their non-commissioned officers, wearing their armor, to be erected in Edessa (XIX, 6, 12). Ammianus does not even tell us the names of any of the latter.

In spite of his military background or, more probably, because he saw the military environment with the clear eye of the Greek, Ammianus was not the kind of soldier who believed that the military could handle civil administration more effectively and, if given the authority, could set the crooked straight with drastic dispatch. He does not scorn or depreciate civil officers and civilians, but judges them in the light of their virtues and vices as human beings and the way in which they perform the functions of their respective offices. In his obituary of Constantius, he counts it among the Emperor's virtues that no military leader was promoted to the *clarissimate* (a rank enjoyed by senators and their sons), that the civil governor of a province was not obliged to come out to meet the commander-in-chief of the country and that the latter was not allowed to touch a civil matter. Military and civil officers alike, he continues, held the praetorian prefects, who were then civil magistrates ranking just below the Emperor in traditional respect. Constantius did not allow the military to raise their "horns" (XXI, 16, 2-3).

Ammianus saw that the most crucial task which confronted the Empire in his time was its defense. He was not unaware of some of the internal problems, which to us, who can look back upon them with historical perspective, appear to have reached the point where they were insoluble. Ammianus saw these problems in the simplest terms: the abuses of his time were the work of bad or incompetent men, not inherent in the system under which the body politic functioned, but subject to correction by the application of honesty and justice. He gives no indication that he yearned to see radical changes effected in the proliferating imperial bureaucracy, the rigidly stratified society, the methods of collecting revenue in money or in kind. He wished to see able and decent civil servants, an upper class which was as aware of its obligations as it was of its privileges, taxes fairly imposed and fairly collected.

This rather simple approach may have been formed under the influence of a profession in which the integrity, honesty and ability of an individual often made the difference between failure and success, defeat and victory. But we must now bring our discussion to a close. There are many other elements in the historical writing of Ammianus which we have hardly mentioned or completely ignored. They would find their due place in any total description of his work. Here we have had to be content with indications of the way in which his military background affected important aspects of his writing.

The history of Ammianus' own times was military in the essence. It was a continuous battle on the part of the Empire to maintain its frontiers and everything civilized within them. We are fortunate to have in Ammianus a historian who was professionally competent to take the large view. His preoccupation with warfare on the frontiers and in the provinces, with the Emperor as a commander and his court as headquarters, is the product of his soldier's experience. To it was wed a high esteem for education and the cultivated mind, a hatred of injustice and, above all, a passionate and unswerving love of the truth which impelled him to describe events and to judge men as he saw them—impartially.

These qualities give to his *History* a stamp of greatness of its own. I should not pretend, as some have done, that every page captures our interest. The cruel trials for treason have often a sickening monotony and certain engagements against the barbarians have patterns, which become all too familiar. But there is the siege of Amida, Julian's Persian expedition, the battle of Adrianople and the death of Valens, the execution of Gallus, the drunken dinner party in Illyricum which cost some men their lives, the flight of the Armenian king, Pappa, and his treacherous murder, the bears of Valentinian, named Goldflake and Innocence, the gradual development of the characters of the several Emperors and their incomparable obituaries. The great scenes crowd in on one. Here is wonderful reading as well as great history, the like of which we shall not find for centuries to come.

Homer and the Homeric Problem

BY GERALD F. ELSE

Delivered January 21 and 22, 1965

FOREWORD

I too should like to pay my share of tribute to Mrs. Semple. The generosity with which she and her husband fostered the Classics has its memorial not only on the windy heights of Troy and near sandy Pylos but here at home, in Cincinnati. For their benefactions were never limited to archaeology but embraced the whole of classical studies, and your department has always honored that larger commitment. Thus it is appropriate that Greek literature should be represented in this series of Semple Lectures. But unlucky is the man who closes a series that was begun by Professor Blegen, and who proposes to speak of Homer. The inadequacies of these two lectures will be only too evident. What excuses the attempt—if it is excused—is the greatness and perennial fascination of the two poems with which Western literature began. The first lecture deals with the complex problem that has grown up around them, the second with the poems themselves and some of the kinds of experience they can bring us if we are prepared to listen.

GERALD F. ELSE

8

HOMER AND THE HOMERIC PROBLEM

I: THE PROBLEM

THE HOMERIC problem, or, to give it its traditional name, the Homeric Question (*die Homerische Frage*), has been with us for 170 years, by the official reckoning, and there are those who would say that it appears to be no nearer a solution now than it was when Friedrich August Wolf broached it in 1795.[1] It seems to me that this pessimistic view is not justified. In spite of the setbacks and dead ends and wrong turnings in which the venerable Question has repeatedly gotten itself entangled, the endless labor expended on it has not gone quite in vain. Not that we have definitively flushed the quarry from its covert, much less caught it. Some of the problems connected with the Homeric poems will probably never be solved, but nevertheless on certain fronts we have moved forward. We have come closer to asking the right questions and using the right measures. We have exemplified the truth that science consists not in a neatly tied bundle of final answers but in a series of ever closer approximations. And in so doing we have brought into sharper focus another characteristic of scientific knowledge: that the truth is complicated. The increase in our knowledge of the historical and linguistic background of Homer, and of his poetic technique, places us today in a new position vis-à-vis the Homeric Question; above all, it enables us to define with much greater accuracy than in the past the *limits* of our knowledge and our ignorance.

Wolf, in launching the Homeric Question, began with the problem of writing. Being convinced that structures as massive and complex as the Homeric poems could not have been achieved with-

---

[1] *Prolegomena ad Homerum. I* (Halle, 1795). The second part was never published.

12

Minoan Civilization

11

Mycenaean Civilization

I

The Dark Age

10

Linear B

The
Poems:

metre,
style,
structure,
achievement

2

Mainland and
Ionian epic

9

Linguistics and
linguistic geography

3

Oral composit

8

Athens
(Pisistratus)

4

Writing

7

Text tradition

5

Analysis and
Unitarianism

6

Echoes in art
and literature

Fig. 1

out the aid of writing, and being convinced further that "Homer"
lived in the tenth century B.C. and could not write, he was led to
deny that they could be the work of a single poet. Instead he accepted the notion suggested by certain ancient notices about the so-
called "Pisistratean recension,"[2] that the poems as we have them
were put together out of scattered songs in sixth-century Athens.
We shall see that writing still remains closely entangled with the
problem, to such an extent that some modern scholars, equipped
with the most up-to-date ideas of oral composition, accept Wolf's
premises but invert his conclusion: they conclude that the poet (or
poets) must have used writing. The question of the invention of
writing—i.e., alphabetic writing—has also entered recently on a

[2] See J. A. Davison, "Peisistratus and Homer," *Transactions of the American
Philological Association*, LXXXVI, 1957, pp. 1-21.

new stage of close definition, but the central mystery has not been solved.

What, then, do we know and not know that might help to explain the poems? It can be said at once that most of the significant knowledge we have gained, including that which enables us to define more closely the limits of our knowledge, has to do with the background of the poems rather than with the poems themselves as completed structures. Here is a diagram (fig. 1). It can hardly be said to have a clear and rigorous logical order; all I hope is that nothing important has been omitted. The poems, with their verse-form, style, structure, and achievement, stand where they belong, in the middle, while the areas of knowledge and/or ignorance are grouped around them as a frame. The rubrics from the top to the center of each side (from "9 o'clock" to "3 o'clock" on the dial) represent the background. Those below (from 4 to 8 o'clock) represent other areas or issues which have a bearing on the *dating* of the poems but cannot be used, or even defined, without using criteria developed out of the poems themselves (to a lesser extent this is also true of the upper rubrics).

Like any analytical scheme, the diagram grossly oversimplifies the real situation. In order even to approximate the true state of affairs it ought to indicate the intricate web of relationships and modulations which criss-crosses it from every rubric to almost every other. Thus there ought to be a line running straight across the board from "Linguistics" to "Oral composition," another from "style," in the center, to "Analysis and Unitarianism," one from "achievement" to "Writing," and so on. Graphic methods are wholly inadequate to representing these complexities, but it is essential to remember that they exist and that the larger the questions we ask, the more they tend to involve the whole body of relationships.

However, we will use the scheme as an organizing device for passing in review what we know about the background of the poems. First, and of prime importance, the three rubrics at the top (11, 12, and 1 o'clock on the dial) stand under the joint sign of archaeology and history. The two words are bracketed together here in spite of the differences of denotation and connotation between them. Conventionally, history begins when written documents begin, so that we can reconstruct something of what people did and what they said and thought about it, not merely how they lived. Archaeology, unless it brings such documents to light, is "dumb." But in the case of Greek and Aegaean archaeology, at least from the time of the late Bronze Age, the situation is somewhat different. The world of Troy and Knossos and Mycenae and Pylos was already well known to us before Schliemann's spade ever bit into the hill of Hissarlik. We had a rich tradition about it, from the Homeric poems themselves—and that is a part of our problem—but also from later Greek literature and the remnants of ancient scholarship upon it. We knew a good deal about the persons and places of the heroic world; what we did not know was whether they had ever really existed. Schliemann and his successors have put an end to that doubt. He began the process of bringing Troy and Mycenae back from the realm of fantasy to that of reality. But we need not take undue pride in this reversal, as such. The archaeologists have only proved what the Greeks had never doubted: that the world Homer sang of was real, a part of their own past. Most important of all, perhaps, Homer himself never doubted that the world he sang of was real. If he had, he might not have sung at all.

A real world, then. But that is not enough for history. If it was real, then we want to know what happened in it and when, in what order. We want a chronology and a historical sequence. And here the difficulties begin. For one thing, the archaeological record is still very spotty. We know a good deal about the palaces at Knossos and Mycenae and Pylos, less about the country-side around them, very little about Thebes, and less about the Mycenaean sites north of Thebes. For another thing, our two kinds of evidence, archaeological and literary, mostly glance past each other. There are good reasons for this. The bedrock foundation of archaeological chronology is stratigraphy (a relatively recent and correspondingly sophisticated branch of science), and stratigraphy works essentially with pots. Pots are a wonderfully firm basis, since baked clay is one of the most durable of materials. But the chronology they give us is not necessarily complete and sufficient for all purposes. Pottery styles enlighten us on a people's visual taste and imagination; they do not necessarily provide us with a reliable clue to its thoughts, institutions, or literary ideals, or to the changes in them.

Conversely, the kind of historical recollection that is embodied in the poetry of a people (and most of the Greek literary testimony I spoke of a moment ago either is in or is derived from early poetry) often differs sharply from what we call history. It has a way of getting changed, adapted, inverted, padded or cut, concentrated around a few great events and great men. The distortion can go as far as in the *Chanson de Roland*, which brings together people from three or four centuries of actual history, or in the *Nibelungenlied*, where the spread appears to be six centuries. There cannot be much doubt that something like this concentration upon a few great events took place in the Greek poetic cycles which dealt with Thebes and Troy, and that it happened or began to happen long before anybody we can call "Homer." Moreover it is evident that these things are more likely to happen when poetry is purely oral, subsisting in an illiterate society whose poetry is, if not the only, at least the major recorder and interpreter of its own past, without the continuing check of independent written records.

Concerning this ambivalent character of poetry as a recorder of the past we must set down two different, possibly conflicting considerations. First, there are remarkable examples of the tenacity with which oral poetry can transmit both particular details and a correct sense of the general outline and bearing of events which belong to a distant past. The heroic songs of the South Slavs, though with many changes, have maintained a central focus on the battle of Kossovo (fought in 1389) down to the present day; and the Russian *byliny*, which were still flourishing at least down to the Revolution of 1917, kept in memory the siege of Kiev in 1240. We shall note shortly some cases where the Greek bards faithfully preserved a recollection of particular precious objects down through four or five centuries. The question is, is their picture of, say, the Trojan War, and of its supreme importance, equally faithful? Was there in fact a Trojan War? We do not really know.[8] It may have been no more than a large-scale raid.

There is another limiting, if not controlling, factor; unfortunately its incidence upon our problem cannot be gauged. The oral poetry of an illiterate people tends to be, or to become, its national

---

[8] D. L. Page, *History and the Homeric Iliad* (Sather Classical Lectures, vol. XXXI, Berkeley and Los Angeles, 1959), chap. III, "The Historical Background of the Trojan War," evokes some very attractive possibilities but no certainties.

memory. But the collective memory of a people is no more perfectly reliable, over a period of time, than the memory of an individual man about his own past thoughts and actions. Suffering, frustration, success and failure, interest and passion, the desire to make the story more dramatic or entertaining, above all, perhaps, the deep human need to *structure* our memories so that they can accompany and sustain us: all these factors can distort the literal record. And the sad fact is that in the absence of unequivocal external evidence, preferably documents, we cannot be sure where the distortion is, or even whether it has taken place.

Thus we approach Greek heroic poetry with uncertain, even conflicting, expectations. We need not be surprised if in the same poem, even the same part of the poem, old and new, tradition and innovation, historical fact and dramatic imagination, stand side by side. In any case, as we said before, Schliemann and his successors have demonstrated that the Homeric poems deal with a real world. We Americans feel particular pride that Professor Blegen has given the most conclusive and perfectly rounded proof of that, the one for which all other classical archaeologists admire and envy him: the Palace of Nestor. But before we deal with the Mycenaean world and Mycenaean culture, I should like to say a little about Minoan Crete.

Mycenae and Pylos are already distant forms to Homer; Knossos, that is, the great palace and the life that it implies, seems to be almost completely over his horizon. Yet it is possible that his art has ultimately a Minoan, not just a Mycenaean, base. Here it is unfortunate that we have no verdict in the current dispute between Professor Palmer of Oxford and others over the history of Knossos between 1400 and 1200 B.C. (I will be brief, because Professor Blegen has touched on this question in his second Semple Lecture.) If Greeks were indeed at Knossos during that time, or most of it, the hypothesis which I am about to mention might gain added plausibility. At all events Antoine Meillet[4] concluded many years ago on the basis of a wholly different kind of evidence, namely a comparison of early Greek verse-forms with those of Old Indic, that the dactylic hexameter could not be a native Greek (i.e., Indo-European) metre but must have been borrowed from another lan-

---

[4] *L'origine indo-européenne des mètres grecs*, Paris 1923.

guage; he suggested "Minoan." If this suggestion is correct, it would help to explain certain facts about the heroic hexameter. For it is evident that this verse-form must have been cultivated long before Homer: an unremitting effort clearly had to be devoted, over a very long time, to making the language fit the metre, i.e., to fabricating and preserving dactylic sequences of syllables instead of the iambic and trochaic ones which were more natural to it. Again, the versification of the Greek hexameter as we see it in Homer is formal and rigid far beyond anything we find in the heroic verse of other Indo-European peoples; and that rigidity might ultimately be due to borrowing from another language of different rhythmic character and a poetic tradition having other techniques and conventions. Continued contact of Greeks and Minoans at Knossos over several generations, in the fourteenth and thirteenth centuries B.C., would provide a suitable *milieu* for a cultural borrowing of this scope and importance. But the hypothesis remains, at least for now, only a hypothesis.

Passing now to the next rubric at the upper left on our diagram ("11 o'clock" on the dial), Mycenaean civilization, we are on slightly, but only slightly, firmer ground. It is clear that Homer knows in general outline the political structure of the Mycenaean world, its major sites and configuration of power, including the overlordship of the King of Mycenae. He also has an imposing fund of knowledge of heroes' names, genealogies, and undertakings warlike and other, including many that he only alludes to in passing—e.g., the voyage of the Argo, the two expeditions against Thebes, the exploits of Heracles—which can only belong to the Late Bronze Age. Martin P. Nilsson[5] showed many years ago that the basic stock of Greek mythology is Mycenaean (and here we must remind ourselves again that much of what we call "Greek mythology" is in some sense buried history). Finally, the more we understand the nature of the epic language and of oral composition (both of which we will discuss in a moment), the clearer it is that a long period of poetic development must lie back of Homer. We have reason, then, to posit a continuous epic tradition going back to Mycenaean times: in other words, the existence of a body of

[5] *The Mycenaean Origin of Greek Mythology* (Sather Class. Lects., vol. VIII, Berkeley, 1932).

Mycenaean epic poetry which was in some sense an ancestor of Homer.

Prof. Webster[6] has made heroic efforts to flesh out this rather abstract idea, suggesting many possible features of both content and form. On the side of content he particularly emphasizes possible borrowing of Near Eastern themes: Creation myth, the deeds of Gilgamesh, the siege of a city for the sake of a woman (the poem of *Keret*); and certain objects, especially of armor: the tower- or body-shield of Ajax, metal corselets and greaves, silver-studded swords, Hector's gleaming helmet, and the golden lamp of Athena in the nineteenth book of the *Odyssey* (line 34). Certain of these objects are referred to in standing formulaic phrases, e.g., the "silver-studded sword," *phasganon* or *xiphos argyroêlon*; "bright-helmeted Hector," *korythaiolos Hector*; and Webster suggests others such as "Agamemnon king of men," *anax andrôn Agamemnon*. To this list we may add the well-known cases of Nestor's cup (*Il.* XI 632-5), the boar's-tooth helmet of Meriones (X 261-5), the Shield of Achilles (XVIII 478-608), and the brooch of Odysseus with its group of lion and fawn (*Od.* XIX 226-9).

It is one thing to suggest a provenience from Mycenaean poetry for these features, another to prove it. The best and only entirely conclusive proof would have to marshal two converging lines of evidence; namely, it would have to show that neither the object or theme in question nor the language in which it is expressed could have entered the poetic tradition after the Mycenaean Age. So far as the *realia* are concerned, such a proof is a kind of argument *ex silentio*: we have not found such an object from any period after the Bronze Age, *ergo*, it must have entered the tradition during the Bronze Age. Such seems still to be the case with the silver-studded sword—pending further discoveries. But body-shields appear, though distorted, on Geometric vases; a bronze helmet has been found in a Submycenaean grave; Odysseus' brooch has a parallel, though perhaps not a complete one, in ninth-century Boeotian fibulae; the structure of the Shield of Achilles was perhaps suggested by the concentric story-telling bands of eighth-century Oriental bowls, together with some vague recollections of Mycenaean inlay technique; and so on. Although archaeology has occasionally turned

[6] T. B. L. Webster, *From Mycenae to Homer* (London, 1958).

up confirmations of a Homeric description, and from the "right" period (Nestor's cup, the boar's-tusk helmet), more often it has complicated the problem by reducing the number of sure cases. And one final consideration raises its disturbing head. The collapse of Mycenaean civilization must have been different from any other similar catastrophe known to us if the survivors did not carry away with them *some* precious objects, to be preserved and handed down as heirlooms. Thus it is by no means impossible that a Geometric grave will present us, one of these days, with a late Mycenaean silver-studded sword.

The case for Homeric knowledge of the Bronze Age rests much more solidly on various general features of the poems—their Mycenaean political geography, the wealth and power of the Achaeans, the exclusion (generally though not totally consistent) of iron weapons, the ignoring of the Dorians—than on the exact remembrance of particular Mycenaean objects. And what the bard does remember has been subjected to various strains and distortions over the centuries-long span of the poetic tradition—as for example Homer fairly often confounds the tactics of the single Mycenaean thrusting-spear with those of the later pair of throwing spears—or has been preserved but its real purpose forgotten—as he knows of war-chariots but usually shows little conception of their use except as battle-front taxis.

Beyond the particular question of Mycenaean and post-Mycenaean elements, the development of Homeric studies has brought a steadily growing awareness that no class of *realia*, weapons or drinking-cups, houses or pins, is an assured clue by itself to the dating of the poems or any part of them. This growing awareness is the result of our growing understanding of the nature of oral epic poetry: its techniques, its ways of organizing experience, its use of language. We must therefore turn to the side of language.

We said a moment ago that a complete proof of provenience from Mycenaean poetry would have to include a demonstration that not only the object or practice in question but the language in which it is expressed is Mycenaean and cannot be later. For this and many other reasons an electric shock ran through the body of Homeric scholarship when the news came in 1953 that Michael Ventris had found Greek in the Linear B tablets.⁷ (In what follows I shall assume that the decipherment is correct in its main lines, though with still a considerable margin of uncertainty and possible error.)⁸ Here at last was a chance to measure the language of Homer against a form of Greek at least several centuries earlier. (How many centuries, depends not only on our dating of the Homeric poems but on the still unresolved question of the dating of the Knossos tablets; in any case it was clearly a major time-span.) Beyond this was the hope that perhaps the tablets would bring us some specimens of Mycenaean poetry, or at least clues to its existence.

A naïve hope, as it turned out. Instead of poetry the tablets contained inventories; instead of heroes, oil allotments and chariot-wheels, some of them in poor repair. I am not repining at this fact. The tablets are valuable—if we can depend on the decipherment— for the sociology and economics of the Mycenaean palaces. They open up to our startled gaze a world we would never have dreamed existed in Greece at any period: a centralized, bureaucratic, accountant's world in which every transaction is recorded, every pig and jar of oil is counted, the hair on the head of every mother's son is numbered—down to the sons of bath-attendants (?) and the servants of the least shrine. But so far as their contents are concerned the tablets tell us very little of value for Homer (we already knew that Nestor had chariots and wine-cups). On the contrary, the ordered, not to say regimented way of life they reveal is very different from anything in the poems; it is in fact alien, even hostile to the Homeric conception of life and of man, for it implicitly negates the idea of human freedom.—Except perhaps for the King, the *wanax*, and a few others who stood at the apex of the pyramid. We will return to this question in a moment.

⁷ M. Ventris and J. Chadwick, "Evidence for Greek Dialect in the Mycenaean Archives," *Journal of Hellenic Studies*, LXXIII, 1953, pp. 83-105; *idd.*, *Documents in Mycenaean Greek* (Cambridge, 1956); Chadwick, *The Decipherment of Linear B* (Cambridge, 1958).

⁸ Just a few days before this lecture was delivered the newest study of the problem came to hand: Saul Levin, *The Linear B Decipherment Controversy Re-examined* (State University of New York, 1964). Though he accepts the general correctness of Ventris's transcription, Levin finds that a majority of his values have neither been verified nor refuted and points to a "dark area" consisting of an "indeterminate but not inconsiderable amount of non-Greek" (p. 246). "Judged objectively," he says further (p. 245), "the interpretation of the wording of practically every tablet is pure guesswork."

No, the tablets do not help us substantively in the interpretation of Homer. Their importance for us is on the linguistic side ("9 o'clock" on our dial), in that they document a stage in the development of the Greek language, and therefore of the language of Homer, which far antedates any other direct evidence. (One caution may be in order here. The decipherment was achieved, at least in part, by filling in spaces on Ventris's "grid" with Greek words, or rather their syllables, which were already known to the decipherer either from Homer or from comparative linguistic sources. The extreme obliquity of the Linear B spelling system leaves it possible to match known words and phonemes with the written signs, but makes it very difficult if not impossible to elicit unknown ones from them.) Thus we now know that the Greek of Pylos in the late thirteenth century B.C.—and, if Evans's chronology was correct, of Knossos in the late fifteenth—still pronounced the digamma and maintained the Indo-European labio-velars as a distinct phonetic series; still used the uncontracted genitive singular ending -ojo and the instrumental-locative ending -phi (cf. Latin -bus); employed words like aisa, 'portion,' variant forms like ptolis (for polis, 'city'), a connective idé, 'and'; and so on. All these phonemes, morphemes, and words, or unmistakable traces of them (the clearest case is that of digamma), are still found in the language of Homer although they were obsolete or obsolescent in the current Ionic of his day.

Thus the first fact of importance for us which emerges from the tablets is that some of the elements in Homer's language are very old, at least of Mycenaean date. It might seem that the evidence suffices to prove a comparable antiquity for the poetic language as a whole. But even aside from the clear counter-indications in the language itself (widespread neglect of digamma, generalization of the Ionic fronting of long a [eta, long e, for long a], etc.), the tablets themselves do not prove so much. To demonstrate it we would have to prove, once again, that its elements not only go back as far as Mycenaean times but could not have entered the poetic language at any later date, e.g., during the Dark Age; and we are seldom in a position to do this. Nevertheless the survivals of old words and forms in Homer do establish a presumption that the core of the epic language, and not merely some isolated elements in it, belongs to a continuous tradition going back to the Bronze Age.

Another potentially valuable contribution which the tablets can make to the study of Homer—if we had ampler material and knew what to do with it—lies in certain implications for the linguistic geography of Greece, i.e., the history and distribution of the Greek dialects. No consensus has been reached on this problem, but one or two guiding lines may be indicated. First, certain vocabulary elements, such as *aisa*, *ptolis*, and *idé* mentioned above, are shared by Mycenaean Greek (the language of the tablets) with Arcado-Cypriot and Homer. Arcadian and Cypriot, though geographically widely separated in historical times, bear witness to what we can call the Achaean *diaspora*, the displacement of the speakers of Mycenaean Greek from the best parts of Peloponnese after the fall of the palaces. Marginal speech-areas tend to be conservative. In this partial affiliation of Homer with Arcadia and Cyprus we seem to find a parallel conservatism inherent in the epic language; and the common source appears to lie before us in the language of the tablets.

Secondly, the evidence of the tablets perhaps suggests, though it does not prove, that the main dialect divisions of the Greek language are younger than had been thought, i.e., go back to the end of the Mycenaean Age (ca. 1200 B.C.) but not earlier.[9] South Achaean, which includes Arcado-Cypriot, Attic, and Ionic, perhaps began to separate only then from North or East Achaean (Boeotian, East Thessalian, and Lesbian). Among the corollaries that might flow from this revision, two stand out as most interesting: (1) that much in the Homeric language which we have been accustomed to label "Ionic," with the corresponding assumption that it developed in Ionia after the Ionian Migration, may actually be an inheritance from Mycenaean Greek, and similarly (2) much in it that we have labelled "Aeolic," with the corresponding assumption that it came to the (Ionian) epic from the Aeolic dialect of Lesbos and the Troad, may actually reflect a much older state of affairs on the mainland; in which case Boeotian and Thessalian might turn out to be as important as East Aeolic (Lesbian).

[9] E. Risch, "Die Gliederung der griechischen Dialekte in neuer Sicht," *Museum Helveticum*, XII, 1955, pp. 61-76; and see the concluding remarks in Chantraine (note 11 below), vol. I, pp. 495-513, "Les éléments dialecticaux de la langue épique."

It is too early for a clear verdict on these questions, but surely the longer vista which the Linear B tablets have opened up on the development of the Greek language will end by putting the epic language also in a new historical perspective.

I will interpolate here one further remark about the language of Homer. It perhaps belongs at a later point in the story, but is also relevant to what has just been said. After various aberrations in the nineteenth century, such as Fick's retranslation of both poems into Aeolic, we have slowly but surely come to see that the epic language was a *Kunstsprache*, with laws and a life of its own.[10] It was never actually spoken by anyone at any time in the long history of the Greek language; it existed only for purposes of epic song. Anybody who wishes to understand it must peruse the magisterial pages of Chantraine's *Grammaire homérique*.[11] It has (subject to the eventual reservations suggested above) elements from several dialects, but in a mixture which is unhistorical because it is dictated above all by the needs of the verse. Within this mixture some elements can be distinguished as older (e.g., the phrase *Iliou propa-roithen*, "in front of Troy," which must be read as *Ilioo propa-roithen*, with a disyllabic ending of the noun which must have disappeared from the living language after *ca.* 900 B.C.), and some as younger (e.g., *meliêdeos oinou*, "of honey-sweet wine," where the digamma is ignored; cf. the "older" model *meliêdea (w)oînon*, where it is observed).[12] But the fatal fact about the epic *Kunst-sprache* is that older and younger linguistic phenomena within it cannot be separated into clean strata; they are merged in an indissoluble unity in this immortal language which never, in the usual sense, lived. Thus language cannot automatically tell us, any more than weapons can, whether a given line in Homer is "old" or "young."

We spoke a moment ago of the extreme difference, in fact contrariety of spirit, between the regimented life revealed by the tablets and the free, not overly ordered world of Homer. This may be an illusion imposed by the angle of view. The Linear B script was a highly artificial tool developed for a special purpose. Its

[10] K. Meister, *Die homerische Kunstsprache* (Leipzig, 1921).

[11] P. Chantraine, *Grammaire homérique, I: Phonétique et morphologie*, 3ème tirage (Paris, 1958); *II: Syntaxe* (Paris, 1953).

[12] A. Severyns, *Homère, II: Le poète et son oeuvre* (Brussels, 1946), pp. 86-93.

practitioners must have been a professional guild, perhaps even a caste: in any case a part of the bureaucratic system which they recorded so minutely. They were very possibly not Greeks, any more than most of the other workers were. The masters of these human beehives were certainly Greeks, i.e., speakers of Greek, and nothing requires us to assume that *they* had the bookkeeping mentality of the tablets—any more than we are required to assume that they were literate, or wanted to be. It is perfectly possible that the lords of Mycenae and Pylos had an adventurous, rough-and-ready, even tumultuous spirit like that of Homer's heroes, and that they possessed an oral poetry (in Greek, of course) which glorified similar exploits and similar values.

These possibilities may have a bearing on the next aspect of our subject, to which we now turn ("1 o'clock" on our dial): the "Dark Age." Kirk[13] especially has insisted on the probable importance of this period, roughly from 1100 to 900 B.C., not merely for the preservation and transmission but for the development of epic poetry in Greece. He cites evidence for continued habitation, e.g., in most parts of Peloponnese after the fall of the palaces, and rightly says that heroic poetry does not require cities or a high level of material culture in order to flourish. The village, or even the mountain, may give it a home during times of trouble when it is barred from the main centers: witness the songs of the medieval Greeks and the South Slavs. A book by Maximilian Braun[14] on the latter brings out clearly what it is that gives an epic tradition the inner strength to survive such a period of outward deprivation. It is that heroic song assures a depressed and defeated people of its national identity, by holding up the great deeds of its ancestors for it to remember and glory in. The South Slavs did not surrender to their humiliation at the hands of the Turks so long as their bards kept the memory of Kossovo alive.

I suggest that we need a cause of similar scope and weight to account for the survival—and not just a survival but a probable growth and elaboration—of the Greek epic tradition during the Dark Age. Mere interest in battles and techniques of warfare is not enough. But let us be clear what this means in the frame of Greek

[13] G. S. Kirk, *The Songs of Homer* (Cambridge, 1962), pp. 126-156.
[14] Maximilian Braun, *Das serbokroatische Heldenlied* (Göttingen, 1961).

history. When we speak of the collapse of Mycenaean civilization we mean the collapse of the great palaces, in which it centered. Writing, i.e., the Linear B script, and the structure of that whole elaborately centralized economy was swept away with the palaces. No doubt many of the kings and warriors, the Greek-speaking upper crust—a very thin crust, for all we know—were destroyed also. But not all. Codrus, the last king of Athens, claimed descent from Neleus and Nestor, and so did the Athenian tyrant Pisistratus and the royal family of Miletus.[15] Meanwhile, surely, many if not most of the common folk (and goodness knows what we should call *them*, ethnically or linguistically) went on living, in the same place or another not too far away; they survived this catastrophe as they had survived others.

Now surely it is suggestive, if no more, that although there is evidence of life going on at a humble level in Peloponnese after the fall, there is no sure trace of a later survival of epic activity anywhere in the peninsula except at Corinth—and Corinth is on the way to Boeotia and Athens—while on the other hand the most conspicuous seat of epic poetry in the historical period is Ionia, which according to Greek tradition was settled from Athens by refugees from various Achaean lands including Messenia (Pylos). Is it not likely that the nucleus of these Achaean refugee groups was provided by the remnants of the Achaean kings and warrior class? If so, we need not wonder that they cherished and indeed expanded the tradition of epic song, even in distant Ionia: it was precisely because the songs reaffirmed their Achaean identity and their heritage of heroic valor.

With this we have crossed the line, unawares, to our next rubric ("2 o'clock" on the dial), "Mainland and Ionian epic." In the past our thinking about the Greek epic has centered in Ionia, with a bow to the neighboring Aeolians of Lesbos and the Troad. This being the focus, Hesiod and the "Hesiodic school," along with Agias of Troezen, Eumelus of Corinth, and the other scraps and tatters of tradition about epic poetry on the mainland of Greece, were an embarrassment, a marginal intrusion with no clear relationship to the

---

[15] Neleus the twin brother of Pelias: *Odyssey*, XI 254. Codrus: Herodotus, V 65; Pausanias, II 18, 2. Pisistratids: Hdt., *loc cit.* Miletus: Mimnermus, frags. 9 and 10 Diehl; Strabo, XIV 633.

main center of epic activity. Recently Prof. Notopoulos[16] has marshalled evidence to show that the poems of Hesiod, and others
which are surely of mainland origin or inspiration such as some of
the Homeric Hymns, employ the same formulaic methods of composition as the *Iliad* and *Odyssey*. It is becoming clear that all these
works are ultimately derived from the same general tradition, so
that we no longer need to consider Hesiod as merely a belated,
rustic imitator of Homer. The new vistas which are thus opened
up remind us of the new linguistic perspectives suggested by the
language of the Mycenaean tablets. In short, we are beginning to
see the Greek epic tradition in something like its proper dimensions.

But only beginning. The way is very obscure, and direct evidence from the Dark Age is still wholly lacking and likely to remain so, since it was illiterate. I will only venture a few comments
and suggestions. First, if the chief function of the epic in that period
was to preserve and fortify the Achaeans' national memory and self-
esteem, we may discern a reason for their bards fixing on, and perhaps beginning to augment, the tale of the expedition against Troy.
Depressed or defeated peoples seem to tend, for whatever reason,
to remember especially the most recent episodes of their days of
glory. The historical foundations of the Trojan *geste*, as now defined and delimited by Prof. Blegen's work at Troy,[17] are slender
but solid. It is clear that Troy VIIa fell to a siege, and whether that
happened around 1270-1260, as he believes, or somewhat later, the
event falls within a generation or two before the destruction of the
great palaces. It would have been fresh, therefore, in the memory
of the survivors. The difficulty is to see how the Mycenaean world
could have mounted so massive an attack in the middle or late
thirteenth century B.C., when it itself may already have been in
trouble. But we must leave some room for bardic amplification, and
if the poetic tradition can be trusted at all this was a pan-Achaean
effort—the last one before the collapse.

In both the Homeric epics Pylos and Nestor and his sons have a

[16] James A. Notopoulos, "Homer, Hesiod, and the Achaean Heritage of Oral
Poetry," *Hesperia*, XXIX, 1960, pp. 177-197; "The Homeric Hymns as Oral
Poetry; A Study of the Post-Homeric Oral Tradition," *American Journal of
Philology*, LXXXIII, 1962, pp. 337-368; "Studies in Early Greek Oral Poetry,"
Harvard Studies in Classical Philology, LXVIII, 1964, pp. 1-77.
[17] Cf. C. Blegen, *The Mycenaean Age* (Semple Lectures), pp. 13-15.

strikingly prominent place. If refugees from Pylos were indeed among the leaders at Athens and in the Ionian Migration this feature may have entered the tradition early, in the first generations after the collapse. On the other hand I am sceptical about the central position which Professors Whitman[18] and Webster assign to Athens at this time. It is possible to imagine Pylian and other Achaean refugees at Athens vigorously cultivating the poetic testament of their ancestors' deeds, but then carrying it away with them to Ionia without leaving any great residue behind them. By any reckoning, Athens' part in the Trojan War was a modest one; there is no record of the Athenians having especially cultivated the epic tradition, and no discernible reason for their doing so. I should add that I am also sceptical about the analogies with Geometric, i.e., Athenian vase painting which have been urged so strongly by Whitman and Webster.

There remains the great enigma: Boeotia. The Theban cycle; the Catalogue of Ships in the *Iliad*, with Boeotia as its center; Aulis, the staging point for Troy; ninth-century bronze fibulae with heroic scenes; Hesiod, with his echoes of Oriental cosmological or theological poetry as well as of heroic traditions; catalogues of women, and the other productions of the "Hesiodic school": we have nothing but tantalizing scraps. And Boeotia in the Bronze Age had close ties with Euboea and with southeastern Thessaly: Achilles' Phthia, the Gulf of Pagasae, and Iolcus, home port of the Argo and the site of a Mycenaean palace. Neleus came from Thessaly; he was an uncle of Jason. Boeotian, though mixed with Doric elements, is a sister-dialect of East Thessalian and Lesbian: the North Achaean group. And so on. It is no use; we cannot put the pieces together. But some day we may be able to bring into focus a North Achaean line of development: a line which surely has something to do with our *Iliad* and many of the so-called "Aeolic" features in it.

The touchstone which Notopoulos used to demonstrate the affinity between Hesiodic and Homeric verse was the presence of "formulae." This brings us to our last rubric under the general heading of background ("3 o'clock" on the dial): "Oral composition." I

---

[18] Cedric H. Whitman, *Homer and the Heroic Tradition* (Cambridge, Mass., 1958), chap. III, "Athens, 1200-700 B.C.," pp. 46-64; T. B. L. Webster, *op. cit.* (above, note 6).

trust that at this point in the history of Homeric studies I do not
need to dilate on the nature of Milman Parry's great discovery, or
its momentous consequences.[19] It is beyond doubt one of the most
important contributions this country has ever made to classical
scholarship. Parry himself only lived long enough to make a beginning, but a beginning *sans pareil*. His proof of Homer's use of formulae, and of the "scope" and "economy" of the system, is a classic
of scientific demonstration which need not be repeated here. I am
more concerned with the general concept of oral composition and
with the implications it has for the Homeric poems.

Parry's next step was to seek a "control," i.e., an independent
body of material to check his conclusions; and he found it among
the oral bards of modern Yugoslavia. The most important results
of that field work have been summarized by Prof. Lord in *The
Singer of Tales*.[20] Other scholars have helped to corroborate the
findings and to broaden the concept of "formula" to include not
only phrases and whole lines but "typical scenes" (the arming of
the hero, the reception of visitors, etc.) and themes of still larger
scope. What emerges from the work done so far is the awareness
of a poetic repertory of truly staggering scope and complexity, embracing elements all the way from single words and short phrases
to poetic structures which can fill an evening's recitation. And from
Professor Lord's account[21] we get something else equally important:
a sense of what the actual singing is like: the setting, the audience,
and the reciprocal relation between it and the bard.

Two things at least are entirely clear about oral composition: that
it differs *toto caelo* from memorization of a text, and that the system as a whole is far too complex and finely adjusted to be the work
of any one man or one generation of men, or even two or three generations. The first fact establishes a *prima facie* probability that oral
composition cannot very long survive widespread literacy, while
the second one gives powerful support to the idea that the Greek

[19] Parry's key articles were "Studies in the Epic Technique of Oral Verse-
Making, I. Homer and Homeric Style," and "II. The Homeric Language as the
Language of an Oral Poetry," *Harvard Studies in Classical Philology*, XLI, 1930,
pp. 73-147, and XLII, 1932, pp. 1-50. A complete bibliography of Parry's work
is given in Albert B. Lord, "Homer, Parry, and Huso," *American Journal of
Archaeology*, LII, 1948, pp. 43-44.
[20] Albert B. Lord, *The Singer of Tales* (Cambridge, Mass., 1960).
[21] *Op. cit.*, pp. 13-17.

epic tradition stretches far back of Homer, into the Dark Age and perhaps into the Mycenaean. But some other points are less clear. It is often said that since the singer is a composer, not a mere memorizer, he never sings the same song twice. Obviously, in the literal, tape-recording sense this is true. But much of the difference between versions seems to consist of addition or suppression of lines, or of whole scenes or episodes. An unlimited and unregulated variation is not proved. Indeed the song as a whole (limiting "song" for the moment to the normal size for a single uninterrupted recitation, from 500 to 800 lines) must have some characteristic traits, structural or stylistic, which mark it as one man's work rather than another's; and if those traits, or enough of them, recur in successive recitations then the song is still, in an important sense, "the same." We need a closer definition of "difference" and "sameness." Again, the Yugoslav material and that from modern Greece, collected by Prof. Notopoulos, clearly defines the normal limit of an uninterrupted recitation, the one mentioned a moment ago, and indicates that a song of more than a few thousand lines (spread over several recitations) is exceptional. The longest sustained effort recorded by Parry, and only after considerable encouragement from him, was 12,000 lines. But our problem is precisely to understand two poems which are of that or even greater length and which, by a growing consensus, are agreed to have a large amount of coherent structure. Finally, Parry was led by his observations to assert that the singer never consciously tries to innovate, to change a formula or a song. This assertion was premature and has been rebutted; but it remains difficult, when one is faced with a formulaic system so vast and yet so efficient, to see just where innovation can indeed take place.

It seems to me that the concept of oral composition, *as a means for understanding the Homeric poems*, is still beset with two unresolved questions. One of these has to do with the method itself, the other with the comparative materials which it has brought to bear on the problem.

Parry's first and real triumph was won out of the *Iliad* and *Odyssey* themselves. It dealt with formulas in the strictest sense, the noun-epithet and verb-predicate combinations which fill a part of a line. These are the blocks out of which the building is built. The method loses rigor in proportion as it leaves that level and climbs to larger units, where the "economy" is less and less strict. The unresolved question is whether this is not inherent in the method; or, to put it another way, whether as we go on from formulae to formulaic lines to themes to episodes to songs to longer poems, the specific differences between oral composition and its alleged contrary, literary (or literate) composition, do not begin to fade away. How different is Homer from Vergil or Milton (also an oral poet, by the way, in *Paradise Lost*) when it comes to marshalling the major elements in his grand design? Some think that he must have had recourse to writing to achieve the design; but I am not convinced. It seems to me that this kind of poetic strategy is always shaped in the poet's mind, without benefit of pen and paper except as a secondary resource; so that at this level oral composition, as a specific method, merges into poetic composition *per se*.

The second question is whether the oral singers of modern Greece and Yugoslavia provide an adequate parallel to Homer. I myself do not think they do. At one end of the scale, neither their verse-form nor their use of formulae is anything like as rigorous as Homer's (Parry deduced the principles of the formulaic system from Homer, not from them), and at the other end they have nothing to show—or at least nothing of theirs has been published or described—which is really comparable to the large-scale organization of the Homeric poems. This is not said in disparagement of Avdo Meḍedović and his confrères. They are, or were, honorable practitioners of an ancient craft. But under modern conditions it is a dying craft, relegated to the illiterate fringes of society and unlikely to recruit the best talents. Everything we know about early Greece suggests that the situation there was very different. Clearly the Greek bard, whatever his birth, was in close touch with the leading people in his society. His art made him the admired of all observers, and he was central, not peripheral, to the mainstream of spiritual life. Under these circumstances poetry can recruit some of the finest talents. This must be particularly true of the *Iliad* and *Odyssey*: whatever one thinks of their origins, it is clear that they are the work of exceptionally gifted singers.

It is not, however, just a question of talent, but of the function of epic poetry. If it is true that epic song survives a time of troubles because it ministers to a people's felt need to relive, reaffirm its national identity through memories of a greater past, and if this need is subject to change as the national life moves into new phases, then no contemporary slice from a parallel tradition of song can tell us all we want to know. For that we need a diachronic comparison, based on as full a history of the other tradition as we can get. For the South Slavs, at least a sketch of such a history is offered in the book of Maximilian Braun which has already been mentioned, and glimpses of other relevant traditions are provided by the monumental work of the Chadwicks on *The Growth of Literature* and by Bowra's book *Heroic Poetry*.[22]

This is not to say that we are to abandon the gains made by Parry and his successors. They are priceless and uniquely illuminating. But what they reveal to us of the technique of oral composition needs to be supplemented by a broader view of the historical factors which sustained and fostered the prolonged development of that technique. And it needs to be supplemented by a consideration of what happens when a supremely gifted singer is confronted by a significant shift, a major change of direction, in the life of his people. Heroic song has an innate tragic cast, since heroes must die —the greatest, indeed, die young—and so many of the works of men are ephemeral. What happens if the tragic burden of traditional song impinges on a new era, a time of new stirrings, conquests, explorations, when great deeds are again in motion or in prospect?

Here we come upon a discouraging situation. On the one hand, in the heroic poetry of other lands and ages that can be mustered for our inspection we find few historical developments that are really comparable to the Greek and can be studied in sufficient detail—just because they are oral and therefore elude our search. And on the other hand we find few if any traces of a genius comparable to that of the man or men we call "Homer." All the indices seem to point to one conclusion: ultimately, we can only understand Homer out of himself, that is, out of the poems.

In this connection, however, one fact is perhaps encouraging. A notable consensus has grown up in the last twenty years or so, among most scholars, that the Homeric poems should be dated to

[22] H. M. and N. K. Chadwick, *The Growth of Literature*, 3 vols. (Cambridge, 1932-1940); C. M. Bowra, *Heroic Poetry* (London, 1952).

the eighth century. The reasons are too many and too complex to be recited here, including the thorny question of *unmistakable* echoes of the two poems in Greek art and literature ("6 o'clock" on the dial). The most judicious summary of the evidence is given by Kirk,[23] who does not exclude the late ninth century (for the *Iliad*) but considers the eighth more probable. Others would more confidently date the *Iliad* to the middle of the eighth century (±750) and the *Odyssey* a generation or so later (±720).

This consensus would no doubt be even broader were it not for a persistent disagreement over the problem of writing ("4 o'clock" on the dial) and over the so-called "Pisistratean recension" (8 o'clock). We have noted that the *Homerische Frage* arose from Wolf's conviction that the two poems as we have them could not have been produced and transmitted without the aid of writing. Some recent scholars, even among those most strongly committed to the basic principle of oral composition, tend to agree with him.[24] Again, certain people are convinced that the poems were completed more or less in the shape in which we now have them in the eighth century, while others believe that they reached that shape only in sixth-century Athens; and this controversy is partly connected with the other one, whether the "final" shape could be attained without, or only with, writing. At the moment the battle-line seems to be drawn between Ionians and Athenians, as we might call them. Indeed it appears that the historic war between Analysts and Unitarians ("5 o'clock") may now be concentrating upon this sector of the front. But that fact, if it is one, perhaps gives some ground for hope. For few scholars would now deny that our manuscript tradition of Homer ("7 o'clock") passed through a decisive phase in Athens in the sixth century,[25] while conversely few would date the main development of what Kirk calls the "monumental" poems to the period after 700. We are coming more and more, it seems to me, to focus our attention on the two centuries between ca. 750

---

[23] Kirk, *op. cit.* (above, note 13), pp. 282-287.

[24] H. T. Wade-Gery, *The Poet of the Iliad* (Cambridge, 1952), pp. 37-39, and Bowra, *op. cit.* (above, note 22), pp. 240-241, suggest that the poet wrote. Lord, "Homer's Originality: Dictated Texts," *Trans. Amer. Philol. Assn.*, LXXXIV, 1953, pp. 124-134, prefers the hypothesis of dictation to a scribe or scribes; similarly in *The Singer of Tales*, pp. 155-157.

[25] See G. M. Bolling, *Ilias Atheniensium* (Spec. Publ. of the Amer. Philol. Assn., Lancaster. Pa., 1950), preface.

and 550. They represent the new Critical Gap, one at least as decisive—and as difficult—as the Dark Age.

The newest conclusions about the date of alphabetic writing in Greece give further definiteness to this focus. Thanks to the magisterial work of Miss Jeffery on the archaic scripts,[26] we can now say with some confidence that the invention was made around the middle of the eighth century and spread rapidly, although few if any of the extant specimens can be dated much before 700. In other words writing became available—theoretically available—at almost exactly the time to which, as we have said, a growing consensus tends to assign the completion of the poems. Beyond that the way is still dark. Whether an orally trained poet, as Homer certainly was, could and would resort to writing, what his motives would be for doing so, and through what channels the written text would be transmitted initially, we cannot say.

At the end I should like to return to the sequence of thought which I interrupted in order to discuss writing and related problems. Among those who have spoken out for dating Homer to the eighth century, Schadewaldt's voice is one of the most impressive. And Schadewaldt is precisely the scholar who, bent as he is on understanding the inward reasons for this new creation, has most emphasized the new burst of energy and activity that distinguishes the eighth century, after the long night of the Dark Age.[27] The century of the *polis*, of the beginnings of hoplite tactics, of exploration, of colonization, of the first organization of the great Games, it marks a decisive turning-point away from the Mycenaean and the Dark Age, towards the future. It is the beginning of Hellas as we know it. How do the poems present themselves in relation to this new thrust of energy? From their tradition they are oriented towards the past. In what ways and to what degree do they also look forward to the Hellenic future? Finally, if we do indeed find evidence of a new orientation, combining past and future, to what extent must it and can it be the work of a single mind? It is not certain that answers to these questions can be given, but one thing is certain: only the poems themselves can give them.

[26] L. H. Jeffery, *The Local Scripts of Archaic Greece* (Oxford, 1961).
[27] W. Schadewaldt, "Homer und sein Jahrhundert," in *Von Homers Welt und Werk*, 3rd ed. (Stuttgart, 1959), pp. 87-129.

II: THE POEMS

In the first lecture we surveyed the Homeric Problem: that is, we passed in very summary, not to say sketchy, review the chief kinds of evidence we have for the background, character, and date of the Homeric poems. If our scale of ignorance and knowledge tipped towards the former oftener than the latter, leaving great blanks in the record, that is in the nature of the case, and the situation is not likely to be changed by any foreseeable external discovery. The iron fact remains that Greeks could not write between the thirteenth century B.C. and the latter part of the eighth. What we now know about the character and procedures of oral poetry makes it certain that the epic tradition in its long life passed through many changes: migration to new areas, expansion, concentration, variation of themes, incorporation of new material, creation of new formulae and polishing of old ones, gradual admission of new linguistic forms. But the details of this incessant process of change, balanced always between conservatism and innovation, will remain forever beyond our ken, barring some new and quite unforeseeable source of light.

Thus for better or worse we are left with the poems themselves. In a sense this is the natural and happy ending to our quest. For the poems are greater than the problems to which they have given rise; their greatness is in fact the *raison d'être* and final justification of the whole Homeric Question. And unlike most of the background, the poems are "there" before us, ready to be experienced. In this lecture I propose to talk about the poems as experience. But this is not a simple matter either. For one thing, we cannot go far in an hour towards experiencing the full reality of nearly 28,000 lines of poetry. Yet the length, the cumulative weight and mass of the *Iliad* and *Odyssey* are an essential part of their being and their effect. We cannot cite more than snippets here. What kind of snippets shall they be, then: "representative" passages—standard fare, so to speak—or some of the great climactic moments? This problem is intimately connected with another which, put as briefly as possible, is this:

As was indicated in the first lecture, the age-old controversy between Analysts and Unitarians has recently entered on a new phase of sophistication. In the light of what we now know about oral composition, it has become evident that the poems can no longer be treated as literary texts out of which earlier texts can be quarried by a simple process of extraction. (The only place in either poem where this can be done cleanly is Book X of the *Iliad*, the *Doloneia*.) The old concept of intact layers is dead. Whatever earlier material exists in the poems must have gone through that process of total ingestion—adaptation, expansion, ornamentation, and so on—which we know to be the standard procedure of oral poetry. It has been not merely incorporated but absorbed into a new whole and can be recovered, if at all, only by new and subtler techniques.

On the other hand, it is equally out of the question for the modern Unitarian to claim that his Homer is the only begetter of the poems, in the sense of having invented everything in them. Homer did not invent the versification, the formulae, the style, the basic narrative techniques, or most of the material. The final singers, the monumental poets, as Kirk calls them, stand on the shoulders of all the bards who went before, and those bards, though we cannot identify them or their work, have left their mark everywhere, not in large, separable blocks but in the very texture and fabric of the poems. Conversely, and this must never be lost to view, if the monumental poems did indeed attain their characteristic (one hesitates to use the word "final") shape in the eighth century but were not written down till the sixth, we have no guarantee that a similar process of adaptation, expansion, etc., did not go on during those two centuries. This is perhaps the most troublesome problem of all.

The upshot of these reflections is that it is very hard, perhaps impossible, when we cite particular passages, to be sure whether they more nearly represent the tradition as such, the "monumental" poet or poets, or what was added to their work by later singers.

But, you may well say, millions of listeners and readers have experienced the magic of the poems, from Homer's day to ours, without being disturbed by these subtleties. Wolf himself recorded that when he left the plane of scholarship and returned to the poems he almost repented of his doubts. In the words of Jebb[1] (a translation from Wolf):

[1] R. C. Jebb, *Homer: An Introduction to the Iliad and the Odyssey* (Glasgow, 1887), p. 110, quoting from p. xxii of Wolf's preface to the *Iliad*.

As he steeps himself in that stream of epic story which glides like a
clear river, his own arguments vanish from his mind; the pervading
harmony and consistency of the poems assert themselves with irresistible power; and he is angry with the scepticism which has
robbed him of belief in one Homer.

It is time for us to plunge into the river. Whatever Homer did
to the epic tradition, we can be sure that he was not the first who
knew how to tell a story or the first to use the formulaic apparatus.
And we can be equally sure that single combats between heroes
were a standing feature of the epic from its beginning, whenever
that was. It is not likely that Homer fundamentally changed the
narrative patterns for such a scene. Here is an episode from Book V
of the *Iliad*, the *aristeia* of Diomed. It is very like dozens of others
in the poem. Pandarus has wounded Diomed with an arrow from
his famous bow, but Athena has healed the wound. Now Diomed
goes after Pandarus and Aeneas, who have joined forces. Pandarus
hails him (line 277 ff.):[2]

"Valiant and strong-spirited, o son of proud Tydeus,
you were not beaten then by the bitter arrow, my swift shot.
Now I will try with the throwing-spear to see if I can hit you."
    So he spoke, and balanced the spear far-shadowed, and threw it,
and struck the son of Tydeus in the shield, and the flying
bronze spearhead was driven clean through and into the corselet,
and the shining son of Lykaon cried aloud in a great voice:
"Now are you struck clean through the middle, and I think that
    you will not
hold up for much longer; you have given me great claim to glory."
    Then strong Diomedes answered, not frightened before him:
"You did not hit me, you missed, but I do not think that you two
will go free until one or the other of you has fallen
to glut with his blood Ares the god who fights under the shield's
    guard."

As connoisseurs of heroic combat, that is, of the traditions of com-
bat as transmitted by epic poetry, we are on familiar ground here.
The contestants challenge each other and announce their intentions.
Pandarus does so in full form, with a whole line of ceremonial

---

[2] Unless otherwise noted, all passages from the *Iliad* are in the translation of
Richmond Lattimore (Chicago, 1951).

address: "Valiant and strong-spirited, o son of proud Tydeus." In the next line Lattimore's translation has transposed two phrases, "bitter arrow" and "swift shot." In the original the former stands second, at the end of a line: *pikros oïstos*, which also fills the end of a line, after the "bucolic diaeresis," at IV 118, 134, 217, V 99, 110, and elsewhere. In other words it is a formula. It appears only in the nominative and accusative cases: *pikros oïstos* and *pikron oïston*. Closely related to it are *âlto d'oïstos*, "and the arrow leapt," IV 125; *autar oïstos*, "but the arrow," V 399; *ôkyn oïston*, "the swift arrow," V 395; *helken oïston*, "he drew (out) the arrow," IV 213; and other formulae, still involving a noun and adjective and denoting a weapon, but in the dative case: *oxeï douri*, "with the sharp spear," IV 490, V 73, 238, 336; *oxeï chalkôi*, "with the sharp bronze," IV 540, V 132; *nêleï chalkôi*, "with the pitiless bronze," IV 348, V 330; *aithopi chalkôi*, "with the glittering bronze," IV 495; *encheï makrôi*, "with the long spear," V 45; *douri te makrôi*, "and with the long spear," V 297. Belonging to the same over-all group, defined by the metrical space of the last two feet, are formulae like *patrida gaian*, "his fatherland," IV 180; *isotheos phôs*, "godlike man," IV 212; *thouridos alkês*, "of furious valor," IV 234, 418; *aithopa (w)oinon*, "sparkling wine," IV 250, V 341.

This list of parallels has been gleaned from the immediate neighborhood of our passage; the citations could be multiplied manifold. Similarly Pandarus's "far-shadowed" or "long-shafted spear," line 280, flies from the hand of a dozen or so heroes in the *Iliad*—in the last two and a half feet of a line—and the whole line is repeated seven times in the poem. The spear penetrates Diomed's shield (*tês de diapro*, "and right through it," 281; cf. *hê de diapro*, "and it right through," 66; *alla diapro*, "but right through," XII 184; *oude diapro*, "but not right through," XII 404) and "comes close to the corselet" but stops there. Pandarus shouts exultantly, "Now you have been hit." He has some reason to exult. When he last shot a "bitter arrow," in Book IV 125 ff., it penetrated Menelaus's baldric, his corselet, and the guard (*mitrê*) beneath, and ended by drawing blood, 140. But this time is different. Diomed rejects the claim and boasts in his turn, ending with an ancient formula, *talaurinon polemistên*. Then (line 290):

He spoke, and threw; and Pallas Athene guided the weapon
to the nose next to the eye, and it cut on through the white teeth
and the bronze weariless shore all the way through the tongue's base
so that the spearhead came out underneath the jawbone.
He dropped then from the chariot and his armour clattered upon him,
dazzling armour and shining, while those fast-running horses
shied away, and there his life and his strength were scattered.

This time Athena herself guides the spear, the same Athena who
guided Pandarus's arrow against Menelaus in Book IV; but more
of that anon. For the moment she merely signifies that this spear-
cast will not fail. Pandarus's time has come; in modern fighting
men's parlance, his number is up. The course of the weapon past
his eye and through his jaw is described with the clinical precision
which we associate with Homer's battle-scenes, and the end is entirely formulaic: "he dropped from the chariot and his armor clattered upon him." etc.

"But Aineias sprang to the ground with shield and with long spear,
for fear that somehow the Achaians might haul off the body,
and like a lion in the pride of his strength stood over him
holding before him the perfect circle of his shield and the spear
and raging to cut down any man who might come to face him,
crying a terrible cry."

The hero bestrides his friend's body like a lion (the lion is the
commonest analogue for the hero in the *Iliad*), to keep it from
being dragged off and despoiled by the enemy. But Diomed picks
up a huge stone—a weight that no two men could lift nowadays,
the poet tells us, as he tells us again when Hector (XII 449) and
Aeneas himself (XX 285) perform the same feat—and smashes
Aeneas's hip-joint. The latter falls on his knee, propping himself
up with one hand, and then "black night covered his two eyes":
i.e., he passes out, as Hector does in Book XIV, line 439, when the
stone cast by Ajax has felled him. In our case Aeneas would have
been done for, had not his mother Aphrodite thrown a fold of her
white robe around him and carried him off the field—as she had
previously smuggled Paris from the field under even more humiliating circumstances in Book III, 375 ff.

Before we go any farther I should say that this little passage
was not chosen initially with malice prepense, for the sake of the

parallels and ramifications which spread out from it in all directions, but simply because it offered a good compact example of Homeric fighting.

Compact the episode certainly is; it does its work with a minimum of time and effort. It exemplifies the four cardinal qualities that Matthew Arnold found in Homer (but not in most of his translators): rapidity, simplicity of thought and expression, and nobility.[3] And it is in no way exceptional in these respects. A large part of the *Iliad* is taken up with just such fighting, and with some variations almost all these combats show the same qualities. If we enjoy them, why do we enjoy them?

Here, however, we must take notice of a difficulty which is specifically modern. It is questionable whether most modern readers— perhaps especially twentieth-century American readers—of the *Iliad* do particularly enjoy the battle passages, at least the mass of them that confronts us in Books IV through VIII and XI through XVII. And readers who approach the poem with strong pacifist sentiments, like the lamented Simone Weil,[4] may even emerge with a fundamentally distorted view of what it is about. We have to discount these changes of taste and feeling as best we can, if we are to experience fairly the burden of the whole.

Granting, then, that we are capable of enjoying battle passages at all, why do we enjoy Homer's narrative of them? Basically, because his art equips him to tell them rapidly, simply, and nobly. In each of these respects the formulaic method provides the key. It is the secret of the incomparable *ease and security* we feel in every part of the poems, even when a speech or a piece of narrative grows long—as many of them do. And if this sense of security communicates itself even to us, through the medium of translations and in a world more and more alienated from the heroic way of life, how much more powerful it must have been to Homer's own listeners! If we can trust the modern analogies recorded by Lord, Notopoulos, and others, those hearers, or at least some of them, were connoisseurs not only of the tales but of the language and technique with which they were told. In any case it is not true, as some treat-

[3] Matthew Arnold, *On Translating Homer* ("popular edition," London, 1896), p. 10.
[4] Simone Weil, *The Iliad; or the Poem of Force*, reprint from *Politics* magazine, November, 1945.

ments of the subject seem to imply, that the formulaic technique exists only for the convenience of the bard, to help him sing the song. It exists just as much for the sake of the listener, to enable him to listen. The oral art, with its rich and intricately organized store of formulae, type-scenes, etc., gives the practised singer the firm base he needs, the confidence that he can develop the song in whatever direction and whatever depth of detail he chooses. By the same token, and to exactly the same degree—for the two things are strict correlatives—it gives the listener the confidence that·he can follow the song wherever it leads without getting lost, that he will understand it and enjoy it.

When heroic speeches and actions recur again and again in much the same way and are told, each time they recur, in much the same language, a rudimentary kind of *generalization* has taken place. Parry remarked on this generalizing character of the epic language. But the process remains well below the level of anything we can properly call abstraction. Although the modern singers have more or less complete mastery of their system, they are quite incapable of expounding its rationale; nor do they have an explicit, theoretical conception of man, his character, his actions. No more did the Greek bards. Nevertheless their language and their narrative technique has a structure, is a structure, which gives more than firmness to their work. The qualities which Matthew Arnold attributed to "Homer" are in the main a function of the technique.

To return to our passage: When Pandarus speaks of his "bitter arrow," in line 278 of Book V, he is not merely using a formula. The phrase also recalls—whether Pandarus himself intends it·so does not matter; the *poet* intends it so—the episode of his treacherous bow-shot in Book IV. Pandarus was put up to that act by Athena, and Athena was carrying out the direct command of Zeus, IV 70-72 (my translation): "Go very quickly to the field, among the Trojans and Achaeans, and make trial so that the Trojans may be first to injure the far-gloried Achaeans, against the truce." Pandarus, as it turned out, was the man chosen for this heinous but necessary deed. Can it be a coincidence that now, just 700 lines after his first "bitter arrow" drew Menelaus's blood, he himself falls? Pandarus is the first major Trojan to die since the general fighting began at IV 422 ff. He is paying the penalty for his act of treachery; there is no other reason why his death should come so soon, just here. When he cries out the formula "bitter arrow" and then is killed, we are meant to recall the other scene. Yet no overt allusion is made here to the treacherous bow-shot. No explicit cloud of moral disapproval hangs over Pandarus. He is linked very closely with the major hero Aeneas: they are identified together by Sthenelus, lines 244-245, as men of might and valor, and Aeneas later bestrides his body just as Menelaus does that of Patroclus in Book XVII. Pandarus is not called by name again, after Sthenelus's first identification of him, but is twice referred to by the honorific title "Lycaon's glorious son." We are reminded by this of a strange feature of that earlier passage in Book IV, where Pandarus is identified before the bow-shot (lines 88-89) as "godlike", "Lycaon's blameless and mighty son"; and this identical line is repeated in V 169. Blameless indeed, when he is about to commit an act of infamy! The word has puzzled many readers; it has even been cited to prove that the poet's use of epithets is purely mechanical: Pandarus is "blameless" because the epithet is customary and fits the meter, regardless of the context. Is it not possible on the contrary that the poet indeed imputes no blame to Pandarus? The most he permits himself is the one word (IV 104; as a predicate, not an epithet) *aphroni*, "witless" or "foolish." Pandarus has been chosen by a god to perform the indispensable function of starting the fighting, after the truce. It was foolish of him to do it, but he personally is blameless. What matters is not that he is Pandarus but that he is a Trojan, and Zeus was determined that the Trojans (plural in his speech, line 71) should be guilty of the breach.

But why was Zeus determined that the Trojans should be guilty? We may note that he was only approving and echoing an utterance of Hera (65-67). But let us essay a psychological rather than a theological answer. The song is being sung before a Greek, i.e., an Achaean audience. Everybody knows that the Trojans were to blame for the war. One of them, Paris, stole Helen; we have been on this beach, fighting and suffering, for nine years to get her back, and they have only just now (in Book III) made the first constructive proposal looking in that direction. Everything was to depend on the outcome of a duel between the seducer and the injured husband.

And then what happens? After the most solemn exchange of vows, Menelaus beats Paris in fair fight and is dragging him off the field when suddenly—Paris is not there. Somebody, it is not sure who, has spirited him away. (Aphrodite, who did it, took care not to let her hand be seen). A hundred lines later Menelaus is still stalking the field like a beast of prey, looking for Paris to no avail. The Trojans say they are sorry but *they* cannot help him; they have no love for Paris and would be glad to turn him in, but they didn't see which way he went.

It is a very unsatisfactory situation. The one thing that is clear is that the Trojans are to blame. Paris was the one who violated the bonds of hospitality before, and now he has done another unforgivable thing. Trojans cannot be trusted. If anyone breaks the truce, it will certainly be one of them. And they will be punished for it.

This may seem a superficial way of dealing with Books III and IV, especially when we have seen Aphrodite at work and the gods in council, debating what to do next. It is, however, the official Achaean view of the matter. Agamemnon, after Menelaus has been wounded by the arrow, announces with all possible solemnity (IV 163 ff.) that the Trojans are guilty and will suffer the consequences:

"For I know this thing well in my heart, and my mind knows it.
There will come a day when sacred Ilion shall perish,
and Priam, and the people of Priam of the strong ash spear,
and Zeus son of Kronos who sits on high, the sky-dwelling,
himself shall shake the gloom of his aegis over all of them
in anger for this deception."

And this prophecy is implicitly accepted, in an episode pregnant with tragic forebodings, by Hector in his parting from Andromache (VI 447-49). Hector only repeats the first three lines; he does not echo the words about Zeus and his anger at "this deception." Hector indeed is innocent of the deception, even more clearly than Pandarus, but he too is caught in the web; the war will bring his death, the destruction of his city, the agony of Andromache and Astyanax and the wives and children of all the other Trojan heroes—guilty or innocent, which shall we call them? Does it matter? By the time Hector's death comes before us as a thing actually to be experienced, it will have become evident to us—emotionally evident—that guilt and innocence are only very obliquely related to human suffering. But that is a dimension that Homer has added to the poem; it remains to be spoken of later.

If we now return and ask once more why Zeus was so determined that the Trojans should be the first to break the truce, the answer should be obvious. He was determined because this accords with the set of our emotions as we reach this part of the poem. Hera spoke for us, and Zeus ratified it. Zeus is the authority for our feelings, the guide-line for the direction the poem must take—at present. Dare we say it? Zeus is another name for the poet.

The implication of these remarks about Books III through VI is that in some sense they form an emotional whole. In them the theme of Trojan guilt is broached and reinforced. When Pandarus dies in Book V we are reminded of Book IV, and through that of Book III. This network of emotional affiliations is clearly intended. In itself it does not exceed the limit of three or four successive recitations, according to the norm we have previously mentioned (500 to 800 lines per recitation). Some Analysts, like Mazon, would be prepared to admit that III through V or VI are from a single bard. But that is not enough. III through VI could never have been an independent, self-sufficient song. They have meaning only as a *Vorspiel*, a prologue to the *Iliad*, our *Iliad*. The web of affiliations, echoes, anticipations we have uncovered here (and there are others which we have neglected) is already too extensive for anything but a long poem.

In proceeding to sketch a little of the profile of this long poem we will sight again upon our passage in Book V. The heart of our *Iliad* is the *Patrocleia*, Books XVI and XVII, which grows out of the fabric of the action in XI through XV and in turn precipitates the crisis of Achilles' remorse in XVIII and, through it, his supreme *aristeia* in XIX-XXII.

The *Patrocleia* falls into two halves, Patroclus's *aristeia* and death (XVI) and the fight over his body (XVII). This second half is not only, in a sense, the climax of the *Patrocleia*, it is also the climax of the second third of the poem (I-VIII, IX-XVII, XVIII-XXIV). At the beginning of that second third the Achaeans beseech Achilles to help them, but are repulsed; at the beginning of the last third he undergoes a decisive change of feeling and embarks on the course which will lead to Hector's death, the burial of Patroclus, and the ransoming of Hector's body.

Book XVII, the fight over Patroclus's body, though it occupies a special climactic position, has much in common with the other Books of the second third, which narrate the Great Battle. I will deal with just two aspects of it, because I think that they give important clues to the way in which the poet has expanded a tale of battle into the poem we have before us, the *Iliad*.

Book XVII is a long (some have said too long, but they are impatient readers) set of variations on the theme of the Defense of the Body, which we saw in germ in Book V (Aeneas over the body of Pandarus). The theme has already been repeated, expanded, varied, again and again in the course of the Great Battle; now it is chosen to mark a major turning-point. Menelaus begins in line 4, bestriding Patroclus's body "like a mother cow over her first-born calf." Menelaus disposes of Euphorbus, the killer of Patroclus, as Diomed had disposed of Pandarus in Book V. But Hector approaches, spurred on by Apollo to defend the body of Euphorbus in turn, and Menelaus gives way (line 108). Hector strips the arms of Achilles from Patroclus's corpse; but Ajax comes and stands over the naked body like a lion over its young (133). Hector, after hearing and answering a long reproach from Glaucus, puts on the armor; Zeus shakes his head, thinking of Hector's own death, now so near (200); but for the moment he breathes new life into Hector's attack. Ajax despairs of holding out alone and calls upon Menelaus to summon the other Achaeans. He does so, and the battle over the corpse is joined in full fury (262). Then the Achaeans "might have driven the Trojans back into Troy," had not Apollo breathed special might into Aeneas. Aeneas attacks; the battle reaches a new pitch of desperation. A mist closes over the fighters at the center, around the body. The immortal horses of Achilles refuse to move, but Zeus inspires them to obey the charioteer Automedon (442) and Automedon has his moment of glory. Athena strengthens Menelaus, but Apollo strengthens Hector, and a rout of the Achaeans begins (597). Ajax surveys the situation and makes his famous prayer to Zeus: "In the daylight destroy us, if destroy us you will" (645-47). Menelaus goes and gives Antilochus the sorrowful message for Achilles (685). Then he resumes his place over the body, with the two Ajaxes (707). Finally, at the suggestion of the Telamonian Ajax, Menelaus and Meriones lift the corpse and carry it from the field, with the two Ajaxes guarding the rear, and the little procession moves toward the ships accompanied by a symphonic burst of five similes in a row; meanwhile the fighting rages on without check or pause.

Book XVII shows the motif Defense of the Body fully expanded. The scale of the expansion (761 lines, enough to fill a recitation) is justified by the importance of this corpse; or perhaps we should say more truly that the importance of the corpse is established, emotionally, by the scale of the expansion. The actual building up of this mass of incidents follows a pattern which pervades all the fighting in the *Iliad*: attack and retreat, rout and rally, or to give it the simplest possible designation, Back-and-Forth. Idomeneus or Ajax or Antilochus gains a momentary success and the Achaeans threaten to break through, but Hector or Aeneas or Sarpedon restores the balance and the Trojans press forward. Almost always these surging counter-movements are actuated by gods. And the back-and-forth in each Book—each song—finds its echo in the still larger counterpoint of the Great Battle as a whole, where the Trojans sweep forward toward the ships in XV and XVIII but are pushed back on their heels, to and then into the walls of Troy, at the end of XVI and XXI.

Throughout this whole middle section of the poem, and with mounting insistence as the Battle approaches its climaxes, the gods dominate the action. Athena and Apollo especially are on hand every other moment. And as the density of their participation grows, the pattern back of it emerges into clearer and clearer light. These events are the will of Zeus. That *boulê Dios*, the counsel or plan of Zeus which was mentioned in the fifth line of the poem and was formally pledged by Zeus to Thetis in I 500-527—that he would give increased power to the Trojans until the Achaeans restored the rights and the honor of her son—is now in process of fulfilment. The promise has been recalled and renewed in two speeches of Zeus, in VIII 473-477 and XV 62-71. The first of these prophesied the death of Patroclus; the second is still more explicit and more frightening:

> "Let him [Hector] drive strengthless
> panic into the Achaians, and turn them back once more;
> let them be driven in flight and tumble back on the benched ships
> of Achilleus, Peleus' son. And he shall rouse up Patroklos
> his companion. And glorious Hektor shall cut down Patroklos
> with the spear before Ilion, after he has killed many others
> of the young men, and among them my own son, shining Sarpedon.
> In anger for him brilliant Achilleus shall then kill Hektor.
> And from then on I would make the fighting surge back froun the vessels
> always and continuously, until the Achaians
> capture headlong Ilion through the designs of Athene."

Here Zeus takes direct responsibility for the back-and-forth pattern which pervades the *Iliad*. After Hector's death, i.e., after the end of the poem, it will give way to a single, irreversible forward movement ending in the fall of Troy. What must happen will ultimately happen. Meanwhile, so far as the fighting is concerned, the whole *Iliad* is nothing but a monumental delaying action: fifteen thousand lines thrown into the breach to hold up the inevitable.

Why? Why is this Zeus's will? No clear answer is given in this passage or in the poem, except his promise to Thetis that he would honor Achilles—and, incidentally, Hector. After that, he says, he will let Hera and Athena wreak their vengeance on Troy. But this answer does not entirely satisfy us, and we may doubt whether it satisfied even Homer's original audience. It does not satisfy us because it does not accord with our experience of the poem as a whole. Another answer is possible, but before we essay it we must do justice to some other aspects of that experience.

The similes are a peculiar glory of Homeric poetry, especially the *Iliad*. Comparison with other poetic traditions discloses nothing comparable either in bulk or beauty, and when we meet similes in Vergil or Milton we cannot but be aware that they are derivative: they would not be there were it not for the Homeric model. What is the compelling secret of this model? Among the many things that can be said about the similes, two are of paramount importance. First, they invoke a store of common experience; second, they provide a rhythmic counterpoint to the action, a change of pace which is necessary to the success of the poem.

It is a commonplace that the similes are drawn chiefly from nature, and from a nature that is incessantly moving, changing, in action. The sea dashes against the cliffs; snow descends, sent by Zeus in masses that obliterate the landscape; fire crackles in a forest; boars or lions hold their own or charge against the encircling ring of dogs and hunters; a hero falls like a young tree; Ajax resists like an ass in the meadow, harried by small boys; or the blaze from the head of Achilles goes up as signal-fires blaze from a beleaguered city, calling to men of the neighboring islands to see and come and help. Whether men are present or not—and sometimes they are introduced just as auditors or spectators, like the shepherd who hears the distant roar of trees falling in the mountains, blown down by the storm—it is the voice of nature that speaks in most of the similes. Nature that is eternally in motion but eternally the same, the same in the Troad and Boeotia, Ionia and Oregon: the nature that we all know unless we are city-bred and have never been beyond the suburbs.

The Nature of the similes is a world of forces in never-ending contention, but also of the peace that lies behind the contention: the *palintonos harmonia*, the harmony that balances against itself, of Heraclitus. It is an eternally *valid* realm, bespeaking that piety for all things permanent and true yet immediate, which is the core of Hellenism. It brings into the tense, nerve-racked world of battle a largeness and a sense of understanding which makes it bearable.

The content of the similes accords with the linguistic evidence, marshalled by Shipp[5] and others, for their lateness. At least in their developed form, they are not part of the traditional epic baggage. Nothing forbids our thinking that they were developed especially by the monumental poet, and for the audience he knew in Asia Minor and the adjacent islands in the eighth century: an audience composed, if we trust the similes themselves, not of mail-clad heroes but of hunters and farmers, shepherds and woodcutters, mariners and fishermen, adventurers and citizens.

What, then, is the function of the similes? They cluster particularly in the battle books, and more and more thickly as the battle

[5] G. P. Shipp, *Studies in the Language of Homer* (Cambridge, 1953).

draws to a climax, in Books XI through XVII. These five thousand lines of fighting are interrupted only by relatively short interludes: Patroclus in the tent of Nestor (XI), the seduction of Zeus (XIV), Zeus's prediction (XV), and the sending out of Patroclus by Achilles (XVI). This continuous stretch of attention to a relatively monotonous subject—and coming as it does on top of 5700 lines of preparation (I through IX, omitting X)—is unprecedented in oral poetry. Homer is concerned to provide relief, not simply by making the battle situations more graphic and more universal through comparisons with nature, but by providing a counterpoint to them in another rhythm, the calmer, unhurried rhythm of the world around us.

Thus counterpoised, yet not robbed of their dense, serried action, the battle books move forward to the climax of the poem, the last 4300 lines (XVIII through XXIV). In this climax the massed fighters fade to the edge of the scene; the spotlight is now focussed not on the battle as such, and not on Olympus, but on two men, Achilles and Hector. Like the mist that enveloped the battlefield in Book XVII, the uncertain cloud of fighting gives way to a confrontation. Time does not suffice to speak of the episodes that illuminate this final sequence. The important thing is that Homer has shaped the poem to lead to this particular end: two heroes confronting each other. By now we know them pretty well: Achilles the demi-god, raging at Agamemnon in council (I), passionately resisting the Embassy (IX), betraying his affection and his concern for Patroclus (XVI); Hector the loving husband and father, conscientious defender of his city, a brave but uneven fighter, subject to dangerous lapses of judgment, who has really been sustained for so long only by the oblique mercy of Zeus, to do honor to Achilles and to him.

In preparing our feelings for the final encounter, Homer has repeatedly risked alienating them from "our" hero, Achilles, to the "enemy," Hector. This process of preparation too has features of the delaying technique. Achilles had all our sympathy in Book I; in IX he forfeits most of it, to regain it only after the death of Patroclus. But Hector also forfeits some of the sympathy he won in Book VI, at his parting from Andromache, by rash boasts and actions, e.g., in Book XII, 230 ff., when he rejects the omen of the eagle, and by less than heroic conduct, as in XVI, 830 ff., where he brags over Patroclus who was really brought low by Apollo and Euphorbus. (Similar ambiguities appear in the brief battle career of Patroclus: he too acted recklessly, and bragged in unseemly fashion over Cebriones, XVI 745-750.) Yet by and large modern readers tend to sympathize with Hector as the climax approaches, certainly in his death-scene, and there is no reason to suppose that ancient listeners did otherwise. Has the poet allowed our feelings to slip out of his control? That is not very likely.

In Achilles and Hector, Homer has measured two worlds against each other, the old single-minded heroic world of battle and glory and death and the new realm in which man is son and husband and father and citizen as well as fighter: a world less grand than the other but closer to the experience and sympathies of ordinary mortals. Far from masking the contrast, the poet pushes it to its farthest extreme at the moment of Hector's death: Achilles the unapproachable, pitiless warrior, alone except for the gods who "set up the kill" for him, Hector running for his life and dying under the agonized eyes of his dear ones and his countrymen. On one side stands the half-divine hero glittering like the Lord of Battles, on the other a frightened, all-too-human human being who can hardly nerve himself to face his enemy.

Achilles comes straight out of the epic tradition, though he ends by transcending it. I have done less than justice to his many and sometimes contradictory qualities, his absoluteness and his limitations. Cedric Whitman has written a brilliant chapter on Achilles, showing how his passionate speeches in Books I, IX, and XVIII progressively explore the emptiness of the traditional code—fighting, glory, gifts, honor—and reach beyond it for something more permanent and real, more absolute. But although this quest for the absolute takes him beyond the limits of mortality, to a realm where the only enduring answer is death, there is nothing in him—except the special brilliance and the insistent desire to *passer outre*—that does not spring from the heroic tradition. He is something more than, but not different from, the incarnation of "epic hero."

Measured against Achilles, Hector is all too clearly only human. But his humanness also includes a new range of experiences and values that are alien, or at best marginal, to the old *beau ideal* of the epic hero: the involvement of man in family and community, the fabric of love and loyalty to and with others in a social bond which makes him not merely a hero but a civilized human being.

The funeral of Patroclus restores Achilles in a measure to humanity, through suffering. Then, after the gracious interlude of the funeral games, where he shines with all the tact and magnanimity of a great gentleman, Homer takes another splendid risk with our feelings—and imposes another delay—by making Achilles continue his maltreatment of Hector's body. It is cruelty in the extreme; it is also self-castigation. Finally the gods intervene, but the ending of the tension is not brought about by them directly, it springs out of the confrontation of Achilles and Priam. The sight of the old man brings back to vivid life Achilles' only remaining link with humanity: his father. And it is Achilles, at the end, who achieves a new understanding of the common lot of men (XXIV 517-551). The new understanding is a tragic understanding: that life is short and most of it is suffering. Not a new idea, perhaps, *qua* idea, but new in spirit and effect because it has grown out of suffering and responds to the suffering of others. *Pathei mathos*, "through suffering, learning": the *Iliad* anticipates Aeschylus. And we, the audience? The poem was made for us; the song is always for the listener. It has led us to this moment through long delays and endless battles. If we have suffered, we have learned; the learning is proportionate to the experience.

Now, perhaps, we can answer the question why Zeus willed the fall of Troy only after all the immense work of delay. He willed it because *it happened*; it is an irremovable part of the legend, that is to say, of history. Zeus represents what must be, will be. But he willed it in this way because through this long action, through Hector's death, which prefigures the death of his city, and Achilles' final reconciliation we are led to a new point of vantage from which to feel the infinite pity of that death and all the others that have preceded it and are still to come. Zeus's will is the poet's will; it stands for the meditative force that has added a new dimension to our experience of heroic song.

The *Iliad* draws its basic material and its technique from the epic tradition, but it writes a spiritual *finis* to the tradition; an end and a new beginning. It goes irrevocably beyond the old naïve acceptance of fighting, glory, honor as ends in themselves. And it goes beyond all nationalism. If the function of epic song during the Dark Age was to comfort and uphold the survivors of the Mycenaean collapse against their enemies in Greece or Asia Minor, this new epic speaks to all men alike, high and low, Greek and barbarian, with a message of heroism *and* humanity, valor and compassion. The *Iliad* stands at the end of the heroic tradition, in its narrower sense, and announces the Hellenic world.

As so often happens when one treats of Homer, I have left too little space for the *Odyssey*. There is no time to discuss its structure: a structure much more complex and sophisticated than that of the *Iliad*, though still based on the same story-teller's technique of grandiose delay. Aristotle is responsible for the dictum that this poem is more like comedy—by which he means not that it is funny but simply that it has a happy ending. The *Iliad* saw life as a tragic mixture of little good and much evil, and the most conspicuous result of divine activity was the deaths of men and cities. In the *Odyssey* the gods stand for Odysseus' return and future happiness; they represent order and settled life.

But perhaps the most striking difference is in the heroes of the two poems. Achilles is the epic hero *par excellence*, with the virtues and faults of the old breed magnified to the farthest degree. As a warrior Odysseus has an honorable but minor role in the *Iliad*. His fighting career is cut short abruptly in Book XI; he appears to best advantage in other situations like the Achaean panic in Book II or the Embassy in IX. The *Odyssey* is his avowed partisan, alleging that he was one of the greatest heroes at Troy, the special confidante and best friend of Agamemnon, Menelaus, Nestor, etc. We are not required to believe all these claims. The *Odyssey* itself provides evidence, later on, which suggests that his favorite and best weapon was the bow, in which case he cannot have been originally a major hero but only a minor one like Teucer or Pandarus.

Whatever the truth about the origins of his acceptance into the epic tradition, it is clear on the one hand that the *Odyssey* knows and presupposes the *Iliad*, and on the other that its Odysseus is a new kind of epic hero. The crucial test is our experiential relationship to him. Seldom if ever can the listener be said to identify himself with Achilles. Thetis's son is too frighteningly different from ordinary men, too remote from ordinary experience. With Odysseus, on the contrary, we are in sympathy from the beginning. We want him to win his way home to Ithaca, dispose of the suitors, and regain his wife and kingdom. For although Odysseus is a king, a talented and resourceful speaker, equally handy with a quoit or the making of a raft, and so on, his abilities do not frighten us; we have no difficulty in identifying with him.

Some of this came home to me with special force when I read an article recently in the third issue of the new periodical *Greek Heritage*, on the sponge divers of Kalymnos.[6] Among the sponge divers the poorest kind, and the one that represents the lineal tradition going back to remote antiquity, is the *yimnos* (*gymnos*), who plunges into the depths stark naked except for a knife between his teeth and a stone to carry him down. As I looked at a photograph of such a *yimnos* going overboard with the stone in his hands, I thought of Odysseus at the crisis of the storm off Scheria, when Poseidon smashes his raft to bits:

"But Odysseus mounted on a beam as if he were riding a horse astride and stripped off the clothes that the goddess Calypso had given him. He tied the veil under his chest [so Odysseus had one thing that the *yimnos* has not; a special veil, an amulet given him by the sea-nymph Leucothea] and plunged headlong into the sea, stretching out his arms, determined to swim." (*Odyssey* V 370-375)

In spite of the amulet, Odysseus is one of those who have faced death in the sea. He is a hero in the sense in which the writer of the article says that the divers are called *pallikaria*, heroes, by the people of Rhodes and Kalymnos. But no longer quite a hero of the old epic breed, since death confronts him in the sea or in the Cyclops' cave or at the hands of the Laestrygonians, not by the spear on the battlefield, according to the rules. The *Odyssey* widens the range of heroism to include situations that any man might find himself in (making due allowance for imagination), and Odysseus is in fact Everyman, questing through the world in search of home and loved ones and his own property. These are universals of a different stamp from the narrow code of the old epic: available to all men, not

[6] Willard Manus, "Kalymnos and its Sponge Divers," *Greek Heritage* (publ. by the Athenian Corporation, Chicago, Ill.), I, no. 3, 1964, pp. 53-63. Pictures of the *yimnos* on pp. 59 and 60.

merely kings and aristocrats. Odysseus is the first Hellene. It is no accident that he has been the prototype of the Greek race ever since: prepared to die if necessary, but preferring to live and take possession of his inheritance.

I should like to cite just one other episode of the *Odyssey*, not from the Adventures but from Ithaca, very near the end of Odysseus's quest. He has come home, but in disguise, unknown except to his son and the swineherd Eumaeus. On the eve of the final dénouement, the Trial of the Bow and Slaughter of the Suitors, he sits in the hall of his own house, alone (*Od.* XIX 51). Penelope comes. A chair is placed for her before the fire. It is an heirloom, made long ago by the carpenter Icmalius (and therefore, of course, well known to Odysseus), with spiral work of gold and ivory and an attached footstool. The poet of the *Odyssey* likes to dwell on such details of background, setting, *ambiance*. A fleece is thrown over the chair and Penelope sits. The maids clear away the remains of the suitors' feast—a procedure familiar to Penelope, we assume, but necessarily painful to Odysseus, although the poet does not say so. After a short interlude between him and the "bad" maid Melantho, Penelope has a stool brought for the stranger and placed near her, it too covered with a fleece for warmth and comfort. Then she begins to question him: "Who are you, stranger? From what country? Where are your city and your parents?"

Before we go farther, however, we must take note of a structural anomaly in the immediate background of this scene. In XVIII 280-283 Odysseus rejoiced to see Penelope coquetting with the suitors and winning gifts from them, "charming their hearts with pleasing words, while her mind had a different purpose." But how could her husband know what her purpose was, before he had even spoken to her? Again, just before the present interview prophecies of Odysseus' imminent return, nay, that he is already in Ithaca, have begun to cluster thick and fast. These facts make it very probable, as Kirk[7] and others have argued, that there was an older version of the story in which the husband revealed himself to his wife immediately upon his return and the two of them plotted the destruction of the suitors together. Our *Odyssey* has not completely obliterated the traces of that version, but as a whole it is committed to another

[7] G. S. Kirk, *The Songs of Homer* (Cambridge, 1962), pp. 245-248.

order of events in which the recognition takes place after the destruction of the suitors. Why this transposition?

To Penelope's question Odysseus replies with a tactful evasion: The queen's fame is like that of a just and pious king who is the mainstay of his people. But let her not fill his (the speaker's) heart with still more pain by reminding him of his sorrows. Penelope rejects the implied praise of her beauty (actually, Odysseus had not mentioned it), and she continues by recounting the device of the web which she wove by day and unravelled by night to put off the suitors. The trick has now been discovered and she is at her wit's end. And she renews her question.

So Odysseus tells her one of those lying yarns that we have heard him spin before, "telling many falsehoods that were like the truth" (XIX 203). He is a Cretan, the brother of Idomeneus. He did not get to Troy, but he did see and entertain Odysseus who was driven to Crete by a storm on his way there. He describes the reception. "And as she listened her tears began to flow and her flesh was melted. As the snow melts in the high mountains, when it has been softened by the south wind and the west wind has showered it [with rain], and as it melts the rivers run full with it, so her fair cheeks were melted as she shed tears, weeping for her husband as he sat by her side" (204-209). *Klaiousês heon andra parêmenon.* But Odysseus does not weep. He pities his wife in his heart, but craft, cunning, keeps his eyes hard as horn or iron. And he goes on to try her still further.

Whatever his predecessors had done, the poet of our *Odyssey* did not want the recognition of Odysseus by Penelope to come now. He wanted to save it for his last climax, the end of the poem. In other words he regarded Penelope as even more important, in the final analysis, than the suitors: the most important thing of all. But her constancy, the inwardness of her love for Odysseus, must be tested in some way comparable to the long testing of his love for her in the earlier part of the poem, when he refused Calypso in favor of the mortal woman (V 215-224) and won through seas and sufferings to come home.

In shaping his poem so as to make the love of husband and wife its climactic theme, the poet of the *Odyssey* has profoundly altered the balance of the epic ideal. In heroic song, which is sung for men, by men, and about men, women figure only marginally, as the desirable bride, the mourning widow or mother. The inwardness of the marital relation in the *Odyssey* is something new, and for us listeners this inwardness first becomes actual experience in Book XIX. The evening quiet of the hall, after the noisy suitors have departed, the two figures sitting close together in the warmth of the braziers: the scene establishes the note of intimacy which is essential. And then Odysseus' false tale begins the process of testing which, painful though it is to Penelope—and to him—*must* be carried through if she is to be established in our hearts as his true wife and worthy of him.

The tenderness of the episode reaches a first climax in the tears that burst from Penelope like the melting snows on the mountain. Similar tears had sprung to Odysseus' own eyes at the court of Alcinous, when the bard Demodocus sang of the strife between Odysseus and Achilles at Troy (VIII 72-92); and when Demodocus sang of the Trojan Horse and the last fighting in Troy (VIII 500 ff.) Odysseus had again wrapped his head in his cloak and given way to tears, "as a woman weeps, embracing her dear husband who has fallen in defense of his city and his people; seeing him dying and breathing his last she throws herself upon him, crying shrilly; but the men behind her, striking her back and shoulders with the spear, drive her into slavery, to suffer toil and grief; and with most pitiful suffering her cheeks are wasted."

The link between that scene and the present one—so mysteriously suggested by the simile of the widow being dragged away into slavery—is human suffering. For in spite of the occasional bursts of gaiety that enliven the poem, and in spite of its happy ending, the *Odyssey* too is a poem of griefs and toils, on the sea, in distant lands, and at home. Penelope's less spectacular years of suffering find their chance to be expressed at last, that is, to become a part of our experience, in Book XIX. The two paths that led so far apart for so many years are joined again, no farther than a hand's breadth, as she weeps for the husband who sits beside her.

It should be evident that I believe the over-all structure of each poem is the work of one poet. But is the poet who planned this reunion of Odysseus and Penelope, and their final reunion in Book XXIII, the same one who shaped the structure of the *Iliad*? It is possible. Both poems deal with suffering: suffering redeemed in the one case by courtesy and magnanimity, in the other by courage, tenacity, and love. Both are, according to the testimony of Aristotle, long and complex beyond any others in the Greek tradition. It is an attractive thought that the man who had brought off such a risky undertaking as the *Iliad* was moved to repeat his triumph with another long poem. And it is certain that the *Odyssey* follows and is indebted to the *Iliad*. But its structure, its style, and its spirit —above all, its interest in setting and its taste for domesticity, intimacy, subtlety—seem to me too different to allow the hypothesis of a single poet. Much more clearly than the *Iliad*, the *Odyssey* breaks the narrow bonds of the old epic tradition of glory and death on the battlefield. Its scene is the wide world, known and unknown, in which we live, and its hero, for all his exceptional endurance and intelligence, is a man like other men. The *Odyssey* transmutes the old epic code into a plausible and possible ideal, for the Hellenic centuries to come and for us.

EPILOGUE

And there comes before me, again and again,
    the ghost of Odysseus, eyes reddened by
    the salty waves
and his burning desire to see again the smoke
    rising from the fireplace of his house,
    his dog, aged by the long wait, standing
    by the door.

He stands like a giant, whispering through
    his bleached beard, words of our lan-
    guage as it was spoken three thousand
    years ago.
He stretches his palm, calloused by the ropes
    and the rudder, with skin roughened by
    the northwind, by the heat and by the
    snow.

> As if he wanted to chase away the super-
> human Cyclops who stares through a
> single eye, the Sirens who steal away
> your memory with their song, Scylla
> and Charybdis that stand among us;
> all those strange monsters which keep us
> from thinking that even he was only a
> man who fought in this world with soul
> and body.
>
> He is the great Odysseus, who ordered built
> the wooden horse through which the
> Achaeans took Troy.
> I imagine him coming to show me how I
> too can build a wooden horse to conquer
> my own Troy.

These lines came to my notice as I was reading the first proof of the lectures. They are from a translation of a poem of George Seferis, "On a Strange Verse," by Elias Vassiliades, a senior in Athens College, first printed in the *Athens College Bulletin*, Vol. VIII, no. 2 (Winter 1965), pp. 10-11, and are reproduced here by permission of Mr. Vassiliades and the Editor of the *Bulletin*. The poet has expressed better than I could the permanence and vitality of the "new" kind of heroism embodied in the hero of the *Odyssey*.

G.F.E.